The (Un)Rule of Law

and the Underprivileged

in Latin America

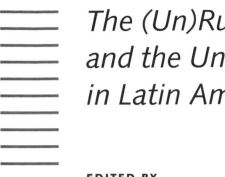

The (Un)Rule of Law and the Underprivileged in Latin America

EDITED BY

Juan E. Méndez

Guillermo O'Donnell

AND

Paulo Sérgio Pinheiro

UNIVERSITY OF NOTRE DAME PRESS

NOTRE DAME, INDIANA

306.098
u 58

Library of Congress Cataloging-in-Publication Data

The (un)rule of law and the underprivileged in Latin America / edited by
    Juan E. Méndez, Guillermo O'Donnell, and Paulo Sérgio Pinheiro.
        p. cm. — (A title from the Helen Kellogg Institute for International
    Studies)
    Includes bibliographical references and index.
    ISBN 0-268-04301-9 (cl : alk. paper). — ISBN 0-268-04302-7 (pbk. : alk.
    paper
        1. Rule of law—Latin America.   2. Minorities—Legal status, laws,
    etc.—Latin America.   3. Discrimination in criminal justice administra-
    tion—Latin America.   I. Méndez, Juan E.   II. O'Donnell, Guillermo A.
    III. Pinheiro, Paulo Sérgio de M. S.   IV. Helen Kellogg Institute for Inter-
    national Studies.   V. Title: Unrule of law and the underprivileged in
    Latin America.   VI. Series.
    KG552.U56   1999
    306'.098—dc21   98-31846

·/oo

Contents

Preface

SINCE 1993 the Helen Kellogg Institute for International Studies at the University of Notre Dame, through its Project Latin America 2000 (generously supported by The Coca-Cola Company), has sought to enlarge its contribution to the understanding of significant political, economic, and social issues facing Latin America at the threshold of a new century. It has done so through its own academic research priorities on these issues and by engaging in constructive dialogue on its research results with distinguished scholars, senior statesmen and stateswomen, government officials, entrepreneurs and executives from national and international businesses, labor leaders, and representatives of nongovernmental organizations, civil associations, and the media. Our hope is that the research and the dialogue together will contribute to policy agendas in public and private sectors by clarifying issues and questions, analyzing options, and pointing the way to more effective and equitable public and private policy alternatives.

The format we have followed for these events begins with an academic workshop, in which distinguished academics write and comment on topics directly related to the main theme. The workshop is followed by a policy forum with a roundtable discussion of the same topics, in which leaders from various venues of public and private life draw upon their own experience and take into account the findings and questions raised in the academic workshop.

The first such event, in 1993, focused on "Economic Integration in the Western Hemisphere." Its main results are presented in a volume of the same title, coedited by Roberto Bouzas and Jaime Ros and published by the University of Notre Dame Press in 1994. For the second event we decided to take stock of the present situation and future prospects of democracy in the Americas. The contributions to the workshop on this topic have been published as Working Papers of the Kellogg Institute and are available upon request.[1]

The next event, held in September 1995, addressed poverty and inequality in Latin America as extremely serious problems in themselves and in terms of their impact on the democratic regimes presently existing in the region. The resulting volume, coedited by Víctor Tokman and Guillermo O'Donnell, was published in 1998 by the University of Notre Dame Press under the title *Poverty and Inequality in Latin America: Issues and New Challenges*. The present volume results from the fourth Project Latin America 2000 event, held in November 1996, at which participants in the academic workshop and the policy forum considered various issues related to the rule of law in Latin America and its failures, especially in relation to minorities and other underprivileged sectors. "The Changing Status of Children in Latin America: Issues in Child Health and Children's Rights" was the topic for the last (September 1997) of the five events planned for the Project Latin America 2000 series. A volume is currently in progress that will publish papers and some of the commentaries presented on this occasion.

The chapters published in the present volume were written by the authors of principal papers in the academic workshop "The Rule of Law and the Underprivileged in Latin America." The coeditors have also included most of the commentaries to these papers, likewise commissioned for the workshop. It may be noted that, in view of the main thrust of most of these contributions, the coeditors have changed the title of this book from *The Rule of Law* . . . to *The (Un)Rule*

1. Project Latin America 2000 Working Paper #1, 1994, Catherine Conaghan, "Democracy that Matters: The Search for Authenticity, Legitimacy, and Civic Competence in the Andes"; #2, Scott Mainwaring, "Democracy in Brazil and the Southern Cone: Achievements and Problems"; #3, Jorge G. Castañeda, with comments by Robert Dahl, "Three Challenges to U.S. Democracy: Accountability, Representativeness, and Intellectual Diversity"; #4, Laurence Whitehead, "The Peculiarities of 'Transition' *a la Mexicana*"; #5, Terry Lynn Karl, "Central America in the Twenty-First Century: The Prospects for a Democratic Region"; and #6, the summary of the workshop, Volker Frank and Charles Kenney, "Democracy in the Americas: Approaching the Year 2000 (A Rapporteurs' Report)."

of Law . . . , as a way of stressing the sharp contrast brought out by this book between the emergence of democratic regimes in most Latin American countries and the severe incompleteness of the rule of law in these same countries.

We were fortunate in this endeavor to have the collaboration of Juan Méndez, Executive Director of the Inter-American Institute of Human Rights, and Paulo Sérgio Pinheiro, professor at the University of São Paulo and Director of the University's Center for the Study of Violence. Méndez and Pinheiro contributed not only their generous dedication and great international prestige, but also their vast professional knowledge and relationships. The academic workshop and policy forum were thereby able to convene some of the most distinguished scholars and practitioners in the diverse fields of expertise represented in this endeavor. Since its inception, the Kellogg Institute has been proud of its ability to establish long-standing relationships of mutual trust, respect, and fruitful cooperation with institutions and individuals based in other countries, especially within Latin America. The present volume is another expression of this spirit of mutual and respectful collaboration.

Finally, we wish to acknowledge the staff of the Kellogg Institute for their extremely helpful contributions to the above-mentioned events. We also thank Kelly D. Askin for editing the chapters that follow, and Caroline Domingo for her valuable contributions to that task in its final stages.

ERNEST BARTELL, C.S.C.
former Executive Director
GUILLERMO O'DONNELL
former Academic Director
The Helen Kellogg Institute
for International Studies

Notre Dame, June 1998

The Rule of Law and the Underprivileged in Latin America: Introduction

Paulo Sérgio Pinheiro

SINCE THE RETURN OF DEMOCRATIC RULE to many countries in Latin America, relations between governments and society, particularly the poor and marginalized members of society, have been characterized by the illegal and arbitrary use of power. The great hope during the democratic transitions in Latin America in the 1980s was that the end of dictatorships would mean consolidating the rule of law. The return to a civilian government brought the hope that the degree of human rights protection achieved for political opponents under authoritarian rule would be extended to all citizens.

Nonetheless, although Latin American societies experienced the transition from dictatorships to civil governments, many authoritarian practices of their governments were not affected by political changes or elections. There is a significant gap between the letter of the bill of rights, present in many constitutions, and law enforcement application and practice. Human rights abuses occur every day, and the majority of the perpetrators are not punished or otherwise held accountable for their heinous crimes. In certain areas, the state monopoly of legitimate violence has been relaxed, and survival may depend on an individual's ability to maintain his or her reputation by displaying a "credible threat of violence,"[1] a process which threatens the development of a democratic society. Growing criminality not only erodes democratic expectations (as many surveys in the continent have demonstrated) but also sanctions arbitrary violence, weakening the legitimacy of the political system. There are large portions of the territory, mainly in rural areas, where the local ruling classes continue to manipulate state institutions, including the judiciary and police. To complicate this situation, we face a paradox which undermines the efforts to fight crime: although the fundamental guarantees are well-defined by most of the democratic constitutions, the exercise of full citizenship is practically nonexistent for the majority of the population. These societies which are based on exclusion—in civil and social rights terms—could be considered "democracies without citizenship."[2]

In most Latin American countries, especially those without traditional practices of protecting civil rights, even after the writing of new democratic constitutions, legal institutions have not been reformed and arbitrary practices of state agents remain unchanged. Despite significant advances in civil society and democratic governance, the poor continue to be the preferred victims of violence, criminality, and human rights violations. The state in much of Latin America has shown itself unable—or more likely, unwilling—to eradicate the impunity for crimes committed by its agents to the same extent that it attempts to punish crimes committed by petty and common criminals.

In this continent, democratic governance has been unable to implement or propose reforms for certain legal institutions, such as the judiciary, the public prosecutor's office, and the police. This book, in attempting to expose the dimensions of these setbacks and to discuss new perspectives for reform, deals with the problem of how the rule of law in Latin America can become an effective instrument for the appropriation of rights by the majority of the population. The principal issues addressed here are the problems of illegal violence, the various methods for overcoming discrimination, and the avenues to institutional reform, including access to justice.[3] An important clarification made by Jean-Paul Brodeur for the debate on the issues proposed by this book is that the rule of law which is discussed here must not be equated with the enforcement of criminal law, precisely because one of the cardinal features of criminal law is its discriminatory character. Indeed, the vast majority of those who are punished or imprisoned in every society in Latin America, with the exception of those committing homicide or other horrendous crimes against persons, are the powerless and the underprivileged—exactly those whom democracy intends to protect through the rule of law. Democracy must not support a rule of law which punishes primarily the poor and marginalized.

Lawless Violence

The first section of this book deals with lawless violence, a phenomenon which continues to plague the non-elites, in particular the poor and the destitute. In comparison to the small groups of political opponents during the authoritarian regimes, the number of the poor and the vulnerable groups after the political transitions is much higher. Those victims, the traditional targets of arbitrary power under democracy and dictatorship, are much more difficult to identify, since they do not constitute a homogeneous group. The democratic state, in most cases, is no longer directly responsible for committing these abuses. Its responsibility lies in its failure to control the arbitrary practices of its own agents or to fight impunity, a failure which is a consequence of the precarious functioning of the judiciary.

The return to democratic constitutionalism did little to eradicate the authoritarian practices present in the state and in society. Despite constitutional protection, violence continues unabated. Civilian governments have failed to control abuse of power. One of the most visible signs of the failure of Latin American democracies to rein in the police by imposing greater civilian controls is the prevalence of abusive practices against suspects and prisoners, practices which continue to be entrenched in the system. One major failure of the new democratic state is its incapacity to end the ill-treatment of common criminals under arrest. Torture under police investigation and the abominable conditions of prisons throughout most countries in Latin America are still pervasive even after political transition. In effect, as Nigel Rodley points out in his chapter, even if the gravity and scope of torture have abated substantially as and where armed political opposition has diminished, the limited information on current practices of torture could give an inaccurate picture of the problem. Undertrained, underpaid, and underrespected law enforcement officials continue to practice torture during police inquiries. In many countries, these practices are exacerbated by the absence of systems of accountability: accusations of torture are rarely investigated; when they are investigated, those responsible are seldom punished. Additionally, Rodley reminds us that such practices are encouraged by legal systems that rely heavily on the written dossier, thus placing great value on confessions and other declarations by suspects and witnesses.

Prison conditions are characterized by overcrowding in most institutions in the region. Food, health conditions, and medical assistance are poor. In most cases, the management of these establishments is arbitrary and oppressive, and frequently, the internal running of prisons is left to the inmates themselves. The consequences for the hundreds or thousands of inmates who are concentrated in very limited spaces and subjected to sheer oppression from the guards and sexual violence from each other include frequent riots and mutinies. The reaction of the police forces to these protests has been, in several countries of the region, massacres committed in the name of restoring "order." The prison in Latin America is the space of disorder which is unveiled for a limited time as a consequence of prison revolts.

Discussing the work of Nigel Rodley, Ligia Bolívar stresses that being underprivileged is both a source and a result of human rights violations in the spheres of physical integrity and conditions of detention. She argues that judicial systems which consider confession as key evidence stimulate the use of torture. In her comments, Bolívar also analyzes the ambiguous role that the state, the NGOs, and the international community play in enforcing the rule of law regarding the use of torture and the conditions of detention. She additionally calls attention to the myth of stable democracy in certain countries, which can contribute to tolerance of serious human rights violations, and which undermines democratic stability when abuses are allowed to continue without punishment.

Police and other institutions of the criminal justice system tend to act as "border guards," protecting the elites from the poor. Police violence remains cloaked in impunity because it is largely directed against these "dangerous classes" and rarely affects the lives of the privileged. Crime-prevention policies, especially those proposed during election time, are aimed less at controlling crime and delinquency than at diminishing the fear and insecurity of the ruling classes. Elite perceptions of the poor as part of those "dangerous classes" are encouraged by a judicial system which prosecutes and convicts for crimes committed by poor people, while crimes committed by the elites remain largely unchallenged. Middle-class and elite crimes—such as corruption, financial scams, tax evasion, and the exploitation of child or slave labor—are not perceived as threats to the status quo. The same is generally true for the activities of organized crime, including drug trafficking, money laundering, contraband, and even the very profitable arms trade, which are not, in many countries of the region, targets of consistent enforcement policies.

In Latin America, police officers see the rule of law as an obstacle to, rather than an effective guarantee of, social control; they believe that their role is to protect society from "marginal elements" by any means available. As Paul Chevigny shows in his chapter, the police also have special powers in some countries that serve to emphasize their independence of the laws that govern the rest of the criminal system. In Argentina, for example, the federal police can detain a person for up to thirty days for vagrancy, drunkenness, or even cross-dressing; in Venezuela, the police can detain persons deemed to be a threat to society for up to five years, thus confirming the belief that the police are primarily intended to control poor people.

Besides the practices of torture, mentioned above, police in many countries have been criticized for their policy of "shoot first, ask questions later." Indeed, summary executions of suspects and criminals are common practices in many countries of the region. Chevigny notes that the abuse of deadly force by the police varies from country to country, but a common characteristic is that it is justified as a way to control ordinary crime in poor neighborhoods. The victims tend to be from the most vulnerable groups—the poor, the homeless, and the African descendants. This police violence can be considered a form of vigilantism, a version of the police effort to eliminate the "undesirables." But what complicates this picture even more is the acquiescence of the majority of the population, including the poor, to these practices. Such killings enjoy broad support not only from elites, but also from the poor, even though the poor represent the largest category of victims of violent crime.

In Brazil, the democratic constitution did not change the decision made during the military dictatorship that common crimes committed by the military police were to be tried by military police courts. These courts, made up of military officials and based on shoddy criminal investigations, often condoned the excessive use of force, including unnecessary deadly force. In the face of this bleak picture, Chevigny reminds us that reform is needed against these abuses. Action is needed to decrease violence and corruption and to increase security. Legislatures could augment accountability and reduce violence not only by procedural changes which limit the practice of police abuse, but also by procedural changes which limit the powers of the police.

In his comments on Chevigny's chapter, Jean-Paul Brodeur expresses skepticism towards the possibility of convincing the upper classes that it is in their own best interest to have a police force which impartially respects the rule of law. Brodeur argues that human rights defenders are fighting a losing battle as long as they frame the debate in terms of individual risks and individual victimization. For example, the greatest toll of police bribes and police corruption in general is collective, because it strikes against the wealth of the nation. He believes that only when collective rights and the collective impact of deviant policing come into the foreground can a persuasive argument be marshaled. Brodeur agrees with Chevigny that there should be an effort to persuade the middle and the upper classes that it would be in the interest of all to have a police observant of human rights and governed by the rule of law. But he is not convinced that there is full recognition in Latin America that the word "all" should be interpreted in its inclusive sense. Until this happens, attempts to convince certain classes that observing the rule of law is in the best interest of all are fraught with difficulties.

Brodeur also remarks that one of the words most frequently used in the chapters and comments in this book is "impunity." He notes, however, that direct responses to specific groups urging severe prison terms for perpetrators of crimes will simply aggravate the overflow of inmates in every country. He makes a plea for the need to find alternatives to punishment in attempting to solve problems of crime and repression, which I think must be present in our minds every time we are concerned with challenges to strengthen the rule of law.

Gross human rights violations under democratic rule are much more visible in urban areas than in the countryside because of their number and their exposure by the media. Nonetheless, police brutality and massacres are also frequent in rural areas of the continent, particularly concerning conflicts over control of the land, indigenous communities, or peasants rights. As Alfredo Wagner indicated in his presentation at the Notre Dame workshop, based on a study of massacres in the state of Pará (a rural area in Brazil), violence, as an instrument of control and oppression, has become the main form of communication between the ruling powers, the peasants, and the indigenous communities. The repetition of these massacres, accompanied by the absence of effective measures for investigating these crimes, contributes to their banalization. The criminal justice system has failed to investigate and prosecute numerous cases of rural violence against poor peasants. According to Brazil's Pastoral Land Commission, of the 1,730 killings of peasants, rural workers, trade union leaders, religious workers, and lawyers committed between 1964 and 1992, only thirty cases had been brought to trial by 1992. A mere eighteen of the thirty resulted in convictions. Throughout the continent, impunity is virtually assured for those who commit offenses against victims considered "undesirable" or "subhuman." Most frequently, peasants, rural workers, and indigenous peoples fall under this classification and do not have access to guarantees of the rule of law. In the cases mentioned by Wagner, access to judicial instruments, for instance to seek redress for criminal damages as a result of the frequent rural massacres, is not available for those groups. The law and the police exist primarily as instruments of oppression on behalf of the elites. The military police, in charge of patrolling, act as an extension of the militia of gunmen of the owners of the latifundia.

At the Notre Dame workshop, Roger Plant called attention to the fact that massacres in the Amazon region are connected to unresolved problems of land reform, a situation most recently aggravated by the neoliberal approach to agrarian issues. In his chapter, Plant identifies the urgent need for accountability at all levels of government and for guarantees of access to justice, including the availability of civil and penal law, for labor workers and peasants. He emphasizes that nothing will have a significant, long-term impact on rural violence as long as broader economic and social policies turn a blind eye to the current patterns of rural landlessness and desperation. The main issue is to define how those without resources can have a stake in national development.

Overcoming Discrimination

The second section of this book discusses various ways to overcome discrimination by equalizing the content and the application of law among the population, regardless of race, gender, or socioeconomic status. Despite the positive developments in the democratic transition and consolidation processes, most democracies in Latin America are still far from being capable of assuring liberty and justice for all.

During the past decade, a large number of Latin American countries have adopted constitutional reforms or new constitutions which include provisions concerning the rights of indigenous peoples. These measures were the result of considerable debate and organized pressure by civil society organizations and support groups, and were accompanied by a veritable avalanche of laws and regulations. In his chapter, Jorge Dandler reminds us that this phenomenon requires a particularly vigilant strategy by indigenous organizations to ensure that their constitutional rights are safeguarded in various subjects, including land rights, forestry, biodiversity, mineral and petroleum laws, and environment laws. Without these efforts, democracy for indigenous peoples will mean little. Latin America, concludes Dandler, has a unique opportunity to peacefully construct multiethnic societies and to thrive in diversity, avoiding interethnic conflicts and war.

In his discussion of Dandler's chapter, Shelton Davis agrees that there has been some evolution of international and legal standards in relation to the rights of the more than 40 million indigenous people in Latin America. Nevertheless, he insists that we must recognize that most of the recent constitutional reforms have not addressed the area of legal process or administration, that is, "access to law" or "access to justice." Thus, there is still a great distance to go before one can say that the rule of law reigns in the relationships between nation states and indigenous peoples in Latin America. Davis determines that much more attention must be focused upon the procedural aspects of the law before indigenous peoples and the rule of law have a real chance in Latin America.

In many aspects, the situation of women in Latin America has several points of contact with that of the indigenous peoples: despite a substantive advance in the recognition of women's constitutional rights, the laws regulating these rights are sparse and democracy has not yet meant full realization of the guarantees of the rule of law. Mariclaire Acosta, in her chapter on the situation of women in Mexico, addresses some of the limitations imposed on women in daily life. Over the last fifteen years, losses in income and job opportunities for most people, but particularly for women, have been devastating. Women and their children have borne the brunt of the processes of privatization and economic globalization. Acosta explains how, in practice, equality of men and women continues to be mostly a formal right. Women are systematically targeted by sexual and domestic violence, and most perpetrators count on and receive impunity. The future prospects are somber; ending discrimination against women will require, in addition to the full implementation of constitutional guarantees and governmental programs, a thorough change of economic policies, which does not appear likely in the near future.

Dorothy Thomas, in her comments on Acosta's chapter, compares the situation of women in Mexico with that in other countries, like Peru, Haiti, and Brazil, and reminds us that gender discrimination is often deeply intertwined with other forms of discrimination, such as discrimination based on race, ethnicity, sexual orientation, social class, or economic status. If the rule of law is really to encompass the underprivileged, society will have to change this pervasive character of discrimination and the degree to which it is embedded in the structure of the law itself, in order to ensure that the rule of law is truly a rule for women rather than an exception.

Constitutions in Latin American countries usually incorporate broad provisions for the protection of individual rights, which are then systematically disregarded. A context of broad economic inequalities has widened the gap between rich and poor and has doomed millions of Latin Americans to lives of poverty and social exclusion. Race discrimination is one of the most evident expressions of unequal access to resources. This issue is treated in the chapter by Peter Fry. Latin American societies tend to present themselves as liberal democracies, but the equality of all before the law is regularly challenged by unequal distributions of power. Contemporary data analyzed by Fry demonstrate that "racial democracy" in Brazil is a myth, evidenced by the fact that almost 90 percent of the population of all colors agree that racial discrimination is rife in the workplace and in relation to the police. This discrimination is also present in the criminal justice system, as Sérgio Adorno noted during his presentation at the Notre Dame workshop. Indeed, color is a powerful trigger of discrimination in the distribution of justice. People of color confront greater obstacles accessing criminal justice and have more difficulty utilizing their right to an adequate defense. As a result, they are more likely to be punished than whites and they tend to receive more rigorous penal treatment. After discussing recent trends of research, Fry concludes that recognizing the existence of racism accomplishes more than merely denying the myth of racial democracy: he suggests that the myth has the powerful function of masking discrimination and prejudice and has prevented the formation of a large-scale black protest movement. He then poses a practical question: what is being done and can be done to reduce prejudice and discrimination against the poor in general and against people of darker color in particular? After describing the struggles of the black social movements and the initiatives taken by the federal government under the Cardoso administration to implement specific policies in favor of blacks in Brazil, Fry discusses the broader and unexpected implications of these new developments.

Discussant Joan Dassin points out that the central "paradox" addressed by Fry's chapter is that despite the demonstration of the reality of racism in Brazil, and the fact that most Brazilians of all colors agree that racism exists, most also claim they do not discriminate or even suffer from discrimination. This suggests that the real debate should be around the myth of racial democracy—a "dream," a principle of such strength that it impedes the recognition and subsequent punishment of those who deny it. Dassin notes that one of the merits of Fry's chapter is that his nuanced, historically-grounded contextualization of both "race" and the "law" holds both concepts up to serious examination. This perspective could prevent well-intentioned policymakers from being lulled into simplistic solutions which are doomed to fail, as have many of the programs established to promote legal and judicial reform, to alleviate poverty, and to end race- and gender-based discrimination.

Access to Justice

The final section of this book deals with institutional reform, including access to justice. State institutions charged with providing law and order are widely perceived as dysfunctional. A large percentage of Latin American citizens do not believe that their government implements, or attempts to implement, the law with equality and impartiality for all citizens. Formal guarantees enshrined in the constitution and the legal codes are systematically violated, largely because of the glaring gap between what the law says and the way the institutions charged with protecting and implementing the law—i.e., the police and the judiciary—function in practice. In Latin American countries, the poor often see the law as an instrument of oppression in the service of the wealthy and the powerful.

The judicial system has been widely discredited for its venality, inefficiency, and lack of autonomy. It is deficient in every respect: material resources are scarce; judicial procedures are excessively formalistic; judges are insufficiently trained; and too few judges oversee too many cases. Because of these obstacles, courts often frustrate plaintiffs. Many judges have been impotent to prosecute cases of organized crime, and some have even been linked to drug trafficking. In most countries of the region, the investigative capacity of the police is very limited, and only a low percentage of investigated cases reach the courts. In general, the way the courts function is intimately linked to the hierarchical and discriminatory practices that mark social relationships.

Certain of these problems are being tackled in Latin America through the framework of international programs. In his chapter, Reed Brody discusses the international dimensions of current efforts of judicial reform, concentrating on the recent Haiti experience. He emphasizes that one of the key principles of development assistance

concerning judicial reform should be the participation of intended
beneficiaries in determining the priorities and modalities of this assistance. International assistance of judicial reform, like all international development assistance, must be shaped by those who will be
most immediately affected, and should be in accordance with international human rights norms. In turn, Leonardo Franco concludes
that it is impossible to separate judicial reform from human rights.
Disjointed approaches to judicial reform cannot succeed unless they
are linked to measures addressing the deeply rooted political, technical, and structural factors which inhibit effective functioning of the
judiciary. Another decisive aspect emphasized by Franco is that judicial reform is not neutral in any society; the change process will suit
certain societal interests and will conflict with those of other powerful groups.

Jorge Correa Sutil provides a comprehensive presentation of the
process of judicial reforms in several countries in Latin America. He
begins his chapter by pointing out the common trends in these reforms, including amendments to the constitution to guarantee a percentage of the budget for the judiciary; revising the rules which
govern the ways judges are appointed and their terms of and conditions in office; adopting more oral and less inquisitorial procedures;
and including measures to improve the education of judges. He then
explains why changes are occurring at this moment in Latin America.
One important factor is the increased importance of the judiciary
after the return to democratic political systems. The Argentinean
transition is a good example, because it coincides with the public trials of the generals who had been in power. In many cases, these reforms are the answer to the perceived need to establish new relations
between the judiciary and the other branches of power. Another important element is that open market economies have decentralized
the fora of dispute resolution; indeed, the process of opening the
markets and allowing them to allocate resources has multiplied the
amount of litigation. The chapter concludes that there is a clear trend,
caused by the opening of markets, towards increasing the importance of the judiciary as a forum of dispute resolution. There is also a
recent trend of some marginalized groups in the region to use the judicial forum, through public interest litigation, in order to advance

their interests. The judiciary is probably being reformed in Latin America in order to respond to social demands for a wider and stronger role, and the underprivileged may benefit from that process. At the Notre Dame workshop, Leopoldo Schiffrin agreed with Correa that the connection between judicial reforms and improving access to the legal process for the underprivileged is not clear enough. An important precondition is that politicians must renounce any manipulation of the judicial system. The struggles for a fair deal for the underprivileged in the legal field are fights for the rule of law, which will exist only when all have the same chance to find judicial protection for their rights.

The chapter by Alejandro Garro deals with issues involving access to justice for the poor in Latin America, and asserts that the terms of the debate on "access to justice" should be centered on making justice more accessible to the poor and marginalized. The chapter considers different approaches that have been adopted, their potential for progress, and approaches that have the greatest chance of making a difference in the search for access to justice. Garro and his discussant at the Notre Dame workshop, Sérgio Adorno, agreed that reducing the costs of litigation, adjusting prevailing procedural mechanisms to satisfy the overwhelming needs for justice of the marginalized, and embracing the ideal of "public interest lawyering" as an essential component of legal education and training, are essential reforms that must be carried out in order to improve access of the underprivileged to justice and to reinforce institutional effectiveness.

The different approaches to the multiple subjects covered by this book confirm the assertion that the new democracies in Latin America are far from capable of assuring liberty and justice for all. In this context, governments that attempt to promote reforms to address the multifaceted problems of crime and impunity may find themselves in a no-win situation. The failure of these democracies to require their own institutions to respect internal laws and international obligations has seriously compromised their legitimacy. As a result, governments are likely to have difficulty garnering popular support for their reform efforts. But in order to make the rule of law a notion with real meaning for the underprivileged in Latin America, these governments must address the desperate need for social reforms.

Legal recognition and exercise of political and civil rights must be stressed in settings where basic human, social, and economic rights are systematically violated. In many Latin American societies, there exists a profound gap between social citizenship and political citizenship in the context of a democratic institutional framework.

We must also recognize that the current international conjuncture is not the most propitious for implementing redistributive policies which would reduce social polarization or for instituting principles of social justice. The shift to neoliberal economic policies has provoked a deepening of inequality which threatens to undermine the legitimacy of the new constitutional regimes. Perhaps the basic condition to overcome the extremely limited content of the rule of law for the underprivileged in Latin American democracies is to grapple with the problem of poverty generated by technological competition and increasing globalization. Extreme economic and social imbalances, which lie at the root of inequality and victimization among the underprivileged, cannot be corrected by the market alone.

Civil society organizations and the state have important roles to play in achieving the rule of law in Latin America. Social movements were able to reshape the face of politics by helping to dismantle authoritarian regimes. When rights continue to be violated under democratic rule, the role of civil society is crucial because the state alone cannot provide solutions. These movements in civil society have introduced a new dynamism and a capacity for innovation into the state's system. Civil society organizations monitor state compliance with international standards, help promote changes in institutions, and challenge institutions in the interest of human rights.

The state—as the primary defender and promoter of human rights—has a critical role to play if Latin American societies are to tackle the growing problems of poverty and the associated problems of lawless violence, racial and gender discrimination, and obstacles to the access to justice. Only the state can provide consistent national programs to promote health and education—the prerequisites for a social order—based not on the silence of official abuse and impunity, but instead on democracy, development, and conviviality. Unhappily, as Guillermo O'Donnell argues in his concluding chapter, the studies in this book indicate a severe incompleteness of the state, especially in terms of its legal dimension. Paradoxically, this deficiency has increased, not decreased, during political transitions and democratic consolidations, in large part due to economic crises and the anti-statist economic policies adopted throughout the last two decades.

Despite the obstacles which are discussed and analyzed in this book, including the failure of present state institutions to enforce the rule of law, it is important to acknowledge that civilian rule and "formal democracy," to use Agnes Heller's expression,[4] with all its limitations in Latin America, have opened new perspectives for democratic consolidation processes which now necessarily encompass the appropriation of rights by the underprivileged. As O'Donnell reminds us, the full effectiveness of the rule of law has not been completely reached in any country, as social change and acquisition of rights trigger new demands and aspirations. Seen from this angle, concludes O'Donnell, democracy is not a static political regime but a moving horizon.

NOTES

1. For a discussion on the state monopoly of physical violence, *see* Norbert Elias, *Violence and Civilization: The State Monopoly of Physical Violence and Its Infringement*, in CIVIL SOCIETY AND THE STATE (John Keane ed., London: Verso, 1988). The expression "credible threat of violence" is from MARTIN DALY & MARGO WILSON, HOMICIDE (New York: A. de Gruyter, 1988), *passim*.

2. I have developed these ideas most recently in Paulo Sérgio Pinheiro, *Democracies without Citizenship*, 30(2) NACLA REPORT ON THE AMERICAS 17–23 (Sept./Oct. 1996); and P.S. Pinheiro, *Popular Responses to State-Sponsored Violence in Brazil*, in THE NEW POLITICS OF INEQUALITY IN LATIN AMERICA 261–80 (Douglas Chalmers et al. eds., Oxford University Press, 1997).

3. In writing this introduction, besides reading the chapters and comments, I have benefited from the summary of the academic workshop, "The Rule of Law and the Underprivileged in Latin America," held November 9–11, 1996, at the University of Notre Dame, as the fourth annual program of Project Latin America 2000 sponsored by the Helen Kellogg Institute for International Studies, with the cooperation and support of The Coca-Cola Company, published in Andreas Feldman & Carlos Guevara-Mann, *The Rule of Law and the Underprivileged in Latin America*, no. 27 (Kellogg Institute, Fall 1996).

4. Agnes Heller, *On Formal Democracy*, in CIVIL SOCIETY AND THE STATE, *supra* note 1, at 129–45.

I

Problems of
Lawless Violence

1 Problems of Lawless Violence: Introduction

Juan E. Méndez

THE TRANSITION from dictatorship to democracy in most of Latin America has, undoubtedly, improved in many different ways the quality of life and the exercise of freedoms for most Latin Americans. However, it has not made much of a dent in the violence that affects the region. Political violence, though still present in some countries, has decreased enormously with the advent of democracy. But there remains a sweeping and deadly epidemic of violence of a nonpolitical sort, the extent of which affects the quality of the democracy in which we live. It is not only urban areas that are experiencing an ever-growing sensation of insecurity due to the rise in criminality; rural conflict is also increasingly subject to violent resolution. While there are many sources of and many actors in the violence, state agents continue to contribute a great deal to the lawlessness and the brutality.

This is not to say that nothing has changed since elected governments succeeded military dictators. In the first place, there is a vigorous exercise of freedom of expression and investigative journalism, and that factor makes it possible for the problems of violence to be openly discussed and publicly aired, something that was done under dictatorships only at great risk to life and freedom. When it comes to state actors, the quality of violence has changed, even if that change is not an improvement. Targets of state violence are different now: police and military officers no longer direct their actions against a political adversary, however defined, as was the case during dictatorial regimes. The victims of torture, extrajudicial execution, and the occasional forced disappearance are now anonymous; these victims are not the well-known political prisoners with whom the rest of the world instantly sympathizes, but instead tend to be young persons from a poor district whose victimization hardly merits a newspaper story.

There is no evidence of a deliberate, planned pattern of systematic infliction of gross violations of human rights on a specific segment of the population. As we have since learned, the military elites that controlled the governments not long ago carefully planned and supervised large-scale disappearances, the use of secret detention centers, and the murder of those caught in the system. No such evidence has surfaced about systematic plans to kill persons from socially marginal districts. There is, however, strong evidence that those whose duty it is to stop those murders and other abuses do little to bring the perpetrators to justice and even less to discipline them administratively. It may well be that impunity for these nonpolitically-motivated crimes is not evidence of a conscious, deliberate decision to sanction them, although we would do best to hold final judgment. On the other hand, there is no question that these crimes go generally uninvestigated and regularly unpunished, and that a clear duty on the part of the state is thus violated.

Even without the use of secret detention centers, and with no clear signal that state violence is officially sanctioned, the number of cases of police killings in dubious circumstances and of instances of torture is still staggering. An indisputable feature of the kind of democracy that Latin America offers at the end of this century is that violent and illegitimate behavior by state actors is so pervasive that it is part of the ordinary way of doing business by many law enforcement bodies. Some observers call these violations "endemic," in the sense that they do not seem to rise or decline with any change of government. The adjective "endemic" appropriately dramatizes the problem, but it is also dangerous if it gives the sense that little can be done about the problem. On the contrary, living with routine torture and murder is inconsistent with democracy: it shows a clear abdication of democratic authority, it tarnishes the reputation of democratically-elected offi-

cials, and it undermines the public's confidence in democratic institutions. For that reason, democracies that coexist with alarming inci-
dences of state violence do not deserve to be called democracies.

Police killings by excessive use of force, death squad–type murders, and routine use of torture to elicit information are the more visible aspects of this lawless state violence, but they are only part of the
phenomenon. We must also reckon with an increasing deterioration
in prison conditions that is caused both by neglect and by corruption.
In many parts of the world, prisons rank at the bottom of budgetary
priorities. In Latin America, the result of this neglect is evidenced not
just by overcrowding and inhumane conditions, but also by periodic
explosions of mutiny and hostage-taking, and the subsequent harsh
and indiscriminate use of force to put them down, sometimes claiming dozens of lives. In the countryside of many Latin American countries, conflicts over land or over working conditions are increasingly
resolved through violence conducted by private armies of powerful
parties or by state agents manipulated by these parties.

The emergence of a variety of violent criminals who are not
clearly identified as state actors is also a salient feature of this picture.
Private armies and vigilante squads complicate the matter of assign-
ing responsibility. It is not always clear that their actions are conducted under color of authority, or even that they are officially
tolerated, although in certain regions evidence to that effect is not
lacking. Yet, even if no policy exists of encouraging these actions,
their existence and growth demonstrate a signal weakness in the
ability of the state to keep peace and maintain order. As a practical
matter, it is difficult to imagine that large and visible groups could
consistently take the law into their own hands over long periods unless some in authority believe such behavior is useful to the interests
they defend.

The reasons for this state of affairs are complex and varied, as the
chapters and comments included in this section suggest. Some factors, however, seem common to most of the continent at this junc-
ture, even if by themselves they do not explain the whole situation.
In the first place, there has been little or no change in personnel
among law enforcement and security bodies, except for the fact that
in many places—though certainly not everywhere—the armed forces

are no longer asked to conduct security-related actions. Many law enforcement officials who have to deal with common crimes are the same ones who were previously asked to fight subversion, and they are accustomed to fulfilling their tasks with tactics and methods imposed in dictatorial times. Even more importantly, they have traditionally been shielded from outside investigations and have come to believe that they do not have to account to courts or other civilian authority for their actions. For these officials, impunity has always been the norm. In the transition to democracy, they saw how elected leaders thwarted efforts by civil society to break the cycle of impunity through pseudo-amnesties and pardons justified under a false theory of "reconciliation." They probably think that their current crimes will be overlooked as well, if the society that gives them uniforms and weapons shares their belief in fighting crime by any available method.

A major contributing factor to this lawless state of violence is, then, the twin effect of a legacy of authoritarianism and the ingrained habit of law enforcement bodies of resisting all attempts to bring them under democratic controls. The result is that police and security bodies are, for all practical purposes, unaccountable to civilian authority and immune to serious scrutiny by any institutional mechanism. In fact, they even seem impervious to many serious efforts by civil society to throw light on their actions. On the positive side, those civil efforts have not been lacking and, in some places, they have met with limited success—another undeniable advantage of at least partially democratic times.

But it may well be that those civil society efforts have not grown in intensity or in influence because of another factor that seems present almost everywhere: the largely unsympathetic view of those efforts by what we may loosely call "public opinion." In many countries, preoccupation with a perceived rise in criminality and with citizens' insecurity is fostering a dangerous tendency to justify police brutality, or at least to consider it only an unfortunate fact of life. At best, public outcry against torture and police brutality is loud but generally short-lived; at worst, it takes the form of active support for such actions. Public attitudes toward crime, in no small way fostered by sensationalistic and scare-mongering press rituals, are often marked by a sense of Rambo-like "justice" that can only be achieved by skirting the legal processes and doing away with niceties like the presumption of innocence.

Those who defended human rights during the dictatorship obtained well-earned legitimacy in the eyes of most of their countrypersons, especially during the transition to democracy. When they persist in their message in our present time, however, they tend to be discredited by the mass media and dismissed by political leaders. If, in the past, human rights organizations were viewed as "defenders of terrorists," now they are accused of defending criminals. It makes little difference to insist on the proposition that even criminals have rights, or that suspects are not to be considered criminals until found guilty by a court of law. The prevalent authoritarianism that justifies lawless violence does not listen to arguments based on facts, such as the real, as opposed to the perceived, crime rate, or the relationship between the proliferation of arms in the populace and the actual increases in some forms of crime. On the other hand, even those who justify lawlessness in the police do not necessarily feel better protected by them. As a result, our cities are in the worst of all possible situations with respect to this kind of violence: our fears paralyze any meaningful effort to deal effectively with crime, and the perceived spiral of violence only widens the gap in confidence and credibility between the citizenry and the police.

This is not to say that there are no solutions. However, the problem will probably get worse before this dangerous complacency with brutality is shaken and our political leaders decide to redress it. It is clear that the more we delay the solutions, the harder it will be to preserve any part of the police forces that are not already corrupted by this system. In some notorious cases, it is increasingly clear that some police bodies will have to be disbanded and rebuilt from scratch, much like what is being done in Haiti after the return of democracy. In the meantime, some broad sketches of paths toward positive change can be outlined.

First, we need to impose accountability in the form of serious investigations and prosecution and punishment of wrongdoers, be they common criminals or police agents. Judicial attempts to bring torturers and killers to justice must be consistently supported. Politicians would also do well in not interfering with those efforts and in not contributing to their delegitimization by playing to the public's fear of crime or by supporting the police at any cost. Obviously, common crime should also be vigorously prosecuted and punished, as long as due process and fair trial guarantees are respected. If the citizenry regains some trust in the effectiveness of the law, a large though faulty justification for lawless police action will be taken away.

Second, the police forces must understand that their job can only be done with community support and that a terrorized community is no support at all. For that reason, we must encourage constructive involvement of civil society in issues of citizen insecurity, premised clearly on the need not to give up a single fundamental human rights principle. Training of police forces in human rights will probably yield long-term results, but only if it is not seen as a lame alternative to vigorous efforts to break the cycle of police impunity. In fact, human rights training should be seen as training in the rule of law and, more specifically, training on the principle that in a democracy nobody is above the law, especially not if he or she wears a uniform.

Lastly, the main point is to understand the phenomenon of lawless violence in all its varied dimensions and with its dramatic consequences for the quality and even the existence of democracy. The following chapters, and the insightful commentaries they provoked, provide a useful contribution to this important task.

2

Torture and Conditions of Detention in Latin America

Nigel S. Rodley

IF THIS CHAPTER were being written as recently as ten to fifteen years ago, its main focus would have been on the systematic torture and enforced disappearance of political undesirables by brutal military regimes. Resort to these atrocious means of maintaining illegitimate power characterized the Latin American region. Of course, not every country had such a regime, nor did all those that did resort to the worst practices on the same scale as, say, Argentina, Chile, Guatemala, and El Salvador. But the overall "style" of the region was set by such countries as these. Most attention was paid to the treatment of political prisoners, not least because they were the main victims of enforced disappearance and, I suspect, of the most exorbitant torture techniques. Another reason was the access of political exiles to national and international media and to international governmental and nongovernmental organizations. They also had the skills to develop national groups capable of professionally gathering data on human rights violations and distributing it in a way that international bodies could use.

A closer look might have also noted some, albeit insufficient, attention was also being paid to the situations in Colombia and Peru, where human rights violations were, in numerical terms, equally if not more serious. What made them less noteworthy, in terms of international attention, was both the fact that these countries' governments had plausible democratic credentials and the existence of extremely violent armed insurgencies (of unparalleled ruthlessness in the case of Peru), complicated by widespread drug-related organized crime (of unparalleled ruthlessness in the case of Colombia).

We were not paying much attention to the situation of common criminals in the hands of the police, or to their conditions of detention on remand or under post-conviction imprisonment. Indeed, in those days, once political prisoners found themselves detained on remand or serving a prison sentence, by and large, the worst was over (Uruguay being a notable exception). Extreme torture for the purpose of securing information or confessions was no longer being inflicted and the detention was acknowledged, substantially reducing the likelihood of permanent disappearance or death.

Yet these are now the problems to which particular thought will be given in this chapter, even though, as will be seen, the worst practices still exist in Colombia and, as far as torture is concerned, in Peru. Nor have the most heinous practices been eradicated in Guatemala and some other countries. Serious ill-treatment in police custody, sometimes amounting to torture, is still meted out to common criminal suspects, probably in more countries than we know. And institutions of detention in many countries impose cruel, inhuman, or degrading conditions on their inmates, conditions that must sometimes be described as torturous.

The latter problem requires a caveat. I am not a penologist or criminologist. I am a public international lawyer, specializing in human rights. My visits to places of detention in Latin America (Chile, Colombia, Guatemala, Mexico, Venezuela) and elsewhere have usually been with a view to discovering facts relating to the reasons for detention and to treatment under interrogation. The main purpose of the visits, therefore, has been to interview individuals, not to inspect the institutions as such. This suggests the limits both of my experience, which I suspect a professional from the International Committee of the Red Cross would find severely wanting, and of my focus. As far as the latter is concerned, I am mainly addressing the most problematic aspects that unmistakably fall under the international prohibition of torture and cruel, inhuman, or degrading treatment or punishment. Penal reformers would properly find much more worthy of attention.

Enforced Disappearance

As already indicated, the practice of enforced disappearance has sub-stantially retreated in the region. In the 1970s and 1980s, hundreds and even thousands of such disappearances took place in Argentina, Chile, Colombia, El Salvador, Guatemala, Honduras, Mexico, Nicaragua, and Peru. In five of these countries (Argentina, Chile, El Salvador, Honduras, and Nicaragua), the number of cases taken up by the United Nations Working Group on Enforced or Involuntary Disappearances had declined to zero no later than 1995; in some of these countries, the decline was substantially earlier. In Chile, for example, there were 16 cases between 1978 and 1989, with none since then. Even in the four countries where the incidence is still a matter of justified concern, the trend, except for Mexico, has been downward. Thus, in Colombia, there were 86 cases in 1990, but apart from 51 in 1992, the figure was in the low 20s until 1995, when it decreased to 16. In Guatemala, from 77 cases in 1990, the number dropped to single figures in 1994 and 1995. The annual rate remained in the hundreds in Peru until 1993, but with the effective suppression of Shining Path, fell to 32 in 1993 and to 3 for each of 1994 and 1995. Only in Mexico has the downward trend been reversed. There the incidence had been in single figures from 1982 to 1991, with none reported in 1992 and 1993. Unfortunately, the Chiapas uprising seems to have seen a grave recrudescence of the problem: 37 cases in 1994 and 21 cases in 1995.[1]

We can take encouragement from the elimination of the practice of forced disappearance from most of the region and the marked downward trend in its use in three of the four countries from which it does not seem to have been eradicated. However, the example of the one country that is bucking the trend, coupled with the continuing, albeit reduced, use of the practice in three others compels a disturbing observation; where the authorities of a country faced with an effective armed challenge resort to the military to deal with the problem, the military does not yet consider the technique to be a no-go area. Worse, civilian authorities seem prepared to acquiesce in the tacit Faustian bargain that the military seems to impose: we'll do the dirty job, but you must let us do it our way.

Also disturbing is the international community's willingness to turn a blind eye to countries faced with serious internal problems and engaging in such practices. It was only in 1993, after two visits to Peru (the first in 1989, the second in 1991), and after the authoritarian constitutional changes brought about by President Fujimori, that the Inter-American Commission on Human Rights issued a report on the human rights situation in that country.[2] Similarly, the Commission, having visited Colombia in 1980 and having issued a report on that country in 1981,[3] waited until 1990 before visiting Colombia again. That visit was followed by another in 1992, with a report being published only in 1993.[4] Also, at the U.N., both countries have escaped substantial scrutiny. For example, country-specific special rapporteurs in the Commission on Human Rights failed to level severe criticism against Colombia or Peru; however, for the last two years critical statements by the chairman of the Commission have been adopted on Colombia.[5]

Torture under Interrogation

It is much more difficult to track the evolution of the practice of torture in the region. In the dark days of the military regimes, torture could be masked by the enveloping enforced disappearance. When disappearance did not conceal torture, its general prevalence, coupled with outright resort to extra-legal executions, made torture seem a matter of lesser concern.[6] Nevertheless, victims, being from the political domain, did emerge. Reports of NGOs, of U.N. country-specific and thematic machinery, and of the Inter-American Commission on Human Rights are replete with information about torture and other extreme violations.

A cursory reading of recent reports of the U.N. Special Rapporteur on Torture predictably reveals that a substantial number of allegations of torture come from Colombia, Mexico, and Peru, with most of the complaints being in respect of acts allegedly committed by the military or other security agencies upon suspected "subversives." Mexico is also a source of allegations in respect of common criminal suspects. In addition, Chile and Venezuela give rise to allegations of torture and similar ill-treatment, both of persons held in connection with suspected political armed activity and of suspected common criminals. It became clear from a U.N. visit to Chile that the torture of "politicals" had diminished by 1993 (the number of arrests had also diminished), but that there remained a problem of sometimes serious ill-treatment of common criminal suspects—a practice that had existed, but been largely ignored, before the 1973 military coup.[7] Most of the cases of alleged torture of politicals in Venezuela arise in connection with spillover problems on the Colombian frontier and land dispute issues. Common criminal suspects are also at risk. While the U.N. report did not confirm either the incidence of allegations reaching the U.N. before the visit, or the routine use of torture or similar ill-treatment, it determined that the problem was more than just an isolated, occasional aberration.[8] Information from Ecuador suggests a similar pattern. Sporadic reports are precisely what reach the U.N. with respect to Argentina and Brazil (mainly of torture of common criminal suspects and, in the case of Brazil, social "undesirables" and local group activists) and Guatemala. Other Latin American countries are also mentioned in similar sporadic reports (Bolivia, Dominican Republic, El Salvador, and Haiti).[9]

What conclusions does the foregoing suggest? Is the level of torture no higher in these countries? Is there none in other countries of the region? I doubt that we have the full picture. Certainly, in countries such as El Salvador, Guatemala, and Haiti, the U.N. or U.N./OAS presences serve as a major deterrent. In the absence of serious political convulsions, some of the worst forms of torture, usually resorted to by the security forces, are not used. This can lead to people not considering other forms of coercion as torture. In Chile, for example, "politicals" who had been gravely physically assaulted and sometimes threatened with death did not describe themselves as having been tortured. When asked why not, they explained that they had not been subjected to electric shocks.[10]

This then leaves us with common criminal suspects, social "undesirables," and local activists. These are all categories that tend to be overlooked. NGOs created in response to, or galvanized into action by, the emergence of unconstitutional regimes tend to be less interested in these types of victims. In Chile, for example, only one of the several NGOs active during the military period and still in existence has been actively engaged in working on behalf of common criminal suspects (CODEPU). The victims themselves are not organized and tend not to expect redress. Communications are often poor outside major urban areas. The priorities of NGOs, national and international, are such that these problems only get examined from time to time, with information being transmitted to official intergovernmental bodies on an *ad hoc* basis, assuming the NGOs are aware of those bodies.

So while we might conclude that both the gravity and scope of torture and similar ill-treatment have abated substantially, as and where armed political opposition has diminished, it would be a mistake to conclude that the limited information available for other categories of victims reflects an accurate picture of the problem. Factors that might suggest otherwise should also be considered. Undertrained, underpaid, and underrespected law enforcement officials are often tempted to abuse their power criminally in discharging their functions, and regrettably, those three adjectives apply to many Latin American police forces. Historical practices of coercing information and confessions from witnesses and suspects no doubt continued during the military regimes, although obscured by the worst excesses. Furthermore, the experience of the police, often called upon to collaborate with the security forces during periods of political unrest, cannot be immediately unlearned after a change of government or the collapse of an insurgency. Such practices are encouraged by legal systems that rely heavily on written dossiers, thus putting a premium on confessions and other declarations by suspects and witnesses. Judges, responding to increasingly insistent public demands for more effective protection of public order, prefer to turn a blind eye to police malpractices. For example, in Chile, judges can and do order incommunicado detention for up to five days for investigative purposes.

Remand and Correctional Institutions

Conceptually, there should be separate treatment of remand institutions, on the one hand, and correctional institutions where sentences are served after conviction, on the other. I deal with them together for two interrelated reasons: first, in many countries the problems are similar; and, second, all too often the same institutions house both remand and convicted prisoners. Indeed, one of the most frequently encountered problems is the failure to separate different categories of prisoners, as required by international standards and often by national law itself.

Separation of Categories of Prisoners

As already indicated, the separation of remand and convicted prisoners is required by international standards. Thus, according to Article 10(2)(a) of the International Covenant on Civil and Political Rights (ICCPR) and Article 5(4) of the American Convention on Human Rights (ACHR), accused and convicted persons are, "save in exceptional circumstances," to be segregated from each other, with accused persons being given "separate treatment appropriate to their status as unconvicted persons." This language points to the crux of the matter: by virtue of being unconvicted, accused persons are subject to the presumption of innocence. The purpose of the detention is not to punish, correct, or rehabilitate; it is merely precautionary. Rule 8(b) of the U.N. Standard Minimum Rules for the Treatment of Prisoners (SMR) also requires separation of these two categories, while Rule 84(2) stresses the importance of treatment consistent with the presumption of innocence.

In practice, institutions called upon to cope with a demand for space far in excess of their capacity (see below) have found themselves ignoring this important rule. Thus, in Brazil, where a relatively low 30 percent of prison inmates are on remand,[11] Human Rights Watch (HRW) reported that pretrial detainees often "live alongside those serving time for murder."[12] Chillingly, HRW notes:

> Among the 111 known fatalities of the 1992 massacres [at the Casa de Detenção São Paulo], eighty-four were pre-trial, while the rest were serving sentences ranging from two to thirty years. All were housed together.[13]

Separation of unsentenced from sentenced prisoners is mandated by Mexico's constitution. Nevertheless, HRW, referring to problems of overcrowding and prison design, cites Mexico's National Human

Rights Commission as finding the practice of mingling the categories in thirty-three prisons it visited between June 1991 and June 1992. HRW notes that 49 percent of prisoners charged with federal crimes and nearly 70 percent of those charged with state crimes were unsentenced as of November 1992.[14] The same organization also notes that national provisions in Peru (where 77 percent of prisoners were unconvicted), which contemplate separation of various categories of prisoners, are "frequently violated." More specifically, it cites Chiclayo's Picci prison, where "people who are charged with crimes live in the same areas as those already convicted and repeat offenders."[15]

At the time of the 1992 massacre at the Retén de Catia in Caracas, Venezuela, some sentenced prisoners were still housed in this pretrial facility. The same was true in 1996 when I visited the country in my U.N. capacity, both in respect of La Planta (Caracas) and Sabaneta (Maracaibo), a prison where another massacre took place in 1994.

Articles 10(2)(6) of the ICCPR and 5(5) of the ACHR envisage the separation of juveniles (ICCPR) or minors (ACHR) from adults. Rule 8(d) of the SMR takes the same position in respect of "young" prisoners. My experience is that this rule tends to be respected, but there can be a problem as to whether all minors are to be treated as minors for all purposes: in some cases the criminal justice system may treat minors above a certain age accused or convicted of certain crimes as ordinary criminals, both for the purpose of trial and of deprivation of liberty. For instance, in Chile, I came across a young person held in solitary confinement by judicial order for seven days, pending transfer to an ordinary prison.[16] HRW reports that in Peru, "minors are frequently treated as adults and incarcerated in the same areas."[17] In Mexico, HRW found four prisons where minors and adults mingle.[18] In Venezuela, I visited a police station given over to pretrial detention of juveniles which held children as young as thirteen. These children were kept in four bare cells, three cells holding ten or so males, with one cell holding three females. This was deemed necessary because proper juvenile institutions were full.

The requirement in Rule 8(a) of the SMR of detention of males and females in separate institutions, or at least with females being kept in "entirely separate" premises in an institution also housing males, seems generally to be followed. However, male prisoners could see the premises housing female prisoners in San Miguel prison in Santiago de Chile and the female prisoners had to pass through parts of the insalubrious male premises when meeting personnel, lawyers, etc.[19]

One requirement of the SMR that seems to be widely ignored is the notion of separation on grounds of criminal record (Rule 8), which requires that some prisoners do not come into contact with other prisoners "who, by reason of their criminal records or bad characters, are likely to exercise a bad influence" (Rule 67(a)). Some of the latter category may be housed in institutions of maximum security detention, but the purpose of this is not primarily to shield others from their influence. Political prisoners are often kept in maximum security detention prisons, but it may well be that these inmates would have a more beneficial influence on first-time or petty offenders or suspects than would hardened, recidivist, or serious common criminals. Yet it is precisely the latter type of mingling that one finds most frequently. Indeed, I have not encountered a general remand institution or prison for convicted persons where such mingling does not exist.

Capacity/Overcrowding

Many of the problems discussed so far are attributable to the broader problem of overcrowding of institutions in countries of the region (a problem not confined to this region). According to Penal Reform International (PRI), there are about 130,000 prisoners in the Brazilian penitentiary system, representing some 250 percent above capacity. This does not take account of another 70,000 prisoners (convicted and pretrial) in the custody of the police. Indeed, "[c]ells built for six are holding 30. Jails built for 70 are holding almost 400."[20] Elói Pietá observes:

> In some cases, there's not even space sufficient for the detainees to lay themselves down at the same time; they tie themselves to the iron bars in order to sleep standing up or in a sitting position.[21]

In addition, "many facilities—though not all—are filthy and smelly. We observed rats and giant cockroaches in some cells; inmates routinely showed us insects they had collected in their cells and displayed the bites on their bodies."[22] The report continues:

> Most cells we visited had a hole-in-the-floor toilet with a faucet directly above it for washing and drinking. We heard many complaints about the temperature: very hot and stuffy during the summer, cold and damp in the winter. In one prison we observed puddles of water on the floor of several cells; regarding one of these, an inmate commented simply: "We call it our swimming pool."[23]

HRW also reports Mexico's prisons as "vastly overcrowded." In fact, the population (86,334 prisoners) was 126 percent of capacity (70,435 places) at the time of the report.[24] My own experience was of a 1975 Amnesty International mission, including a visit to the Lecumberri prison in Mexico City. Parts of this notorious institution were clearly severely overcrowded, in a general climate of oppression and terror. Fortunately, the institution was decommissioned a few years later. At the same time, a new model prison had been built that did not suffer from the same problem. It may be that in this country overcrowding problems depend on the actual dispersal of prisoners among the various institutions. This seems to have been the case in Peru, where overcrowding was, according to HRW, "one of the most serious problems in Peru's prisons." In 1991, Lurigancho prison, with a capacity of 1200 prisoners, was housing "at least 5000," while Miguel Castro Castro (Canto Grande) prison, with a capacity of 800 prisoners, held 2,500; that is, respectively, 416 percent and 312 percent of population above capacity.[25]

During my visit to Venezuela in early 1996, I found an overcrowding problem of between two and five to one.[26] In La Planta prison in Caracas (the situation is reputedly as bad or worse at the Retén de Catia), I saw a situation in which prisoners in a cell could only find sleeping room by lying next to each other in the cell and outside it (not a comfortable option in cold or wet weather). I could not see how it could be done, but the prisoners said it was possible.

The reasons for the overcrowding are not hard to find: public anxiety about "law and order" is reaching psychotic proportions in many countries. Judges are responding by sending ever more suspects and convicted persons to jail. They turn a blind eye to the criminogenic, not to mention frequently unlawful, conditions of detention that they are complicit in creating. In any event, the general situation is all a far cry from the SMR provisions on accommodation, which specify:

9. (1) Where sleeping accommodation is in individual cells or rooms, each prisoner shall occupy by night a cell or room by himself. If for special reasons, such as temporary overcrowding, it becomes necessary for the central prison administration to make an exception to this rule, it is not desirable to have two prisoners in a cell or room.
(2) Where dormitories are used, they shall be occupied by prisoners carefully selected as being suitable to associate with one another in those conditions. There shall be regular supervision by night, in keeping with the nature of the institution.

10. All accommodation provided for the use of prisoners and in particular all sleeping accommodation shall meet all requirements of health, due regard being paid to climate conditions and particularly to cubic content of air, minimum floor space, lighting, heating and ventilation.

11. In all places where prisoners are required to live or work,
    (a) The windows shall be large enough to enable the prisoners to read or work by natural light, and shall be so constructed that they can allow the entrance of fresh air whether or not there is artificial ventilation;
    (b) Artificial light shall be provided sufficient for the prisoners to read or work without injury to eyesight.

12. The sanitary installations shall be adequate to enable every prisoner to comply with the needs of nature when necessary and in a clean and decent manner.

13. Adequate bathing and shower installation shall be provided so that every prisoner may be enabled and required to have a bath or shower, at a temperature suitable to the climate, as frequently as necessary for general hygiene according to season and geographical region, but at least once a week in a temperate climate.

14. All parts of an institution regularly used by prisoners shall be properly maintained and kept scrupulously clean at all times.

Management

The SMR contains rules on discipline and punishment (Rules 27–32), on complaint procedures (Rules 35–36), on the qualifications and functions of institutional personnel (Rules 46–54), and on regular inspection by a competent authority (Rule 55). Although it is not explicitly stated, these rules are aimed at ensuring an orderly and fair system of management. Yet what one finds all too often is either arbitrary and oppressive management or no management at all, in that the internal running of the place is abandoned to the inmates themselves.

HRW mentions reports of beatings by staff in almost all the Brazilian institutions they studied: "Beatings occur both as extra-official punishment for disciplinary infraction—ranging from arguing with a guard to attempted escape—as well as a means of intimidating and controlling prisoners." Violent inmates are reported as abusing and exploiting younger or weaker ones. In one jail, "every cell has a chief." Homosexuality is "rampant," including homosexual rape: "[Y]oung people are sold by guards who then place them in the same cells as the buyers."[27] The Mexican National Commission on Human Rights is cited by HRW as condemning beatings and mistreatment by prison officials in eleven prisons in a twelve-month period in 1991–1992. In some institutions, the Commission has denounced "self-government," that is, in effect, some prisoners taking control of part of the prison population or buying off or intimidating custodians and officials.[28]

In Venezuela's Sabaneta prison at Maracaibo, I was able to see an institution effectively divided into two camps, each run by the prisoners with the most weapons. The inadequate personnel (numerically and in terms of training) confined themselves essentially to taking regular censuses and guarding the perimeter. Prisoners who got into trouble with the leadership of one camp would be transferred to the other one.

These conditions do not necessarily correspond to the wishes or policies of the governments. Rather, the problem is not given the budgetary priority that could furnish the resources necessary to overcome it.

Massacres

In the light of the conditions that I have described so far, it will probably come as no surprise to anyone familiar with prisons that some
of the institutions mentioned have experienced riots and mutinies.
What is shocking is how frequently the authorities responsible for
restoring "order," be they the penitentiary authorities or other law
enforcement or public security agencies, have resorted to widespread
and indiscriminate use of lethal force to quell the uprisings.

In Brazil, where, it will be recalled, over a third of prisoners are
held in police custody, there was a disturbance in a police lock-up in
1989. The Military Police called to São Paulo's Precinct 42 forced 51
men into a cell of less than fifty square feet with a heavy metal door
and no windows. After more than an hour in the cell, 18 of them were
found to have suffocated to death. In 1991, at Agua Santa prison in
Rio de Janeiro, guards threw an incendiary device into a cell after discovering an escape plot, resulting in 31 prisoners dying of burns.
In response to a prison disturbance in 1992 at the São Paulo Casa de
Detenção, the Military Police killed 111 inmates, 84 of whom were
awaiting trial. As of 1993, "not a single member of the police or
prison staff [had] been criminally prosecuted for the killings."[29]

The notorious suppression of three 1986 prison rebellions in Peru
is succinctly described by Human Rights Watch:

> On June 18, 1986, Shining Path inmates staged coordinated uprisings
> in Lurigancho, in the island prison of El Frontón, and in the women's
> prison of Santa Bárbara, in Callao. The government of President Alan
> García reacted violently and desperately: it declared a war zone in the
> prisons and called in the Armed Forces to quell the riots. The army
> took command of the operation in Lurigancho, and the navy did the
> same with El Frontón. Judges and prosecutors, prison authorities and
> the government's own Peace Commission members were denied ac-
> cess to the prison as well as permission to try to negotiate a peaceful
> solution. Four prison guards were killed by the rioting inmates. A day
> later, the riots were over. In Santa Bárbara, the riot was quickly sup-
> pressed: two rioting inmates died. In Lurigancho, about twenty in-
> mates died during the battle for control of the cell block, and all of the
> survivors, more than 110, were murdered after their surrender. In El

Frontón, the navy destroyed the cell block with explosives with most inmates and hostages still inside. Some thirty inmates (of a total of around 135) were apprehended and taken to hospitals or to other prisons. Of the more than 100 dead in El Frontón, many were captured alive, some were killed on the spot and others were taken away, apparently to naval installations, never to be seen again.

The total number of inmates' deaths for these tragic episodes is well over 200. A military court investigation ended in prison sentences for only a handful of army and Republican Guard officers. The navy never accounted for its actions in El Frontón.[30]

In January 1995, the Inter-American Court of Human Rights found violations of the right to life and the right to habeas corpus in respect of the El Frontón massacre.[31]

A disturbingly similar incident occurred at Castro prison in May 1992, a month after the presidential coup of Alberto Fujimori. Again, I can do no better than to quote Human Rights Watch:

> This maximum-security prison houses most prisoners accused or convicted of belonging to Peru's two guerrilla insurgencies: the Communist Party of Peru–Shining Path and the Túpac Amaru Revolutionary Movement (MRTA). On May 6, the security forces entered in order to transfer some women to a new facility. The women resisted, apparently with the aid of some male prisoners. In the ensuing battle, three policemen and ten prisoners were killed. Mediation by third parties was rejected by the government, which opted for a frontal assault on May 10. A total of thirty-nine prisoners died and many more were wounded.
>
> Although the government declared that there were no excesses or abuses committed, Human Rights Watch believes there is evidence to suggest that at the very least excessive force was used and there is a strong possibility that several inmates were executed after surrendering. At the time of this writing, no internal investigation of the clash has been made public, and no outside group has been allowed to conduct an impartial investigation.[32]

In 1994, at Venezuela's Sabaneta prison in Maracaibo, one group of prisoners set fire to the premises of another group and then killed over 100 of those escaping the fire, while prison staff and National Guard personnel (responsible for perimeter security) stood by.

Conclusions

The 1990s have seen a marked reduction in the incidence of enforced disappearances along with the end of military rule and the restoration of constitutional government across the region. Nevertheless, some cases continue to occur in situations of internal conflict. A similar pattern occurs in respect of torture of suspects, some of the more extreme manifestations being reserved for suspected offenders believed to be associated with the parties involved in the conflict. Torture or similar ill-treatment also continues to be a problem as far as ordinary criminal suspects are concerned, even though the techniques may not always be as afflictive or used as routinely as before. Indeed, some of the practices may just be a continuation of the style of treating suspected common criminals that prevailed among police forces before the systematic torture of suspected political opponents drew attention to itself.

As far as treatment of suspects in remand and correctional institutions is concerned, the situation in a number of countries that have been reported on by NGOs is dismal. Separation of the sexes and of juveniles from adults is generally adhered to, but separation of other categories of prisoners contemplated by international standards, notably of remand and convicted prisoners on the one hand, and of serious or recidivist offenders and petty or first-time offenders on the other hand, is ignored. This is partly due to the overcrowding problem which leads people to be held in conditions that would, in some countries, create an outcry if farm animals were subjected to them.

Circumstances like these would tax the skills and resources of the most professional prison administrators. Inevitably the underpaid, undertrained, and understaffed administrations found in several countries tend either to abandon the running of institutions to the inmates or rule with brutal severity; when disorders occur, they have sometimes been repressed with murderous ferocity.

The causes are not hard to find: public clamor for ever greater repression in response to a perceived breakdown in law and order, and the lack of political will to accord the necessary financial priority to the administration of justice in general and the penal system in particular. The one bright spot is the growing regional awareness of the problems, as evidenced by the decision of the Inter-American Commission on Human Rights to study prisons. It has already preliminarily highlighted the violations addressed in this chapter and other problems.[33] It can only be hoped that this will herald some real improvements in places of deprivation of liberty.

NOTES

1. U.N. Doc. E/CN.4/1996/38, Annex IV.
2. Report on the Situation of Human Rights in Peru, Organization of American States (OAS) Doc. OEA/Ser.L/V/II 83, doc. 31 (1993).
3. Report on the Situation of Human Rights in the Republic of Colombia, OAS Doc. OEA/Ser.L/V/II 53, doc. 22 (1981).
4. Second Report on the Situation of Human Rights in Colombia, OAS Doc. OEA/Ser.L/V/II 84, doc. 39 rev. (1993).
5. U.N. Commission on Human Rights, Report on the 51st Session, Economic and Social Council Official Records, 1995, Supp. No. 4, para. 595; U.N. Commission on Human Rights, Report on the 52nd Session, Economic and Social Council Official Records, 1996, Supp. No. 4, para. 24.
6. Thus, the Chilean Truth and Reconciliation Commission concentrated on killings and enforced disappearance, with torture being addressed only when it resulted in death. MINISTRY OF FOREIGN AFFAIRS OF CHILE, SUMMARY OF THE TRUTH AND RECONCILIATION COMMISSION REPORT (1992).
7. U.N. Doc. E/CN.4/1996/35/Add.2.
8. U.N. Doc. E/CN.4/1997/7/Add.3, para. 75.
9. *See* U.N. Doc. E/CN.4/1997/7/Add.1, paras. 115–17 (Ecuador), 144 (El Salvador), 20 (Bolivia); U.N. Doc. E/CN.4/1996/35/Add.1, paras. 32–41 (Argentina), 167–70 (Dominican Republic); U.N. Doc. E/CN.4/1995/34, paras. 66–73 (Brazil), 303–06 (Guatemala), 307–14 (Haiti).
10. U.N. Doc. E/CN.4/1996/35/Add.2, para. 73.
11. Penal Reform International (PRI) Newsletter, no. 18, Sept. 1994, at 4. According to a study by Carranza et al., of thirty countries in the region, the percentage of non-sentenced prisoners in civil law countries ranges between 50 and 90 percent with a mean of 69 percent, while in common law countries the percentage ranges from 2 to 38 percent with an average of 23 percent. Pérez Perdomo, *La Justicia Penal en la Investigación Socio-Jurídica de América Latina*, in COMPARATIVE AND PRIVATE INTERNATIONAL LAW: ESSAYS IN HONOUR OF JOHN HENRY MERRYMAN ON HIS SEVENTIETH BIRTHDAY 257, 272–74 (Berlin: Duncker & Humblot, 1990). I am grateful to Alejandro Garro for drawing this work to my attention.
12. THE HUMAN RIGHTS WATCH GLOBAL REPORT ON PRISONS 133 (1993) [hereinafter HRW GLOBAL REPORT].
13. *Id.*
14. *Id.* at 193.
15. *Id.* at 200–01.

16. U.N. Doc. E/CN.4/1996/35/Add.2, para. 33.

17. HRW GLOBAL REPORT, *supra* note 12, at 201.

18. *Id*. at 196.

19. U.N. Doc. E/CN.4/1996/35/Add.2, para. 32.

20. PRI Newsletter, no. 23, Dec. 1995, *quoting* ELÓI PIETÁ, PRISONS IN BRAZIL (1995).

21. *Id*. at 7.

22. HRW GLOBAL REPORT, *supra* note 12, at 132.

23. *Id*.

24. *Id*. at 193.

25. *Id*. at 200.

26. U.N. Doc. E/CN.4/1997/7/Add.3, para. 60.

27. HRW GLOBAL REPORT, *supra* note 12, at 133.

28. *Id*. at 195.

29. *Id*. at 131, 134–35.

30. *Id*. at 206.

31. Inter-American Court of Human Rights, *Neira Alegría et al.* Case, Judgment of January 19, 1995, Series C. No. 20.

32. HRW GLOBAL REPORT, *supra* note 12, at 207.

33. OAS, Annual Report of the Inter-American Commission on Human Rights 1995, OEA/Ser.L/V.II 91, doc. 7 rev. (1996), at 221–23.

3 Comments on Rodley

Ligia Bolívar O.

El problema no es el fusilado.
El problema es el fusilador.
Cuando se dispara en frío a un ser humano
indefenso—criminal o no—se aprende a matar.
Terrible oficio.
Se crea una máquina de matar.
Y esa máquina represiva nadie la para más.
Necesita una materia prima. Un combustible.
Y cuando no lo tiene, lo inventa.

CARLOS FRANQUI, Retrato de familia con Fidel

COMMENTING ON Nigel Rodley's chapter is both a privilege and a challenge: a privilege, because one rarely has the opportunity to share views with someone as rigorous and articulate as Rodley; a challenge, because there is very little one can add to his news. Therefore, I would add very few new elements, and will focus most of my comments on the relationship between poverty, discrimination, and human rights violations.

Since English is not my first language, I decided to look up the word "underprivileged" in the dictionary, and found the following definition: deprived of fundamental social rights and security through poverty, discrimination, etc. I will look at Rodley's chapter from the lens of poverty and discrimination, both as a source and as a consequence of deprivation of fundamental rights, such as the right to physical integrity and the right to adequate prison conditions.

According to the World Health Organization (WHO), the main factor of mortality and the principal source of disease and suffering around the world is listed almost at the end of the International Classification of Diseases under code Z59.5: extreme poverty. If, as the WHO suggests, "health is a state of complete physical, mental and social well-being and not merely the absence of disease or infirmity," then it is easy to establish the link between poverty and deprivation of the right to physical integrity and adequate conditions of detention, as part of a holistic understanding of the concept of health.

I fully agree with Rodley's views that torture, ill-treatment, and poor conditions of detention have existed but have been largely ignored both before and after the wave of Latin America's military dictatorships; it is also true that such illegal practices do not take place only under dictatorships but also under constitutional regimes (allow me not to call them "democracies"). While such practices have always existed in the region, the main targets seem to be different under dictatorships and under constitutional governments.

In the past, dictatorships were responsible for torturing political prisoners. Now, emerging constitutional governments which have embraced rigid economic structural adjustment programs are responsible for acts of repression and exclusion, including torture and deplorable prison conditions, affecting particularly the underprivileged who already existed and the new underprivileged that have been generated by these programs.

In general, Latin American societies have inherited a culture deeply rooted in authoritarian patterns that began in colonial times. Peace, democracy, and consensus have been the exception, not the rule in this region. Corporal punishment, for example, was used early on as a normal means to ensure obedience from indigenous peoples and slaves. This explains why, as Rodley rightly points out, people may not consider certain forms of coercion as torture, and will not report them as such. Some victims, especially poor people, may even think that they *deserve* such treatment. Some years ago, a street child detained and severely tortured at a police detention center in Caracas told a priest who visited him: "I know they have to beat me, but they went too far."

The same applies to prison conditions. The general view is that deprivation of personal freedom is not the only punishment associated with imprisonment: prisons are not supposed to be comfortable and people should expect to be subjected to a variety of additional suffering, physical coercion being one of them. Authorities often echo these views, while prisoners—most of them from the lower levels of society—take such additional miseries as the normal course of events. Or else they prefer not to complain in order to avoid additional punishment. Their relatives rarely complain of abuses due to fear of retaliation against their loved ones, and public defenders are too busy to deal with such "technicalities."

When poor people do understand that there is something wrong with the way they have been treated, they may see no reason to report such abuse to the authorities. After all, poor people are excluded from society, not only economically, but also from a political and legal point of view. They are victimized twice: first by the perpetrator of abuses and then by a system unwilling to take action on their behalf. Yesterday's torturers knew that their acts could occur with impunity due to the complicity of their superiors. Today's perpetrators of abuses know that impunity is almost guaranteed by the low social and economic status of their victims, who would not dare file a complaint.

Interestingly enough, most members of security forces and prison personnel come from the same shantytowns as their victims. They are the empowered underprivileged, those who become a convenient instrument for governmental repression—the dirty job to which Rodley refers.

Actors

Rodley has referred to three different actors who play a key role in promoting respect for the rights to physical integrity and to adequate conditions of detention: states, NGOs, and the international community. I would like to make a few comments on how these actors contribute to or become an obstacle for the enforcement of the rule of law in the field of torture and conditions of detention for the underprivileged in Latin America.

The State

Although Latin America has experienced a change from dictatorial to constitutional regimes, the security apparatus remains unchanged, sometimes as part of the "deal" reached with former military rulers so that they would leave. Rodley's chapter provides a number of examples in this regard. The worst part of this tragedy is that once the unlawful techniques of repression are learned, they can be used at any time. As Cuban writer Carlos Franqui said, a man who learns how to kill becomes a machine that, when it runs out of fuel, will fabricate it. The same can be applied to torture. After the February 1989 national protests in Venezuela, I was horrified to listen to the testimonies of sixteen victims of torture who were taken to a military unit. The kind of torture methods they described were not just those we are used to hearing from people who are taken into police custody, but exactly the same ones I had heard from torture victims from the Southern Cone in the 1970s.

Lack of adequate training for law enforcement officials is one of many reasons that explain the persistence of torture within the region. I am convinced, however, that introducing human rights issues in training courses for law enforcement officials is not as important as specific training on investigative skills. As long as our judicial systems encourage confession as the key evidence, police and security forces will continue detaining in order to investigate, instead of investigating in order to detain a person. The use of up to five days of *incomunicado* detention in Chile, as mentioned by Rodley, is clear evidence of the persistence of poor investigative skills.

With regard to conditions of detention, the enormous gap between international standards and national legislation and practices is sufficiently described in Rodley's chapter. I would only add a minor point that, in my view, illustrates the link between rules governing life in prison and their effect on rights such as physical integrity. When looking at Human Rights Watch's account of homosexuality in Brazilian prisons, one could think that this is just another manifestation of some prisoners' depravity. I was shocked to see that there is nothing in the United Nations Standard Minimum Rules for the Treatment of Prisoners (SMR) regarding prisons' policy on inmates' sexual life, such as marital visits. The SMR's stipulate how often a prisoner should shave (SMR 16) or change his or her underclothing (SMR 17.2), but say nothing about his or her sexual life, despite the fact that it is expected that the penitentiary system should reduce differences between life in prison and life on the outside, especially when this can affect prisoners' dignity (SMR 60.1). Undoubtedly, lack of policies on prisoners' sexual life contribute to a deterioration of their sense of dignity, and in that context homosexuality and homosexual rape can become a normal practice. Although it is true that certain conditions do not necessarily correspond to the wishes or policies of the governments, as Rodley expresses, a policy on the inmates' sexual life is one area in which authorities could and should play an active role to avoid prisoners' depravity, exploitation of other prisoners, and deterioration of their dignity as human beings.

Nongovernmental Organizations (NGOs)

I entirely agree with Rodley's critical account of the role of human rights NGOs in the region regarding different standards used to deal with human rights violations under dictatorships and under democratic regimes, on one hand, and different approaches according to the kind of victim involved (e.g., political dissidents as opposed to common crime suspects), on the other hand.

I visited a wide variety of human rights NGOs in the mid-1980s in countries undergoing "transitions to democracy," and I was surprised by what I then characterized as the NGOs' "identity crisis."[1] Regardless of the reasons, the fact is that many NGOs were so focused on the evils of dictatorships and so keen to achieve democratic rule that, once military regimes were over, they lost sight of their main purpose: defending human rights regardless of the context and of the identity of the victim.

Deciding how to deal with past human rights violations without ignoring endemic human rights problems remains today one of the major challenges confronting NGOs. An adequate approach to these violations is essential if they are to address the human rights situation in their respective countries with some degree of effectiveness.

Eight years of monitoring economic structural adjustment programs has given those of us at the Venezuelan Program for Human Rights Education and Action (PROVEA) the opportunity to identify different ways in which such programs tend not only to increase but also to criminalize poverty. As a consequence, crime rates increase and tougher measures against crime are demanded by the public. When NGOs decide to intervene in this field, they confront a hostile public opinion that is willing to compromise fundamental rights in exchange for more security. An emerging challenge for human rights NGOs is how to reconcile the rights of common crime suspects with the rights of crime victims. Torture and poor prison conditions are not good for either side, but very few human rights groups have been able to narrow the gap and to propose alternative ways of securing rights for both criminal suspects and victims. In the meantime, human rights NGOs continue to be unfairly regarded as "obstacles" to an effective fight against crime.

International Community

Coming from a country where constitutional governments have ruled for the past forty years, I can only thank Rodley for his approach to the myth of democracy.

Democracy, even where it truly exists, seems to provide a cover under which human rights violations become invisible in order to avoid scandal, while a blind trust is placed in the system's ability to correct its own "excesses." But when entire official institutions are involved, the excesses become normal practice and they are covered up rather than investigated and punished.

The myth of a "stable democracy" has allowed human rights violations under constitutional regimes to remain hidden for many years. We need only remind ourselves of the case of Mexico, which has been ruled fraudulently by the same political party for more than sixty years, and of Colombia, where a decades-long agreement between liberals and conservatives, providing for alternation in the control of government, was enforced through the use of successive states of emergency, a practice that has far outlived that original agreement. These two cases should be sufficient to understand that democracy is more than periodic elections.

The myth of democracy contributes to tolerance of serious human rights violations, without regard to the fact that the stability of democracies has come increasingly under jeopardy as abuses are allowed to continue without punishment. As Rodley suggests, the myth of stable democracies results in the application of a double standard by the international community. This double standard not only affects the credibility of intergovernmental organizations, but also contributes to creating a climate of neglect, both at domestic and at international levels, for human rights violations that undermine the moral bases of the state.

Final Remark

I hope these comments contribute to our need to stress how being underprivileged is both a cause and a result of suffering human rights violations in the spheres of physical integrity and conditions of detention, and how different actors could contribute to changing this situation.

NOTE

1. Ligia Bolívar O., *Estrategias de defensa de los derechos humanos en regímenes de democracia formal* (Buenos Aires: Instituto Latinoamericano de Servicios Legales Alternativos [ILSA], 1989).

4

Defining the Role of the Police in Latin America

Paul Chevigny

> *The rules of the game are changing. Police forces were created not to protect but to control the population, and they were given permission to steal and extort bribes in exchange for loyalty to authority. But now there are complaints about corruption everywhere, and the police are in the crossfire.*
>
> SERGIO AGUAYO

IT IS DIFFICULT to define the role of the police in any society, particularly because the police are so ubiquitous and their job so protean. We can approximate the scope of the police role by speaking of the jobs of protecting persons and keeping order through patrol, as well as investigating past crimes through detectives or "judicial police."

As in so many cases, it is easier to say that the role is not being filled than it is to specify the scope of the role; so, for example, the adoption of a military role for the police seems to me always a mistake. Thus it is clear that in many Latin American countries, the role of the police is misdefined. Many politicians unthinkingly accept a semi-military model in which it is the job of the police to "fight" the enemy "crime," embodied in the person of the criminal. The model blinds them to the simple perception that the police are citizens, as are those with whom they work, and that there is no enemy. Furthermore, some politicians as well as police administrators have accepted a formula according to which it is the job of the police to reduce crime—to fight it directly, regardless of other institutions of the law and the criminal justice system. This has led to a situation in which the police are ill-equipped either for preventive policing and keeping order or for criminal investigation; they have assimilated everything to a form of semi-military "control" of the sort that Sergio Aguayo mentions in the epigraph quoted above.[1] The consequences can be seen at the extremes in acts of violence such as torture and extrajudicial killings. At the same time, the police have concealed their worst violence, as well as lesser forms of brutality and corruption, by a system of impunity. We can imagine a better role for the police if we do no more than imagine an end to these abuses.

When the problems are stated in such a bare, schematic way, it is difficult to understand why democratic societies, now prevailing in most of Latin America, would tolerate such police systems. This is especially so since most of the official violence is directed against the poor, who are the majority in substantially all these countries. Why has the situation continued? We cannot answer that question, or consider what can be done to change the role of the police, unless we confront the fact that, at least as far as life in the cities is concerned, policies that encourage police violence are popular. Leaders have succeeded in conveying the impression that police abuses are directed not to "the people" as a whole, or even to the large part of it that is poor, but only to a few demonized as antisocial. In São Paulo in 1991, when former governor Fleury was criticized for strengthening the fearsome ROTA in the military police, he asserted:

> The philosophy is what we always try to teach; a police that may be the friend of the worker, the householder and of students, but very hard in relation to bandits. For the bandits there is to be no mercy, no, and the ROTA is going to continue on this path.

And in 1990, when the notorious "tough cop" Luis Patti, an Argentinean police commander, was arrested for torture, residents demonstrated in his support, and even Argentina's President Menem claimed that he had "cleaned up crime," and that he "does everything well."[2]

From Rio de Janeiro, to Buenos Aires, to Los Angeles, and increas-

ingly to Mexico City, elected officials as well as the police complain
that defendants have too many rights, that the courts are a "revolv-
ing door," and that the police have to "crack down" on crime; they
even say we need to mount a "war on crime." I would argue that
crime and personal security are always going to pose a political
temptation in democratic societies such as these that have large social
inequalities. Where there is a free press, the media attracts viewers
and readers by sensational crime stories. Politicians can give an impression of strength and decisiveness by inveighing against crime
and the criminal justice system without having to come to grips with
intractable problems of economic and social injustice; they shift the
blame for some of society's ills onto the poor, or at least onto that portion of the poor which can be labeled marginal and dangerous. The
appeal is effective because it responds to the fears of the elites and
the middle classes, while at the same time it intimidates those who
are most affected by police crackdowns. In fact, this method is so effective that politicians sometimes exaggerate the dangers to keep the
support of the voters through fear. This has happened recently, for
example, in Argentina, where the administration tried to whip up
support for increased security measures even though the problem of
crime did not seem overwhelming, and it is starting to happen in
Mexico.[3] In a case of what Charles Tilly has aptly called the "protection racket," governments sell their people as a source of support.[4]

The rhetoric of fear and personal insecurity is appealing enough
in the United States, where the law has assumed such symbolic importance that it seems plausible that the assertion of rights might
cause, as well as solve, social problems. The rhetoric is perhaps even
more appealing where governments are beleaguered by debt and increased economic misery, and viable political means to alleviate the
misery in the short run seem to be closed, sometimes by the demands
of creditors. The temptation to escape the apparently insoluble by attacking the criminal justice system becomes overwhelming. Where
there has been heavy reliance on the military and security system in
the past, moreover, as in Argentina and Brazil, the appeal to that system is reinforced. As the criminologist Zaffaroni has written, penal
agencies "try to recover their secure position by projecting another
war; because open political violence does not exist any more, there

should be a war against ordinary delinquency."[5] It has reached the point where "human rights" is a term of abuse for some politicians, as though it were a set of privileges for criminals.

We cannot rid our societies of police abuses, not even such extreme abuses as torture and extrajudicial killings, merely by showing that they are against the rule of law. The alliance between democracy and the rule of law is uneasy at best. If we think of democracy in its primordial sense of rule by the mass of the people, there is no obvious reason that the *demos* should care deeply about the generality and continuity of laws. It is familiar ground that one of the reasons democratic governments have constitutions and that the international system has treaty-based and customary laws of "human rights" is that governments, democratic as well as authoritarian, often see little reason to protect those who are outcasts. I think we have to go beyond the assertion of human rights to show why, as a practical matter, changing the police by subjecting them to the rule of law is in the interest of all groups, elite as well as poor, in a democratic society.

The main goal of this chapter is to make that apparent. But before we reach that point, we have to understand the scope of the extremes in police work.

Torture

It is to the credit of the Argentinean government that a vice-minister of defense was forced to resign in 1995 after he had implied the permissibility of torture, by questioning whether "sometimes torture isn't justified."[6] Unfortunately, many police administrators in Latin America behave as though they are still asking themselves that question. Reports of the use of coercion against suspects in Latin American police practices are so routine that they lull the senses like rain on a tin roof.

Torture is reported in the Dominican Republic, Honduras, Nicaragua, Paraguay, Peru, and Venezuela.[7] Torture also appears even in relatively quiet places, such as Chile, Ecuador, and Uruguay, where other forms of violence such as the abuse of deadly force are not so common. Torture is notorious in Mexico, where the investigation of the murder of Jose F. Ruiz Massieu, brother-in-law of the former president, has been stained, if not ultimately ruined, by allegations of spectacular tortures, including pulling fingernails and toenails from a suspect. In Brazil, even though torture is condemned by the constitution, the legislature has been reluctant to make it a statutory crime.

In some places, such as Colombia, Cuba, and Peru, torture is reportedly used against political dissidents,[8] but for the most part, victims everywhere are accused of ordinary crimes. In Rio de Janeiro, the reform chief of the civil police publicly lamented in 1995 that "torture has long been a common practice of the Brazilian police, declaring that society had accepted torture as a just punishment for common criminals and a legitimate means of obtaining information. [He] added, however, that he thought society was gradually coming to reject torture as a legitimate police practice."[9]

Clearly, torture is used against those who are "torturable"—generally, common criminals. It is important to note that it is used as a form of punishment just as much as it is used to seek information. It is rarely used against middle-class people, except in desperate political cases or sometimes for corrupt purposes. Thus, having been tortured by the police is a badge of poverty and degradation. However, for reasons we will discuss more fully in connection with accountability and impunity, the use of torture is decreasing.

Deadly Force

The abuse of deadly force by the police varies enormously from country to country. It is sometimes used, especially in rural areas in Brazil and Mexico, for the outright suppression of social movements. In the Brazilian state of Rondônia, the military police killed ten peasant squatters in 1995, and in 1996 they killed nineteen in the state of Pará.[10] In Mexico, Guerrero state police killed seventeen members of a peasant protest.[11] These are only recent examples of similar incidents stretching back for generations.

In major cities, the use of deadly force does not usually have such an open social or political aim; instead it is justified as a way to control ordinary crime in poverty-stricken neighborhoods. In Rio de Janeiro in 1995, the military police, who do much of the patrol work in Brazilian cities,[12] raided the Nova Brasilia *favela*, killing thirteen people; in the state of Alagoas, the police killed ten people during a search for bank robbers. In both cases, the state governors, claiming that the actions were taken to fight crime, refused to entertain any criticism of police work.[13]

In Brazil as in other countries, the military police claim that the killings are the result of "shoot-outs" with armed criminals. Apart from the many accounts by witnesses that contradict that claim, the statistics about the killings suggest that this story is not often true. In the first half of 1995, there were 338 killings by police in the state of São Paulo (officially admitted). The police killed more than they wounded, suggesting that some of the killings were deliberate. The killings by police amount to a substantial proportion of all the intentional homicides in the state.[14] Moreover, it is clear from the changes in the numbers due to political pressures that police commanders can reduce the killings if they choose. The most sanguinary year in São Paulo was 1992, when the military police admitted to killing 1,470 suspects; the number of deaths caused an international scandal, followed by a plea from the federal government to control police violence. The following year the number dropped by over two-thirds, although it began to climb again in succeeding years;[15] it dropped off again in 1996.

It is clear that many killings have been part of a militarized approach to policing; criminals, or even mere *marginais* (roughly, "low-lifes"), were enemies to be killed. In Rio de Janeiro, the police, under civilian control, were replaced in 1994 by the military in "Operation Rio," and after the army finally left, an army general, a veteran of the dictatorship, was made State Secretary of Public Security. During the last decade in São Paulo, those military police who had killed the most, in one case more than forty suspects, were honored and promoted. Military police commanders claimed that the killings reduced crime directly, by eliminating criminals; they took it upon themselves to bypass the entire criminal justice process, including the courts and the prisons, alleging that the legal system was helpless to control the problem. At the same time, evidence confirms that most of those killed were not the robbers and rapists, the violent criminals, that the public most fears. In his study of thousands of police killings over many years, journalist Caco Barcellos concluded that more than half of those killed who could be identified had never had any previous contact with the criminal process; most of them were not even suspected of a violent crime at the time they were shot. The majority were black in a place where the black population was in the minority.[16] Nevertheless, military police continued to claim that the killings repressed crime, on some unstated theory, apparently, that criminals were intimidated by the number of suspects killed. But this was almost the equivalent of saying that the shootings were a reign of terror, primarily against the poor, since the police rarely kill middle-class people.

The public in Brazil often does not seem to care very much whether police killings can be legally justified; the killings have been popular. When the military police killed 111 prisoners (most of whom were detainees awaiting trial) in the São Paulo House of Detention in response to a rebellion in 1992, a large percentage of the population said that they approved, and when a TV crew filmed the actual execution of a suspect at a shopping mall in Rio in 1995, a majority of those polled condoned the killing.[17]

Although police abuse of deadly force has been much smaller in Buenos Aires than in São Paulo, there is a continuing problem with "trigger-happy" police in Argentina.[18] It appears that a semi-militarized approach to policing has exacerbated the problem there as well. Some of the violence has come from special squads, or brigades, organized on the model of special military groups, who have become a law unto themselves. Within the federal police ranks which work in the capital, the Robbery and Theft Squad accounted for over 30 percent of all police killings during the late 1980s through 1990. During this period, the police did not tend to arrest suspects, but instead lured them into corners where they could be shot.[19] In one of several cases in the province of Buenos Aires (which has its own police force operating outside the capital), a "brigade" group killed five young people in 1994, using 239 bullets to do so. Those killed were innocent; the guilty parties were arrested a short distance away without a single shot being fired. The killing, known as the "Wilde massacre," has turned out to be important in an ensuing scandal concerning the provincial police.[20]

This kind of police violence—shooting suspects of ordinary crimes (or people who merely run away from the police) in the streets—is a form of vigilantism; it is the police version of eliminating undesirables. The problem is most pronounced where civil government is weak, where there is rebellious activity against the government, or where there is a large amount of private vengeance and vigilantism. This is the case in Colombia, Guatemala, and Haiti, where there is civil disorder and vigilantism, and in Venezuela, where there is civil disorder. Similarly, the civil government is weak in Brazil, and vigilantism, in the form of lynching or of organized killers for hire, is notorious. The connection between vigilantism and police violence is emphasized by the fact that in every place where death squads are used against ordinary criminals, the police turn out to be involved. Furthermore, the police help the death squads. Thus, death squads and the police engage in "social cleansing."[21]

Conversely, governments that claim to have a monopoly on legitimate force, and at least tell a story of peaceful urban government, have had less abuse of deadly force by the police, as in Chile, Ecuador, Mexico City, Paraguay, and Uruguay. It is worth emphasizing that authoritarian or repressive governments, at least when they are not run by the military, do not necessarily have the worst problems with the profligate use of extrajudicial killing in ordinary crime cases. The incidence of such abuses at the hands of patrol police is relatively low in Mexico City[22] and they scarcely occur at all in Cuba.[23] Cuba is a highly organized society; while its police appear to have a tight control over people through surveillance, and the government does not hesitate to jail its critics, it does not seem to me that the government would tolerate police shooting of ordinary criminal suspects in the streets. Deadly force is neither democratic nor authoritarian; it is used as an instrument of terror where the control by the government is weak, and where the poor are seen as potentially dangerous.

Impunity

Extrajudicial killings, torture, and disappearances are only the worst, the most notable of violations of the rule of law by police. The police also have special powers in some countries that serve to emphasize their independence of the laws that govern the rest of the criminal justice system. In Argentina, under the use of "police edicts," the federal police have been able to detain individuals for up to thirty days for vagrancy, drunkenness, or even cross-dressing. The police constantly use and abuse these powers. In Venezuela, the police have the power, under the 1939 Vagrancy Law, to detain persons deemed by them to be a threat to society for up to five years (yes, 1,825 days). And they use that power constantly, although they do not actually detain alleged vagrants for five years.[24] Whenever it is proposed that these antiquated instruments of social control be repealed, the police always claim that they are essential to maintain order, and politicians usually agree. Such laws support the proposition of Sergio Aguayo that the police are primarily intended for the control of people.

Broad vagrancy powers do have at least some legitimacy in that the state affirms that the police have such powers, and tries to justify them. In contrast, extrajudicial killing and torture are secret. Fortunately, no present government would openly claim that it tries to keep order in the streets by killing suspects or that successful criminal investigation depends on torture. Therefore, persistence of the abuses is dependent on systems of impunity. These are multifarious, they occur at every level of the system of criminal justice, and they partly reflect the fact that people often do not want the police to be punished for violating the rights of suspects.

At the first level, administrative systems to discipline police have been inadequate or nonexistent. When I participated in an investigation in Buenos Aires in 1991, we found that the systems of administrative discipline were opaque—absolutely unknown to the public. Very little has changed; to this day there is no transparent system of police discipline.[25] Similarly, in Ecuador and Paraguay, the government simply failed to take administrative action in response to complaints of torture.[26]

When police abuses are referred to the courts or other public bodies, the police have myriad ways of interfering in the investigations. In São Paulo, when the military police kill a suspect, in order to remove most forensic evidence, they commonly take the victim to the hospital as if he or she were still alive.[27] In an effort to substantiate the story that the victim was killed in a shootout, they will plant a weapon in his or her hand. In Mexico, during the investigation of the killing of seventeen peasant demonstrators in Guerrero in 1995, it was found that the police had tampered with a videotape of the shooting and had planted weapons. The police in Argentina have sometimes used a particularly effective method of concealing their responsibility when a suspect dies under torture: they simply make all traces of the person disappear, pretending that they never had contact with the victim. Evidence confirms that this was done following the deaths of Miguel Bru and Andrés Núñez in Buenos Aires province, and in the case of Diego Laguens in Jujuy.[28]

Often superior officers will demonstrate, by aiding in a cover-up, that they do not disapprove of the violence. To take just one example, the investigation of the death of Andrés Núñez, who disappeared in 1990 after having been tortured in La Plata, Argentina, has been agonizingly protracted, in part because the chief of the investigation brigade falsified the guard book to conceal the fact that Núñez had been there.[29]

The judiciary has rarely been vigorous either in investigating or punishing police abuses. I recall some judges in Buenos Aires in 1991 telling us that they were investigating a killing by police in the province, while people in the neighborhood were telling them that they hoped the police would not be prosecuted because they had gotten rid of some bad elements. Under those circumstances, it is hard for officials to be very assiduous in prosecuting or punishing police violence. It is reported that in the Dominican Republic, officials have been punished for acts of torture with sentences ranging from suspension from the job to six months' incarceration. In Mexico, the National Commission for Human Rights has recommended that police be prosecuted for acts of torture, and sometimes that criminal convictions be reviewed if they appear to be based on coerced testimony. The courts have often failed to charge police or to reverse convictions based on torture.[30]

Criminal procedure in many Latin American countries makes it difficult to trace the progress of cases against police. The proceedings in a pending case are sometimes available only to those with a legal interest in the case, and the proceedings are in any case often conducted very quietly by an investigating magistrate. There is thus little for the media and public to follow, and if a case against the police is dismissed, it is difficult to mount an intelligent criticism of the actions of the court.

In Brazil and Colombia, the police are subject to their own system of justice, through military courts, although this practice is being revised in Brazil. Such courts are extremely lenient on the rare occasions when they do convict police. For example, in São Paulo, the military court imposed a sentence of six years for killing a transvestite, when the civilian court gave the same person forty-four years in a similar crime over which the military court did not have jurisdiction. The conviction rate is very low, and the military courts are absurdly understaffed and underfunded. Thus, they are unable to complete their work within a reasonable time frame.[31]

It is possible in most jurisdictions to bring claims for damages against the government for the misconduct of its officials. Nevertheless, it is rarely done, partly because there is little tradition of bringing such claims, partly because the victims and their families are intimidated by the violence of the government's representatives in the police, and partly because the success of the civil claim sometimes depends on the success of the criminal case against the police, which may be protracted and ultimately unsuccessful.

These sources of impunity are formidable, but in fact they only scratch the surface. If any of the systems of review—administrative or judicial—show a spark of independence and willingness to find a police official guilty (and they increasingly do so), police have used personal influence, intimidation, sometimes bribery, and ultimately violence to put out the spark. But this is only part of the story of why society as a whole ought to unite to put a stop to police violence, even though it is directed almost entirely against the dispossessed. This is the subject to which I will now turn.

Society's Interest in Controlling Violence and Impunity

If we are going to come to grips with the popularity of police violence, and with the widespread view that the legal system is too slow and too inefficient—too, well, legalistic—to cope with crime, and that the job is necessarily left to what is in fact vigilante justice, we are going to have to get most people to see that the rule of law serves the general interest. We can make a political argument that a society cannot be "democratic" in a modern sense unless it treats all its citizens alike, that it cannot make arbitrary distinctions against the poor and at the same time pretend that the poor are full participants in the democracy. I do not disagree with that argument, but I want to make a more narrow and instrumental argument to appeal to those who do not care very much about the theory of democracy.

During one of my trips to Brazil, I sat next to a very pleasant young woman, the daughter of a prominent journalist family in Brazil, who was then living in the U.S. and on her way home for a visit. She said that she was apprehensive about going home because Brazil seemed so unsettled; there seemed to be a constant danger of kidnapping among people of her class. When I told her what I was doing—investigating police violence, particularly against poor people in the cities—she was bemused. She knew better than to argue with the whims of American liberals, but I sensed that she thought what I was doing was irrelevant. The first thing to do was to reduce crime; then we could worry about rights violations. I would like to make an argument that would appeal to people like that young woman: society cannot obtain "security" through police lawlessness, precisely because it is lawless. I think recent history supports this argument strongly.

The argument is relatively easy to make in the case of torture. In Mexico, where the use of torture by the police is endemic, cases are usually "solved" by confession. The police are frequently not sure whether the person charged is the right person, and it often seems that they do not care. Not only does this lead to innocent persons being convicted, and guilty ones remaining at large, it leads to an inability to resolve cases in a trustworthy way. As it becomes known that torture is used and that innocent persons may be framed, the system of criminal justice loses its credibility;[32] citizens do not know whether they ought to believe the claims of the government, and are inclined not to. In a notorious case in the late 1980s, officers of the Federal Judicial Police were charged by the Mexico City police with a number of rapes. The Federal Judicial Police tried to pretend that the charges were false, even though the victims had identified some of their members, by arresting some Mexico City police for the crimes and forcing them to confess, creating a scenario that is not implausible in Mexico, in which it appeared that the Mexico City police had framed the Federal Judicial Police.[33] The effect of decades of such Byzantine intrigues is obvious in the current investigations of the killings of Luis Donaldo Colosio and Jose F. Ruiz Massieu, in which investigators have advanced theories and then dropped them, in which there are reports that witnesses have been tortured, and where there is a general consensus that the police are incapable of conducting a fair investigation.

The sense of mistrust of civil police investigators is similar in Brazil. The story that we hear is not so much that the police frame the innocent, but that they make use of torture for corrupt purposes. Torture is used in property crimes to obtain the proceeds of the crime to then sell back to the owner, and it is used to obtain a bribe to stop the torture; suspects may even be released without charges being filed. The result is that the police cannot solve many crimes and do not develop the skills to obtain persuasive evidence. It has been reported that 90 percent of the homicide investigations in Rio de Janeiro have produced insufficient evidence for trial.[34] Thus torture creates a situation in which, in addition to the violation of human rights, guilty people remain at large and crimes are not investigated adequately.

The problems for society as a whole and for its elite, created by extrajudicial killings and lesser uses of force, take many forms. The vigilantism that runs parallel to the unlawful use of deadly force by police on duty is not really unofficial crime, as it appears to be; as I noted above, the death squads against putative crimes have always been found to involve the participation of the police. The "social cleansing" by such groups is not restricted to those suspected of specific crimes, for it is also prevalent against outcast groups, such as homosexuals or children who are suspected of living a criminal life. That alone might not be enough to arouse the fears of the elite about vigilantism. The fact is, however, that there is nothing to stop such uncontrolled groups from attacking those who are mere political adversaries of the existing regime. This has already been happening in Mexico for some time. In 1994, the CNDH investigated 140 claims of political violence against members of the opposition PRD, including many murders, and found that almost half of them involved the collaboration of the authorities.[35]

Because of official involvement in vigilantism, dismantling the death squads becomes a problem of overcoming impunity, the same impunity that prevails for the killings on duty in the bogus "shootouts." The parties guilty of violence, whether on or off duty, try to derail investigations of their crimes and discourage witnesses and investigators through intimidation and actual violence. Thus the system of impunity threatens lawyers, judges, journalists—anyone who tries to reveal the facts about violations of human rights and other police abuses. In the Mexican state of Sinaloa, the president of the Human Rights Commission, Norma Corona Sapién, was murdered in 1990, and a police commander was accused of the killing during a trial in the course of which six prosecution witnesses were murdered.[36] In Rio Negro, Argentina, there are reports that a *subcomisario* of police was murdered because he was a witness to the death of a victim under torture by some of those in his command.[37] A prosecutor of the military police justice in São Paulo, Stella Kuhlmann, has been threatened for years because of her investigations, and there are reports of serious threats to judges in Argentina, Brazil, Honduras, and Guatemala.[38]

The threats are crimes, of course, only slightly less serious than carrying out the threats, and they run against people of all classes, although principally against middle-class individuals. They make risky the business of being critical. The most important thing, however, about these crimes for purposes of our present topic—the dangers of police lawlessness to the society as a whole, including its elite—is that the crimes are part of a system of impunity that extends to all police crimes, whether or not they involve police brutality.

The system starts with taking bribes. Corruption has no respect for class, and thus the police will demand money from people at every level of society. All residents of Mexico City fear contact with the police because they know they will have to pay a bribe, and they run a risk of being beaten if they refuse.[39] Indeed, corruption and brutality are interrelated; together they show the power of the police, their independence of the rest of the criminal justice system, and their ability to administer justice as they see fit. In New York City, the

Mollen Commission on corruption wrote words that have a wider application, and thus are applicable in Latin America as well as in the United States:

> [Brutality] strengthens aspects of police culture and loyalty that foster and conceal corruption. For example, brutality, regardless of the motive, sometimes serves as a rite of passage to other forms of corruption and misconduct. Some officers told us that brutality was how they first crossed the line toward abandoning their integrity. Once the line was crossed, it was easier to abuse their authority in other ways, including corruption. Brutality is also used as a rite of initiation to prove that an officer is a tough or "good" cop, one who can be accepted and trusted by his fellow officers not to report wrongdoing. . . . [40]

Thus police officers who have committed crimes, whether of corruption or brutality or worse, have to tolerate the crimes of others; if they try to report them, they risk being exposed themselves and sometimes being assaulted or killed. And because the crimes are concealed by the system of impunity, there is no limit as to how far they may extend, especially if the money from corruption pervades all levels of the police and other parts of the political system.

It is not a long step between taking a bribe to ignore a crime and actually aiding a crime. Under a system of impunity, there is no way to prevent this step from being taken. Thus, in many cases, police collaborate with kidnappers. Particularly where there have been political disappearances and police participation in vigilante death squads, kidnapping is an easy exercise for the police, one for which they already have the skills. And the crime is doubly tempting because it is so lucrative, at least when it is used against the rich. Indeed, in the last few years, there have been scandals about police involvement in kidnapping in Brazil,[41] Argentina,[42] Colombia,[43] Guatemala,[44] and Mexico.[45] Because of continuing impunity, moreover, when one scandal blows over, another succeeds it. And kidnapping is the one crime that most terrifies the upper classes and makes them feel most ill at ease in their own countries. As the elite demand more security, it becomes a classic case of state power acting in a "protection racket" against dangers that the state itself perpetuates. I am tempted to think of kidnapping as the quintessential crime for security forces, who are constantly honing their skills at grabbing people against their will, whether legitimately or not. It has gotten to the point that whenever I hear about a string of unsolved kidnappings, I immediately suspect the police.

Kidnapping is one clear case in which the impunity consequent on police lawlessness is against the interests of elites as well as of society as a whole. But it does not stop there. The primary interest that corrupt police have in kidnapping is money; if the protective net is strong, if they have the protection of the politicians, there is no crime that is too bizarre, provided it pays well. A current scandal in Buenos Aires, which is still missing some pieces, has cast a lurid light on the interconnection between violent crime, corruption, and violation of human rights in police work.

The scandal begins in 1994 with the Wilde massacre, discussed previously, when Buenos Aires provincial police used grossly excessive force to kill five persons wrongly suspected to be robbers. Several police personnel were convicted of homicide in the case, while others took flight. Nevertheless, with typically little explanation, the convictions were reversed by superior courts and the cases dismissed in 1996.

Six months after the Wilde massacre, a colossal car bomb exploded in front of the Asociación de Mutuales Israelitas de la Argentina (AMIA) in Buenos Aires, killing eighty-three people and attracting intense international interest. The government assigned its best investigators to the solution of the crime, which was thought to be the work of foreign terrorists. At the end of that year, they arrested one Carlos Telleldin, who had apparently supplied the stolen car that contained the bomb. Telleldin, who had bribed Buenos Aires provincial police in the past in order to conduct his stolen car business, implicated some police members in the explosion. In 1996, the investigators finally found that the police had moved the stolen car for the bombing, apparently in return for bribes. The most powerful officers in the Buenos Aires police, including Juan Ribelli, the right-hand man of the chief himself, were charged with homicide in the case (the foreign terrorists, if such there be, have never been identified). Perfecting the circle of crime, the investigators linked Ribelli back to the Wilde massacre, finding that he had collected money and paid bribes for the impunity of the police who were ultimately cleared by the courts in that case. According to the Buenos Aires magazine *Noticias*,[46] by the time of his arrest Ribelli had amassed some fifteen million dollars in assets, which surely must have been known to dozens, if not hundreds, of other officials.[47]

The AMIA bombing and the Wilde massacre demonstrate how inextricably intertwined human rights violations are to greed and corruption. These vices drew the police into the bombing and protected their impunity in the Wilde case. If nothing is done about the sort of corruption that permits a police officer to amass a fortune of fifteen million dollars, then there will likely be no crime that is too heinous for the police. This further demonstrates that the lawlessness of the police is in the interest of no one except the police and the circle of politicians with whom they share the spoils. It might be argued that the AMIA scandal is truly exceptional, as some Argentinean politicians would like to claim. I doubt it. However, I do think that it is different from other cases in that, due to international pressure, it has been given an apparently thorough investigation, and this has revealed its interconnection to other crimes in the system.

Reforms in Police:
Less Violence, More Honesty and Efficiency

This has been a bleak picture. The measures we need against the abuses include actions to cut down on violence and corruption, while at the same time increasing security. In 1996, the signs are beginning to be hopeful because the problems have been so starkly revealed.

Particularly hopeful are the measures directed at reducing impunity, at least for acts of violence. Administrative review of police actions is slowly beginning to change. An ombudsman has been appointed in São Paulo, and he is taking complaints against police. In Buenos Aires province, the governor has proposed that a citizen be appointed to oversee police complaints.[48] At an even more basic level, training in the principles of human rights has begun, for example, in São Paulo, Brazil. In Buenos Aires, there is a project which requires police force candidates to have graduated from secondary school and examinations for promotions to be based upon university training.

Furthermore, in São Paulo many of the worst killers have been transferred, and there is now a new program requiring that any police officers who take a life be transferred to a special program for six months that includes counseling. The official figures of 1996 show that the number of military police killings is reducing radically.

In the field of judicial action, the situation is improving. There are several reports from Argentina of convictions of police officers for acts of violence, and it is now possible to conduct homicide trials as open, oral proceedings which the public and the press can attend. In Brazil, the military courts have finally been deprived of their jurisdiction in trials of military police for intentional homicide.[49]

The judiciary has tremendous power to control the abuse of suspects in custody by excluding evidence obtained through coercion. In the early 1990s, the judges in São Paulo reduced the incidence of torture by constantly monitoring the civil police and any suspects in custody. In contrast, the judiciary in Mexico has done little to reduce the incidence of torture.[50] Judges should be trained and encouraged to exclude all evidence that appears to be tainted; criminal procedure should provide that when a defendant presents evidence that a confession is coerced, the state has a heavy burden to justify the confession.

Ways must be found to investigate and redress the chronic problem of threats against judges, officials, lawyers, and witnesses who are involved in cases against the police. In Buenos Aires, a special detective squad has been proposed for the investigation of these matters, an idea that is useful but seems too feeble. The judges should have their own investigators appointed, or better yet, the federal government should have charge of investigations of alleged violations of human rights. In Brazil, it appears that a program has been established to protect witnesses in cases of official misconduct.[51]

The legislatures can increase accountability and reduce violence not only by investigating police abuses, but also by procedural changes which limit the powers of police. Indeed, both in Mexico and Argentina, laws have been adopted that make confessions made to the police alone inadmissible as evidence; this is an important reform to reduce torture. In addition, in Argentina, the arbitrary powers under the police edicts are being eliminated.

In countries with a federal structure, the central government ought to undertake the oversight of human rights for the nation as a whole. This has begun in Brazil, and took effect under the Salinas government in Mexico with the National Commission for Human Rights. Experience everywhere, including the United States, is that federal governments are extremely reluctant to undertake this responsibility because it is not a popular cause. It is important nevertheless that national governments embrace the position advanced here, that accountability for official misconduct is in the interests of everyone at every level of society. Moreover, for any program, it is essential that governments, local or national, undertake reforms systematically and permanently. There is a tendency, in the United States as elsewhere, to treat official abuse as a "scandal" to be dealt with by a one-time investigation, or by replacing officers with other officers. Independent investigative bodies for police violence and corruption have to be established on a continuous, routine basis, and changes in policy must be permanent. The Brazilian government is engaged in a program to foster human rights on a permanent basis and as part of national policy. That is the correct approach because temporary and "crisis" measures do not bring permanent change.[52]

Almost all the actions discussed above are specifically directed at the problem of police violence; they do not come to grips with the broader problems of police corruption and failure to ensure security. It is clear that police must be better paid and that the qualifications for police officers must be raised. In Mexico City, for example, the pay for police has been so poor that taking bribes is obviously expected, and the situation is not much better in many other cities. The qualification of a secondary school diploma for entry to the force and further academic training for advancement, already noted as presently proposed in Buenos Aires, are useful reforms. But we must not be naive; such qualifications are necessary but not sufficient for reducing corruption. Police in the United States have had decent salaries as well as academic qualifications for decades, and corruption persists. Corruption can be eliminated only if superior officers are committed to rooting it out, and are willing to dismiss officers shown to be crooked. The attack on corruption should be maintained by an independent body funded and empowered to investigate and prosecute. Such a program has to be conducted systematically over a long period, and it has to have the support of elected officials and other parts of the political system. If it cannot be carried out at the local level, it should be spearheaded by the national government. But it should never be carried out by further militarizing the police, as has happened recently in parts of Brazil and Mexico.

This leads me to the point that the police cannot be viewed as "a problem" in isolation. If they operate in a society rife with corruption, they will be corrupt, and will in fact probably contribute part of their gains to the politicians. If they are corrupt, they will generally be violent as well, and it will be nearly impossible to break the wall of impunity. The elimination of corruption has to be made part of a program of cleaning the political system generally. Then a program against police corruption and violence can be carried out over a period of time, and the energies of the police can be directed to preventing and solving crime.

NOTES

I would like to express thanks to the Center for the Study of Violence in São Paulo, the Centro de Estudios Sociales y Asesorias Legales Populares in Buenos Aires, and Human Rights Watch. Their help was essential in completing this chapter.

1. *See* Sam Dillon, *Mexicans Tire of Police Graft as Drug Lords Raise Stakes,* NEW YORK TIMES, March 21, 1996.

2. PAUL CHEVIGNY, EDGE OF THE KNIFE: POLICE VIOLENCE IN THE AMERICAS 169, 198–99 (New York Press, 1995).

3. CHEVIGNY, *supra* note 2, at 199–200; *Mexico Politics: Radical Proposals to Beat Rising Crime,* LATIN-AMERICAN WEEKLY REPORT, April 4, 1996, at 152.

4. Charles Tilly, *War-Making and State-Making as Organized Crime,* in BRINGING THE STATE BACK IN (D. Rueschmayer, T. Skocpol, & P. Evans eds., Cambridge University Press, 1985).

5. E. R. Zaffaroni, *The Right to Life and Latin American Penal Systems,* 506 ANNALS 64 (Am. Assoc. Pol. & Soc. Sci., 1989).

6. *As noted in* CHEVIGNY, *supra* note 2, at 198.

7. U.S. DEPARTMENT OF STATE, COUNTRY REPORTS ON HUMAN RIGHTS PRACTICES 1995 (1996) [hereinafter COUNTRY REPORTS 1995].

8. *Id.*

9. As reported in *id.* at 345.

10. COUNTRY REPORTS 1995, *supra* note 7; Michael Sherrill, *Of Land and Death,* TIME, May 6, 1996.

11. HUMAN RIGHTS WATCH WORLD REPORT 1996 112 (1996).

12. The military police are under civilian control. They are organized along hierarchical military lines, however, with *oficiais* and *soldados*.

13. HUMAN RIGHTS WATCH WORLD REPORT, *supra* note 11, at 71.

14. *Id.*; COUNTRY REPORTS 1995, *supra* note 7.

15. CHEVIGNY, *supra* note 2, at chap. 5.

16. CACO BARCELLOS, ROTA 66: A HISTORIA DA POLICIA QUE MATA (São Paulo: Globo, 1992).

17. CHEVIGNY, *supra* note 2, at 177–78; COUNTRY REPORTS 1995, *supra* note 7.

18. Calvin Sims, *Buenos Aires Journal: The Police May Need to Be Policed Themselves*, NEW YORK TIMES, June 17, 1996.

19. CHEVIGNY, *supra* note 2, at 194–95.

20. CISALP (Centro de Estudios Sociales y Asesorias Legales Populares), *Boletín* (on-line news service), no. 22, Aug. 2, 1996, Buenos Aires, *quoting* CLARÍN, Aug. 1, 1996.

21. *See* CHEVIGNY, *supra* note 2, at chap. 5; COUNTRY REPORTS 1995, *supra* note 7; HUMAN RIGHTS WATCH WORLD REPORT, *supra* note 11, at 71, 95–96.

22. CHEVIGNY, *supra* note 2, at chap. 8.

23. COUNTRY REPORTS 1995, *supra* note 7.

24. CISALP, *Boletín* (on-line news service), sup. 5, Sept. 18, 1996, Buenos Aires.

25. CHEVIGNY, *supra* note 2, at chap. 6; Sims, *supra* note 18.

26. COUNTRY REPORTS 1995, *supra* note 7.

27. HUMAN RIGHTS WATCH WORLD REPORT, *supra* note 11, at 71; CHEVIGNY, *supra* note 2, at chap. 5.

28. CISALP, *Boletín* (on-line news service), sup. 4, Sept. 11, 1996, Buenos Aires. *Quoting Clarín*, June 9, 1996, June 22, 1996, and July 20, 1996; U.S. DEPARTMENT OF STATE, COUNTRY REPORTS ON HUMAN RIGHTS PRACTICES 1994 311 (1995) [hereinafter COUNTRY REPORTS 1994]; Sims, *supra* note 18.

29. CISALP, *Boletín*, sup. 4, *supra* note 28.

30. COUNTRY REPORTS 1994, *supra* note 28, at 445–46; CHEVIGNY, *supra* note 2, at chap. 8.

31. COUNTRY REPORTS 1995, *supra* note 7; CHEVIGNY, *supra* note 2, at chap. 5.

32. CHEVIGNY, *supra* note 2, at chap. 8; COUNTRY REPORTS 1995, *supra* note 7.

33. HUMAN RIGHTS WATCH, HUMAN RIGHTS IN MEXICO 14–15 (1990).

34. CHEVIGNY, *supra* note 2, at chap. 5; COUNTRY REPORTS 1995, *supra* note 7.

35. COUNTRY REPORTS 1994, *supra* note 28, at 445.

36. U.S. DEPARTMENT OF STATE, COUNTRY REPORTS OF HUMAN RIGHTS PRACTICES 1993 (1994) [hereinafter COUNTRY REPORTS 1993].

37. CISALP, sup. 4, *supra* note 28.

38. COUNTRY REPORTS 1995, *supra* note 7; CHEVIGNY, *supra* note 2, chap. 6; HUMAN RIGHTS WATCH WORLD REPORT, *supra* note 11.

39. CHEVIGNY, *supra* note 2, at chap. 8.

40. *Commission to Investigate Allegations of Police Corruption and the Anti-Corruption Procedures of the Police Department Report*, Office of the Mayor, New York, 1994 [hereinafter Mollen Commission].

41. COUNTRY REPORTS 1995, *supra* note 7, at 344.

42. CHEVIGNY, *supra* note 2, at chap. 7; COUNTRY REPORTS 1994, *supra* note 28, at 310.

43. HUMAN RIGHTS WATCH, STATE OF WAR: POLITICAL VIOLENCE AND COUNTER-INSURGENCY IN COLUMBIA 27 (1993).

44. M. Moore, *Crime Bedevils Guatemala*, WASHINGTON POST, June 17, 1996.

45. Sam Dillon, *In Shake-up, Army Officers Fill Top Police Posts in Mexico City*, NEW YORK TIMES, June 19, 1996.

46. *See Los Soldados del Diablo*, NOTICIAS (Buenos Aires), Aug. 10, 1996.

47. CISALP, no. 22, *supra* note 20.

48. COUNTRY REPORTS 1995, *supra* note 7, at 342; CISALP, *Boletín* (on-line news service) no. 34, *Buenos Aires*.

49. Sebastian Rotella, *Brazil Tries to Rein in Its Police*, LOS ANGELES TIMES, Aug. 27, 1996.

50. CHEVIGNY, *supra* note 2, at chaps. 5 & 8.

51. Rotella, *supra* note 49.

52. Paulo Sérgio Pinheiro, *Brazil's Bold Effort to Curb Police Violence*, TIME, June 10, 1996; *Programa Nacional de Direitos Humanos* (National Human Rights Program) (Brasilia: Ministry of Justice, 1996).

5 Comments on Chevigny

Jean-Paul Brodeur

DESPITE ITS TITLE, Paul Chevigny's chapter is not so much about defining the role of the police in Latin America as it is about finding ways to change how the police force presently operates there. This is a difficult chapter on which to comment, since I find very little in it with which I disagree.

Chevigny presents a bleak picture of policing in Latin America, where the police systematically abuse their powers with impunity and act more as a force to control the poor, the weak, and the destitute through torture, deadly force, and repressive vagrancy laws than as an institution devoted to the promotion of security for all citizens. Particularly in countries such as Columbia, Guatemala, Haiti, and Venezuela, where the civil government is weak, the poor are seen as undesirables who posit a threat to the state.

I will not dispute the accuracy of Chevigny's description of the situation that actually prevails in Latin America. He has researched this situation for several years, and I have little experience with Latin America. However, I was involved with Canadian-sponsored programs designed to protect homeless youths against police killings in Kinshasa, Zaire (under Laurent Kabila, restored to its former name, the Democratic Republic of Congo); this is a problem which is also very acute in some South American cities, such as São Paulo. Knowing Chevigny's previous work and the fact that he has just published a book on police violence in the Americas, I assume that his description is in the main justified, and I will not attempt to change the picture that he presents. Nor will I try to summarize his chapter. It is a model of clarity, devoid of the usual jargon that provides grist to the mill of commentators.

The argument that Chevigny's chapter develops is expressed thus:

> I think we have to go beyond the assertion of human rights to show why, as a practical matter, changing the police by subjecting them to the rule of law is in the interest of all groups, elite as well as poor, in a democratic society.

In my comment to his chapter, I will address the problem of how the police may be made to change in Latin America. My comments are divided into four parts. First, I discuss some of the points raised in Chevigny's chapter. Second, I make suggestions that go beyond the chapter. Then, I make some brief conclusions. In a postscript, I have added remarks taking issue with comments that were made during the stimulating debates that took place during the workshop held at the University of Notre Dame.

Will Subjecting the Police to the Rule of Law Be Perceived to Be in the Interest of All?

Before addressing the chapter's main argument, I make three brief comments. First, it appears that following the scandal raised by the number of military police killings in 1992—1,470 suspects had been killed in São Paulo alone—the volume of police killings was reduced by two-thirds in 1993. This result was achieved by applying political pressure on military police commanders. This example indicates that when there is a political will to decrease excess in police brutality, results are actually produced. The real problem is to be able to achieve the desirable level of constancy in the political will. As a point in fact, the numbers of killings started to climb again in 1994. Second, as is emphasized by Chevigny, Latin American countries differ widely in their institutions and in their present social and political predicaments. Hence, it may be argued that the strategies to bring the police apparatus under the rule of law in these different countries should reflect their diversity. The case of Peru, where there are still remnants of a once powerful guerilla movement, is different, for instance, from the case of Chile. Third, any attempt to convince the middle and upper classes of a given society that it is in their best interest to have a law-abiding police is bound to fail if it runs against what they are being fed daily by the mass media. If, for instance, the media nurtures the belief that the haves are under the siege of the have-nots and that only the most repressive kind of policing will protect them and their property, then the argument in favor of a law-abiding police will most probably be lost in the panic of the ruling classes.

Chevigny reviews several mechanisms through which police can be made more accountable and respectful of the law. These mechanisms are the appointment of an ombudsman taking complaints against police in São Paulo, a proposal to appoint a citizen to oversee police complaints in Buenos Aires, and programs for training police in the principles of human rights. Some of the more promising of these training programs, such as in São Paulo, include counseling. I have been involved over many years in such programs. For instance, I was part of the external review board of the citizens' complaints against the Quebec provincial police for over four years. I have also taught in several police academies. Based on my experience, I would call these complaint processing and educational strategies only fine-tuning strategies. They are not in themselves conducive to fundamental changes and are in need of bases upon which to build. The problem with complaint boards is that they only target the rank and file and rarely reach above that level. With regard to teaching, police tend to assimilate only what they perceive as heightening their performance in the field. Tricks to circumvent the due process of law are viewed as more useful than training in the principles of human rights, which are often seen (at least in my own country, Canada) as a hindrance to effective policing.

In the field of judicial action, it must be admitted that in the U.S. and in Canada the exclusion of illegally obtained evidence and legal constraints on the admissibility of confessions, which must increasingly be videotaped, are powerful tools for making police respect the due process of law. Consequently, any confession obtained through submitting the suspect to torture or improper pressures would be inadmissible as evidence. However, I am concerned that in Latin America, where the due process of law is perceived as an obstacle to overcome in the war against crime, judicial measures that would be efficient in reducing torture, with the attendant effect of reducing the number of confessions, may incite police to use lethal force even more often in order to balance the uncertainty of obtaining a conviction in court.

As previously noted, however, the main argument developed by Chevigny is that the upper classes must be convinced that it is in their own best interest to have a police respectful of human rights. In trying to convince them of that, according to Chevigny, two points should be made. First, when they are not ruled by law, police may stifle political opposition by targeting political adversaries of the government, by taking revenge upon persons blowing the whistle on police violations of human rights, and by making it a risky business to be a critical person in a democratic society. Such persons are often to be found among the elites, who are thus threatened. The second strand of argument is that police brutality is conducive to police corruption (taking bribes) and to the involvement of police in crime, such as kidnapping and terrorism perpetrated to protect their own impunity. Again, the victims of such practices could be found among the upper classes.

Are these arguments likely to swing the upper classes in favor of police accountability? It is very difficult to say. First, I believe that people tend to differentiate between political policing directed against dissent and criminal law policing directed against crime. Although they might be swayed against political policing that threatens them in their patrician activities, the upper classes may keep on fearing criminals who threaten their lives and their property, and give a blanket allowance to the abuse of power implied by an all-out war against "crime." The point that needs to be made is that the separation between political and criminal law policing is artificial and that excess in the one leads to excess in the other. This is not an obvious point, as the North American example shows. In my own country, Canada, we are extremely vigilant against any form of political policing, while being fairly tolerant of police abuse against persons branded as criminals. I would hypothesize that the situation is much the same in the U.S., with even less indulgence towards criminals.

The second point that I want to make is empirical. Given how the upper classes assess the chances that they will be victimized by a police kidnapping or by a random terrorist act, are they likely to believe that the greatest threat to their well-being comes from the police rather than from deviant members of the underclass against whom police claim to protect them? As I previously said, the answer to this question depends at least in part on what the media are reporting to the public.

In this regard, I offer a suggestion. I would tend to believe that progressives are fighting a losing battle as long as they frame the debate on policing in terms of individual risks and individual victimization. The greatest toll of police bribes and, more generally, police corruption is collective, as it strikes against the wealth of the nation. Corruption begets corruption and can be so pervasive that the whole state becomes a kleptocracy, as happened in certain African countries such as Mobutu's Zaire, which has now collapsed. It is, I believe, only when collective rights and the collective impact of deviant policing come into the foreground that a more persuasive argument against it can be marshalled.

Rule-Governed Democracies and the Social Contract

First of all, let me offer a word of caution against believing that the rule of law guarantees that there will be no recourse to massive penal repression. Depending on whether one takes into account the number of persons in jails and in preventive custody, there were in 1997 between 1.2 and 1.6 million persons incarcerated in the United States. The Afro-American minority is vastly overrepresented in the prison population (Afro-Americans represent some 12 percent of the U.S. population and account for at least 40 percent of the prison population). It is projected that the U.S. prison population will grow to 3.2 million persons by the end of the first decade of the new millennium. In my own country, Canada, we are only beginning to measure the magnitude of the abuse to which whole generations of Aboriginals were submitted by being forced to be educated in boarding schools operated by the Catholic Church. It was recently discovered that at one of these schools (St. Ann), children were not only beaten, they were also sexually abused on a regular basis and even tortured, an electric chair being used to inflict electrical shocks to "undisciplined" children. That Aboriginal children were actually murdered in such institutions is an acknowledged fact in Canada.

This word of caution having been expressed, it might be asked whether there are historical models that we might study in order to learn how society evolved from a period of wanton brutality, which characterized the medieval epoch in Western Europe, to another period where human rights were increasingly recognized and the repressive apparatus governed by the rule of law. The work of the German sociologist Norbert Elias on the civilizing process[1] and of the French historian-philosopher Michel Foucault on the different forms of governance[2] provide interesting case studies, although I do not have the space to discuss these in any detail. Thus, I will only briefly discuss two strategies in the following sections.

The State Monopoly of Physical Violence

Norbert Elias writes that "once the monopoly of physical power has passed to central authorities, not every strongman can afford the pleasure of attack."[3] This monopolizing of physical power by the state was epitomized in Hobbes' great work, *Leviathan*. What history further revealed was that this monopoly was not by itself a progress and might actually mean a regression, if the force to be used by the state was not legitimate and was not explicitly ruled by a covenant between the subjects and the sovereign.

Let me first discuss legitimacy. I begin by making a distinction between the tautological and the substantial sense of legitimacy. In its tautological sense, "legitimate" only means "was performed by agents acting under the authority of the state." This meaning of legitimacy is tautological because it adds nothing to the notion of state agency: everything performed under the authority of the state is *ipso facto* legitimate, whereas anything happening outside its authority is illegitimate. In its substantive meaning, the notion of legitimacy can qualify a practice only if it meets a set of external standards, these standards being potentially of great diversity (moral, religious, legal, political, cultural, and even socio-psychological). The substantial use of legitimacy is closer to that of Max Weber, who viewed legitimacy as the element that leads subjects to obey willfully the diktats of their sovereign.[4] Needless to say, I use the notion of legitimacy in its substantive meaning in the course of this chapter. The first example that I will discuss illustrates the gap between tautological and substantial legitimacy.

Absolute monarchies had achieved the monopoly of physical force by the seventeenth century and were still massively resorting to torture, used either as a way to obtain a confession or as a way to execute as painfully as possible criminals convicted of particularly serious crimes (and also of what we would regard as petty crimes). One crucial difference between torture as it was used before the seventeenth century and as it is used now was its very high visibility. Torture was often inflicted in public for the purpose of deterrence, and the pain suffered by what was called "the patient" was on public display. Although historians have observed that torture may have been seen as a form of public spectacle that was for some entertaining, a case could be made that in the long run the public display of torture becomes intolerable. It first becomes unpalatable to the "enlightened few," who then make their case to convince the rest of the population that torture is indeed evil and morally wrong. This is how it happened in the times of Voltaire and Beccaria, who succeeded with others in having torture banned. They argued persuasively that the mere fact that torture was applied under the authority of the state was not sufficient to make it legitimate, if it contradicted fundamental principles of ethics and of justice.[5]

Police brutality during interrogations never really went away. However, torture codified as a set of practices designed to inflict various degrees of serious pain is now undergoing a resurgence. This resurgence is in a large way covert. That torture is regularly inflicted is known through the testimony of persons who have been submitted to it. However, torture is no longer inflicted in public, and the secrecy that nowadays surrounds it makes it more palatable to public opinion. If I am right in believing that torture becomes an intolerable practice when it is on public display, we should pursue a strategy of maximal visualization in regard to it. Maximal visualization would surely not consist of an absurd attempt to convince those who are practicing it to do it in public. However, it might entail attempts to give it a high media profile (recovered bodies of murdered persons are frequently horribly mutilated) and to try to convince persons who have been submitted to torture to testify about their experience and to have the pain that was inflicted on them put into the record through photographs. I am fully conscious that one of the effects of torture is to break the spirit of those upon whom it is inflicted, and that the last thing that the victims of torture want to do is to reactivate through language or otherwise these experiences. Nevertheless, I am also convinced that torture will continue to spread if it is not publicly shown to be the unbearable evil that it is. Before getting the videocams into the precincts to record whether basic human rights are protected during police interrogations, it may be necessary to force torture out of the precincts' basements and into the open. This process is already under way through the great courage of some victims of torture and should be accelerated.

The Social Contract

I previously said that granting the state a monopoly in the use of physical force and coercion may be counterproductive if the force to be used is not legitimate, that is, if it is not governed by external standards embodied within a covenant between the sovereign or the state and its subjects or citizens.

Here I will very tentatively propose a distinction between two kinds of democracy. The first kind of democracy I call rule-based democracy. It consists of a constitutional and institutional framework of laws, customs, and public agencies that ensure that the body politic is governed by "the people," usually through the election of representatives to a parliament. Such a constitutional and institutional framework is a necessary condition for democracy but it may not be sufficient. The weakness of this kind of democracy, that characterized the government of ancient Greek city-states and the government of the American republic before the Civil War, is that it rests on a highly discriminatory definition of citizenship, which allows, for instance, slavery. Slaves are by definition excluded from the realm of "the people." With the use of such exclusionary criteria, it was maintained by some apologists that during apartheid, South Africa was a democracy.

In theory, there are no more slaves, although slavery is still flourishing in certain countries that use child labor. Whatever may be the case with slavery, there certainly are underclasses in our democracies. They are comprised of the poor, the weak, and the dispossessed, a great many of these happening to be members of underdeveloped countries, ethnic minorities, and migrant workers. What I would call a social contract–based democracy rests on a covenant which explicitly specifies that all those who are legal citizens of a country or who are in the process of becoming citizens are full members of the civil society making up this country, are equally protected by its laws, share the same privileges, and cannot be discriminated against. This social contract tradition has been recently revived in the work of John Rawls.[6] Its basic features are an assertion of social solidarity and the consequent will not to exclude anyone from the covenant, when that person has the legal right to be included. According to Rawls, the only departures from the equal treatment of all which are justified are those which are beneficial to the poorest denizens of a political society.

In reading Chevigny's chapter, I was quite struck by the fact that the abuse of police powers, the torture, the death squads, and the extended preventive detention for vagrants actually enjoyed the favor of the middle and upper classes and were indeed popular. These well-off classes regard the underclass as aliens that threaten their personal security and their property; the state apparatus considers underclasses to be threats to the stability of the government.

I fully agree with Chevigny's point that there should be an effort to persuade the middle and the upper classes that police deviance also threatens them and that having police observant of human rights would be in the interest of all. However, on the basis of Chevigny's own descriptions, I am not convinced that there is a full and conscious recognition in Latin American countries that the word "all" should be interpreted in its inclusive sense. Until it is so interpreted, the attempt to convince the middle and upper classes that police governed by the rule of law are in the best interest of all may be fraught with great difficulties.

This last remark is not intended as a criticism of Chevigny's chapter. He demonstrates that he is fully aware of the need to go beyond the legal framework to solve problems of abuse of power. For instance, he acknowledges that paying police decent wages is an important move towards solving the problems of police corruption. I believe that although he is fully aware of the broader context, it might be useful to articulate a few ideas that explicitly refer to this broader context.

Concluding Remarks

Chevigny says that "the adoption of a military role for the police seems to me always a mistake." I fully share this view. Actually, a strong historical case could be made to the effect that police forces were invented both on the continent of Europe and in England as an alternative to social control by the military, which begot rebellion rather than produced conformity. My own studies for the Canadian government have led me to believe that there is a fundamental difference between what I shall call the constabulary or police ethos and the military ethos. The constabulary ethos is defined by the minimal use of force to solve problems that require the imposition of a solution. The military ethos consists in the use of overwhelming force to gain total supremacy over an enemy in an attack and to ensure that the foe inflicts the least possible damage on its attackers. The military ethos may be suited for war between countries, if suited to anything at all. It is completely unsuited for promoting respect for the law within a society, because what defines a society is precisely its will to put an end to the warlike predicament according to which every one is in conflict against every other one. To the extent that a militarized police fans the winds of war within a society, it defeats the very purpose for which this society came into being.

Postscript

The discussion that took place during the Rule of Law workshop held at the University of Notre Dame was stimulating, and I would like to react to some of the things that I have heard. Most of my comments are centered on the notion of punishment.

Impunity

If I were to be asked what was one of the words most frequently used during the debates, I would say that it was "impunity." The fact that aggressors of all kinds could harm their victims without having to answer for their behavior before the criminal courts was perceived by many participants at the workshop as a major source of scandal. Although I believe that the spectacle of impunity is obnoxious, I would like to make a plea for the need to find alternatives to punishment in attempting to solve problems of crime and disorder. Being a criminologist by profession, I often attend conferences on crime and repression. I am then struck by two things. The first one is that all pressure groups are clamoring for the most severe punishment to be inflicted on their own favorite *bête noire*: bankers want to put armed robbers in prison for life, parents want child molesters to be castrated and homosexuals to be jailed, feminists are asking for ever more serious sanctions for rapists, and the military seek to execute or imprison for life all terrorists and political opponents. This list could go on endlessly, with every penal lobby having its own prized target. When, after having listened to all these indignant voices, I make the sum of all the offenders that should be imprisoned for life, I come up with an astounding number of persons. It is precisely at this point that the second thing that strikes me most during these conferences comes to mind: all those groups calling for more imprisonment also recognize that prisons are overflowing with inmates in their own country, the problem of prison overcrowding being a worldwide plague. These people also admit that we cannot build more jails, because that would mean divesting money from health services, child care, and educational programs which have a higher priority, at least in a society that still pretends to be humane. Since I cannot reconcile both the outcry for more punishment and the recognition that we are penally bankrupt, I sometimes wonder if each society should not surround the space in which it lives by (cost-profitable) barbed wire so that it could legitimately pretend that *everyone* within the society is now in custody. Thus having gotten rid of their obsession with incarceration, they could move on to solve in a more imaginative way all the problems which are afflicting them. Whether this is a dream or a nightmare proposal, I do not profess to know.

The Rule of Law

The point that I want to make here is quite simple. It is just a reminder that the rule of law is not to be equated with the enforcement of the criminal law. The price of drawing such an equation is the transformation of society into a penal colony, a direction into which the U.S. is now swiftly moving. Because it is punitive, the criminal law is certainly the most dramatic kind of legislation, and through this dramatization it has usurped its status as the paradigm for all law. But there are of course other kinds of law, such as constitutional law, civil law, administrative law, and international law, just to mention some main categories. As Hart[7] and many other legal theorists have shown, it is not all law that can be defined as a prescription that entails a sanction if it is not followed. Besides its provisions for punitive sanctions, the other cardinal features of the criminal law are its discriminatory character and its discretionary application. For instance, in the U.S., the federal sentencing guidelines instruct judges to multiply by a factor of one hundred the quantity of crack cocaine of which an offender was found to be in possession. According to this rule, an offender charged with the possession of ten grams of crack must be sentenced as if he or she were charged with the possession of 1 kilogram of powder cocaine; the effect of the rule is to transform simple possession of crack into possession for the purposes of trafficking, which carries a much higher penalty. In the U.S., crack is the Afro-American way of consuming cocaine, whereas powder is the favored way of whites.[8]

In any society that I have investigated, the answer to questions such as "who is being punished in this society" or "who is in prison" generally is: those segments of the population which are powerless and underprivileged. With the traditional exceptions of homicide and some of the more heinous crimes against persons, the criminal law mainly targets, in its definition and application, street crime, which is perpetrated by the poor and by excluded members of society. Hence, if one wants to use exclusively the criminal law to deal with wife and children beaters or with sexual offenders, it is only the poorest of them that will end up in prison. Medical doctors and police, who according to victim surveys on domestic violence are among the most frequent offenders, rarely end up in jail. The same applies to other upper-scale offenders.

A point related to that which I have been arguing is the question of whether mediation is "second-class justice," as was heard several times during the debates at the workshop. When the so-called "first-class justice" is as punitive and discriminatory as the criminal law, any mediation process that would be fairer and less harmful should be seen as progress. If the Simpson trial, of which most of us at least caught a glimpse, is first-class justice, one wonders how much worse economy-class justice could be.

International Declarations of Rights Are No Substitute for the Criminal Law

This is perhaps one of the most potentially devastating misunderstandings that can occur with respect to declarations of human rights. It was repeatedly stressed during the debates at the workshop that persons who systematically violated other persons' human rights generally behaved with complete impunity. Not only is this not at all surprising, but it is deemed "normal." The most severe sanctions are meted out against serious offenders because they have committed a *crime*, that is, because they have violated the *criminal law*, which, we claim, is entirely different from charters of human rights, although criminal law embodies some of the values and principles enshrined in these charters. In other words, in no country governed by the rule of law, for example, is the offence of murder prosecuted as a violation of the bill or charter of rights.[9] The offence of murder is prosecuted under a criminal code. If the application of the criminal law completely collapses in a country, it is for me a *complete delusion* to try to convince people ignorant of the law that international declarations of rights can be relied upon to fill the void. International tribunals are notoriously slow and to a very large extent impotent in the prosecution of crime. What must be done is to reform with all possible energy the national system of criminal law of a country and to stop mystifying people by urging them to place their hope in international declarations of human rights, which cannot legally be used as an *ersatz* for the failed criminal law within a state that has forfeited the rule of law.

War Criminals and Dictators in Exile

There is one last point on which I would like to briefly reflect. There were questions raised during the workshop on why the military thugs who had toppled President Aristide were not brought to justice when he came back. There are compelling reasons for that. Until very recently, the only time in modern history when war criminals (deviant military) really stood trial was in Germany and, to a lesser extent, in Japan after the Allies had won the Second World War.[10] It is crucial to see that the generals and other military persons who were convicted of various crimes against humanity had been stripped of all power through their defeat and were, for all practical and political purposes, submitted to the law of the *victors*. Such is not at all the case when General Cedras went into golden exile after having negotiated the conditions under which he would depart. President Aristide did not come back as a victor but was imposed by the U.S. through great travails. This meant that the Haitian military and their accomplices who stayed behind were never stripped of all their power, as were the German and the Japanese militaries. For instance, the former never were disarmed. When they retain their power it becomes extremely difficult to prosecute them. Such is generally the case when dictators, like General Pinochet, are eventually forced or persuaded to accept a reinstatement of civilian democracy. Such a transition towards democracy is usually the product of a strenuous process of negotiations between the ousted military oligarchy and the forces of democracy, most often backed by foreign powers. Dictators and their accomplices are generally granted immunity for whatever crimes they may have committed in return for their leaving the government. The overwhelming point is that the forces of democracy are very far from being in the same position of strength as were the victorious Allies at the end of the Second World War. The military who leave the government in Latin American countries and elsewhere are by no means vanquished. On the contrary, they remain a very powerful force within the country attempting to become a democracy and they must be coddled to prevent their return to power. Within this context, it is hopeless to expect the kind of purge that occurred (to a very limited extent) in Europe and in Japan, after the Axis powers had been defeated. It is even more of a delusion to wait for the U.N. to enforce the law of the victors when there never was any war or victor or vanquished.

NOTES

1. Norbert Elias, The History of Manners (Vol. 1 of *Über den Progress der Zivilization*, Edmund Jephcott trans., New York: Pantheon Books, 1982).
2. Graham Burchell, Gordon Colin, & Peter Miller, The Foucault Effect: Studies in Governmentality: With Two Lectures by and an Interview with Michel Foucault (University of Chicago Press, 1991).
3. Elias, *supra* note 1, at 202.
4. Max Weber, Essays in Sociology (H.H. Gerth & C. Wright Mills trans., eds., New York: Oxford University Press, 1958); *see also* Max Weber, Science as a Vocation (Peter Lassman & Irving Velody eds., Boston: Unwin Hyman, 1989).
5. *See* Cesare Bonesana Marchese di Beccaria, An Essay on Crimes and Punishments (Brookline Village, MA: Branden Press, 1983); *see also* David P. Bien, The Calas Affair: Persecution, Toleration and Heresy in Eighteenth-Century France (Princeton University Press, 1960).
6. *See generally* John Rawls, A Theory of Justice (Cambridge, MA: Belknap Press of Harvard University Press, 2d ed., 1972); *see also* John Rawls, Political Liberalism (Columbia University Press, 1993).
7. H.L.A. Hart, The Concept of Law (Oxford: Clarendon Press, 1961).
8. For this issue of crack versus powder cocaine in the U.S. and the federal sentencing policies, *see* Michael Tonry, Malign Neglect—Race, Crime, and Punishment in America 41, 188–90 (New York: Oxford University Press, 1995).

9. One possible exception to this principle is the U.S. federal law. Since persons who had murdered African-Americans were either not prosecuted or systematically acquitted in the Deep South states, the central U.S. government enacted a federal law that allowed for the prosecution of offenders for depriving victims of their civil rights by killing or harming them. This is the rather unusual law that was used to prosecute the Los Angeles police officers who had beaten Rodney King, after they had been acquitted by an all-white jury. The important point to see is that such human rights legislation is invoked for the prosecution of crimes only when there is a breakdown in the normal application of the criminal law.

10. In her thought-provoking book, Tina Rosenberg has shown the devastating effects on society of the *Lustrace* (purification) laws that were enacted in the former communist countries of Eastern Europe (particularly Czechoslovakia, Poland, and the former East Germany) after the collapse of the communist regimes. Intended to punish former Communists, these laws were arbitrarily applied and thus added to the social chaos, rather than reducing it. *See* TINA ROSENBERG, HAUNTED LAND (New York: Alfred Knopf, 1996).

6

The Rule of Law and the Underprivileged in Latin America: A Rural Perspective

Roger Plant

Introduction

As the twentieth century draws to a close, it is important to take stock of Latin America's emerging legal tradition and law enforcement machinery insofar as they relate to the rural poor and underprivileged. As elsewhere in the world, the twentieth century saw huge transformations in Latin America's legal and political systems, and even more so in its agrarian systems. At the beginning of the century, Mexico experienced its profound social revolution, the legacy of which was later to have a significant impact on constitutional, social, and agrarian law throughout Latin America. The mid-twentieth century saw social revolutions in countries such as Bolivia and Cuba, which were largely agrarian-based. Land reform laws provided for the distribution of the large *hacienda* among tenant farmers in Bolivia; in Cuba, after a more moderate start, the Castro government then launched a Latin American experiment with agrarian socialism and collectivism.

The third quarter of the twentieth century, between approximately the early 1950s and the mid-1970s, saw a series of moderate land reforms launched by modernizing governments, many of them of Christian Democratic or similar persuasions, aiming to abolish feudal land tenure regimes in the countryside, to effect a limited land redistribution among poor peasants and tenant farmers, and eventually to pave the way for more capitalized agriculture built exclusively around wage-labor relationships. The nature and extent of these reforms changed by country, depending on political circumstances and the extent to which organized peasant movements were able to exert strong pressure on the governments of the time. Colombia, Ecuador, and Venezuela are examples of the more limited and moderate reforms. Brazil, Chile, and Peru are countries where the agrarian reformists tried to go further, pressed on by militant peasant movements, but where (at least in the Brazilian and Chilean cases) the rural militancy was one factor behind the consequent military backlash.

The last quarter of the twentieth century has seen, at least in official policy and developmental circles, an end to agrarian reform and agrarian reformism. There are a number of reasons for this, mainly economic and demographic ones that will be examined in more detail below. As the continent becomes increasingly more urbanized, most governments and policymakers have abandoned the earlier concept of an agricultural sector based on small-scale farming. Agriculture has become increasingly large-scale and commercialized, and there has been a renewed emphasis on both traditional and alternative export crops. Whether the crop is fruit in Chile and northwestern Mexico, citrus and sugar in Brazil, soya in eastern Bolivia and Paraguay, or the more traditional coffee and sugar in some Central American republics, the broad picture reveals many similarities. The large farmer can again feel protected, often paying negligible taxes and derisory salaries to the rural work force, as long as the farmer produces with some degree of efficiency for the market.

As Latin American economies have expanded, there has also been pressure on remote and hitherto uncoveted lands. The agricultural expansion in the Amazon, the Chaco, the Guatemalan Peten, and Mexico's Chiapas has led to conflicts between agricultural or cattle-raising entrepreneurs and the indigenous peoples or peasant squatters who have long held customary rights over these regions. When violent conflict breaks out, all too often the local or national security forces take the side of the larger landowner, seeing the weaker party as the aggressor rather than as the victim of aggression. This is not always the case. One of the most positive developments in Latin

America over the past decade has been the greater degree of legal protection for indigenous peoples and their lands. All too often, however, the new laws are simply not enforced.

Altogether, economic trends in rural Latin America over the past quarter century have entailed considerable human cost. Statistics tell part of the story. While Latin America may be becoming more urbanized, over one quarter of its population still lives in rural areas, and the patterns of rural poverty are desperate by any standards. A global study on rural poverty carried out in 1992 by the International Fund for Agricultural Development (FAO)[1] found that the proportion of the rural population whose income and consumption fell below nationally defined poverty lines was higher in Latin America and the Caribbean than in any other developing region. Out of a total rural population of 123 million, 76 million, or 61 percent, were below the poverty line.

Rural poverty has also been on the increase since the land reform era came to an end. FAO observed some years ago that the number of rural poor in Latin America had been increasing since 1970, now comprised approximately two-thirds of a total rural population of some 126 million, and was likely to rise by a further 27 million by the end of the century.[2] More recent estimates of rural poverty can point to little change. A 1997 study by the Economic Commission for Latin America found that rural poverty had diminished by only one percentage point, from 56 percent to 55 percent, between 1990 and 1994, and that one-third of the rural population still lived in extreme poverty.[3]

But statistics of rural poverty in themselves are not enough to explain the types of conflict that are now breaking out in diverse parts of Latin America. It is important to understand the economic and social factors which have created new categories of rural poor, now living almost outside the framework of protective social legislation, and without much chance of improving their situation through the customary legal and political channels. It is a particularly serious example of social exclusion, in which there is increasingly less room for marginal groups within the modern nation-state.

There have been major changes in the patterns of rural poverty. Generally, there has been a reduction in what FAO has termed "dependent" peasant agriculture, meaning the small-scale farming practised under the tenures such as renting, sharecropping, and usufruct rights provided in exchange for labor services. Together with the decline in the number of small farm tenancies, there has been an increased use of wage labor and a massive expansion of temporary employment. In Brazil, for example, temporary employment in agriculture increased by 85 percent, and in Chile by 46 percent, in the 1980s.

These trends are the key to understanding the nature and character of much of the rural conflict in Latin America today. Not so very long ago, the clashes were between traditional landowners and tenant farmers who fought for greater land security or against eviction. But by the end of the twentieth century the panorama has changed radically. Millions of desperately poor rural inhabitants are now uprooted from the land. They are not struggling against feudal conditions of work, as in the traditional Andean *hacienda*. Nor, for the most part, are they striving for improved tenancy conditions, because the poorest of the poor are rarely peasant or tenant farmers.

A new feature of the Latin American countryside is the mass migratory movements of landless or near-landless peasants, moving to different areas of commercial agriculture in accordance with the agricultural cycle. There may be as many as ten million of these floating workers in Brazil, known as the *boias frias,* who migrate to sugar, fruit, coffee, and other harvests, picking up work by the day or the week. Much of the migrant labor is performed by indigenous peoples, such as the Guatemalan Indians who move from their highland villages to commercial plantations on the Pacific coast; or the Mexican Indians who migrate from the southern states to the fruit-farming regions of Sinaloa and Sonora in northern Mexico. Moreover, the distinction between "urban" and "rural" poverty and employment is becoming increasingly blurred in the light of the new productive trends. The workers who pick up the occasional jobs in commercial agriculture often reside year-round in small towns on the fringes of the estates, or even in larger towns including capital cities.

While these are some recent trends of rural poverty and employment, the prevailing orthodoxies are now to terminate agrarian reform legislation, to strengthen private property rights, and to "flexibilize" labor legislation in order to provide less rigidities in the labor market and generally to reduce the costs of hiring labor. While the latter group of measures are usually targeted at the urban sector with its higher labor costs, rather than at rural areas, the implications can be an overall drop in labor protection. Seasonal workers, and above all indigenous migrant workers, are bound to prove more vulnerable in all aspects of recruitment and employment than organized estate workers with regular labor contracts.

In the contemporary structural adjustment era, the thrust of "neoliberal" economic policies is to reduce the role of the state in economic management, and insofar as possible to promote free and unfettered markets. Property regimes should be clarified and strengthened, similarly to promote market forces in agriculture. Yet in some ways this is a mere repetition of the economic philosophies that prevailed in Latin America in the late nineteenth century. Neoliberalism is, after all, not so different from classic laissez-faire liberalism in its approach to property regimes, markets, and economic management. In most parts of Latin America, classic nineteenth-century liberalism had a fairly disastrous effect on social equity, leading to a high degree of land concentration, landlessness, and impoverishment. Latin America's social constitutionalism of the twentieth century was devised largely in response to this, seeking the middle ground between western and socialist traditions of property rights. This involved a strong role for the state in social law and its implementation, implicitly allowing the state to reallocate property rights in the social and economic interest. The "social function of property" was a key aspect of Latin America's social constitutionalism.

Thus, an important part of Latin America's recent legal tradition has been that the law can be an instrument of social justice, affecting the redistribution of wealth and assets in accordance with social need. This does not mean that the law will automatically be implemented to the advantage of the poor. In many cases the opposite has occurred, because of the basic conservatism of local judges and other law enforcement officials and their typical alliances with agrarian oligarchies. But this does mean that the law could be a banner around which the rural poor could mobilize in claims for their land and other social rights. And this fact helped give legitimacy to rural pressure groups in their alliances with political parties and other interest groups.

In recent years, despite the growing academic and policy literature on rule of law and democratization issues in Latin America, rather little attention has been paid to this aspect of the rule of law. The discourse on rule of law issues, whether in Latin America or elsewhere, tends to focus on respect for civil and political rights. By this criterion, a state can be said to abide by the rule of law when there is a functioning democracy with free and fair elections, when there is an independent judiciary, when there is respect for press freedoms, or when governments refrain from arbitrary arrest or maltreatment of individuals. These are the classic "Western" principles of the rule of law, embodied in a number of internationally recognized human rights instruments. And by the classic standards of individual freedoms, of civil and political rights, all of Latin America has made considerable headway over the past two decades. The political democracies which predominate throughout the continent today represent a sea change from the repressive dictatorships which characterized all too many Latin American countries until the 1980s.

Yet there is, and has to be, another aspect to rule of law discussions in Latin America, most particularly where vulnerable groups are concerned. A legal tradition and judicial machinery governs not only individual freedoms, often seen as freedoms and rights against the state, but also economic relations within society. The extent to which the law and its enforcement provides for social justice, measured as the equitable distribution of resources and fairness of opportunity to economic welfare and advancement, is an issue of immense relevance in Latin America today.

This chapter thus examines the role of constitutional, agrarian, labor, and other social legislation in addressing economic and social conflicts in Latin America, with particular reference to the rural sector. An attempt is made to provide some historical perspective, examining the tensions within the legal tradition and the reasons for this, and then tracing the evolution of agrarian and other social legislation over different periods of the twentieth century. A final section contains some reflections on present-day debates concerning the strengthening of the judiciary and law enforcement in the adjustment era. The main concern is that Latin America as a whole may now be going too far in rejecting those "corporate" elements of its recent legal tradition, which enabled the state to redress economic imbalances to the advantage of some vulnerable groups, without creating alternative mechanisms to address the severe and sometime growing poverty in many rural areas. The trend can be attributed to the conventional orthodoxies of structural adjustment and privatization policies. But it risks provoking ever greater tensions in marginal rural areas, unless attention is given as a matter of urgency to social protection and income generation for the most vulnerable rural groups.

The Law and Economic Reform in Rural Latin America: An Overview

For centuries there have been tensions between different aspects of Latin America's legal tradition as it affects rural areas and agrarian policies. During the colonial period, the tendency was to have one system of property law for Spanish colonists and another for indigenous peoples. While both law and colonial practice provided for severe exploitation of indigenous peoples, through tribute and various coercive labor systems, measures were adopted to protect indigenous communal lands.

After independence from Spain, policy differences between liberal and conservative factions were reflected in frequent changes to the law. Liberals were keen to construct new Latin American nations on a platform of equal rights for all. Their models tended to be the French and North American constitutions, while civil law was naturally influenced by the Spanish as well as French civil codes. Liberals also fought for open economies, aiming to attract foreign investment and to find overseas markets for agricultural as well as mineral exports. Conservatives were more inward-looking, aiming to maintain both church privileges and a separate regime for indigenous lands. Neither of the political factions, however, had much interest in abolishing Indian tribute, in those countries where indigenous peoples played an important role in national economies.

By the second half of the nineteenth century, liberal economic and political philosophies were in the ascendancy throughout Latin America. Countries from Mexico down to Argentina and Chile sought to promote European immigration, and most countries sought to amend their legal systems to bring them more squarely into line with laissez-faire economic principles. In rural areas this meant a concerted effort to register property with private title and to abolish by law the status of indigenous communal lands. The extent to which land privatization actually occurred depended on patterns of immigration, the treatment of indigenous populations, and the success of each country in developing export crops with an overseas market. Where export agriculture did develop, requiring an extensive labor supply, there was a very rapid process of dispossession of indigenous peoples from their traditional lands. This was the case in southern Mexico and parts of Central America, where plantation economies developed around coffee in particular. In part of the Andes, indigenous land tenure systems tended to survive in practice despite the civil law, though in countries like Bolivia there was also extensive land accumulation by large landowners by the early twentieth century. Altogether, the years between 1850 and 1900 saw the rapid extension of large private farms throughout Latin America, and a parallel rise in feudal forms of labor. Rural landlessness similarly increased, and there was no protection for farm workers.

The first half of the twentieth century brought a reaction against the excesses of late-nineteenth-century liberalism, with the progressive development of Latin America's rather unique model of social and agrarian legislation. A watershed was certainly the revolution in Mexico, where the land accumulation had been perhaps the most flagrant and the land hunger the most serious. Over a period of several years, the Mexican revolution introduced a new legal tradition based on the principles of equitable land distribution, recognition of communal and inalienable forms of land ownership, the "social function of property," and limitations on private land ownership with absolute title to the land vested in the state. A key provision of the 1917 Constitution was that all land was owned by the nation, which in turn had the right to transmit this land to individuals and to constitute private property. The constitution empowered the federal government to restore alienated land to the indigenous peasantry, either through donation or through restitution in cases where *comuneros* could prove valid title to the land. Ceilings were placed on the size of individual landholdings (the exact amount to be determined by the separate states in the federal Republic), and expropriated estate lands were to be redistributed to the peasantry in the form of inalienable common lands (*ejidos*). The Mexican labor code of 1924 was also the first to recognize the labor rights of rural workers. It provided for the abolition of unpaid personal services, debt-peonage and other feudal labor, and tenure relationships; for minimum wage legislation; and for a series of welfare rights in which the obligation to provide social benefits for the agricultural workforce (including health care, housing, education, and social security) fell not on the state but on the individual landowner in the countryside.

The novelty of Mexican revolutionary legislation thus lay in its limitations to private property rights, its reaffirmation of communal rights to the land, and also in the linkages established between land rights and rural labor rights. In practice, land reform was a staggered and uneven process over several decades, with most redistribution occurring in the 1930s. It nevertheless provided the inspiration for future agrarian and labor law, and also much constitutional law, in the rest of Latin America.

The concept of the social function of property spread to the constitutions of other Latin American republics. Yet the actual experience was very limited until the 1960s, when concerns to eliminate and modernize the now anachronistic *hacienda*—and also to prevent a repeat of the Cuban revolution—sparked off a wave of moderate land reform programs throughout the continent. Until then there was only a short-lived land reform experiment in Guatemala, broken up by a military coup in 1954; and a more comprehensive reform in Bolivia, following a social revolution in 1952. In Guatemala, the 1947 Constitution declared the social function of property, and redefined the legal basis of land ownership as its proven use, rather than the often dubious land titles that had been produced by new landowners over the past century. The aborted land reform law, enacted in 1952, had provided for the expropriation of all rural properties over 300 hectares, all uncultivated farms over 100 hectares, and also for the abolition of all servile and unpaid labor systems. The Bolivian reform law, enacted in 1953, provided for the abolition of the large *hacienda* and subdivision of expropriated estates among the workforce.

Latin America's agrarian reform era can be dated, very approximately, between the early 1960s and the mid-1970s. During this period, agrarian reform laws were adopted in almost every Latin American republic, often complemented by labor laws extending the benefits of labor legislation to the countryside. The links between new land and labor laws were often very direct, in that violation of minimum wage and other labor laws could be one of the reasons for expropriating land.

In 1959, Fidel Castro's revolutionary movement took power in Cuba, where the land had been extensively monopolized in large sugar plantations, many of them under foreign ownership. Cuba's first land reform law, enacted in May 1959, provided for the expropriation of all farms over 400 hectares. It also prohibited foreign ownership of land, as well as tenancy and share-cropping arrangements. The expropriated non-sugar lands were distributed to the former squatters, tenant farmers, and sharecroppers, over 100,000 of whom now received titles of ownership. Expropriated landowners were entitled to compensation according to the declared taxable value of their properties. The large sugar estates were nationalized and brought under state ownership, as cooperative or collective farms in which the former seasonal workers were taken on with guarantees of permanent employment. The second major land reform law, enacted in 1963, provided for the expropriation of all rural properties over 5 *caballerias* (approximately 67 hectares). Most of this reformed land went to the state, though a further 40–50,000 peasants received land titles.[4] Though the reforms of the early 1960s left approximately one quarter of the land under private ownership, there has been a progressive consolidation of land ownership by the state, and a gradual decrease in private property. Under Cuban law, individual plots could not be inherited, but reverted to the state upon the death of the owner. The long-term aim was thus the progressive socialization of all agrarian property.

The land reforms of the 1960s in the rest of Latin America were motivated at least in part by political concerns to prevent a repeat of the Cuban revolutionary experience. The overall principles behind the land reform laws and programs of this period were spelled out in the Punta del Este Declaration, which was adopted by the Organization of American States in 1961:

> To encourage, in accordance with the characteristics of each country, programmes of comprehensive land reform leading to the effective transformation, where required, of unjust structures and systems of land tenure and use; with a view to replacing latifundia and dwarf holdings by an equitable system of property so that, supplemented by timely and adequate credit, technical assistance and improved marketing arrangements, the land will become for the man who works it the basis of his economic stability, the foundation of his increasing welfare, and the guarantee of his freedom and dignity.

The above suggests that the underlying philosophy was to be one of "land for the tiller" on the East Asian model, breaking up the large traditional estates and converting tenants and estate workers into small farmers. In practice however, the national laws rarely provided for ceilings on private landholdings, usually requiring only that the land should be brought under efficient and active cultivation in order to evade expropriation. There were exceptions to this. In Chile, for example, the 1967 land reform law provided for an 80-hectare ceiling, which had been further reduced to 40 hectares by the end of President Salvador Allende's three-year socialist government (1970–1973).

Of all the reforms of this period, the most significant land redistribution occurred in Peru during a period of military government between 1968 and 1975. In coastal regions, where commercial agriculture predominated, a 1969 land reform decree provided for the expropriation of all private farms over 150 hectares and all agroindustrial complexes. In highland areas it placed the ceiling at between 15 and 55 hectares, depending on such factors as irrigation. Landowners were required to live and work on the land, and expropriated large estates were to be owned and operated as co-operatives. A special agrarian jurisdiction was created, through Agrarian Tribunals represented at all levels of the judiciary up to the Supreme Court. Peasant farmers were granted free legal assistance to register their land claims and have effective access to the legal machinery.

The creation of the agrarian tribunals, and the interpretation given by agrarian judges to their responsibilities, had a major impact on the land reform process. In accordance with instructions given by the president of the Agrarian Tribunal, agrarian judges were to apply existing legal norms in favor of the peasant whenever there were ambiguities in the law itself. Before then, the decisions of both civil and criminal courts had generally been biased towards landowner interests, usually resulting in the eviction or even imprisonment of the peasants involved in litigation. But forgotten laws dating as far back as the 1820s were now invoked to support land claims based on possession rather than written title. Over ten million hectares of land were expropriated in Peru between 1969 and 1976, and redistributed to over 300,000 peasant and indigenous families. Yet *hacienda* lands were redistributed to former permanent workers, to the exclusion of various categories of other salaried and seasonal workers.

In hindsight, it can be argued that none of the Latin American land reforms of this era were predicated on the needs of the landless. The more skeptical analyses have argued with much justification that they usually aimed to modernize traditional agriculture rather than to break up the large holdings, and to replace feudal and servile labor arrangements by wage labor systems. In practice, unless there was strict implementation of tenancy protection laws, this meant the widespread dispossession of tenants and sharecroppers from the estate lands to which they had previously enjoyed rights of subsistence. This process has already been observed for Brazil, following the enactment of a Rural Labor Statute in 1963. Similarly in Colombia, a 1968 law aimed at the gradual abolition of sharecropping and tenancy arrangements served in practice only to accelerate land eviction.

While the reforms were legislated from above, the level of implementation depended on the degree of pressure from below, from peasant and rural worker organizations mobilized in demands for land and labor rights. The governments that did press for land redistribution (in Brazil before a military coup in 1964, in Chile before 1973, in Colombia in the late 1960s, and in Peru between 1968 and 1975) actually built up peasant organizations to provide political support for their reformist initiatives. Not surprisingly, the demands of these peasant groups were for a radicalization of the reform process. Frustrated by the slow implementation of reforms, or by the tendency of the courts to side with landowners, they often turned to spontaneous occupation of the lands which were either idle or over the legal limit. Such extralegal methods usually met with repression. Even the governments that pledged commitment to significant reforms were concerned to control the process through their own political organizations, and feared that the land reform issue would be exploited by radical opposition groups.

The agrarian laws of this period have to be analyzed in the context of the wider transformation of Latin American agriculture and society. The agrarian reform debates took place at precisely the time when the rate of expansion of the modernized subsector of agriculture was expanded, with the adoption of highly developed technologies. Modernization was in practice concentrated on the medium and large commercial farms, to the virtual exclusion of peasant farmers. And governments played a key supporting role in accelerating this modernization, through the provision of concessional credit and subsidies, price supports, and infrastructural investments. Thus, the land reforms began with much consensus among new entrepreneurial elites and politicians, modernizing farmers, some sectors of the military, and also foreign investors, all of whom wished to break down the feudal remnants of rural society and make increasing use of wage labor. But equity considerations were arguably secondary to those of economic efficiency, and the concept of the "social function of property" was for the most part interpreted by the criterion of efficient production alone. As the subsidized modern sector of agriculture did begin to register high productivity growth, the official impetus for redistributive reforms melted away.

The transition was often a violent one, involving serious crises of political legitimacy. In countries such as Brazil and Chile, the military interventions were sparked off at least in part by conflicts over the land, and by a determination to stamp out the increasingly militant peasant organizations. In countries under formally democratic rule, such as Colombia, there was effective militarization of the countryside as security forces moved against peasant organizations that had hitherto received official support. The most serious conflicts occurred in such Central American republics as El Salvador and Guatemala, where a longstanding militarization of the countryside had blatantly served the interests of landowners, and where a rapid growth of commercial farming after the 1960s (of new crops, including cotton and sugar, on top of the longer-established coffee estates) sparked off a wave of violent evictions of peasants from their subsistence lands.

In the course of the 1980s and 1990s, the issue of redistributive land reform has barely remained on the policy agenda. There have been some very few exceptions, including the controversial reforms carried out in El Salvador in the early 1980s, in the midst of a civil war situation; and the reforms implemented by the Sandinista government in Nicaragua after 1979. The concept of the social function of property is still entrenched in many constitutions, in principle allowing for challenges to private land title on the grounds of social needs. But constitutional reforms of the late 1980s, in countries such as Brazil and Guatemala, provided stronger protection for private property and now seem to rule out the redistribution of private agricultural land. In recent years there has been a policy shift towards market-based solutions, through land titling and registration programs designed to increase security of tenure for small as well as large farmers.

Social Protection and the Rural Underprivileged: Future Challenges

In the interest of brevity, it has been necessary to make some rather broad generalizations about Latin American processes. In a large and diverse continent there is no uniformity in agrarian structures, legal texts, law enforcement machinery, or the nature of rural conflicts. The Southern Cone countries, with their small indigenous populations, are obviously very different from Mexico, Central America, and the Andes. And Brazil, with its vast land area and acute conflicts in its Amazon Basin, normally has to be considered apart.

Despite the differences, it is still possible to identify some common features, problems, and challenges in the continent as a whole. Some basic social principles, which were quite widely shared in Latin American legal traditions, are now under attack. Remnants of corporatism, which permit the state to affect free market operations by any criteria, are at variance with very powerful economic orthodoxies. At the same time, the international financial institutions, which have such strong influence on Latin American governments, are concerning themselves increasingly with issues of governance, state modernization, the strengthening and modernization of the judiciary, and in some cases with the causes of civil conflict and their possible remedies. And the fight against poverty, often with a particular emphasis on rural poverty, is among the highest of declared priorities of both Latin American governments and the international financial institutions.

For the rule of law to have any real meaning for Latin America's rural poor, at least two things have to be achieved. First, governments must have the political will and the means to eradicate violence against the rural poor by landowners and the armed bands employed by them, and even by elements of the state's own security forces. But second—and equally important—the rural poor who, as a result of the economic and political trends referred to above, simply do not have access to a subsistence livelihood, must feel that there is some scope to improving their situation through use of the legal system.

The continued violence in isolated rural areas is one of the weakest points of the democratic regimes in Latin America over the past two decades. Killings, sometimes multiple killings, have been a regular occurrence in the conflict-ridden areas of northeastern Brazil. Over one thousand assassinations have been reported in the "Grande Carajas" region alone over the past two decades, while only eight cases have been taken to trial and only six murderers incarcerated. In the state of Maranhão, over three hundred intentional homicides have been reported against rural workers involved in land conflicts since 1972, and over six hundred in Para during the same period. Seventy-four deaths in agrarian conflicts were reported during the first fifteen months of the government of President Fernando Henrique Cardoso after 1995. Human rights organizations have detected a situation of generalized impunity, also arguing the involvement of state military police and other law enforcement officials in the killings.[5] Similar repression against indigenous peasant movements in Chiapas over the past two decades has been extensively documented and is often seen as one of the factors behind the growing peasant radicalism and the growth of the Zapatista movement.[6]

Rural violence and impunity is an issue that needs to be addressed by human rights organizations, both nationally and internationally. In recent years, these aspects of rural violence have indeed been addressed by such international human rights groups as Amnesty International and Human Rights Watch, among others. Their reports on rural violence in countries including Brazil, Colombia, Mexico, and Paraguay all need to be widely read and circulated. And they should be distributed in mass to the international development banks and other donor organizations. All one can do here is to ask for more of the same, and perhaps urge that the issue of rural violence with state complicity be placed as a thematic concern on the agenda of the United Nations human rights organs.

A second issue is that of access to justice, civil and criminal justice more generally, and labor and agrarian justice in particular. There is a need for swifter legal mechanisms. Land cases in civil courts often drag on interminably, at a cost that peasant groups cannot afford. Special programs of legal assistance to peasant and rural worker organizations are a vital necessity. And human rights ombudsman's offices, of growing importance throughout Latin America, need to develop assistance programs in this area. Labor law generally needs to be revised, taking account of the fact that an increasing proportion of rural workers have no direct employment relationship with the landowner. Contractual systems where the recruitment is carried out by intermediaries need to be regulated by law, and rural labor inspection systems need to be massively improved, allowing for more direct access and participation by rural worker organizations.

There have been some recent innovations in this respect. An Agrarian Attorney's Office (*Procuraduría Agraria*) was created in Mexico in 1992, with a broad mandate to protect both communal and small farmers and salaried rural workers. Its functions are partly those of conciliation and arbitration, representing rural workers before the agrarian tribunals and federal, state, and municipal authorities. It also has an investigatory mandate, to oversee the administration of justice in rural areas and to report on law enforcement. And in Guatemala, as one of the commitments in the 1996 peace agreement signed between the government and armed insurgent groups, a presidential office for legal assistance and land conflict

resolution has now been created. Its functions include legal assistance to peasants and rural workers and their organizations; intervening in land conflicts at the request of any party; and receiving
denunciations of abuses committed against peasant communities
or individuals, and transmitting these to the requisite human rights
organizations.[7]

But such procedural mechanisms cannot have a significant long-
term impact on rural poverty and conflicts as long as broader
economic and social policies fail to address the current patterns
of landlessness, precarious employment, and in many cases, real
human desperation. Here the question is not of legal remedies, in
terms of access to the existing justice system. The issue is how the re-
sourceless and most marginal groups can have a stake in national development, in countries with no effective social security systems, no
unemployment benefit, and a dismal recent record in employment
creation outside the urban and rural informal sectors.

In this sense, it is vital to consider how principles of law can tem-
per market forces, providing social protection for the vulnerable,
and also shielding from market forces those groups who simply do
not wish to run their economic and political affairs by the rules of
the free market economy. There are some basic differences between
late nineteenth-century liberalism and the "neoliberal" trends in the
average Latin American country. A century ago, radical liberals were
determined to stamp out all nonmarket and corporate institutions in
the interests of economic progress. In the medium term, they failed.
Today, many governments pay some lipservice to the concept of the
"social market economy." There is also a growing willingness to permit indigenous communities to run their affairs on partly nonmarket
lines, perhaps under a special land tenure regime which prohibits
land sales and mortgaging outside the immediate community.

Even as regards indigenous peoples, current policies are far from
uniform. The 1992 reforms to the Mexican Constitution—perhaps
symbolically enacted five hundred years after the Spanish conquest
of the Americas—were designed to put a definitive end to the agrarian reform process, and also to pave the way for the privatization of
agricultural land. Though the Mexican reforms did not abolish the
status of indigenous communal lands (instead, they grant indigenous

communities the right to decide whether they wish to maintain a special communal legal status), they are nevertheless part of an overall policy to remove subsidies and to reform the agricultural sector along free market lines. Bolivia, interestingly, has moved in a different direction. Its most recent land reform law, enacted in 1996, places more restrictions on the alienation and transfer of indigenous lands (not only for forest-dwelling peoples in the tropical lowlands, but also for Aymara and Quechua indigenous peasants in the highlands) than the earlier land reform laws. Under the new law, agrarian property is clearly divided between the commercial sector and the indigenous or peasant sectors. In other countries where indigenous peoples are either a majority or large proportion of the national populations, the tensions between market and nonmarket principles have as yet to be resolved. It is clear that indigenous peoples in such countries as Ecuador, Guatemala, and Peru do produce extensively for national—and sometimes international—markets, but that for them the land still has a special cultural and spiritual significance beyond agricultural production. Thus it is interesting that the recent Guatemala peace agreements place most emphasis on market approaches to agricultural development and to the clarification of property rights, while a sectoral Indigenous Accord also recognizes the importance of indigenous communal land rights.

But while the situation and demands of Latin America's indigenous peoples tend to receive much international attention, the deteriorating plight of the non-indigenous landless—the many millions of uprooted workers in such countries as Brazil and Colombia—tends to be ignored. It is unlikely that there will be a new round of land reforms in the style of the 1950s and 1960s. Though the rural poverty is arguably more acute now than it was then, the conditions are different. It is far from certain that the floating migrant workers, who endure such miserable and unstable conditions in the commercial agricultural belt, all desire to be small farmers. Their demands are as likely to be for stable and year-round employment, for health protection and education, all necessary to give them a chance of an adequate human existence. But this is all part of the social function of property, as recognized in Latin America's earlier legal and social tradition. Under feudal conditions, an individual landowner had obligations to a specific work force. Under today's different conditions of capitalist agriculture, landowners as a whole must have obligations to the work force as a whole, whether migrants, day laborers, or more permanent workers. The answer may not lie in redistributive land reforms, but in higher and more efficient land taxes, in more effective enforcement of rural labor legislation, in official support for strong and independent rural worker organizations, in improved welfare services, and in training programs. In some situations, however, the land occupations will grow and the rural violence will intensify as long as economic and social policies fail to address the demands of the rural underprivileged.

NOTES

1. *The State of World Rural Poverty: An Enquiry into Its Causes and Consequences*, International Fund for Agricultural Development, Rome, March 1992.

2. *Potentials for Agricultural and Rural Development in Latin America and the Caribbean. Annex II, Rural Poverty*, Food and Agriculture Organization of the United Nations, Rome, 1988.

3. *Panorama Social de America Latina 1996*, Economic Commission for Latin America, Santiago de Chile, 1997.

4. For the Cuban experience, *see* DHARAM GHAI, CRISTOBAL KAY, & PETER PEEK, LABOUR AND DEVELOPMENT IN RURAL CUBA (Macmillan Press, 1988).

5. *See* Alfredo Wagner Berno de Almeida, *Amazonia: Rite of Passage from Massacre to Genocide*, paper presented to Rule of Law workshop, University of Notre Dame, November 1996.

6. *See* NEIL HARVEY, REBELLION IN CHIAPAS (Center for U.S.-Mexican Studies, University of California at San Diego, 1994).

7. Agreement on Socioeconomic Aspects and the Agrarian Situation, signed between the Government of Guatemala and the URNG in Mexico City, May 6, 1996. The agreement came into force in December 1996 upon the signing of a final peace agreement, and the presidential office was created in mid-1997.

PART

II   Overcoming
Discrimination

7

Overcoming Discrimination: Introduction

Rebecca J. Cook

AN IMPORTANT POINT raised by this volume is the recognition that discrimination of marginalized groups is not simply a misfortune associated with their particular status, but an injustice. Accordingly, justice systems at national and international levels must become committed to remedy this injustice. Most societies confront the challenge of devising effective strategies to overcome discrimination of marginalized groups as a step toward achieving overall justice. The following chapters provide important insights into the nature of discrimination, particularly against indigenous peoples, women, and racial minorities, and of the contextual challenges to achieving equal protection of their rights. They suggest ideas on fostering compliance with equality norms in a variety of Latin American countries.

Jorge Dandler's chapter on indigenous peoples demonstrates that assimilationist policies that have attempted to integrate indigenous cultures into dominant national cultures have themselves been a source of discrimination. Dandler explains that assimilationist policies are being replaced through reforms that require compliance with new national constitutional provisions and regional and international instruments protecting the rights of indigenous peoples. He describes the recent constitutional reforms in nine Latin American countries that provide indigenous peoples with varying degrees of constitutional guarantees of their communal property rights, their cultural and linguistic identities, and autonomy in their governance.

Shelton Davis, commenting on Jorge Dandler's chapter, identifies some of the challenges to achieving equitable treatment of indigenous peoples. He stresses the need for research to develop sound empirical understanding of the socioeconomic realities of these peoples[1] and to apply the written law to remedy the actual injustices that such peoples experience. He explains the related need for improved understanding of and training in the rights of indigenous peoples, particularly regarding the collective nature of these rights, in law schools and in judicial education programs. This is particularly important if domestic and international law is going to continue to evolve in ways that are effective in overcoming discrimination against indigenous peoples.[2]

Mariclaire Acosta's chapter on discrimination against women in Mexico explains that a cause of discrimination against women is that laws are generally not framed to cover many of the abuses that women face in the privacy of their homes. For example, criminal laws neither consider forcible intercourse within marriage as rape nor allow for punishment of men guilty of domestic violence. Acosta adds that where laws are framed to cover abuses that women face, it is rare that they are effectively applied. She cites the example of abortion laws that permit abortion in cases of rape, but that are not applied to the approximately one in five victims of rape who become pregnant as a consequence. Despite many criticisms of the lack of access to lawful abortion in such cases, Mexico has not established procedures to enable pregnant rape victims to obtain safe abortions, unlike some public hospitals in Rio de Janeiro.[3]

In commenting on Mariclaire Acosta's chapter, Dorothy Thomas observes the injustice that "the rule of law for women is not a rule, it is an exception." Thomas emphasizes that Mexico is not the only country to neglect domestic violence. She refers to studies showing that Brazil does not guarantee its female citizens equal protection of the law, given its widespread failure to prosecute wife murder, marital rape, and domestic assault and battery.[4] Key to the equal application of the law is building the capacity among women themselves to use national and international human rights instruments to prevent and remedy the pervasive abuses that they face.[5]

Peter Fry's chapter on race in Brazil challenges the Brazilian claim of racial democracy and argues that it is only a myth. He cites studies showing that blacks tend to be more persecuted than whites by police vigilance, confront greater obstacles in access to criminal justice, and have greater difficulty in the protection and promotion of their constitutional rights. He explains that biased functioning of the systems of criminal and constitutional justice results in a lack of faith in the overall rule of law. Reasons for unreliability of the legal system to correct injustices vary, but include corruption of the judiciary, congestion of cases in the courts, and lack of modern concepts in the legal system, particularly the criminal justice system, that would make the system responsive to marginalized groups.[6]

Commenting on Peter Fry's chapter, Joan Dassin explores the advantages and disadvantages of different strategies for fostering compliance with equality norms in Brazil. She argues that despite the lack of faith in the rule of law, nongovernmental organizations are vigorously pursuing the more effective application of rights to remedy racial discrimination through recourse to the courts. She explores the questions that Fry raises about the advisability of an affirmative action strategy in Brazil, and addresses his concerns that formalizing race as a criterion for defining and targeting policy will exacerbate and not relieve the problems of racial inequality. Dassin assesses Fry's preference for policies aimed at relieving economic inequality, believing with him that such policies would automatically benefit large numbers of Afro-Brazilians.

At least three overarching themes emerge from these chapters that signal the need for further reflection and policy development: multidimensional discrimination, the use of social science research, and market globalization and state responsibility.

Multidimensional Discrimination

The chapters analyze discrimination from the perspectives of three different groups of people. No single form of discrimination occurs in a vacuum. Each is intertwined with other forms of discrimination and with the ways in which societies organize themselves. Minority feminist scholars have begun to question the effectiveness of single-axis frameworks to expose discrimination against minority women.[7]

Unidimensional applications of gender equality provisions are inadequate to expose the full depth of discrimination suffered by women within social groups exposed to additional discrimination on grounds unrelated to sex and gender. Further, stereotyped discrimination may exist within racial or other social subgroups that is not a feature of the wider society.

More refined work of this nature is required for improved understanding of the interaction of racial, gender, economic, and other discrimination, and to translate this understanding into the legal prohibition and elimination of multidimensional, composite forms of discrimination.

Use of Social Science Research

The chapters use the findings of social science research to expose the gap between written law and the reality of indigenous peoples, the lack of the equal application of laws to the violent abuses women face, and the racist nature of the criminal justice system in different countries. The authors use these research findings to challenge prevailing assumptions about how different groups live and their vulnerability to different forms of discrimination. Some contributions to knowledge from social sciences have changed, in profound ways, the perception of marginalized groups in certain societies.

In order for policies more effectively to overcome discrimination, social scientists and lawyers need to be trained to work together. Careful interdisciplinary work is needed to expose the differences between written law and the social realities of all marginalized groups. Moreover, that work needs to be applied to argue for more effective implementation of laws and, where needed, for legal reform in ways that respond to those realities. Critical to effective legal enforcement of accountability of agencies and individuals mandated to eliminate discrimination are tools and measures that lawyers and enforcement tribunals cannot create unaided.

The development of appropriate enforcement tools depends upon legal, judicial, and legislative collaboration with social scientists who apply their own skills and imagination. The details and techniques of the law are responses to the social conditions from which facts can be determined through evidence, and to social circumstances from which remedies can be fashioned and enforced. Lawyers may have a more informed understanding than others of due process, and a wider range of experience of the proper functions and dysfunctions of legal processes, but a sense of justice is not simply concerned with processes of inquiry and resolution of disputes. The sense of justice and the satisfaction that it has been achieved comes from a whole community or society, created from the ideals, hopes, and values of all its participants.

Social science research is most productively employed to place governments on notice of their failure to conform to standards of nondiscrimination. Governments are thereby afforded the opportunity to remedy their failings and to avoid condemnation for violations of legal duties arising both under their own constitutions and domestic laws and also under international legal obligations. Lawyers before courts and tribunals may use evidence from social science research that shows breaches of legal standards, but many other groups may also apply such research by political means to press for reform of inadequate practices and to achieve remedies.

If governments take their obligations to foster compliance with equality norms seriously, they have to think carefully about how to encourage and facilitate social scientists and lawyers to work together for the effective reform and implementation of laws.

Market Globalization and State Responsibility

Various authors identify market globalization as exacerbating particular forms of discrimination, and decry state policies that rely exclusively on the market to achieve equality among social groups. While efforts to employ private means to achieve public goals are important to relieving discrimination, they cannot replace the central role of government in ensuring effective implementation of nondiscrimination laws. States remain responsible under their own constitutions and under regional and international treaty obligations for violations of equality norms. Violations can consist both of individual instances of discrimination and of systemic patterns of discrimination, such as persistent and gross discrepancies in access to criminal justice, education, and, for example, health services, that cumulatively disadvantage one group in contrast to another.

States have duties to respect, protect, and fulfill equality norms, and if they fail to abide by these duties, they are legally responsible to the victims of discrimination to remedy injustices and to prevent recurrence of abuse.

The duty to respect requires states bound by human rights conventions to refrain from direct violations of rights and to respect the ability of those entitled to the rights to enjoy them by their own means. Thus, indigenous peoples' right to nondiscrimination is violated by such state action as official expulsion from native territories or the government leasing of indigenous territories to mining companies without the consent of those peoples.

The duty to protect requires states to prevent violations of rights committed by private persons and organizations. Private individuals and institutions as such are not bound by international law, except in extreme circumstances, such as commission of war crimes and crimes against humanity. However, states and their governments are legally bound under such conventions "to organize the governmental apparatus and, in general, all the structures through which public power is exercised so that they are capable of juridically ensuring the free and full enjoyment of human rights."[8] States whose governments leave private violations of human rights unremedied or unaddressed are in breach of their duty to protect human rights.

The duty to fulfill requires states to take appropriate legislative, administrative, judicial, budgetary, economic, and other measures to achieve individuals' full realization of their human rights. Thus, governmental failure to ensure Afro-Brazilian citizens reasonable access to education or the criminal justice system, for instance, places the state in breach of its duty.

The following authors and their commentators indicate that some governments have made important beginnings to meet their obligations to ensure respect, protection, and fulfillment of the rights of marginalized groups. They contribute to our understanding of the systemic and multidimensional nature of discrimination, and suggest that fostering equality norms will not be accomplished through simplistic approaches. Understanding the underlying causes of discrimination is a necessary first step in the advancement of justice for marginalized groups, but identifying the cultural, socioeconomic, and other dynamics of discrimination is a precondition to their remedy. The following chapters show how the work of dedicated lawyers and judges can be reinforced through data established, among others, by investigators in the social sciences in the quest to overcome discrimination.

NOTES

1. INDIGENOUS PEOPLE AND POVERTY IN LATIN AMERICA: AN EMPIRICAL ANALYSIS (George Psacharopoulos & Harry Anthony Patrinos eds., Washington, D.C.: World Bank, 1994).

2. JAMES ANAYA, INDIGENOUS PEOPLES IN INTERNATIONAL LAW (New York: Oxford University Press, 1996).

3. Jacqueline Pitanguay & Luciana Sarmento Garbayo, *Relatório do Seminário: A Implementacão do Aborto Legal no Serviço Público de Saude* (Report of the Seminar: The Implementation of Legal Abortion in the Public Health Service) (Rio de Janeiro, Brazil: Cidadanía, Estudo, Pesquisa, Informação e Ação, 1995).

4. Human Rights Watch, *Criminal Injustice: Violence against Women in Brazil* (New York: Human Rights Watch, 1991).

5. Cecilia Medina, *Toward a More Effective Guarantee of the Enjoyment of Human Rights by Women in the Inter-American System*, in HUMAN RIGHTS OF WOMEN: NATIONAL AND INTERNATIONAL PERSPECTIVES (Rebecca J. Cook ed., Philadelphia: University of Pennsylvania Press, 1994), also available in Spanish: Cecilia Medina, *Hacia una manera más efectiva de garantizar que las mujeres gozen de sus derechos humanos en el sistema interamericano*, in DERECHOS HUMANOS DE LA MUJER: PERSPECTIVAS NACIONALES E INTERNACIONALES (Bogotá, Colombia: PROFAMILIA, 1997).

6. Lawyers Committee for Human Rights and the Venezuelan Program for Human Rights Education and Action, *Halfway to Reform: The World Bank and the Venezuelan Justice System* (New York: Lawyers Committee for Human Rights, Caracas: Venezuelan Program for Human Rights Education and Action, 1996).

7. Kimberle Crenshaw, *Demarginalizing the Intersection of Race and Sex: A Black Feminist Critique of Antidiscrimination Doctrine, Feminist Theory and Antirascist Politics*, UNIV. OF CHIC. LEGAL FORUM 139–67 (1989); Mary Ellen Turpel, *Patriarchy and Paternalism: The Legacy of the Canadian State for First Nations Women*, 6 CANADIAN J. WOMEN & LAW 174–92 (1993).

8. *Velásquez Rodríguez* Case (Honduras), 4 Inter-Amer. Ct. H.R. (ser. C) at 92, para. 166 (1988).

8

Indigenous Peoples and the Rule of Law in Latin America: Do They Have a Chance?

Jorge Dandler

"There are few left or they are already integrated."

"We no longer have indigenous people."

"How are we going to sit with them at the same table if they are not integrated to civilization?"

"They are bound to disappear."

"Who, after all, is indigenous?"

"They are poor because they are indigenous and as development and modernization become more generalized, they will no longer remain poor and therefore also will no longer remain indigenous."

"The majority of the indigenous we have in my country come from your country [Bolivia] or are Chilean Mapuches who have come from across the border to obtain land here."

"To protect this forest reserve and the fauna it is better to relocate indigenous communities."

"The best way to develop our jungle region is to bring colonists from the highlands and farmers from other countries, with a vocation for work and progress."

"They are not trustworthy, they can bring division of the country as in Yugoslavia."

"Our poverty eradication program is for all the poor. Why should we discriminate between indigenous and non-indigenous?"

"They have a long way to go until they are integrated and the main way is through education."

WE ARE CLOSE TO THE END of the millennium and no one doubts that economic globalization is here to stay and thrive at all costs.

Nevertheless, as Margarita Retuerto, former Defensora Adjunta del Pueblo of Spain, stated at a seminar in Lima: "Economic globalization is a fact of life in today's world, but let us not forget that there is also a globalization of human rights as a guiding principle: globalization in communication also makes it increasingly difficult for nations to commit human rights abuses with impunity."[1] No doubt there are global economic tendencies that are increasingly affecting the economic, social, cultural, and political lives of indigenous peoples in all the countries they inhabit. At the same time, there is a growing awareness, at least in some countries, that the strengthening of democracy is also linked to the need for taking effective measures to recognize the rights of indigenous peoples. Such an agenda is part of a larger problem: Is it possible to effectively recognize cultural diversity as a permanent dimension of national society? Do Latin American nations have a historical debt to indigenous peoples which needs to be redressed? Indigenous peoples are increasingly asserting their organized presence, posing demands, dilemmas, questions, and proposals to which governments and the wider national societies in which they live are slow to respond.

The End of *Indigenismo*?

A number of problems in international and national settings have historically hampered recognition of indigenous peoples' rights. First, constitutions in Latin America, as in other regions, formally guarantee that no individual shall be discriminated against for reasons of race, ethnic origin, culture, religion, or gender. At the same time, they contain provisions that guarantee fundamental individual human rights. Nevertheless, the human rights of indigenous persons and their communities both as individuals and as collectivities are frequently violated in practice since basic constitutional principles recognizing their existence and permanence have been, until recently, relatively absent.

Second, the legal vulnerability of *indígenas* as individuals and communities is closely linked to the lack of appropriate legal provisions or guarantees in the majority of existing national legislation. In spite of considerable progress in the adoption of international and national standards concerning fundamental individual and collective human rights, the collective rights of indigenous peoples have been systematically violated on many occasions and in many circumstances.

Third, the prevailing historical premise that has guided the construction of nation-states in Latin America has been "integration," understood as the necessity that indigenous peoples, as they "benefit" from modernization and development, become acculturated and thus no longer identify themselves as indigenous (i.e., as Mayas, Quechuas, Aymaras, Shipibos). The dominant goal, in this context, was to create a homogeneous national culture or an "integrated" national society which has no indigenous peoples. A variant of this perspective was the glorification of an integrated "mestizo" culture, which also implied downgrading indigenous culture, regarded as a remnant of the past, mixed with the "positive" ingredients of the nonindigenous culture or "occidental" influence.

Fourth, development projects and programs quite generally have not been able to transcend an integrationist or patronizing approach, including those implemented by *indigenista* institutions or policies that attempted to take into account cultural specificities. And finally, the ideology of benevolence in many national legislations and constitutions gave rise to elaborate mechanisms of tutelage that denied indigenous individuals and communities effective participation along with the necessary legal security to exercise their citizenship rights and to defend their cultural identity and their livelihood.

These prevailing views regarding indigenous peoples have been strongly challenged in the past two decades, particularly as indigenous organizations and their leaders increasingly have voiced their demands. In addition, of course, many intellectuals, NGOs, and development practitioners have contributed to this rethinking, touching on issues such as social and cultural exclusion, sustainable development, and social equity in the overall context of democratization.

Changing Perspectives in International Law and Other Agreements

As the Universal Declaration of Human Rights, the American Declaration of the Rights and Duties of Man, the American Convention on Human Rights, the International Covenants on Human Rights, the International Convention on the Elimination of All Forms of Racial

Discrimination, and other international instruments have taken root, collective social, economic, cultural, and political rights have gained greater recognition. In this context, some progress has been achieved in the debate and adoption of new principles concerning fundamental rights of indigenous peoples. These advances would not have been possible without a growing international and national presence of indigenous organizations. In the following section, I summarize some of the major recent normative developments at the international level.

ILO Convention No. 169

In response to a growing international consensus on the shortcomings of ILO Convention No. 107 (1957), in particular its integrationist and patronizing underpinnings, as well as the need to adopt new international standards that respond more adequately to the demands and needs of indigenous peoples of the world, in 1989 the International Labor Organization (ILO) adopted Convention No. 169 (Indigenous and Tribal Peoples in Independent Countries), replacing the earlier instrument.[2] This new convention is currently the most comprehensive international instrument on the rights of indigenous and tribal peoples. It takes the approach of a fundamental respect for the cultures, ways of life, traditions, and customary laws of these peoples as enduring peoples (understood as within the boundaries of existing states), with rights and an identity derived from their historical and contemporary presence in the countries where they live. The convention holds that self-identification is to be regarded as a fundamental criterion for determining the groups to which the provisions of this international instrument apply. In other words, no social group or state has the right to deny the identity that indigenous and tribal peoples may hold or affirm.

The convention recognizes that these peoples have the right to decide their development priorities and to exercise control over their economic, social, and cultural development. This can be achieved in several ways. They should be able to participate in the decision-making process, and they should be able to identify themselves as being indigenous or tribal. There are also provisions that give these peoples the right and the responsibility to run programs that affect them. For example, they have the right to participate in the provision of health services or to undertake overall responsibility and control over these services. Governments are required to secure for these peoples the highest standards of physical and mental health, and to achieve this goal, health services must be adequate, i.e., community-based and drawing upon their traditional preventive and healing practices and medicine. Participation in managing educational services and programs is also provided. Indigenous education should be bilingual and bicultural.

Convention No. 169, in contrast to the earlier ILO instrument, establishes clear general principles on consultation and consent. Governments are required to consult indigenous and tribal peoples, through adequate procedures and their representative institutions, whenever consideration is given to legislative or administrative measures which may affect them directly. It is specified that consultations have to be undertaken in good faith and in a form appropriate to the circumstances, with the aim of achieving an agreement or consent to the measures proposed.

Land rights are absolutely fundamental to the continued survival of indigenous peoples. Land and its natural resources are the principal source of livelihood, social and cultural integrity, and spiritual welfare of these peoples. The convention requires governments to respect the special importance of the cultures and spiritual lives of these peoples and, in particular, the collective aspect of their relationship with the lands or territories which they occupy or use. The recognition of land areas to which indigenous and tribal peoples have special rights is intended to give them a stable base for their economic, social, and cultural undertakings and future survival. When the state or nation retains the ownership of mineral or subsurface resources, it has to consult these peoples in order to determine whether and to what degree their interests would be prejudiced before it allows any programs for the exploration or exploitation of the resources to be undertaken. Special attention should be drawn to the fact that this impact assessment has to be undertaken before allowing exploration or prospecting. In this connection, the convention provides that these peoples shall be able to participate in the benefits of the exploitation of resources, and shall always receive fair compensation for any damages they may sustain as a result of these activities. Indigenous peoples are often displaced from their lands, mainly because of the denial of their customary rights, and when relocated, both compensation and resettlement arrangements are woefully inadequate. The convention demands that these peoples shall not be removed from the lands which they occupy; if relocation is necessary as an exceptional measure, governments are required to apply rigorous procedural requirements, including public inquiries and effective representation.

The convention requires governments to establish deterrent measures to prevent nonindigenous persons from taking advantage of indigenous and tribal peoples' lack of knowledge of national laws or to intrude on or use their lands without authorization. In the latter case, adequate sanctions shall be determined by law. Traditional procedures for the transmission of land rights among indigenous and tribal peoples shall be fully respected. Whenever governments consider adopting measures affecting the ability of these peoples to alienate or transmit their rights to nonindigenous people, consultations have to be held with indigenous and tribal peoples. This is a crucial principle, especially as a growing number of countries, as part of their economic liberalization and modernization, are amending their land laws and constitutional provisions. The major aim is to lift restrictions, introduced through agrarian reform laws and programs, on ownership, size, and use of agricultural lands, including those belonging to indigenous peoples. In these cases, the convention stipulates that these peoples have to be consulted on the scope and implications of these amendments prior to their enactment.

Convention No. 169 holds that indigenous peoples have the right to retain their customs and institutions, including traditional methods for dealing with offenses committed by their members, where these are not incompatible with fundamental rights established by national and international law. Governments are required to have due regard to the customary law and the social, economic, and cultural characteristics of indigenous and tribal peoples when applying national laws and regulations and when imposing penalties.

The convention includes a number of other provisions, such as the requirement that governments adopt special measures to ensure the effective protection of these peoples with regard to recruitment and conditions of employment, including equal remuneration for work of equal value, medical assistance, and special protections for seasonal, casual, and migrant workers. With regard to indigenous women workers in general, there is a specific provision protecting them from sexual harassment and abuses.

Since in many cases indigenous and tribal peoples have been separated by national borders which were established without their consultation, the convention provides that governments shall take appropriate measures, including international agreements, to facilitate contacts and cooperation between these peoples across borders.

Finally, the convention requires governments to establish agencies or other appropriate institutional mechanisms to administer programs and policies affecting indigenous peoples, and to ensure that they have the resources necessary to carry out the functions assigned to them. Furthermore, these programs shall include planning, coordination, execution, and evaluation, with the participation of the indigenous peoples concerned, on the measures provided for by the convention. They should also include legislative and other measures which should be drawn up in cooperation with these peoples.

As the most recent and specific international instrument pertaining to the rights of indigenous and tribal peoples, the convention represents a significant advance in translating many of their demands into internationally established rights. Similar to other promotional ILO Conventions, Convention No. 169 contains what are considered universally agreed-upon minimal standards. A state that ratifies No. 169 is committing itself to develop a more adequate legislation and administration of justice, as well as to put into action other requirements to ensure the livelihood and future of indigenous and tribal peoples.

Convention No. 169 should be seen in the context of various international fora which contributed to its adoption in 1989. Since then, there have been evolving discussions concerning additional instruments by the U.N. and the OAS, other international agreements, and initiatives by multilateral and bilateral development agencies to include guidelines or policy directives.

The U.N. Working Group on Indigenous Populations
and Draft Proposal for a Universal Declaration
on the Rights of Indigenous Peoples

Since 1982, as a result of a decision by the U.N. Economic and Social
Council and the U.N. Commission on Human Rights, the Working
Group on Indigenous Populations of the Sub-Commission on the
Prevention of Discrimination and Protection of Minorities (Sub-
Commission) was established. The creation of the Working Group
coincided with the growing internationalization of activities by indigenous peoples. For example, two nongovernmental conferences
were held in Geneva, the first in 1977 ("Discrimination Against Indigenous Populations of the Americas") and the second in 1981 ("Indigenous Peoples and the Land"). Both conferences called for, among
other things, urgent measures to adopt international instruments, to
revise Convention No. 107, and to guarantee basic land rights.

The Working Group has become an important international
forum which annually gathers representatives of indigenous organizations, governments, international agencies, and nongovernmental
organizations to examine issues affecting indigenous peoples world-
wide. Although the Working Group has no authority to process complaints, the publicity and exchange of information, including specific
studies, working papers, and proceedings have stimulated a greater
awareness of issues. In both the Sub-Commission and the Commission, this awareness has been translated into greater coverage in its
monitoring of human rights violations and country reviews, insofar
as indigenous peoples are considered (inadequately for many situations) as minorities or as part of a problem of cultural or racial discrimination under the existing U.N. human rights instruments.

A significant product of the Working Group has been the preparation of a draft Universal Declaration on the Rights of Indigenous Peoples. This proposal is being examined by a special intergovernmental
working group (initiated by the Commission on Human Rights)
specifically established in 1995. The proposed text will need approval
by the Commission on Human Rights; it will then be submitted to
the Economic and Social Council, and finally to the U.N. General Assembly for final adoption. The procedure is lengthy and will no

doubt take several years. The Working Group on Indigenous Populations, in response to indigenous organizations of many countries, was instrumental in promoting adoption by the U.N. General Assembly of the International Year for the Indigenous Populations of the World (1993) and subsequently the International Decade (1995–2004). There is now a discussion to transform the Working Group into a Permanent Indigenous Forum within the U.N. system, which would contribute to a greater international presence of indigenous peoples, systematically monitor their situation, and hopefully obtain a more adequate response by the U.N. and member states.

The draft declaration shares many provisions similar to Convention No. 169 but, as indigenous organizations insist, the proposed text should go further in a number of new concepts and definitions concerning indigenous rights. One of the crucial issues is the use of the term "self-determination." Many governments express concern over the issue of whether the use of the term "peoples" in connection with the use of the term "self-determination" (as used, for example, in the two international covenants on human rights) would mean that their right to secede from the countries in which they lived would be recognized in international law. In the context of the discussions leading to the adoption of Convention No. 169, after much debate, it was decided that the only correct term for the new convention was "peoples," but "that the use of the term 'peoples' [in this Convention] shall not be construed as having any implications as regards the rights which may attach to the term under international law."[3] It was determined that it was outside the competence of the ILO to determine how the term "self-determination" should be interpreted under international law. However, it was understood that the convention does not impose any limitation on self-determination nor take any position for or against self-determination.

So far, the special intergovernmental working group has not yet resolved the issue. Similar difficulties have arisen, as a number of Asian and African governments do not recognize that they have "indigenous populations or peoples" (one reason why the ILO Convention refers to indigenous *and* tribal peoples). It is important to note that while the Working Group on Indigenous Populations had amply debated these and other issues, the intergovernmental working group provides a new venue for governments, *together* with representatives of indigenous organizations and accredited NGOs, to discuss and reach a satisfactory text proposal for further deliberation and approval.

A Future Inter-American Instrument

In 1989, the OAS General Assembly resolved to initiate consultations leading to the adoption of an Inter-American instrument on the rights of indigenous peoples in the hemisphere and requested the Inter-American Commission on Human Rights (IACHR) to undertake consultations and prepare a draft proposal. Although the type of instrument is yet to be defined (convention, declaration, etc.), it is significant that member states agreed in principle on the need for a specific instrument. If adopted, it should provide, among other positive factors, a much clearer mandate to the IACHR to promote and protect the rights of indigenous peoples. Also, it would enable this important body to monitor human rights of indigenous peoples within the region and to include a more systematic treatment of violations of these rights in annual reports and country studies. In addition, such an instrument would give the Inter-American Court of Human Rights an opportunity to strengthen its role regarding indigenous rights.

The first draft, resulting from an initial consultation with governments, indigenous organizations, and experts, was approved by the IACHR in September 1995, to stimulate further consultations and revisions before submission to the OAS General Assembly. The text incorporates much of the new philosophy of respect and participation contained in Convention No. 169; many specific provisions are similar to this instrument or to the draft U.N. Declaration.

This important effort should be closely linked to another evolving issue within the Inter-American system, this being the revision of the Pátzcuaro Convention of 1940, which established the policy and juridical framework for the creation of the Instituto Indigenista Interamericano and its national counterparts, the *institutos indigenistas*. Indigenous organizations have only been able to participate at recent Inter-American Indian Congresses on a consultative basis, a status clearly unacceptable to them. In addition, the basic underpinnings of *indigenismo* have been profoundly questioned. As a result, the Inter-American Indian Congress (Managua, 1994) took the decision that the Pátzcuaro Convention should be revised. Since such modification would provide the framework for a reorganization of the Inter-American Indian Institute and its national affiliates, the preparation of this new or revised instrument should be carefully tied to the adoption of an Inter-American instrument on the rights of indigenous peoples.

Other International Agreements, Guidelines, and Policy Directives

In recent years, provisions concerning the rights of indigenous peoples have been adopted in various international agreements of a more general nature, such as the Rio Declaration, the World Charter for Nature, and Chapter 26 of Agenda 21. The inclusion of these provisions, as well as references concerning the rights of indigenous women, indigenous children, or indigenous rights in general at various world conferences (Beijing, Vienna, Copenhagen, etc.) were largely possible as a result of arduous work by indigenous organizations. If indigenous peoples had not made their presence felt, these agreements, plans for action, and declarations would likely have remained silent on the plight and human rights of indigenous peoples.

A number of international financial institutions and government international cooperation agencies over the past few years have adopted policy directives or guidelines regarding indigenous peoples. In 1991, the World Bank adopted Operational Directive 4.20 on indigenous peoples, which revised an earlier Operational Manual Statement (OMS 2.34) on the rights of "tribal people," outlining procedures for protecting the rights of indigenous peoples in World Bank–financed projects. The World Bank is currently in the process of revising its Operational Directive 4.20, which will be reissued as Operational Policy 4.10 on indigenous peoples. The World Bank's Operational Directive on Environmental Assessment (OD4.01, 1991) of lending operations and related types of environmental analysis also includes provisions regarding indigenous peoples. The United Nations Development Program (UNDP) has circulated a draft of a possible operational guideline to orient the work of its country offices and resident coordinators in support of indigenous peoples. In its "Strategies and Procedures on Socio-Cultural Issues," adopted in 1990, the Inter-American Development Bank (IDB) outlines some principles and actions required when projects and lending operations affect indigenous communities. Additionally, the governments of The Netherlands (1993), Denmark (1994), and Belgium (1994) have issued policy guidelines or development cooperation strategies regarding indigenous peoples.

The common concern of these international agreements and policy guidelines is to provide indigenous peoples with equal opportunities to influence and benefit from development, on their own terms and based on their cultures, recognizing that these peoples have an enduring presence in the societies where they live but have been especially subject to discriminatory practices, loss of their lands, and violation of their basic human rights. Convention No. 169 is quoted in most of these agreements and policy guidelines, or the wording of these instruments is often similar to that of the convention. In relation to policy guidelines, international development actors are gradually moving toward a common understanding of the problems, aspirations, and rights of indigenous peoples in the context of lending operations or technical cooperation programs. This awareness also opens the possibility of ensuring mechanisms of consultation and consent by indigenous peoples in national contexts where programs and projects are likely to affect them. Although not yet fully tested, many of these guidelines should also directly serve to remind governments of their own commitments regarding the rights of indigenous peoples. Above all, if more widely informed about these guidelines, indigenous peoples and their organizations have more elements to exert their own influence on development institutions and governments.

Recent Constitutional and Legislative Changes

During the past decade, a number of Latin American countries adopted constitutional reforms or new constitutions which include significant new provisions concerning the rights of indigenous peoples. In almost all cases, the reforms are the result of considerable debate and organized pressure by indigenous organizations and support groups.

Guatemala's Constitution (1985), adopted in a context of the democratic transition from a military regime, devotes five articles to indigenous communities, specifically granting them recognition of their way of life as "ethnic groups of Maya ancestry," and protection of their customs, traditions, forms of social organization, use of indigenous dress by men and women, languages, and dialects. The constitution states that the lands of cooperatives, indigenous communities, or any other form of communal or collective tenancy or property of land, will be accorded special protection by the state: "Indigenous communities and others which have lands that historically belong to them and that they have traditionally administered in a special way, will maintain this system." These provisions, including the mandate for Congress to develop a special law regulating the five articles, remained a declaration of good intentions. Indigenous organizations and their leaders, at the time the new constitution was adopted, were hardly in a position to present their proposals directly or to press for effective compliance, legislative development, or administration of justice in regard to gross human rights violations, discriminatory practices, and violence that prevailed in Guatemala.

A decade later, as the democratic process opened and the peace prospects renewed hope for a better future, human rights no longer were considered a subversive subject. In this context, indigenous rights soon followed as an issue that could also be discussed more explicitly. A broad spectrum of indigenous organizations and leaders has emerged in recent years, enabling the Mayas to more openly voice their grievances and proposals regarding their future role in Guatemalan society. Undoubtedly, the Nobel Peace award to Rigoberta Menchú in 1992 not only provided indigenous peoples worldwide an important momentum to their demands, but also brought an international focus on the plight of indigenous peoples in Guatemala and encouraged the latter to further their cause.

The peace agreement on Identity and the Rights of Indigenous Peoples signed by the government and the URNG (*Unidad Revolucionaria Nacional Guatemalteca*) in March 1995, based in large part on the proposals that were put forward by indigenous organizations, for

the first time opens the possibility of building a new relationship between the state and indigenous peoples in Guatemala. The peace
agreement, which will be analyzed later in this chapter, contains an
agenda for a much clearer recognition of indigenous rights, including a commitment to proceed with a constitutional reform.

The Nicaraguan Constitution (1986) and the Statute of Autonomy
for the Communities of the Atlantic Coast Region were adopted during the Sandinista government in the context of a major internal conflict and the danger of a secessionist movement generated by outside
support for the *Contras*. Although in practice there is still a long way
to go, the Statute of Autonomy constitutes an important innovation
in Latin America, since the right of regional autonomy and self-
administration is constitutionally recognized. Indigenous organizations in Nicaragua have thus far been effective in preventing a
reversal of these provisions.

The Brazilian Constitution (1988) contains a chapter relating to indigenous peoples. This chapter would have been impossible without
the mobilization of indigenous peoples and their organizations, and
was supported by the Catholic Church, ecumenical groups, NGOs,
and intellectuals. There was a strong campaign against indigenous
rights promoted by conservative groups, economic interests, and
some newspapers. The proposed text put to a vote at the Constitutional Assembly would have been highly damaging to the rights of
indigenous peoples. For example, it would have given rights only to
those Indians having no prior contact: those having contact were excluded from the text and had no special rights to land or their social
organization, customs, or traditions. After heated debates, sit-ins in
Brasília, and an effective presentation at the Assembly's plenary by
the president of the Union of Indian Nations (Airton Krenak), the approved text ended the deep-rooted and discredited integrationist
legal framework that had provided the basis for assimilationist policies. For the first time, the constitution recognized the enduring existence of Indians in Brazil.

The new constitution recognizes original rights to Indian lands
(meaning prior to law), not only those considered necessary for their
habitation, but also rights concerning production, preservation of the
environment, and physical and cultural reproduction. Although

Indian lands belong to the Federal Union, the new constitution recognizes that lands traditionally occupied by Indians are inalienable and undisposable and the rights over them are not subject to prescription, granting Indian communities exclusive usufruct of the existing soil resources, rivers, and lakes within their lands. For the first time in Brazil, the new constitution recognizes the existence of collective indigenous rights, acknowledges indigenous social structure and organization, and grants Indian communities the right to express their opinion about the utilization of natural resources. The constitution provides procedural safeguards regarding exploitation of natural resources, especially minerals, by requiring previous congressional approval, and prohibits removal of Indian populations, specifying that Congress should study the established exceptions and consider new ones. The constitution also recognizes the rights of Indians as citizens, their social organization, and their traditional practices, religions, languages, and beliefs. The right to plead in courts is specifically acknowledged, terminating the special state tutelage that was often used to violate, rather than protect, their rights. A number of favorable sentences by higher courts have introduced significant precedents and have raised hopes that the judiciary may provide a useful recourse.

Brazilian Indians face staggering challenges to have their constitutional rights effectively protected. Within three years after the constitution was adopted, some 140 amendment proposals had been presented to Congress, most of them relating to the constitutional safeguards on indigenous lands and natural resources. So far, no amendments have been approved. The process of revising the existing *Estatuto do Indio,* in conformity with the new constitutional norms, has lingered for years. Also, the process of definitive land demarcation was not concluded after the five-year deadline stipulated by the constitution, and the recent Supreme Decree no. 1775 (January 1996) has generated considerable uncertainty over lands that were in the process of demarcation.

Colombia's Constitution (1991) includes considerable advances regarding indigenous rights, recognizing and protecting the ethnic and cultural diversity of the nation. The languages and dialects spoken by ethnic groups are also official in their territories and education should be bilingual, in order to promote the maintenance of traditional languages. Building on established jurisprudence regarding *resguardos indígenas* (administrative areas that encompass more than one community), the new constitution recognizes, for the first time in Latin American constitutions, the concept of indigenous territories or indigenous territorial entities, thus consolidating the far-reaching territorial domains in the Amazon region that were established during President Barco's government (about 18 million hectares). The constitution also introduces into the region the use of the term *pueblos indígenas* (soon adopted by other constitutions, as will be observed below). Authorities of indigenous peoples are given the right to exercise jurisdictional functions within their territories, in conformity with their own norms and procedures, when these are not contrary to the constitution and laws of the Republic. Indigenous territories are given the right to exercise local autonomy and to be governed by *consejos indígenas* made up and regulated according to the uses and customs of their communities. The latter are to design policies, plans, and programs of economic and social development of their territory, to promote local public investment, and to watch over the preservation of natural resources, among other functions.

The exploitation of natural resources in indigenous territories is to be carried out with due respect to the cultural, social, and economic integrity of indigenous communities; in relation to decisions regarding these undertakings, the government will favor the participation of the respective communities. The goods for public use, natural parks, communal lands of ethnic groups, and *resguardo* lands (the archeological patrimony of the nation, and other goods determined by law) are inalienable, and therefore cannot be sold or mortgaged.

Concerning representation in Congress, the Colombian Constitution specifies that two Senate seats are to be reserved for representatives of indigenous peoples (this provision is not guaranteed in any other Latin American constitution); and in the Chamber of Deputies, a number of seats can be occupied by indigenous deputies elected as representatives of their territorial entities.

Adopting provisions regarding indigenous rights was made possible by the considerable pressure and lobbying that indigenous organizations were able to exert, enhanced by the direct participation of three indigenous senators, including a representative of the indigenous guerrilla group *Quintín Layme* that had just signed a peace agreement and qualified to participate in the Constitutional Assembly, as did the M-19 insurgent group.

After these constitutional achievements, Congress has been rather slow in implementing various laws favorable to indigenous peoples, including the *Ley Orgánica de Ordenamiento Territorial*, a law regarding the regulation of the special indigenous jurisdictions with the national justice system and other laws and regulations that the constitution required. Nevertheless, perhaps the most far-reaching results so far have been the channeling of significant state financial resources to territorial entities and *resguardos* regarded as municipal districts, as part of the constitutional decentralization of public investment. Also, the Constitutional and Supreme Courts have adopted at least thirty sentences favorable to indigenous peoples, establishing important precedents in Colombian jurisprudence.

In Mexico, a constitutional amendment of Article 4 was adopted in 1992, as a result of a broad debate and consultation undertaken by the government with indigenous organizations. The amendment recognizes, for the first time since the 1917 Constitution, that the Mexican nation is pluricultural, derived originally from the existence of its indigenous peoples. In a rather long and contested article that did not satisfy indigenous organizations, the provision also stipulates that the law shall protect and promote the development of their languages, cultures, uses, customs, resources, and specific forms of social organization, and shall guarantee their members effective access to the jurisdiction of the state. Furthermore, the same article recognizes that their practices and customs shall be duly regarded in agrarian suits and procedures. Although the controversial revision of Article 27 of the Mexican Constitution regarding *ejido* lands includes recognition of indigenous communal property rights, its regulations are linked to the constitutional requirement of a special regulatory law for the amended Article 4. Such a law has not yet been adopted by Congress.

The Chiapas rebellion, in spite of the protracted peace negotiations, no doubt generated a qualitatively different opportunity for indigenous peoples in Mexico to have their grievances and demands taken into account by the rest of society and the government. This new situation pertaining to the issue of indigenous peoples' rights in Mexico will be dealt with in the next section of this chapter.

Paraguay adopted a new constitution (1992) in the aftermath of the Stroessner dictatorship. Although Paraguay has an appalling record of violations of the rights of indigenous peoples, the constitution recognizes for the first time in this century that Paraguay has an indigenous population. The two previous constitutions (1940 and 1967) ignored this reality. Congress (acting as an interim Constitutional Assembly) considered a proposal presented by indigenous organizations, enabling the presence of four representatives to participate without vote. A salient provision is the recognition of the existence of indigenous peoples defined as groups of culture predating the formation and organization of the Paraguayan state. The constitution also recognizes communal property rights and requires that the state provide these lands at no cost and that they are not transferable, subject to rental, or taxation. The constitution prohibits removal from their habitat (as does the Brazilian Constitution) except under the condition of prior explicit consent. The status of sacred sites is also recognized. Although Spanish and Guaraní are recognized as official languages, the right of indigenous peoples to maintain their languages is also provided. As in the case of Colombia, indigenous persons are exempt from military service. Acknowledgment of customary laws is made, with the proviso that such laws must be compatible with the national judiciary system.

The new Argentinean Constitution (1994) recognizes for the first time that Argentina has an indigenous population and states that (similar to the Paraguayan Constitution) indigenous *peoples* are descendants of populations that existed prior to the formation of the state. It guarantees respect for their identity and the right to a bilingual and intercultural education and recognizes the juridical status of their communities and the rights of communal possession and property of the lands they traditionally occupy, which are not subject to transfer, sale, mortgage, or taxation. The right to participate in the management of natural resources is also afforded.

Bolivia's reformed constitution (1994) for the first time acknowledges the multiethnic and pluricultural character of the nation, uses the term *pueblos indígenas*, recognizes indigenous communities as legal entities, and provides that the traditional authorities of indigenous peoples can exercise administrative functions and alternative procedures, in accordance with their customs, with the proviso (similar to other constitutions previously reviewed) that such procedures (understood as traditional norms or *derecho consuetudinario*) are compatible with the constitution and national laws. As in other constitutions, when indigenous traditional norms are acknowledged, the Bolivian Constitution states that a special law shall regulate the compatibility of traditional indigenous authorities with the prerogatives of state powers.

The same provision (art. 171) recognizes the social, economic, and cultural rights of indigenous peoples, especially relating to their *tierras comunitarias de origen*, original communal lands, guaranteeing the use and sustainable exploitation of natural resources, and their identity, values, languages, customs, and institutions.

These significant provisions were the result of considerable heated debates and lobbying efforts exercised by leaders of the national lowlands indigenous organization (*Confederación de Pueblos Indígenas del Oriente Boliviano*, CIDOB), a Guaraní deputy, and the negotiating ability of the vice-president of the country and president of Congress (Victor Hugo Cárdenas, an Aymara). The term *tierras comunitarias de origen* was a last-minute compromise as an alternative to *tierras de la comunidad* (an atomized notion already present in the previous constitution) and *territorio,* a more inclusive concept, emphasized by indigenous peoples and their organizations, in accordance with the use of this term as already phrased in a number of presidential decrees and in conformity with ILO Convention No. 169, which has been ratified by Bolivia. Congress has also adopted the use of the term *organizaciones territoriales de base* ("grass-roots territorial organizations") in the Law of Popular Participation, referring to the organization of new municipal districts. This recent law has generated a broad process of decentralization, direct access to public funds on a per capita basis, and establishment of many indigenous municipal districts in both highland and lowland areas where rural and indigenous populations are predominant. In effect, this policy has opened the way for greater local autonomy and empowerment of indigenous peoples, who are a majority of the country's population.

The new Peru Constitution (1993) has a number of innovations regarding indigenous peoples' rights: the use of the term *pueblos indígenas;* the state recognizes and protects the ethnic and cultural plurality of the nation; Quechua, Aymara, and other aboriginal languages are recognized as official languages in the areas where they are predominant; and authorities of *comunidades campesinas y nativas* can exercise jurisdictional functions in conformity with customary laws so long as these do not violate the fundamental rights of a person. The constitution also states in relation to these functions that the law will establish the forms of coordination of such special jurisdiction with the *juzgados de paz* and other instances of the judiciary. Regarding education, the constitution provides that the state will promote bilingual and intercultural education. *Campesino* and native communities, as in the 1979 Constitution, are recognized as legal entities and autonomous in their organization.

Concerning land rights, the new constitutional provisions are a setback. Whereas in the prior constitution communal lands were inalienable, not subject to liens or prescription (*inalienables, inembargables, imprescriptibles*), the present text drops the first two restrictions and holds that communities are free to dispose of their lands and that their lands are not subject to prescription, except in the case of abandonment. These provisions are to be regulated by a specific law. The new constitution provides a more generic treatment of land rights than the previous one. The Law for the Promotion of Private Investment in the Development of Economic Activities in Lands of the National Territory and of Campesino and Native Communities (July 1995) reinforces the underlying rationale that private investment in land should be given priority. This is possible only if land is freed to market forces and deregulated. For instance, the long-standing agrarian tribunals have been replaced by regular civil administrative procedures. Regarding the promotion of investments, the government has already taken administrative measures to stimulate the organization of *empresas multicomunales*. Such entities could be helpful to promote economic activities in the countryside. However, if not properly regulated, they could also serve as a venue for groups of individuals or families within indigenous communities to hoard communal resources at the expense of the communities.

There is thus considerable controversy over this law and its regulatory statute that has yet to be adopted. A first proposal of the latter was submitted by the Executive for consultation to Congress; a second proposal later presented also by the presidency focuses primarily on the privatization of coastal valley lands, possibly recognizing that property arrangements in the Sierra and Selva are more complicated than the recent law envisages. So far, this law and draft statute have faced considerable adverse criticism by Amazonian indigenous organizations, agrarian experts, Catholic bishops, and NGOs. In contrast, Andean and coastal *campesino* organizations have not been as active against the constitutional setbacks on land rights or the recent law, possibly because their national organizations are presently quite weak.

Regarding the above summary of constitutional changes in various Latin American countries, a few observations are in order. The evolving normative developments show significant trends, as enumerated below.

A number of constitutions use the term *indigenous peoples* and recognize that national societies are multiethnic or pluricultural; some go further, recognizing that today's indigenous peoples are descendants of populations that existed prior to the founding of the state or nation; one constitution recognizes the rights of Indians as prior to law; all of them have references to special collective land rights; one stipulates the concept of indigenous territory; several refer to special rights regarding surface natural resources on their lands; most constitutions refer to the right of indigenous peoples to an education in their own languages and promotion of bilingual and bicultural education; a few recognize official status for indigenous languages in areas where they are predominant; most provide explicit recognition of customary laws and the role of traditional authorities, while some go as far as recognizing the latter as first instances of the administration of justice system; one provides direct representation of two senators; most constitutions grant various forms of local administration or autonomy, although the latter term is not widely adopted; one constitution recognizes a regional autonomy.

The new constitutional provisions in Latin America regarding indigenous rights were often the result of arduous debate and difficult compromises in legislatures where direct indigenous representation is woefully inadequate or entirely absent. Nevertheless, the evolving norms now tend to shift away from piecemeal, "top-down," or benevolent approaches, to a conception recognizing the rights inherent to indigenous peoples or derived from their enduring existence. In general, constitutions no longer explicitly or implicitly require "integration" as a basic underpinning (Venezuela is one of the exceptions). Similarly, the new constitutional provisions in most cases do not specify or necessarily imply the development of a single, all-inclusive law regarding indigenous rights (for example, a *ley indígena* or *ley agraria*), but instead require a "transversal" treatment and inclusion of indigenous rights in many laws and regulations, most of them not necessarily specific to indigenous peoples. The new constitutional recognition of the multiethnic or pluricultural composition of the national society presupposes that the state now has the challenge to develop legislation, regulations, policies, and administration of justice that indeed reflect cultural diversity.

Although some significant progress has been achieved in constitutional norms, in all the countries concerned there has been sparse development of derived legislation or regulatory laws to reflect these changes. Few legislators and political parties seem to have a clear political will to undertake such reforms. People seldom appear to have the concepts and tools necessary to translate cultural diversity into a workable backbone for the rule of law. This is indeed a major gap. The legal profession and law faculties have been slow to develop the necessary expertise on the evolving rights of indigenous peoples or to propose a new framework sensitive to cultural diversity in law and administration of justice. Not surprisingly, these deficiencies are reflected in the output of legislatures and the judiciary. For example, grave problems remain in such issues as the role and scope of customary law. The proviso included in the constitutions is that customary norms are to be recognized insofar as "they are not incompatible with national laws or the national judicial system." This in practice tends to downgrade the role of traditional norms or relegate them to further study, special legislation, or other future measures which are not easily forthcoming, and few higher courts have provided helpful jurisprudence on this matter.

As most constitutional reforms or new constitutions were adopted in an era of democratization and economic liberalization, an avalanche of laws and regulations is occurring. This phenomenon requires a particularly vigilant strategy by indigenous organizations, who need to muster all the expertise within and outside their ranks to ensure that their rights are properly safeguarded in subjects as varied as civil and penal codes, land rights, forestry, biodiversity, mineral and petroleum laws, environmental law, intellectual property rights and patents, educational laws, and tourism. In addition, they have the difficult task of struggling to develop adequate provisions in the maze of derived procedural and regulatory laws. Without all these efforts, the rule of law concerning the rights of indigenous peoples cannot be easily achieved.

In the following sections, I will draw attention to three situations. The first two deal with peace agreements (Guatemala and Mexico) that specifically address the rights of indigenous peoples. As such, these represent new comprehensive statements of principles and commitments by governments, resulting from negotiations with armed insurgents (indigenous or nonindigenous). The third example (Bolivia) draws on a situation where especially Amazonian or lowland indigenous peoples have managed to organize themselves in recent years, gain a wider audience nationally, and show a sustained ability to press for their rights and negotiate not only significant constitutional reforms, but also crucial provisions in a number of laws and regulations.

The Guatemalan Peace Accord on Identity and the Rights of Indigenous Peoples

The peace negotiations between the government of Guatemala and the URNG gained momentum during the government of President De León Carpio (May 1993–January 1996) and especially the present government of President Arzú, which concluded the final comprehensive peace accord at the end of December 1996. The peace negotiations were able to break the stalemate when De León Carpio both requested the U.N. Secretary General's Office to assist in the moderation of the peace negotiations and verification of the peace accords, and also established the *Asamblea de la Sociedad Civil* (Assembly of Civil Society) to engage the participation of representatives of various social sectors of Guatemalan society in the discussion and presentation of proposals on the various subjects of the peace agenda to the two parties in the negotiations. A milestone in the peace talks was the conclusion of a comprehensive agreement on human rights, which initiated the presence of the United Nations Mission for the verification of human rights. Accords have since been reached on the return of refugees and resettlement of the displaced; the rights of indigenous peoples; socioeconomic aspects and the agrarian situation; the role of the army in a democratic society and strengthening of civil society; reinsertion of the guerrilla forces; and constitutional reforms and the electoral regime. The comprehensive final agreement established full verification by the U.N. of all the agreements, among other important measures.

The *Asamblea de la Sociedad Civil* gave an opportunity to a number of Maya organizations to participate in a coordinated way vis-à-vis other "sectors," such as universities, journalists, political parties, labor organizations, NGOs, private academic institutions, and employers' groups. The Mayas presented a proposal containing their basic views and demands, constituting an occasion for other sectors of Guatemalan society to hear and respond to a position regarding the rights of more than half of the national population. As several nonindigenous delegates observed, the Mayas were actually the only "sector" that presented their views in a comprehensive manner as a *pueblo* or people. Although others also presented proposals on the indigenous issue, the Maya project served as a basis for the consensus Assembly document that was presented to the government, the URNG, and the U.N. moderator.

The peace talks on the issue of indigenous rights lasted nine months. Understandably, indigenous organizations and their leaders, including Rigoberta Menchú, complained that there was no indigenous person representing them. The URNG did not include in its delegation an indigenous person, although the government delegation did (Manuel Salazar Tetzaguic, a Kakchikel, then Vice-Minister of Education). Each party had position papers, but the Assembly consensus document and the Maya proposal became essential, and ILO Convention No. 169 provided a conceptual and legal framework for the negotiating parties and the U.N. moderator.

The agreement on Identity and Rights of Indigenous Peoples is a remarkable document which covers a wide range of issues and commitments. The following are highlighted for the purpose of my analysis:

Identity of Indigenous Peoples:
— the Government agrees to promote a reform of the Constitution in order to define and characterize the Guatemalan nation as being of national unity, multiethnic, pluricultural and multilingual;
— the identity of Maya peoples (21 socio-cultural groups), Garifuna and Xinca peoples is recognized and the Government undertakes to promote in the Guatemalan Congress a reform of the Guatemalan Constitution to that effect;

Struggle against Discrimination:
— regarding de jure and de facto discrimination, the Government will promote in the Guatemalan Congress, the classification of ethnic discrimination as a criminal offense and promote a review of existing legislation with a view to abolishing any law or provision that could have discriminatory implications for indigenous peoples;
— in relation to the rights of indigenous women, the Government will promote legislation to classify sexual harassment as a criminal offense, considering as an aggravating factor in determining the penalty for sexual offenses the fact that the offense was committed against an indigenous woman; and will establish an Office for the Defense of Indigenous Women's Rights, with the participation of such women, including legal advice services and social services;

Cultural rights:
— in relation to international instruments: (a) legislation incorporating the provisions of the International Convention on the Elimination of All Forms of Racial Discrimination, in the Penal Code; (b) approval of ILO Convention No. 169 by Congress [ratification was registered in June 1996]; and (c) approval of the draft Declaration on the Rights of Indigenous Peoples, and its adoption by the appropriate forums of the United Nations and subsequent ratification by Guatemala;

— Maya culture is the original basis of Guatemalan culture and the development of the national culture is inconceivable without recognition and promotion of the culture of indigenous peoples; educational and cultural policy must focus on recognition, respect and encouragement of indigenous cultural values; the Maya, Garifuna and Xinca peoples are the authors of their cultural development and the role of the State is to support that development, eliminating obstacles to the exercise of this right, undertaking necessary legislation and administrative measures to strengthen indigenous cultural development;

— promotion of a constitutional reform regarding the official status of indigenous languages where they are predominantly used; programs for the training of bilingual judges and court interpreters, among other measures;

— the right to register indigenous names, surnames and place names; and the right to use indigenous dress, and the necessary measures to combat de facto discrimination in this connection;

— recognition of Maya, Garifuna and Xinca spirituality and promotion of a constitutional reform;

— the right of indigenous peoples to participate in the conservation and administration of temples and ceremonial centers of archaeological value, and access to sacred sites, including regulations to provide access where these are located in private properties;

— promotion of indigenous scientific and technological knowledge;

— the role of mass media to promote respect towards indigenous peoples;

Civil, political, social and economic rights:
— recognition of the role of community authorities in the management of their own affairs, in accordance with customary norms;

— recognition of the role of communities, within the framework of municipal autonomy in exercising the right of indigenous peoples to determine their own development priorities, particularly in the fields of education, health, culture and infrastructure;

— reform of the municipal code to promote participation of indigenous communities in the decision-making process;

— educational reform: greater role by linguistic communities to manage educational programs; promotion of intercultural bilingual education; changes in curricula, etc.;

— effective decentralization of the State apparatus and indigenous participation at the local, regional and national levels, including the necessary legal and institutional reforms;

— mandatory mechanisms for consultation with indigenous peoples whenever legislative and administrative measures are likely to affect them; guaranteed access by indigenous persons to the various branches of public service;

— customary law: the Government recognizes that both the failure of national legislation to take into account customary norms which govern life in the indigenous communities and the lack of access by indigenous peoples to the national judiciary system have resulted in the denial of rights, in discrimination and marginalization; promotion of free legal advisory services, obligation to make court interpreters available to indigenous communities free of charge; in cases where the intervention of the courts is required, and in particular, criminal matters, the Government will promote a continuing program for judges and government officials on the cultures of indigenous peoples and on the norms and mechanisms which govern their community life;

— land rights: these include both communal and individual land tenure, rights of ownership and possession, as well as of use of natural resources for the benefit of the communities without detriment to their habitat; the situation regarding lack of protection and plundering of indigenous communal lands merits special attention within the framework of the agreement; the Government will adopt measures to regularize the legal situation of communal possession; will guarantee the right of communities to participate in the use, administration and conservation of the natural resources existing in their lands; reestablish communal lands and compensate for lost rights; undertake the constitutional mandate to provide State lands for indigenous communities with insufficient lands; and undertake other specific measures to protect the land rights of indigenous communities.

The provisions on indigenous land rights in the above agreement need to be linked to the peace agreement on Socio-Economic Aspects and Agrarian Situation, signed nearly a year later, which contain a number of specific measures, such as modernization of the land registry.

Joint commissions

The agreement on the rights of indigenous peoples is intertwined with a commitment to establish a number of specific mechanisms of dialogue, consultation, and formulation of proposals between the government and indigenous organizations. Specifically, a number of joint commissions or *comisiones paritarias* are to be established to deal with educational reform, increased participation, and land rights. In addition, a commission (not defined as having strict parity) is to be formed of representatives of the government, indigenous organizations, and indigenous spiritual guides to identify sites considered sacred by the Maya, and to establish rules for their preservation and access. Although these are the commissions to be established, no doubt there will be other issues of the agreement which will generate dialogue and negotiations between the government and indigenous organizations, including constitutional reform, customary law, administration of justice, measures to eliminate *de facto* discrimination, and recognition of indigenous women's rights.

Verification

The agreement, and the mechanisms for its implementation, require verification by the United Nations. This is the first time that the United Nations was specifically called upon not only to moderate but also to verify a specific peace agreement regarding the rights of indigenous peoples within a country. In accordance with the initial Framework Agreement for the peace agenda, the government and URNG requested the U.N. Secretary General to verify the implementation of the indigenous rights agreement, in which "it is suggested that, in planning the verification mechanism, he should take into account the views of indigenous organizations." Furthermore, it is stated that the aspects of the agreement which relate to human rights (in accordance with Guatemalan legislation, treaties, and other international instruments regarding human rights, to which Guatemala is a party) shall have immediate force and application. Such verification is to be undertaken by MINUGUA, the U.N. Mission for the Verification of Human Rights in Guatemala. Finally, it is stipulated that the rest of the agreement will enter into full force at the time of the signing of the final Comprehensive Accord.

The First Chiapas Peace Agreement

Since Mexico has the largest indigenous population in the hemisphere (about 10 million), the way in which the Chiapas conflict is resolved will undoubtedly influence how other Latin American countries deal with their own indigenous peoples.

The Chiapas rebellion, as many authors have pointed out, certainly is not a movement to overthrow and take over the Mexican (or the Chiapas) state. The *Zapatistas* firmly entrenched themselves in a "liberated territory" to communicate to other indigenous peoples of Mexico, the wider Mexican society, the Mexican state, and to the world, that they were speaking for indigenous peoples in Chiapas and in Mexico and that they wanted to be heard—*para ser escuchados*—and they wanted to negotiate a new relationship with Mexican society and the state. Essentially, the Chiapas rebellion is a movement of indigenous peoples that want a hearing with all Mexican society to reach a negotiated settlement with the federal and state governments; they refuse to get back to normal life because they have not negotiated all their demands and they feel that they have not yet been taken seriously by the Mexican government. And so, the stubborn stance of getting a hearing and negotiating continues, while the government often appears to hope the problem may go away and that sooner or later the *Zapatistas* will get tired and exhaust the grassroots communities that support them. In essence, the rebels seem to be saying, "We are here to contradict and we are here to stay, to permanently remind you that we are here. We are not 'the problem,' 'you' are the problem. We are different and we need to be taken into account. So long as we are not taken seriously and our demands do not receive a permanent response by the state, a state which is also ours, we are not going to fall into the trap of becoming silent. We are tired of promises. Getting back to normal life as you see it, without fundamental changes, is not what we want."

The first (and so far, the only) peace agreement signed in San Andrés on February 16, 1996, between the federal government, the

Chiapas state government, and the EZLN (the Zapatista National Liberation Army), needs to be understood in this perspective. The text has quite a different flavor than the Guatemalan peace agreement. The Guatemalan text is the result of a negotiation between the government and the URNG, which is not the same as a negotiation between a government and an insurgent indigenous force and its representatives. The Guatemalan agreement provides a framework of normative goals and commitments to be developed *in situ* between the government and indigenous peoples through their organizations. Thus the agreement is intertwined with the notion of mechanisms (commissions) for its specific contents to be implemented and verified.

In contrast, the Chiapas agreement is the result of a negotiation between the government and indigenous peoples. The *Zapatistas* managed to convince the government to negotiate with the latter. The resulting text consequently appears as a "lesson" and "charter of good governance." If read in this light, the agreement is a remarkable document which does not detract from its fundamental purpose, i.e., the negotiation of principles and commitments that are envisaged as necessary toward the establishment of a new relationship between the Mexican state, society, and indigenous peoples, based on tolerance, respect, participation, and social equity.

The joint *Pronunciamiento* spells out the basic principles and ingredients for a new social pact between the state, indigenous peoples, and civil society. The document states that "this social pact for a new relationship arises from the conviction that a new national and local situation for indigenous peoples can only take root and develop with the participation of indigenous peoples and the society at large, within the framework of a profound reform of the State." The principles on which the social pact is to be grounded are: (a) respect of the rights of indigenous peoples as enduring and permanent pueblos (peoples) with identity, a social organization, culture, and way of life, thus contributing to the cultural pluralism of Mexican society today; (b) conservation of the natural resources of the territories they occupy or otherwise use, their role in the sustainable management of the environment, and the right of indigenous peoples to obtain adequate compensation for extraction of natural resources, especially when their habitat has been affected; (c) integrity and transparency, through involvement of indigenous peoples in decision making and control over public expenditure; (d) participation of indigenous peoples in their own development, through comanagement of projects and plans; and (e) recognition of the autonomy and self-determination of indigenous peoples within the framework of the state. These principles are to be adopted in a new juridical framework at the federal and state levels.

The Joint Proposals of the federal government and the EZLN contain reforms and amendments to the federal and state (Chiapas) constitutions and adoption of corresponding legislation to reflect the above principles. Particular attention is drawn to reform Articles 4 and 115 of the federal constitution. Effective measures are to be adopted to recognize traditional authorities and procedures for electing them, secure access to the judiciary, and recognize the procedures and customary law by which indigenous communities resolve their own affairs. Other proposed measures include a broad conception of economic rights to enhance their capacity to implement economic activities and administer natural resources. Land tenure security and effective protection of the integrity of indigenous territories, as provided for in ILO Convention No. 169 (art. 13[2]), is considered a matter of utmost urgency. Indigenous communities are to be guaranteed preferential rights regarding exploitation of natural resources in their lands. Adequate participation by indigenous men and women in public administration and political representation at national, state, and local levels is reiterated in various paragraphs.

The government is to revise the municipal law in order to facilitate the creation of indigenous municipalities where the indigenous population is predominant, and to ensure adequate representation where they are a minority. Effective protection is also sought for indigenous workers, especially migrants. Discrimination of indigenous women requires effective remedial measures, including legal services. Indigenous women and children are also identified as particularly vulnerable groups deserving priority attention by social policies and programs.

The Joint Commitments and Proposals signed by the federal and state governments of Chiapas and the EZLN provide for the establishment of: (a) a Commission for Municipal Reform and Redistricting in Chiapas; (b) an Inspector General responsible for indigenous affairs within the National Commission for Human Rights; (c) a special *Defensoría de Oficio Indígena;* and (d) an Agrarian Board *(Mesa Agraria)* to resolve land conflicts. Proposals are agreed upon for a more adequate definition of sexual crimes and sanctions in the penal code and its procedural law and the recognition of specific gender and labor rights of indigenous women. Regarding access to communication, the radio stations belonging to the National Indian Institute (INI) are to be transferred to indigenous communities. Indigenous institutes are to be established (to be understood as a revamping of the *centros* or *institutos indigenistas)* to promote indigenous languages; textbooks should accordingly convey the country's culturally diverse character. Opportunities must be provided for traditional medicinal uses, with due regard to an effective extension of public health services at the national, state, and local levels. A fundamental review and transformation of existing public institutions that deal with indigenous peoples are to be undertaken by indigenous representatives, in coordination with the national and state governments.

The Commitments for Chiapas signed by the federal and state governments and the EZLN specify the articles of the Chiapas Constitution which should be modified, and resulting from this process, reforms of state laws such as the Civil and Penal Codes, the Chiapas Basic Law of the Judiciary, the Electoral Code, and the Municipal Law are to be undertaken. The constitution of the state of Chiapas should recognize the pluricultural character of the society as well as the autonomy of indigenous peoples as culturally distinct societies, and their capacity to decide their own affairs within the framework of the existing state.

The above is a synthesis of a long and reiterative list of principles, proposals, and commitments. As mentioned before, its style and content also convey a "lesson," worked out in protracted negotiations, that might have been reached much earlier. The agreement, only the first of others that have yet to be negotiated and signed, constitutes in effect a new "charter of good governance." If effectively implemented, it would point the way toward a new relationship between indigenous peoples and the state.

The Struggle for Indigenous Rights in Bolivia

An important milestone in Bolivia was the *Marcha por la Dignidad y el Territorio* (March for Dignity and Territory) in August 1991. More than a thousand indigenous men, women, and children from Beni walked to La Paz (about 1,000 kilometers) to press the government for recognition of the Chimane forest area as an indigenous territory. During the approximately forty-five days that this walk lasted, the march gained considerable national and international publicity. Until then, indigenous peoples of the Bolivian lowlands had been ignored by other social sectors. They had been regarded as "the savages" or "the barbarians." Conservation of natural resources and depredation of tropical forests by lumber companies and colonists had been issues defended only by a handful of specialists or NGOs, with relatively minor impact. The march became the first ecological movement in Bolivia led by indigenous peoples and posing the issue of environmental protection as something vitally linked to their lands and survival. Indeed, the *marcha* had a great educational impact, contributing to a much broader awareness of the plight of lowland indigenous peoples and vital issues regarding the environment.

When President Paz Zamora and several of his ministers met the marchers at a halfway point along the road and offered to resolve their demands regarding the demarcation and protection of the Chimane forest "right then and there," Ernesto Noe, the leader of the march, stated that the best solution was for the marchers to arrive in La Paz and for the president to wait for them at the Palace, to be ready with a special decree and available for a meeting between two chiefs (the president and the leader of the march). The president reluctantly agreed that he would be waiting with the duly prepared documents granting recognition of the amount of land for which indigenous peoples of the Chimanes had been pressing (700,000 hectares), instead of the reduced amount of land that the government had offered (400,000 hectares). Two weeks later, when the marchers had reached the outskirts of La Paz and thousands of highland *campesinos*, students, workers, and others joined them, a number of labor and political leaders placed themselves within the front lines of the marchers. But Ernesto Noe and his people remained behind, unwilling to proceed. As the former realized this, they went to ask why, insisting that the march should continue since it was getting late and the whole city was waiting for the massive arrival. Noe responded: "Well, if you wanted to head the march, then why didn't you come and join us back in Trinidad and walk with us these 1,000 kilometers?" Consequently the march proceeded with the lowland indigenous people leading in front and all the others following behind. Noe and other indigenous leaders handled these encounters and political subtleties in ways that symbolically questioned the established social and political hierarchy.

Indigenous organizations of lowland Bolivia and their leaders in recent years have quite frequently shown their strength and ability to press their demands, rally behind wider support, and draw on a well-established tradition in Bolivia (since the 1952 Revolution). Governments quite frequently end up negotiating with mobilized sectors (*campesino* organizations, neighborhood associations, workers' federations, mining cooperatives, etc.) when policies or laws are adopted which affect them adversely.

In this context, the Chimane forest became a powerful symbol of indigenous territorial demands in eastern Bolivia, since it had become a refuge for several indigenous communities that had migrated there as a result of road penetration, lumbering, and encroachment by colonists and cattle *estancias* on the lands they had traditionally occupied.

In recent years, presidential decrees recognizing nine indigenous territories totaling 2.3 million hectares were signed by President Paz Zamora, drawing on a previous decree implemented by President Paz Estenssoro that established the concept of "territorial area" or *espacio socioeconómico* to legally characterize the lands and habitat of indigenous peoples in the lowlands, which also established the objective of recognizing indigenous rights in the Chimane forest. Such decrees adopted by President Paz Zamora came increasingly under attack by lumber companies and other economic interests in eastern Bolivia. Although during the process of constitutional reform in 1994, indigenous organizations did not manage to have the term "indigenous territories" included, nevertheless, the term *tierras comunitarias de origen* was adopted, conveying a broader notion than single community lands. The government's commitment to extend definitive titles and demarcation of the nine territories, as well as several others that were pending, was recently obtained in the context of a mobilization of indigenous organizations in connection with the *Ley INRA*, a draft law that had been submitted to Congress regarding the reorganization of the Agrarian Reform Council and measures concerning property rights and titling procedures. This law was recently passed by Congress (October 18, 1996), reflecting a compromise reached between the government and indigenous leaders, although not wholly endorsed by the large-scale agricultural entrepreneurs of eastern Bolivia. Similarly, indigenous organizations had managed earlier to have at least some provisions included in the new Forest Law, the new Hydrocarbon Law, and the Environmental Law, all of vital interest to indigenous peoples to safeguard their livelihood and lands. In this context, the vice president of Bolivia (Victor Hugo Cárdenas), an Aymara, who was also president of Congress, exercised an important role as a facilitator for dialogue and negotiation between the government and indigenous organizations.

The constitutional provisions and legislative innovations recently achieved in Bolivia regarding indigenous rights were inconceivable a decade ago. They were possible due to sustained organizational pressure and leadership, and the ability to put forward clear proposals and goals as part of a strategy to win bargaining opportunities, including more adequate procedures for consultation and consent on policies and laws that affect indigenous peoples. In this context, the various government administrations showed flexibility to negotiate and reach agreement, a stance which was not necessarily forthcoming as a "concession from above."

Bolivia demonstrates the possibility of building a qualitatively different relationship between indigenous peoples and the state, in a context that is not generated by a situation of internal war (Guatemala) or an indigenous armed rebellion (Chiapas). Events in all three countries show that a more inclusive democratic process is necessary for sustainable development in Latin America. In all three (as well as in other countries), indigenous peoples are clamoring for a hearing and challenging the national societies where they live, to be recognized as an enduring and permanent presence, not as secondary citizens or marginal "social groups." Indeed, Latin America has a unique opportunity to peacefully construct multiethnic societies and thrive in diversity, avoiding interethnic conflicts and wars that some nations in other regions of the world are too blind to prevent.

NOTES

1. International Forum of Human Rights Ombudsmen, organized by the Peruvian Defensor del Pueblo and the Andean Commission of Jurists, Lima, Peru, 1996.

2. Convention No. 169 has so far been ratified by Bolivia, Colombia, Costa Rica, Denmark, Guatemala, Honduras, Mexico, The Netherlands, Norway, Paraguay, and Peru. The Argentinean Congress approved it but registration of ratification is pending. Elsewhere in Latin America, the convention is being considered for ratification by the legislatures of Brazil, Chile, Ecuador, Nicaragua, and Venezuela.

3. Draft U.N. Declaration on the Rights of Indigenous Peoples, Working Group on Indigenous Populations, Art. 1, para. 3.

9

Comments on Dandler

Shelton H. Davis

JORGE DANDLER's chapter on indigenous peoples provides an excellent overview of the evolution of international and national legal standards in relation to the rights of the more than 40 million indigenous people of Latin America. The central argument of the chapter is that there has been a fundamental recognition over the past two decades of the collective rights of indigenous peoples to their ancestral lands, their aboriginal languages and cultures, and their customary governance and legal systems, and that their rights to participate as groups with their own ethnic identities and cultural outlooks in national development policies and programs are incontestable. Dandler is also correct that this huge effort at law reform on both the international and national levels has resulted from the increasing political voice and influence of the hemispheric indigenous movement. This broad assortment of regional and national indigenous organizations has laid to rest the nineteenth-century political image of Latin America as a series of culturally and ethnically homogenous nation states, and in its place the multiethnic, multilingual, and pluricultural reality of almost all the countries of the Western Hemisphere has been affirmed. With nearly five hundred indigenous languages still spoken in Latin America, and with many of them now being taught in remote rural schools and heard in urban barrios and on indigenous radio stations, it is somewhat ironic that it has taken Latin American statespersons and jurists so long to recognize and incorporate into law the ethnic and cultural diversity which characterizes their societies.[1]

Yet, although there have been advances (and they are not to be minimized), Dandler would be the first to admit that the road to legal reform in both the international and national arenas has not been without its obstacles and challenges, its false starts, and its persistent frustrations. Only a minority of countries, for example, have ratified ILO Convention No. 169, and even those which have are not ready to implement all of its precepts. Furthermore, even where domestic constitutions recognize indigenous rights and the cultural and linguistic diversity characteristic of their societies, laws regulating these changes have not been instituted and other laws have been passed which often run counter to or contradict these rights. Examples of the latter are recent land reform laws calling for the privatization of peasant communal lands and waters, or environmental or natural resource laws calling for the establishment of national parks, forestry concessions, or mineral or hydrocarbon developments in indigenous territories.

In places such as Guatemala and Mexico (Chiapas), where Indian rights have been placed on the national agenda through armed conflict or regional rebellion, it is still uncertain what will be the outcome of what have often been fitful negotiations. In some of these negotiations, indigenous peoples were not even present at the negotiating table. And, as some of the quotes which frame the introduction to Dandler's chapter demonstrate, there are strongly held attitudes and prejudices against further recognition of indigenous rights. There are also countermovements of powerful interests in some countries (witness the recent uproar surrounding Decree 1775 concerning indigenous land demarcation in Brazil) which could diminish the many constitutional victories of recent years.

Most of the recent constitutional reforms in relation to indigenous peoples' rights in Latin America have taken place on the level of substantive or normative law and not in the areas of legal process or administration—what is often referred to as "access to law" or "access to justice" in the literature on legal reform. For example, Article 8 of ILO Convention No. 169 states that "[i]n the application of national laws and regulations to the peoples concerned, due regard shall be given to their customs and customary law." (*Derecho Consuetudinario* is the Spanish term used to describe these customary legal systems and procedures.) Other articles in the ILO Convention call upon governments to respect the customary methods used by indigenous peoples for dealing with crimes or other offenses committed by their members, as long as these are not inconsistent with the national legal system and internationally recognized human rights (art. 9); to impose penalties which take into account the economic, social, and cultural characteristics of indigenous peoples (art. 11); and, to provide indigenous peoples with access to legal proceedings for the protection of their rights, including the right to use their own languages in such proceedings (art. 12).

Some of these rights to use customary legal procedures and to have their cultural practices respected within national legal systems are also recognized in domestic law regimes, such as the recent law reforms relating to indigenous peoples in Colombia. Colombia is probably the country in Latin America whose national legal regime and jurisprudence recognize most comprehensively the rights of indigenous peoples to govern and administer their own affairs in their own territories, according to their own customary rules and regulations.[2]

Yet, here again, the differences between written law and the social realities of many Latin American countries are noteworthy. While anthropologists have increasingly come to realize the pluralistic nature of legal systems in Latin America and the persistence of traditional law regimes at the local or village level, the latter remain subjected to national law regimes and little understood by judges and attorneys in most countries.[3] As one knowledgeable observer, a Minister of the Supreme Court of Bolivia, writes of his own country:

> The legal system suffers from a considerable degree of imposition, which is to say that little attention is paid to appreciating, analyzing, and consulting the cultural values, local circumstances, or specific factors involved in a dispute. As a result, a large segment of the population, above all aboriginal or indigenous groups, does not feel that the system will serve them.
>
> In addition to this cultural gap, many are denied access to administration of justice because they cannot afford the high fees involved. Most unfair is that small farmers in rural areas—usually the most de-

prived of the population in economic terms—often fall prey to illegal surcharges that take advantage of their ignorance of the system.

This same observer goes on to write:

> Although corruption in the judiciary has declined in the face of the Supreme Court's recent decisions, it is still prevalent among lawyers, witnesses, and court experts and constitutes one more barrier to the administration of justice.
>
> The ritualistic procedures associated with the legal system, and which the bulk of lawsuits must contend with, erect another formidable obstacle to access to justice. Written proceedings are heavily relied on, which tends to drag out court trials. Add to this the lack of nontraditional methods of conflict settlement, such as conciliation, arbitration, and mediation, and you have a legal system bogged down in long, costly, and overly complicated proceedings—and one that effectively denies access to many of the country's citizens.[4]

Despite (or perhaps because of) these conditions, customary or traditional legal regimes appear to be quite strong at the local level in many Latin American countries. These traditional legal regimes function rather differently from national legal systems, albeit in constant interaction with them. Usually, traditional legal systems are most capable of dealing with domestic disputes, interfamilial conflicts, and conflicts surrounding rights to common property resources (communal grazing lands, forests, and waters). The chief mediators in such disputes are often elders, shamans, or other religious specialists. Their methods are usually based upon trying to reconcile conflicting parties through discussion and the establishment of facts surrounding disputes. In so doing, they try to reestablish social peace in communities where social cohesion and shared values and identities are always threatened by individualism and competition for scarce resources. These traditional systems differ substantially from the Eurocentric judicial systems based upon written documents, legal professionals, adversarial procedures, and judicial outcomes where there are clear winners and losers.[5]

One of the most interesting and progressive trends in Latin America is the attempt to incorporate some of the principles of these indigenous or traditional systems into national judicial reform programs, especially at the local level or courts of first instance. For example, recent reforms in Peru have promoted a widespread system of nonlawyer justices of the peace, many of whom speak Quechua and use customary norms and conciliation methods for resolving disputes which are brought to their offices. Surveys conducted by the Judicial Studies Center of the Supreme Court of Peru and sponsored by the Friedrich Naumann Foundation of the Federal Republic of Germany indicate that roughly 47 percent of the cases that enter into courts of first instance (outside of Lima) are handled by justices of the peace, about 70 percent of whom are nonlawyers. The same surveys found that a majority of the litigants (63 percent) were satisfied by the handling of their cases. The reasons for this were because of the accessibility of the justices, their handling of cases in Quechua, their use of plain language, the simplicity and rapidity of their procedures, their low costs, their residence in the same community as the litigants, and the general perception of them as honest and just.[6]

However, as one moves from the local level to higher courts in the national system, the picture changes in Peru, as in most other Latin American countries with large rural and indigenous populations. The same writer who describes the success of the justice of the peace system observes the following about how poor people view the national system:

> The Peruvian judicial branch is perceived as a system that does not recognize the realities of the peasant's life or of the urban population sectors, that does not take into account the values and customs of the different regions and zones of the country, and that usually requires litigants to express themselves in Spanish, a language that is foreign to many Peruvians. Extreme delays in legal processes and institutionalized corruption contribute to the negative perception. It is estimated that as of 1993 in the Supreme Court alone, there was a backlog of 28,000 cases pending. In the judicial branch overall, there was a congestion of from 250,000 to 500,000 civil and criminal cases.

This same observer continues,

> Thus, it is not surprising that the representatives of the judicial system have such a bad reputation. Our surveys indicated that one-half of

those interviewed had a terrible perception of professional judges, viewing them as "unjust," "immoral," "grafters." Justice, as rendered in Peru, is met with a lack of confidence and elicits fear and a sense of rejection. It seems like there is national consensus in this feeling of discontent. And although there have been many efforts at reform of the judicial branch since the early 1970s, they have had poor results.[7]

The past few years have seen a great deal of interest on the part of private foundations, bilateral aid agencies, and multilateral lending institutions, such as the Inter-American Development Bank and the World Bank, in assisting Latin American governments in modernizing and reforming their judicial systems. While most of this interest results from the need to improve the efficiency of national judicial systems in order to adapt to the opening up and globalization of the regional economies, it also provides excellent opportunities to improve the responsiveness of these systems to the needs of poor and traditionally marginalized and excluded populations. Even if a limited amount of the funds currently going to judicial reform activities in Latin America were directed toward the rural poor, it could have a major impact on the situation of these peoples and ensure that they have the minimal legal security to participate in the new economic order. Such funds could be used to strengthen justice of the peace programs, provide court interpreters for non-Spanish-speaking litigants, provide free or low-cost legal services for the poor, establish special offices for the defense of indigenous peoples and peasant rights, and educate lawyers and judges in the emerging national and international laws relating to indigenous peoples.[8]

In the interim, however, we should probably expect rising expectations in terms of rights and access to justice on the part of indigenous peoples and their organizations and a general failure to obtain their fulfillment through domestic institutions and legal remedies. Given this situation, we should also expect more attempts on the part of indigenous organizations to bring their grievances before international bodies, such as the U.N. Human Rights Commission and the Inter-American Commission on Human Rights (IACHR). As documented elsewhere in this volume, the past few decades have seen several cases involving the violation of land rights and resulting in human rights abuses against indigenous peoples and their communities brought to the attention of the IACHR.[9]

As the IACHR became more aware of the scope and importance of these indigenous rights cases, it drafted an instrument on the rights of indigenous peoples which is currently in the final stages of consultation with governments, experts, and indigenous peoples' organizations. Whatever form this instrument finally takes, either as a stand-alone declaration or convention, it will probably lead most Latin American countries to take more seriously their current commitments to indigenous peoples, as reflected in their own constitutions and laws. It will also, as Dandler suggests, provide new opportunities for strengthening the role of the Inter-American Court of Human Rights in accepting and processing human rights cases relating to indigenous peoples.[10]

There is little doubt that there have been a number of positive steps taken by international human rights bodies such as the International Labor Organization, the United Nations, and the Organization of American States, as well as many national governments, to recognize the land, language, cultural, and other collective rights of indigenous peoples. However, there is still a great distance to go before one can confidently say that the "rule of law" reigns in the relationships between nation states and indigenous peoples in Latin America. This is particularly true in the area of procedural law, where indigenous peoples, like many other poor rural populations, are systematically denied access to justice and the law. Much more attention, I believe, needs to focus upon these procedural aspects of the law if we are to affirm that indigenous peoples and the rule of law in Latin America truly do have a chance.

NOTES

The comments herein are solely my own and should not be attributed to the World Bank, its Board of Directors, or any of its member countries.

1. For an overview of the contemporary indigenous movements and several country studies, *see* INDIGENOUS PEOPLES AND DEMOCRACY IN LATIN AMERICA (Donna Lee Van Cott ed., New York: St. Martin's Press, 1994).

2. FUERO INDÍGENA COLOMBIANO (Roque Roldán Ortega & John Harold Gómez Vargas eds., Bogotá: Ministerio de Gobierno, Dirección General de Asuntos Indígenas, 1994).

3. ENTRE LA LEY Y LA COSTUMBRE: EL DERECHO CONSUETUDINARIO INDÍGENA EN AMÉRICA LATINA 1 (Rodolfo Stavenhagen & Diego Iturralde eds., Mexico City: Instituto Indigenista Interamericano, Instituto Interamericano de Derechos Humanos, 1990).

4. Guillermo Arancibia López, *Judicial Reform in Bolivia*, in JUDICIAL REFORM IN LATIN AMERICA AND THE CARIBBEAN, World Bank Technical Paper no. 280 210–11 (Malcolm Rowat, Waleed H. Malik, & Maria Dakolias eds., Washington, D.C.: World Bank, 1995).

5. For one of the most systematic accounts of such an indigenous legal system, *see* LAURA NADER, HARMONY IDEOLOGY: JUSTICE AND CONTROL IN A ZAPOTEC MOUNTAIN VILLAGE (Stanford University Press, 1990).

6. Hans-Jurgen Brandt, *The Justice of the Peace as an Alternative: Experiences with Conciliation in Peru*, in JUDICIAL REFORM IN LATIN AMERICA AND THE CARIBBEAN, World Bank Technical Paper no. 280 92–99, *supra* note 4.

7. Brandt, *id.* at 93.

8. *See* Bryant G. Garth, *Access to Justice*, in JUDICIAL REFORM IN LATIN AMERICA AND THE CARIBBEAN, *id.* at 88–91; and DERECHOS HUMANOS Y SERVICIOS LEGALES EN EL CAMPO (Diego García-Sayan ed., Lima: Comisión Andiana de Juristas, 1987).

9. SHELTON H. DAVIS, LAND RIGHTS AND INDIGENOUS PEOPLES: THE ROLE OF THE INTER-AMERICAN COMMISSION ON HUMAN RIGHTS (Cambridge: Cultural Survival, Inc., 1988).

10. For a particularly important case brought before the Inter-American Court, involving human rights violations against Maroon (Bush Negro) populations in Suriname, *see* David J. Padilla, *Reparations in Aloeboetoe v. Suriname*, 17(3) HUM. RTS. Q. 541–55 (1995); and Richard Price, *Executing Ethnicity: The Killings in Suriname*, 10 CULTURAL ANTHROPOLOGY 4, 437–71 (1995).

10 Overcoming the Discrimination against Women in Mexico: A Task for Sisyphus

Mariclaire Acosta

The Public and Private Spheres

The greater part of a woman's life in Mexico is spent in the confines of her family. Whether it be the family into which she was born, or the one she makes for herself quite early on, it is in this context that she will make the choices that shape her future.

In this she is not unique: most Mexicans view the family as something quite positive, and relate family life with concepts such as unity, love, welfare, understanding, happiness, and support. In fact, in a recent survey, 85 percent of the respondents considered that family was the foremost entity in their lives, as opposed to politics, which only 12 percent considered as important. Work, recreation, and friends are somewhere in between, having a 67, 28, and 25 percent popularity, respectively.[1]

This fact is central to understanding Mexican society and the role that women play in it. Although the Mexican Constitution explicitly recognizes equal rights for both men and women, female roles are still based on behavior, values, and norms that stress private life over public life. Unfortunately for women, the acute poverty and marginalization of the vast majority of the population mean that survival today depends mostly on family income and support. This situation reinforces the traditional subordinate position of a woman to the male head of the household, and actually perpetuates and escalates gender-based discrimination.

In this chapter, I will argue this point, and try to demonstrate how major economic and political programs directly affect women's rights. In the case of Mexican women, the particular scheme of development chosen by the political and economic elite currently in power, which is based on a privatization scheme and severe structural adjustment requirements of the international financial community, has imposed particular and severe costs on women that are not apparent on the face of these programs.[2] I will also analyze how this situation has affected existing legal norms and practices, reinforcing traditional patterns of discrimination against women.

The Implantation of a Free Market Economy and Its Effect on the Status of Women

Over the last fifteen years, losses in income and job opportunities have been devastating for most Mexicans. The draconian policies of structural adjustment of the economy, implemented by successive governments since 1982, have left at least 16 million people out of the market. Cutbacks on social spending and the reduction of the role of government in providing many goods and services have forced the majority of the population to rely more than ever on family efforts and personal connections—mostly kinship ties—in order to satisfy their basic needs.

For a long time this was not the prevailing trend. For three decades following the Second World War, Mexico enjoyed high economic growth and broad-based development that gave rise to an extensive middle class, a new industrial working class with steadily rising wage levels, and a rural sector that also increased its income thanks to the opening of new lands, rising productivity, and government-sponsored irrigation projects.[3]

Negotiations with businesses conducted under the auspices of government-controlled labor and peasant organizations ensured that a portion of this expanding national wealth trickled down to the lower reaches of society. An aggressive extension of medical and educational services by the government during this period of "stabilizing development" reached vast sectors of the population and provided the illusion that welfare and social mobility were on the increase. But in fact, this inward-looking state-led model of development did not mean that income was being evenly distributed. Mexico has never been able to break its pattern of highly skewed income distribution.[4]

The facade began to crumble in the 1970s, when the development model openly showed its flaws. In 1982, Mexico suffered a severe economic crisis caused by a spiraling foreign debt and the fall of oil prices—its main export—in the international market. In August of this same year, the Mexican government announced that it could not meet its debt payments for lack of foreign reserves. The international banking community and the U.S. Treasury came to the rescue with fresh money. Payments were stretched out and new loans were written, with the result that Mexico has become socially and economically dominated by its foreign debt problems. In order to meet the monumental payments, severe austerity measures recommended by the International Monetary Fund (IMF) and the World Bank were adopted. Thus, wages have been slashed, governmental services and subsidies cut drastically, state-owned industry privatized, and inflation restricted at the cost of higher taxes, higher interest rates, and less credit. The impact of the recovery program has preserved the stability of the international trading and finance system, but it has caused a dramatic slowing of development. Succeeding administrations, especially after the 1994 so-called "peso crisis," have continued and increased the breadth and scope of these economic policies, resulting in a net loss of economic sovereignty.

At the end of the twentieth century, Mexico seems farther away than ever from reaching the goal of a more equitable and inclusive social structure. The economy has never fully recovered after 1982 and is subjected to periodic bouts of currency devaluation, massive capital flight, and increased dependency on foreign lending. Economic restructuring under the auspices of the international financial community has led to the implantation of a free-market economy based on exports of a few goods mainly to the United States and Canada, Mexico's major trading partners. The social cost of this policy has been devastating. Inequality has increased, producing a highly polarized society in which unemployment is rampant.[5]

Social welfare policies and their legal provisions, which for decades provided subsidized food, health, and education for the majority of the population, have been dismantled. Consumption per capita of corn, beans, and wheat has dropped more than 35 percent in ten years since their price increased at double the rate of the minimum wage, which has decreased by two-thirds since 1982. Malnutrition, coupled with a decline of the state's health budget to almost half of what it was in 1980, caused the tripling of infant deaths in 1992. Overall spending on education declined from 5.5 percent to 2.5 percent of Mexico's gross domestic product (GDP).[6]

Given the unique institutional history of the Mexican state, based until very recently on public enterprises and corporativist structures that provided these goods and services in exchange for political support, public institutions such as political parties, legislative bodies, and court systems are insufficiently developed and simply do not provide the framework for solving people's needs. Moreover, there is a generalized tendency toward the breakdown of many institutions, especially in the justice system.

The severe policies of structural adjustment, applied relentlessly since 1982, have deepened the prevailing inequality typical of Mexican society since it was established as an independent nation. Privatization of government services and corporations, economic deregulation and liberalization of trade, and reductions in the civil service and in social services spending have destroyed the social safety net protecting at least half of the population. This inequality, coupled with the reluctance of the current ruling elite to relinquish power and move toward a more democratic and competitive political system in tune with the changes in the economic sphere, has further eroded many of the institutions of the state, which are unable to withstand the strain of such rapid change. This weakness has reached a crisis point in many regions, especially in the least developed ones such as the states of Guerrero, Chiapas, and Oaxaca, where armed violence threatens to replace institutional channels as a means for solving the unmet demands of the predominantly peasant population.[7]

Mexico is no longer a rural nation. Only 27 percent of its population lives in the countryside. However, urbanization has not provided people with stable jobs and security. There is an increasing lack of infrastructure, such as adequate housing, water, and other services, in the overgrown cities. In almost every sphere, people are being forced to rely more on direct action to solve their many problems. Most of this action is undertaken by women at the community level in order to provide nutrition and health care.[8]

Public insecurity and violent crime are on the rise. But so is the impunity of public offenders. The alarming rate of lynchings of suspected criminals throughout Mexico indicates just how much mob action is replacing the inefficient police and the court system in order to punish suspected criminals.[9]

Women's lives have always been under duress in Mexico. Women and their children have taken the toll of the abrupt process of privatization and economic globalization. Without serious action on the part of the state to reverse the unequal access of low-income women and children (the immense majority) to formal employment, as well as to health, education, and other welfare services, they will continue to be in a situation of gross disadvantage with regard to the rest of the population. However, this entails moving away from orthodox free market economics and the servicing of Mexico's enormous foreign debt. Any serious effort to reverse their plight will require a reconsideration of these policies and of the role of the state in society, coupled with the strengthening of nongovernmental participation in every sphere. But unless the political system becomes truly democratic and pluralistic, none of this will happen.

The Female Population

There are 46.5 million women in Mexico, representing a little over half of the total population. Most of them are in the age group of fifteen to sixty-four years of age (60 percent), as opposed to those under fifteen (36 percent) or over sixty-five (4 percent).

Women and girls live with their family (95 percent), and they tend to establish their first stable relationship, whether it be common law or a legal marriage, at around eighteen years of age if they are city dwellers, and a year before if they live in the countryside.[10] Half of them have their first child at approximately age twenty-one, although 16 percent have already done so between the ages of fifteen and nineteen.[11] Thanks to contraception, most of these women and girls have an average of three children (or five in the countryside) over a period of thirteen years; by the time they reach sixty, more than two-thirds of them will be dependent on their children or other relatives for financial support.[12]

Education

It used to be the case that women had fewer educational opportunities than men. There are more illiterate women over sixty (40 percent), than men (28 percent). However, this has changed, and at least as far as preschool and elementary education is concerned, boys and girls have equal enrollment rates. The difference starts later on, during adolescence, when 32.5 percent of the girls at age fourteen leave school, as opposed to 27.5 percent of their male counterparts. Leaving school means entering the labor market in order to help support the family.[13]

When women are lucky enough to continue their education, they attend secondary school in a smaller proportion than males, with a 5 percent difference in enrollment. If they belong to the elite that has access to higher education, it is still less accessible to them than to men: 82 females per 100 males are enrolled in colleges and universities. Furthermore, many more women than men tend to leave school at this stage, since according to figures published in 1990, only 37 percent of the population over twenty years of age, with four years of higher education, were female.[14]

Occupation and Income

Regardless of her education, a woman's life will center primarily around her family. Of course, access to education determines many things in her life. Less educated women have almost twice as many children (5.6 in 1990), and of course, a poorly paid job. Women provide income for their families in one out of every three homes. In one out of five homes, the woman's earnings are the most important source of income for the family, and in one out of ten homes, she will be the sole breadwinner. Most of the time she is also responsible for domestic chores.[15]

A great deal of the work that women do in Mexico is not accounted for in official figures. However, more than half of the women who are registered in the census as part of the economically active population are living in some kind of marital status (54.5 percent). It used to be true that women would abandon the labor market after a few years, but given the dire economic situation of the vast majority of the population, this is no longer the case.[16]

According to the latest census figures, women are employed primarily in the informal sector as domestic workers. More recent studies, however, point to the enormous expansion of piecework *(a destajo* and *maquila)* occupations, in both urban and rural settings, which provide the flexibility that women need in order to balance their work and family responsibilities. Many women are self-employed (more than 4 million), and half of these do not have fixed incomes.[17] Women who *are* employed in the formal economy tend to work as educators, office workers, technicians, and shop clerks, in that order.[18]

In 1970, women represented almost a fourth of the labor force in Mexico City. Twenty years later, after rising to almost 27 percent in 1980, the proportion has been reduced to 18 percent.[19] In 1980, women with stable jobs represented 33 percent of the female population over age twelve, almost four points more than the decade before. By 1990, the figure was down to 30 percent, and five years later only 21 percent of the women over the age of eleven had paid employment.[20]

Whatever the occupation of a woman, her income is considerably less than a man's. According to the last census, 65 percent of the women received an income of less than two minimum wages, as opposed to 53 percent of the men.[21] Access to social security is also considerably less for women, and support services such as day care are out of reach for most women.

In 1970, women with employment were earning an average of $750 pesos for every thousand earned by men. A decade later, in 1980, their income had increased to $822 per thousand. After the economic crisis of 1982, female income began to descend almost to the level of the previous twelve years: $766 to a thousand for males. In 1995, after the severe financial crisis suffered by Mexico in December of 1994, it plummeted to $694 pesos for every thousand earned by men.[22]

Official statistics do not compare wage differentials between men and women for the same jobs. However, analysis of the census data shows the increasing gap between average male and female incomes over the last twenty-five years, a demonstration of the feminization of poverty. In the words of Ruiz Harrell, "It has not been possible to increase female employment. It has been equally impossible to pay women the same as men. It is increasingly difficult for women to reach positions of authority in their jobs, and even sadder than that: whatever was gained in the years between 1970 and 1980, was lost in the following decade."[23]

Political Participation

Opportunities for political and other public participation for women are deficient but improving. Women achieved the right to vote in 1953, and this was gained only after a long struggle. Their participation in elections is indeed equivalent to that of the men. Women tend to vote slightly more in favor of the party representing the status quo. In recent federal elections, female voters claimed to favor the candidate of the ruling party (PRI) in a proportion five percent higher than male voters.[24]

Many women participate in diverse social movements, especially those pressing the government for basic needs, such as education, housing, food subsidies, land, and urban infrastructure. In fact, most of these grass-roots movements are largely female. However, women have little access to leadership positions, especially elected ones. It seems that politics for them are still strongly related to direct action on issues of family welfare. Access to formal politics is still very limited.

According to some estimates, over two million women are unionized, but less than 8 percent of union leadership is in their hands.[25] Only three women have been state governors in the last forty-five years, and less than four percent of the country's municipalities have elected women to preside over local government. Access to mid-level positions in the executive branch of government is higher, and this also holds true in the legislative and judiciary branches. But on the whole, women are discouraged from participating in positions of influence outside the domestic realm.[26]

Finally, there are several hundred nongovernmental organizations (NGOs) active in advocating women's issues. These groups have been very effective in addressing serious abuses against women.

They have also provided important services and leadership training for an increasing number of women. However, they tend to encompass very small numbers of activists.[27]

Health and Life Expectancy

Life expectancy for women has increased to seventy-six years over the last five decades. In the poorer underdeveloped areas of Mexico, like Oaxaca and Chiapas, it is much shorter, and infectious disease is a high cause of mortality. Maternal death during childbirth has diminished over the years, but is still twice as high as in other, more developed countries (61 maternal deaths per 100,000 live children). Access to contraception has reached a national average of 66 percent, but is much lower in the rural areas and in poor urban neighborhoods. There is a high rate of abortions, which are illegal and thus a high cause of mortality (220,000 deaths per year by some estimates). Furthermore, most women between the ages of fifteen and sixty-four die from either malignant tumors in the breast or uterus, or of heart failure, diabetes, injuries, or complications of abortions.[28] In short, life for most women is one of hard work and deprivation for the sake of their family, both in the home and in whatever occupation to which they can aspire. This situation injures their health: in a recent survey, one out of every three women over the age of sixty stated that they were unable to climb stairs or walk for more than three blocks without help.[29]

Legal Rights versus Real Rights

In preparation for the U.N. World Conference on Women, which was held in Mexico City in 1975, the Mexican Constitution was changed to ensure equality of men and women before the law. This change also added provisions for the legal protection of the family. Article 4 now states explicitly that every person has the right to freely and responsibly decide, with full access to information, on the number and spacing of their children. Since then, Mexico has ratified most of the international and regional legal instruments that are intended to ensure protection of the human rights of women and their children; Mexico reports regularly on its perform-ance to the appropriate bodies.[30] In practice, equality of men and women is mostly a formal right. The dynamics of the economy and society undermine any possibility of affirming the rights of women. Discrimination is, as we have seen in the previous section, a fact of daily life. It is institutionalized. Therefore, it exists in the courts and in some state laws; in Chiapas, for example, the penalty for stealing cattle is higher than for rape.[31] As long as the current economic poli-cies prevail, women will continue to be at a disadvantage, and no matter how many human rights treaties are signed and ratified by the Mexican state, gross violation of women's basic rights will result.

In the previous section, I demonstrated how these rights have been violated by the state's general failure to meet the minimum core obligations of human rights of large sectors of the population. In the next section, I analyze other aspects of the discrimination of women that can be immediately addressed by affirmative state actions, but which have nevertheless not been resolved satisfactorily.

In my introductory section, I pointed out the increase of all types of violent behavior as a consequence of both institutional break-down and the general impoverishment of the majority of the popu-lation of Mexico. Women and children are especially vulnerable to this rise in violence. The government has tended to overlook this fact. Sometimes it has actually moved away from its obligation to ensure the full protection of the fundamental right of women to physical integrity. In the following section, I will focus on the pro-tection of women's life and physical integrity in the judicial system. This is an area in which nongovernmental women's groups have been very active, forcing the government to take some, albeit insuf-ficient, steps to end the most severe effects of this type of abuse.

Violence against Women
Sexual Violence

Violence against women takes many forms. It happens mostly in the home and in the context of the family. However, the occurrence of violence, especially sexual, outside of the home, is also common.

Violence for political reasons, including sexual violence, is increasing, especially in regions where there is intense militarization due to the emergence of armed guerrillas, such as in Chiapas, Oaxaca, Veracruz, and Guerrero.

In mid-1989, Mexico City residents were shocked to discover that nineteen young women, over the course of several months, had been kidnapped and gang-raped, mostly in the presence of their boyfriends and spouses, by the bodyguards of the Federal Anti-Narcotics Prosecutor, Javier Coello Trejo. In the ensuing commotion—the agents were eventually prosecuted after enormous public pressure, mainly from the women's movement—sexual violence finally became a serious issue.

As a consequence, the Criminal Code of the Federal District (*Código Penal para el Distrito Federal*), where Mexico City is located, was updated to include crimes against psycho-sexual freedom (*delitos contra la libertad psico-sexual*) and the legal penalties for rape and other sexual offenses were increased. The Public Prosecutor for the Federal District (*Procuraduría General de Justicia para el Distrito Federal*, PGJDF) established four specialized agencies to deal with these offenses, as well as a service for the treatment and rehabilitation of survivors/victims (*Centro de Terapia de Apoyo a Víctimas de Delitos Sexuales* of the PGJDF). Official statistics on sexual violence began to be compiled, but the data are still insufficient.

Sexual violence is one of the least reported crimes (about 7 percent), but some estimates calculate that in Mexico City alone a rape occurs every seven minutes.[32] Figures for the rest of Mexico are not available, since many states do not have specialized agencies for dealing with these criminal offenses. However, statistics compiled by various women's organizations in other parts of the country show similar trends in the larger cities.

From 1989 to 1995, the above-mentioned specialized agencies in Mexico City dealt with a total of 31,255 persons, between survivors (67 percent) and their families. The crime most often reported was rape (47.3 percent), followed by sexual abuse (27 percent). One in four victims of sexual offenses was under the age of thirteen, and three-fourths of them were female. The most frequent offense against these children was sexual abuse (44 percent), followed by rape (35

percent). Sixty-five percent of the children were girls. Overall however, most sexual offenses affect women (90 percent) under the age of
twenty-four, and half of these occur when the victim is under eighteen. It appears that education and social status are not as determi-
nant as age.[33]

According to the latest report published by the Mexico City Prosecutor's office, sexual violence and maltreatment of women and minors represent 26.6 percent of the daily average of crimes. About 70
percent of the offenders are known to the victim: 35 percent are relatives, and one out of three of these are the father or step-father.[34]

Sexual violence also occurs elsewhere: mostly in public trans-
portation, schools and day-care centers, doctors' offices, and by security agents. Since in the overriding majority of situations the aggressor
is known well by the victim, she rarely presses charges, and detention does not happen.[35]

About one in five victims of rape become pregnant as a consequence of the sexual assault. Abortion is not penalized in these cases.
However, once the victim has proven that her pregnancy was caused
by rape, there is no established legal procedure for her to obtain a
safe abortion in a hospital or clinic. This situation has been denounced frequently, but the state has neglected to establish a procedure for women to exercise this right. At best, she will be absolved of
punishment if she obtains an illegal abortion.[36]

Prosecution and punishment of rapists is very low and has decreased as part of the general trend of high impunity of all types of
crimes.[37] In 1971, approximately 37 percent of the presumed offenders were prosecuted; by 1980, the figure had decreased to 24 percent.
It decreased again to 18.5 percent in 1990, and to 14 percent in 1994.[38]

Added to the difficulties of denouncing and prosecuting sexual
crimes against women is the recent position of the Supreme Court of
Justice. In an unprecedented 1994 ruling by five ministers, including
two women, the Supreme Court determined that forcible and violent
sexual intercourse imposed by one spouse over another could not be
punished as rape, but as the undue exercise of a legitimate right.[39]
Recently, this jurisprudence was denounced as an overt violation of
the Inter-American Convention to Prevent, Punish and Eradicate
Violence Against Women, signed and ratified by Mexico in 1995.

However, since the Mexican courts have not recognized international human rights treaties as legally binding, this ruling remains
unchanged.

Domestic Violence

More than a million women every year seek urgent medical treatment throughout Mexico due to injuries caused by domestic violence.[40] According to one study, between 1989 and 1995 an annual
average of thirty thousand patients were treated in the public hospital facilities of Mexico City for serious, intentional injuries; a fourth of
these patients were women.[41]

Attention to this problem and treatment for victims were first
started by nongovernmental women's groups. After ten years of
denunciation and pressure, the Mexico City Police Department established a public facility for battered women. The Center for the
Support of Violated Women, COAPEVI (*Centro de Apoyo a Personas
Violadas, Secretaría de Protección y Vialidad del Departamento del
Distrito Federal*), was the consequence of a written agreement between the government and feminist groups. In the first two years of
its existence, COAPEVI investigated three hundred cases of domestic violence. However, only 15 percent of the offenders were ever
sentenced.[42]

In 1989, the Prosecutor's office established the Center for the Attention of Intra-family Violence, CAVI (*Centro de Atención a Víctimas
de Violencia Intrafamiliar*). The Center has given support to almost
90,000 persons to date. According to its estimates, most victims are
women. The aggressors are either spouses or boyfriends, who consider themselves to be figures of authority in the home. The ages of
the victims range from 21 to 40 years, and a little less than half of
them are housewives, although the majority have a job and earn their
own income. A significant number were pregnant when beaten.
Many claimed that the violence in their homes had been going on for
several years, and that it affected them as well as their children. Studies done in the states of Jalisco and Colima show similar tendencies.

Domestic violence is a very serious public health problem. A survey in the emergency rooms of the public hospitals of Mexico City

conducted in 1988 showed that the injuries of women and children caused by violence in their homes were the most serious, often requiring hospitalization.[43] Health problems, such as hypertension and diabetes, can also be caused by the stress produced by prolonged subjection to everyday violence and abuse.

Sexism and prejudices against women are ingrained in the justice system. Crimes against women's physical integrity, especially injuries caused by domestic violence, are still treated as a private, family affair, not a public offense. The laws may have been changed to ensure higher penalties for these abuses, but in the everyday business of the police stations and courts, violence against women and children is seldom taken seriously. Furthermore, the reduction of the formerly prominent role of the state as a social benefactor has also affected the prosecution of abuses against women in quite a perverse manner. The Criminal Code was changed, once in 1983 and again in 1993, to the effect that visible injuries that do not endanger a person's life and which take less than two weeks to heal will be prosecuted only by complaint (*querella*). Prior to reforms, the state prosecuted regardless of a formal claim. In other words: injuries have become "private" offenses, not automatically prosecuted. The effect of this reform reinforced existing patterns of discrimination: only a fourth of the injured women in the period from 1989 to 1995 presented a complaint, as opposed to 56 percent of the men. Of the annual total of complaints presented by women, an average of 1.4 percent resulted in a sentence for the offender. The figure for the men was also very low, at 5.2 percent, but this still represented a number several times higher than that for women.[44]

A study of the legal process of women and children who present a claim for injuries relating to domestic violence, conducted by a women's group in Mexico City in 1996, describes the agony that they go through during the whole procedure. Insensitive officials, complicated inspections and tests, hostile confrontations with the offender, and endless paperwork take an average of eight months until the case is presented to a judge, who may ultimately consider the whole thing to be a private affair to be resolved by the family itself.[45]

In August 1996, a law against domestic violence in Mexico City was approved (*Ley de Asistencia y Prevención de la Violencia Intrafamiliar en el Distrito Federal).* The law is the result of much pressure from the women's movement. It contemplates a wide array of preventive measures and assistance for victims, as well as rehabilitation of the offenders. Its major shortcoming, however, is that it leaves out any punitive measures for the offenders. It only provides for negotiated settlements between parties by city government officials, and in special cases, administrative fines. But cases reported to the latter will not be taken to the courts unless the victims decide to do so of their own accord. Thus, the law reinforces existing patterns of discrimination. The impact of this law will be assessed in several years. However, in an international meeting on domestic violence held in Mexico City in October 1996, the Minister of the Interior promised that the federal government would undertake a serious reform of the justice system to ensure that both at the prosecutorial level and in the courts, the problems of domestic violence are properly addressed. Additional measures to combat domestic violence promised by the minister include educational campaigns by the Ministry of Health and the media.

Until more forceful actions to combat domestic violence are taken by the state, the pattern of discrimination of abused women will continue. As long as it is regarded as a "private" affair, to be dealt with in the family and not to be prosecuted as a matter of course, battered women and their children will have little real protection.

Homicide

Female homicides have increased greatly. Figures for Mexico City show that the rate for female homicides has grown from 6 percent in 1930, to a little under 20 percent for 1995. Unfortunately, impunity for homicide is clearly in favor of those who kill women.[46] Official figures establish that offenders who kill women are less prone to be sentenced than those who kill men. The figures from 1989 to 1994 show that for every thousand male victims, 225 perpetrators were sentenced, whereas in the case of female victims, only 126 perpetrators received a sentence. The disproportion between men and women in 1995 is even more shocking: 160 per thousand perpetrators of male homicides were given a sentence, compared to 71 for females. The growth of this bias can only be explained as a probable consequence of the breakdown of the justice system and other state institutions after the recurrent 1994 bout of economic and political crises.[47] The pattern of discrimination against women in the criminal justice system prevails. A recent study of female homicide found that women who commit murder are given a sentence 25 percent higher on average than men for the same crime.[48]

The media highlighted a recent legal battle undertaken by the women's movement to try to change the deeply entrenched discriminatory bias against women in the courts. Claudia Rodríguez, a young woman, married, with children, was on her way home after a night out in a nightclub with her best friend and her male companion. She was attacked by the male companion at a subway station, where he attempted to rape her. She drew a gun and shot him. He died on his way to the hospital and she was accused of homicide. Her lawyer alleged self-defense, and her female friend testified in her favor. The prosecutor claimed that she could have evaded the violent attack. She was sentenced to twenty years. The trial showcased prejudices against women. After months of campaigning by the women's movement, she was released on bail, the courts reconsidered her case, and eventually lowered the penalty.[49]

Future Prospects

After the 1995 Beijing World Conference on Women, the Mexican government officially decreed an ambitious National Program for Women (*Programa Nacional de la Mujer*). This program, which came into effect on August 21, 1996, acknowledges for the first time the discrimination of women in Mexico, with a well-documented analysis of the problem. It also provides a detailed list of strategies and mandatory actions to be undertaken by all federal government agencies on behalf of women, with the participation of social and other nongovernmental organizations. The program is under the supervision of the Ministry of the Interior (*Secretaría de Gobernación*), and is mandated to set the standards and to coordinate and ensure the articulation of all the federal government's policies and actions directed toward women. Dulce María Sauri, previously the interim governor of the state of Yucatan, was nominated Executive Coordinator of the program. Two months later, she was mandated by Congress to install a Consultative Council and a supervising body of the program to ensure its operation. However, the program does not yet have a budget, nor have the members of these bodies been nominated. In short, the National Program for Women is still a blueprint.

During the month of October 1996, a broad coalition of twenty-six women's groups and organizations, covering the full range of political positions, including the major parties, organized the National Assembly of Women for a Democratic Transition *(Asamblea Nacional de Mujeres para la Transición Democrática)*. Their first meeting, held in Mexico City on October 5, was dedicated to presenting a common platform of demands, produced after nine months of debate. This platform calls for the full participation of women in the construction of a plural and inclusive society, with social justice and equity. It recognizes that in a globalized economy, women must join efforts to guarantee a sovereign nation, based on self-determination, which is able to guarantee the full participation of women on equal grounds in all aspects of human endeavor.[50]

The Women's Assembly called for full participation in the reform and democratization of the state; the inclusion of all the provisions for the protection of human rights in the international treaties signed by Mexico in the public policies designed for women; access to decisions in the implementation of the government's National Program for Women, as well as affirmative actions, especially in the political arena; and the design of an economic policy capable of eliminating the marginalization and exclusion of the majority of women that the present policy has produced.[51]

Clearly, the Mexico City meeting had an impact on the government, and was responsible for incremental progress in implementing the National Program for Women. Whether the organizations represented at the meeting will have a real voice in the nominations and future life of the program is hard to assess. In any case, it is evident that the small number of elite women who have access to political power are willing to work together, across the spectrum of ideologies and political interests, for the protection and advancement of all the women of Mexico. Unfortunately, a few days after the meeting, the federal government announced its price and wage policy for the year of 1997. Minimum wages were allowed to increase only 17 percent, while the price of gas and electricity was raised 20 percent. Within hours, this announcement had sparked an inflationary increase that affected the price of basic foods, up to 70 percent in some cases. This raise in the cost of living will be at the expense of the majority of the population, especially women and their children.

It will take more than rhetoric and good intentions to ensure full participation of women in Mexican society. An end to discrimination requires not only the implementation of government programs and the formation of broad political coalitions of women; it also requires a profound change in the economic policies based on the indiscriminate cutbacks in public spending and the privatization of institutions and public services that have, for more than fifteen years, adversely affected women. As long as serious steps are not taken to ensure that the basic social, economic, and cultural needs of the majority of the population are met, discrimination against women will only become more entrenched. This discrimination is the result not only of deeply ingrained behavior and value patterns, but also of underlying economic and social forces that, left to themselves, have strengthened these patterns and the institutions that sustain them, such as the traditional patriarchal family. The government has to take serious measures in order to change these patterns of discrimination. These efforts must begin with an aggressive policy of employment and income distribution in order to ease women's burden of caring for society. Cosmetic changes in some laws, and the establishment of yet more bureaucracy to deal with women's issues, are not enough. However, these endeavors do not appear likely in the near future.

NOTES

I express my gratitude to Dr. Rafael Ruiz Harrell for his help in providing an analysis of discrimination against women for this chapter, especially in the criminal justice system.

1. Diario Oficial, *Programa Nacional de la Mujer, 1995–2000* 22 (Mexico, D.F., Aug. 21, 1996).

2. INTERNATIONAL HUMAN RIGHTS IN CONTEXT: LAW, POLITICS,

MORALS 888 (Henry J. Steiner & Philip Alston eds., Oxford: Clarendon Press, 1996).

3. TOM BARRY, MEXICO: A COUNTRY GUIDE 124 (Albuquerque: Inter-Hemispheric Education Center, 1992).

4. JULIETA CAMPOS, ¿QUÉ HACEMOS CON LOS POBRES? LE REITERADA QUERELLA POR LA NACIÓN (Mexico, D.F.: Aguilar, 1995).

5. According to figures published by EL FINANCIERO, November 21, 1995, the number of unemployed and underemployed people in Mexico was 18 million, that is, half of the economically active population of 36 million.

6. CARLOS HEREDIA & MARY PURCELL, LA POLARIZACIÓN DE LA SOCIEDAD MEXICANA: UNA VISIÓN DESDE LA BASE DE LAS POLÍTICAS DE AJUSTE ECONÓMICO DEL BANCO MUNDIAL 4–8 (Para el Grupo de Trabajo de las ONGS sobre El Banco Mundial, Washington, D.C.: The Development Group for Alternative Policies y Equipo Pueblo, 1994).

7. Cf. Lorenzo Meyer, Ramona o la fuerza de la debilidad!, REFORMA, CORAZÓN DE MÉXICO (Mexico, D.F., Oct. 17, 1996).

8. For an excellent study of the role of women in providing services at the community level in San Miguel Teontongo, a barrio of Mexico City, see Clara Brugada, El impacto del ajuste en los pobres de la ciudad: las mujeres y el acceso al consumo en San Miguel Teontongo, in LA POLARIZACIÓN DE LA SOCIEDAD MEXICANA, supra note 6.

9. Thirteen lynchings of suspected criminals were detected in several press reports by the Comisión Mexicana de Defensa y Promoción de los Derechos Humanos, from January to September 1996.

10. Diario Oficial, supra note 1, at 5–6, and 19.

11. Ana Langer y Mariana Romero, Planificación familiar en México, DIAGNÓSTICO EN SALUD REPRODUCTIVA EN MÉXICO, REFLEXIONES: SEXUALIDAD, SALUD Y REPRODUCCIÓN 11 (Mexico, D.F.: El Colegio de México, June 1994).

12. Diario Oficial, supra note 1.

13. Id.

14. Id.

15. Id.

16. Id.

17. Id.

18. INEGI, XI Censo General de Población y Vivienda (Mexico, D.F.: INEGI, 1990).

19. Rafael Ruiz Harrell, La mujer y la justicia penal, Mexico, D.F., 1996 (mimeo), at 3–4.

20. Id.

21. INEGI, supra note 18.

22. Harrell, supra note 19.

23. Id.

24. Jacqueline Peschard, La especificidad está en la diversidad. El voto de las mujeres en México, HUMANISMO, MUJER, FAMILIA Y SOCIEDAD 163 (VII Simposium Internacional, Mexico, D.F.: Instituto Nacional de la Nutrición, 1996).

25. Diario Oficial, supra note 1.

26. ALICIA MARTÍNEZ, MUJERES MEXICANAS EN CIFRAS (Mexico, D.F.: FLACSO, 1991).
27. *Id.*
28. Diario Oficial, *supra* note 1.
29. Diario Oficial, *Encuesta nacional sobre la sociodemografía del envejecimiento, 1994, supra* note 1.
30. *See* DORA PALOMARES, LOS DERECHOS HUMANOS FUNDAMENTALES DE LOS PRINCIPALES TRATADOS INTERNACIONALES (Mexico, D.F.: Comisión Mexicana de Defensa y Promoción de los Derechos Humanos A.C., 1996).
31. Marta Guadalupe Figueroa, *Legislación y derechos de la mujer indígena en Chiapas. Experiencias del Grupo de Mujeres de San Cristóbal Las Casas A.C.*, MESA DERECHOS Y JUSTICIA NACIONAL E INDÍGENA DEL FORO DE MESAS DE ANÁLISIS Y PROPOSITIVAS "CHIAPAS EN LA NACIÓN" (UNAM, Centro de Investigaciones Humanísticas de Mesoamérica y el Estado de Chiapas, Instituto de Investigaciones, Económicas, Colegio de la Frontera Sur y el Consejo Nacional para la Cultura y las Artes, June 26–28, 1996, San Cristóbal de Las Casas, Chiapas).
32. Irma Saucedo González, *Mujer y violencia: entorno familiar y social*, HUMANISMO, MUJER, FAMILIA Y SOCIEDAD 106, *supra* note 24.
33. Héctor Pérez Peraza, *Importancia de las estadísticas que sobre victimas de delitos sexuales se elaboran en la Dirección General de Atención a Víctimas de Delito en la Procuraduría General de Justicia del Distrito Federal*, MEMORIA, 2A REUNIÓN NACIONAL SOBRE AGENCIAS ESPECIALIZADAS DEL MINISTERIO PÚBLICO EN LA ATENCIÓN DE DELITOS SEXUALES 48 (Mexico, D.F., July 6–8, 1995; Mexico, D.F.: PGJDF y Grupo Plural Pro-Víctimas, 1996).
34. Teresa Ulloa, Claudia Rey, & Patricia Olamendi, *Papel de los órganos de impartición de justicia frente a la violencia intrafamiliar*, Mexico, D.F., Oct. 1996 (mimeo), at 2.
35. Pérez Peraza, *supra* note 33, at 48–49.
36. Juventino Castro y Castro, *Conferencia Magistral: La reparación del daño en los delitos sexuales*, MEMORIA, 2A REUNIÓN NACIONAL SOBRE AGENCIAS ESPECIALIZADAS EN DEL MINISTERIO PÚBLICO EN LA ATENCIÓN DE DELITOS SEXUALES 21, *supra* note 33.
37. According to figures analyzed by Ruiz Harrell, only 25 percent of all reported crimes in Mexico City in 1995 were investigated and prosecuted. Rafael Ruiz Harrell, *La impunidad y la violencia policiaca* 5 (Mexico, D.F.: Comisión Mexicana de Defensa y Promoción de los Derechos Humanos A.C., 1996).
38. Harrell, *id.*; Patricia Salcido Cañedo, *La investigación criminológica y la prevención de los delitos sexuales*, MEMORIA, 2A REUNIÓN NACIONAL SOBRE AGENCIAS ESPECIALIZADAS EN DEL MINISTERIO PÚBLICO EN LA ATENCIÓN DE DELITOS SEXUALES 50, *supra* note 33.
39. Tesis de Jurisprudencia 10/94, Aprobada por la Primera Sala de la Suprema Corte de Justicia de la Nación.
40. Ana Langer y Mariana Romero, *Agresión y violencia doméstica contra*

el género feminino, DIAGNÓSTICO EN SALUD REPRODUCTIVA EN MÉXICO 29, *supra* note 11.

41. Harrell, *La mujer y la justicia penal, supra* note 19, at 6.

42. *Id.*

43. Saucedo González, *supra* note 32.

44. Harrell, *La mujer y la justicia penal, supra* note 19, at 6.

45. Ulloa et al., *supra* note 34.

46. Harrell, *La mujer y la justicia penal, supra* note 19, at 7.

47. *Id.* at 8.

48. ELENA AZAOLA, EL DELITO DE SER MUJER: HOMBRES Y MUJERES HOMICIDAS EN LA CIUDAD DE MÉXICO: HISTORIAS DE VIDA (Mexico, D.F.: CIESAS, 1996).

49. *Tempus. Exceso de legitima defensa*, REVISTA SIEMPRE (Mexico, D.F., Feb. 20, 1997).

50. Laura Baptista, *Dejando mezquindades y sectarismos, debemos crear condiciones para abrir la puerta del escenario político para las mujeres* (Mexico, D.F.: CIMAC, Oct. 5, 1996).

51. *Declaración política de la Asamblea Nacional de Mujeres para la Transición Democrática* (Mexico, D.F., Oct. 5, 1996).

11 Comments on Acosta

Dorothy Q. Thomas

MARICLAIRE ACOSTA, in simple and precise prose, has demonstrated that in Mexico, and I would submit in most parts of the world, the rule of law for women is not a rule—it is an exception. Consider these facts:

- Women provide income for their families in one out of three homes in Mexico, but they earn only 694 pesos for every 1,000 earned by men.
- Over 2,000,000 women are unionized, but less than 890 have union leadership.
- Twenty-six percent of all daily crimes in Mexico take the form of violence and mistreatment of women and children.
- Seventy percent of all those who commit violence against women are known to the victim.
- It is legally impossible for a man to rape his wife.
- In some states, the penalty for stealing cattle is greater than for raping a woman.
- Only 14 percent of presumed rapists are prosecuted.
- You are a great deal less likely to receive a sentence if you murder a woman than if you murder a man.

Think again about all of this and then consider the fact that in Mexico, violence and discrimination against women are illegal. If the rule of law is to have any meaning at all, we will have to resolve this fundamental contradiction.

I do not mean to suggest that we do not face the contradiction between legal rights and lived reality in issues unrelated to women.
This volume is evidence enough of that. I do mean to suggest that
when it comes to women, we often accommodate ourselves more
readily to the contradiction between rights and reality and fail to ensure that our own efforts to secure full respect for the rule of law include full respect for the rights of women.

Let me give you an example. In 1996, the Human Rights Watch
Women's Rights Project released a report on rape that occurred during the genocide in Rwanda in 1994. The report found that during the
genocide, Rwandan women were subject to sexual violence on a
massive scale, including rape, gang rape, sexual slavery, and sexual
mutilation. In late 1994, the United Nations established the International Criminal Tribunal for Rwanda. By 1995, it had begun its work
investigating and preparing indictments of those persons responsible
for genocide, crimes against humanity, and war crimes. Yet, by the
time we released our report in September of 1996, the tribunal had
still not conducted a thorough investigation of sexual violence during the genocide; until 1997, there had not been a single indictment
for sexual slavery or rape (in 1997, two indictments were amended to
include sexual assault charges). In effect, the international criminal
tribunal, which is in some sense an ultimate insurance policy for the
rule of law, itself discriminates against women.

The consequences of sex discrimination, whether in Mexico or
Rwanda or anywhere else, are devastating, not only for women but
also for society. As Acosta's chapter so clearly points out, discrimination against women leaves half the population without a proper education; the failure to educate women, in turn, leads to their having
more children; violence against women has emerged as a serious national health problem affecting not only women but also their children; and the children themselves are increasingly dependent on
their mothers for financial support that—as a direct consequence of
the twin forces of discrimination and globalization—women are increasingly unable to supply.

Clearly, gender discrimination does not occur in a vacuum. It is
often deeply intertwined with racial discrimination and discrimination against indigenous peoples, discussed in other chapters of this

volume, as well as with bias based upon other factors, such as sexual orientation or class. To be sure, these forms of discrimination express themselves differently, but they all have one thing in common: they are usually central to the way in which a society organizes itself. It is this, the invidious and embedded structure of discrimination, no matter what form it takes, that makes it so difficult to overcome. If the rule of law is truly to encompass the underprivileged, it will have to grapple with this fundamental and pervasive character of discrimination and the degree to which it serves the interests of those who rule the law and, all too often, are the law.

In a 1992 report on domestic violence in Brazil, for example, we found that women faced a criminal justice system so fundamentally biased against them that even a crime as egregious as wife murder was often exculpated by the courts as a legitimate defense of male honor. In effect, such acts were considered to be consistent with the rule of law, inasmuch as the law recognized male authority in the private sphere and relegated women to a subordinate status therein. Thus, wife murder, marital rape, and domestic assault and battery were routinely tolerated by the state, and women victims of such abuse were left without meaningful legal recourse. At the time, the state's widespread failure to address domestic violence was not commonly recognized as an abuse of human rights. However, we argued that although the government of Brazil was not directly accountable for committing the acts of violence, by failing to prohibit and punish such abuse, it was violating its international obligations to respect and ensure the right to be free from violence and discrimination and to guarantee its female citizens equal protection of the law.

In subsequent reports on Peru in 1992 and Haiti in 1994, we found that even where acts of sexual violence were committed directly by agents of the state, the law itself obstructed justice. At that time, we concluded that women in Peru were frequently subjected to rape by security forces and police, but that few police officers and even fewer security officers were ever held accountable. One key obstacle was that the rape law itself was rooted in inherently discriminatory attitudes towards women. Up until 1991 in Peru, rape was treated as a crime against honor rather than a crime against the bodily integrity of the victim. If it could be shown that the woman was "dishonorable," then the determination followed that she could not have been raped, even in instances where she suffered severe damage to her physical person. As a result of a campaign by Peruvian women's rights activists, the law has since been changed; however, women victims of sexual violence, whether by agents of the state or private individuals, still face *de facto* discrimination that is reflected in the inadequate penalties and low conviction rates for crimes of sexual assault.

In Haiti during the social unrest following the 1991 coup, we found that military forces and *attachés* used rape and sexual assault to punish and intimidate women for their actual or imputed political beliefs. Although few human rights abuses were investigated or punished in that period, women victims of rape faced the added burden of discrimination in the criminal justice system. As in Peru, rape was codified as an "assault on morals" rather than recognized as a violation of the bodily integrity of the victim or a crime of violence. The investigation and prosecution of such abuse routinely stressed not the physical and mental harm done to the woman but the status of her honor or morals. For example, in one 1993 case that we investigated, military authorities tried to dismiss the rape of a thirteen-year-old girl by one of their personnel on the grounds that she was not a virgin. To date, there has been no substantive change in the criminal law in Haiti, and neither judges nor police have received adequate training on how to handle rape cases.

Most recently, in a report on pregnancy-based sex discrimination in the *maquiladoras* in Mexico, we determined that even where the law specifically proscribes discrimination, it is unenforced. In this instance, we found that despite clear labor, constitutional, and international human rights law to the contrary, potential female employees in the *maquiladora* sector were routinely subjected to, as a condition of employment, pregnancy tests and invasive questioning about their contraceptive use and sexual habits. Those found to be pregnant were not hired. Those who became pregnant after being hired were regularly forced to resign. Many of the companies, the majority of which are based in the United States, openly acknowledge the discriminatory practice and defend it as a cost-saving measure. One corporation even went so far as to suggest that in forcing women to choose between having a job or having a baby, they were assisting the Mexican government in its effort to control population growth. For its own part, the Mexican government has done nothing to remedy this practice or to sanction the offending companies.

As Acosta's chapter makes abundantly clear, whether with respect to the private or the public sphere, the rule of law all too often accommodates, rather than challenges, sex and gender discrimination. Thus, if we aim to eliminate such abuse, we must first overcome the widely held notion that it is acceptable. Then we will have to expose both the *de facto* expression of discrimination and the degree to which it is embedded in the structure of the law itself. Only in this way will we ensure that the rule of law is truly a rule for women rather than an exception.

12

Color and the Rule of Law in Brazil

Peter Fry

Tiririca

In July 1996, the Center for the Articulation of Marginalized Populations (CEAP), a nongovernmental organization based in Rio de Janeiro, petitioned for the prohibition of the performance of a song called "Look at Her Hair." It had been composed and performed by Tiririca, a comic who had suddenly become very popular with children after a checkered circus career. CEAP argued that the song presented negative "physical stereotypes of the black woman when it compares her hair to wire wool used to shine pans (Bombril), and going to the extreme of animalizing her when it compares the smell of her body to that of a skunk." Judge Flávia Viveiros de Castro agreed that the song was offensive to blacks and duly prohibited the sale of the CD and its public performance. For a short while, the news caused a furor in the press. Impassioned voices defended and attacked Tiririca as either an innocent dupe or a vicious racist. Others expressed fears that the constitutional protection of the freedom of expression had given way to the constitutional protection of human dignity. Tiririca declared himself amazed, especially as his own mother is black.[1]

Luciano Ribeiro

In August 1996, Luciano Ribeiro, nineteen years of age and black, was knocked down by a BMW driven by a white man, Rogério

186

Ferreira Pansera, who did not stop to help because he assumed that the black youth was riding a stolen bicycle. At the hospital where the lad was taken, the neurologist, also white, gave the same reasons for delaying treatment. Luciano died three days later from brain damage while in another hospital. Fearful of being mistaken for a thief, Luciano always carried the receipt for his bicycle in his pocket. Neither the driver of the car nor the neurologist have been brought to justice for their behavior.[2] There has been no more press reporting on this incident.

Vicente Francisco do Espírito Santo

Together with 1,700 other employees, Vicente Francisco do Espírito Santo lost his job with a state-controlled electricity company as part of a cutback operation. When he asked why his name had been included in the list, his superior responded: "What more does this black guy (*crioulo*) want, now that we have managed to whiten (*branquear*) the department." Vicente took the company to court, accusing it of firing him for racist reasons. Three years later, in October 1996, the Supreme Labor Tribunal, the highest court dealing with labor legislation, upheld—by five votes to one—a previous decision of the regional Labor Tribunal that he be readmitted.[3]

Color in Brazil

In societies that present themselves as liberal democracies, the ideal of the equality of all before the law is regularly challenged by the unequal distribution of power and influence and the moral hierarchization of social categories and groups on the basis of specific characteristics, real and assumed. Wealth can corrupt, and in spite of the demise of Lombrosian criminology, women and people of color, members of "sexual minorities," and immigrants tend to suffer distinct treatment from the police and judiciary, generally against their best interests.

Brazil is, of course, no exception. The wealthy and powerful influence the police and the courts to their own advantage while the poor, bereft of the means of corruption and unable to hire private attorneys, can do little to defend themselves. The potential for the corruption of justice by wealth and power is exacerbated by Brazil's status as a world leader in the inequality of wealth and income.[4]

The population at large has little faith in the rule of law. A recent opinion survey conducted in Rio de Janeiro by the Institute for the Study of Religion (ISER) and the Center for the Research and Documentation of Brazilian Contemporary History (CPDOC)[5] reveals that only 3.6 percent of the population believe that all are equal before the law. As many as 93.8 percent believe that the wealthy are more immune to the rigors of the law. These figures attest to popular recognition of the fragility of the rule of law in Brazil. What they do not convey, however, is that the rule of law does not hold a monopoly over legitimacy. Those who fail to utilize whatever comparative advantage they may have over the police or the courts may be disparagingly referred to as "straight" (*caxias*), while those who do take advantage of their cunning, wealth, and/or social position may even be admired for their "sharpness" (*esperteza*).[6] However strong the collective feelings against corruption in all its manifestations, the ideal of the favor continues strong. As the popular saying goes: "to my enemies the law, to my friends whatever they want" (*aos meus inimigos a lei, aos meus amigos, tudo*).

If over 90 percent of Rio de Janeiro residents believe that wealth assuages the rigors of the law, the ISER/CPDOC survey shows that a lower percentage (68.2 percent) of "white" (*brancos*), "black" (*pretos*), and "brown" (*pardos*) Cariocas agree that "blacks" suffer more than "whites."[7] A public opinion survey conducted prior to the 1986 elections in São Paulo revealed that 73.5 percent of the whites interviewed and 73.1 percent of blacks and browns felt that "black and mulattos are more persecuted by the police than whites."[8] Indeed, one of the most interesting findings of recent surveys on race in Brazil is that almost 90 percent of the population of all colors agree that racial discrimination is rife, in particular in the workplace and in relation to the police.[9]

Recent research suggests that public opinion is not far off the mark. Lívio Sansone, for example, in his ethnography of race relations in Bahia, distinguishes between "soft" and "hard" areas of social life as far as racial prejudice and discrimination are concerned. The soft areas, where being black does not cause problems and may in fact bring prestige, include bars, *festas,* and churches. The hard areas are the workplace and the labor market, the marriage market, and "contacts with the police."[10] Paulo Sérgio Pinheiro found that of 330 people killed by the police in São Paulo in 1982, no less than 128 (38.8 percent) were black.[11] Moema Teixeira notes that in 1988, 70 percent of the prison population of Rio de Janeiro was composed of "blacks" and "browns," whereas they account for barely 40 percent of the total population. In São Paulo, the situation is similar. Quoting a 1985/86 survey, Teixeira notes that the percentage of "blacks" and "browns" in the prison population (52 percent) was almost twice as many as in the São Paulo population as a whole (22.5 percent), stating: "If Blacks do not reach a quarter of the population of the State of São Paulo, they constitute over half the prison population of that State."[12]

Sérgio Adorno is the only researcher to have investigated the significance of racial discrimination in the criminal justice system as a whole. Consulting criminal records for cases of theft, drug trafficking, rape, and armed robbery in São Paulo in 1990, Adorno found that blacks lose out at each step of the system. Fifty-eight percent of accused blacks were arrested *in flagrante delicto* as opposed to only 46 percent of whites. Similarly, a greater proportion of whites (27 percent) await trial on bail than blacks (15.5 percent). As Adorno forcefully argues:

> [N]othing indicates that blacks show a special inclination for crime: on the contrary, they seem to be more vulnerable to police vigilance. The rigors of arbitrary detention, greater persecution and intimidation, a higher number of police officers in collective dwellings where most of the popular classes live, all of this contributes to the fact that blacks are the preferred target of repressive policing.[13]

When brought to trial, 62 percent of the blacks depended on public defense attorneys, as opposed to 39.5 percent of white defendants. Conversely, 38 percent of black defendants hired private attorneys, as opposed to 60.5 percent of the whites. As a consequence, only 25.3 percent of black defendants call witnesses, as opposed to 42.3 percent of white defendants. In the end, 68.8 percent of black defendants were condemned, as against 59.4 percent of whites. Furthermore, notes Adorno, "the proportion of Blacks who are condemned is higher than their proportion in the racial distribution of the population of the municipality of São Paulo."[14] Adorno continues:

> Blacks tend to be more persecuted by police vigilance, confront greater obstacles to access to criminal justice, and have more difficulty in utilizing their right to ample defense, secured by constitutional norms (1988). As a result, they tend to receive more rigorous penal treatment, given that they are more likely to be punished than whites. . . . Everything seems to indicate . . . that color is a powerful instrument of discrimination in the distribution of justice. The principle of equality of all before the laws, independently of social differences and inequalities, appears to be compromised by the biased functioning of the criminal justice system.[15]

Adorno's conclusions for the present are similar, *mutatis mutandi*, to those of contemporary authors writing about the past. Boris Fausto, in his analysis of crime in the city of São Paulo during the period 1880–1924, observes that the proportion of blacks and mulattos arrested in this period (28.5 percent) was more than twice the proportion of blacks and mulattos in the population at large (about 10 percent). Fausto attributes this disproportion to the fact that most of the arrests were for small misdemeanors, which would be characteristic of the impoverished black and mulatto population soon after the abolition of slavery (1888),[16] and also to "an overwhelming discrimination," which he detects throughout his data in the form of deprecating language when referring to black and mulatto defendants. "Frequently," he notes, "pejorative allusions appear in the words of witnesses who are themselves blacks and mulattos. Here one can detect not only the racist finger of the police scribe but something more serious, the internalization of prejudice by members of the discriminated group."[17] Fausto further notes:

> [W]ithin the collective consciousness the associations between the black and laziness, violence and sexual permissiveness are profoundly established. . . . To be black is a negative attribute conferred by nature and which can only be removed partially and exceptionally by the

demonstration of positive characteristics: devotion to work, fidelity to
some white protector, humility, etc.[18]

Fausto also observes that the police often wrote down the color of accused persons "in ink and in very clear letters" on the margins of the
official forms which did not contain a space for this information. It
was as if color, officially excluded from the evidence, crept in literally
"between the lines."

Carlos Antonio Costa Ribeiro conducted his research on the basis
of the records of crimes brought to trial by jury in the city of Rio de
Janeiro from 1890 to 1930. In his analysis of the court records themselves, Costa Ribeiro notes the constant infiltration of popular stereotypes against blacks and mulattos, who, although brought to trial in
the same proportion as whites, have a higher chance of being convicted than white defendants. Taking 357 cases of "blood crimes"
(e.g., homicide, attempted homicide, and grievous bodily harm),
Costa Ribeiro applied multiple regression analysis to reveal the factors and combinations of factors most likely to lead to conviction. He
found that the color of the defendant was the most significant factor
determining conviction: "The blackness of the defendant increases
the probability of conviction more than any other characteristic. . . . A
black defendant has 31.2 percentage points more probability of being
convicted than a white defendant, and a brown defendant has 15.8
percentage points more probability of being convicted than a white
defendant."[19] Inversely, he observes, defendants accused of killing
blacks and mulattos had just over 14 percent less chance of being
convicted than those accused of killing whites.

Costa Ribeiro's argument is that the discrimination against people
of color that he detected in his case material was related to the
strength in Brazil during the period in question of proponents of
"criminal anthropology," of the "positive school" of thought led by
the Italian triad of Lombroso, Ferri, and Garófalo. Indeed, the
strength of their Brazilian disciples should not be underestimated:
the "classical" nature of the republican penal code came constantly
under attack from jurists and forensic doctors who believed that
criminal behavior was in one sense or another inherent to particular
human beings.[20] Arguing against the "metaphysical doctrine" of the

existence of free will, they claimed that criminal responsibility varied from individual to individual. As a consequence, the penal system should provide "unequal treatments for unequal individuals." The most radical proponent of these ideas was the forensic doctor Raymundo Nina Rodrigues, who, in *The Human Races and Penal Responsibility in Brazil*, argued that criminal responsibility decreased from the white "race" to the black:

> [T]he incapacity of the inferior races influenced the character of the mestizo population, transforming or combining in variable syntheses characteristics transmitted through inheritance. The scale goes from a product which is totally useless and degenerate to a product that is valid and susceptible to superior manifestations of mental activity. The same scale should be applied to moral and penal responsibility, ranging from its absence at one end of the scale to full plenitude at the opposite extreme.[21]

Bereft of responsibility for their acts, blacks, Amerindians, and the people of mixed descent would therefore be subject to an undefined "treatment" meted out by the whites:

> Aryan civilization is represented in Brazil by a very fragile minority of the white race whose duty it is to defend that civilization, not only against anti-social acts—crimes—perpetrated by its own members, but also against anti-social acts carried out by inferior races, be these true crimes according to the concept of those races, be they on the contrary manifestations of the conflict, of the battle for survival between the superior civilization of this race and the attempts at civilization made by the conquered or subservient races.[22]

Whether Nina Rodrigues' pseudo-theory innovated or merely brought the dubious authority of scientific racism to support commonly held views about the intellectual and moral quality of blacks and mulattos in Brazil is a moot point. What is beyond discussion, however, is that the ideas he and others expressed, although kept at a distance from the formal apparatus of the criminal justice system—with the notable exception of the Office for Criminal Identification which operated in Rio de Janeiro throughout the 1930s[23]—continued to inform the moral judgments made of all those who were drawn for one reason or another into the web of the criminal justice system. They operated and continue to operate as a semi-clandestine counterpoint to the formal value of equality before the law.

In spite of the positivist onslaught, the constitutions and penal codes of republican Brazil (Brazil became a republic two years after the abolition of slavery in 1888) have remained neutral as far as "race" is concerned. The exception, as Peter Eccles has rightly pointed out, is the 1934 Constitution, which made a veiled reference to race in Article 138, stating that it is the duty of "the Union, States and Municipalities [to implement] in their laws: the promotion of eugenic education."[24] The first truly race-related legislation was introduced in 1951 to *punish* racial discrimination. It followed an embarrassing incident in 1950 when Katherine Dunham, the American dancer and anthropologist, was refused entry to a São Paulo hotel. Afonso Arinos, conservative deputy and author of the legislation, justified it by drawing attention to the existence of racial discrimination which "showed a dangerous tendency to increase" and because "the promises of racial equality in the Constitution and the international agreements signed by Brazil would remain a dead letter unless the law caused them to be subject to juridical imposition."[25] In spite of Afonso Arinos' fears that racial discrimination was on the increase and the massive confirmation of this prediction by a multitude of activists and academics and combinations of the two, few people have been brought to trial under the law. Eccles, for example, was able to find only three cases that came before the courts between 1951 and 1991, two of which resulted in conviction.[26]

The 1988 Constitution innovated on two fronts: it formally recognized the property rights of descendants of maroon (*quilombo*) communities who continue to occupy their lands;[27] and it went beyond Afonso Arinos' law by redefining racist practice as a crime rather than a mere misdemeanor.[28] Later the Afro-Brazilian federal deputy Carlos Alberto Caó presented new legislation which, in accordance with the new constitution, denied bail to those accused of "crimes resulting from racial or color prejudice" and stipulated prison sentences from one to five years for those found guilty. This harsh law also determines that crimes resulting from racial or color prejudice may never lapse.

From the evidence available, the new law has been no more effective than the old in either stemming racism or punishing "racist practice." The Special Police Station for Racial Crimes, which was established in São Paulo in 1993, opened only eight cases in 1996. According to the magazine *Isto É*, "the police station receives a number of complaints which end up classified as defamation rather than as racial crimes."[29] The legal victory of Vicente Francisco do Espírito Santo cited above is the first of its kind and established jurisprudence for other cases of alleged racism in the workplace.

To begin to understand the difficulties in prosecuting under the Caó law and the many complex issues that are at stake in contemporary Brazilian "racial politics," a brief digression on the salient characteristics of "race relations" in Brazil is in order.

The research I have cited thus far, together with recent research into other aspects of race relations in Brazil, has basically one common theme and mission, namely to denounce the "myth of racial democracy." Together with an active, if relatively small, black movement, it has been remarkably successful in contributing to a most drastic reversal of Brazil's image and self-image. Until the early 1950s, Brazil was regarded as the cradle of "racial democracy," as a model of tolerance and "racial harmony." It is now held to be as racist, if not more, than the United States with which it had previously been so favorably compared.

From the turn of the century until the 1940s, blacks from the United States who visited Brazil returned full of praise. Leaders such as Booker T. Washington and W. E. B. DuBois wrote positively of the black experience in Brazil, while black nationalist Henry McNeal Turner and radical journalist Cyril Biggs in the United States went so far as to advocate emigration to Brazil as a refuge from oppression in their own country.[30] In 1944, the Jewish writer Stefan Zweig found Brazil to be the least racially bigoted society he had visited.[31] In DuBois' time, Brazil was widely held to be a "racial democracy" where relations between people of diverse colors were harmonious and trouble-free. Even Nina Rodrigues felt that Brazil, for all its problems, had produced more tolerance than the United States.[32]

As the world took full stock of the horrors of Nazi racism in the years following the Second World War, the United Nations Educational, Scientific and Cultural Organization (UNESCO) agreed to sponsor a pilot research project to be carried out in Brazil with the aim of studying "the problems of different racial and ethnic groups living in a common social environment."[33] As Alfred Métraux, the co-ordinator of the project, explained:

> The generally favorable impression produced by Brazil's race relations has for many years been remarked on by travellers and sociologists who have been greatly surprised to find there such different attitudes from those observed in other parts of the world. Brazil has, in fact, been hailed as one of the rare countries which have achieved 'racial democracy'. . . . The rare examples of harmonious race relations have not, however, received the same attention either from scientists or the public in general. Yet the existence of countries in which different races live in harmony is itself an important fact capable of exercising a strong influence on racial questions in general.[34]

Stolcke notes that "within Brazil concern was voiced, as it turned out prophetically, that a systematic scrutiny into the nature of the country's race relations might open the Pandora's box of 'racial democracy.'"[35] Indeed, the UNESCO project verified the existence of racism in Brazil and set the tone for subsequent research on racial prejudice and discrimination.

Carlos Hasenbalg, one of the most prominent scholars to investigate Brazilian racism after the UNESCO project, has recently compiled an overview of the principal results of this research. The demographers, he reports, have established a higher infant mortality rate for nonwhites than for whites (105 as against 77 in 1980) and lower life expectancy for nonwhites than for whites (59.4 years as against 66.1 years). In the sphere of education, nonwhites complete fewer years of study than whites, even controlling for income and family background. In 1990, 11.8 percent of whites had completed twelve years of education, as opposed to 2.9 percent of nonwhites. As

Hasenbalg notes, these educational differences obviously affect the subsequent careers of nonwhites and whites:

> Resuming and simplifying, studies indicate that blacks and mestizos are exposed to diverse discriminatory practices in the labor market. Besides entering the labor market with less formal education than whites, they are exposed to occupational discrimination, by which the evaluation of non-productive attributes, such as color, results in the exclusion or limited access to valued positions in the labor market.[36]

As a result, the average income of blacks and mestizos is a little less than half that of whites. Finally, research on social mobility indicates that nonwhite members of the middle and upper classes experience less social mobility than similarly placed whites, and that they have more difficulty in transmitting their new status to their children. All these studies suggest, then, that racial discrimination has the effect of forcing nonwhites into the least privileged niches of Brazilian society.

Ricardo Paes de Barros goes one step further in his analysis of class and race inequality in Brazil, suggesting that racial discrimination is in itself partially responsible for Brazil's overall inequalities of wealth and income. For example, "in Brazil, since racial discrimination causes the income of non-whites to be 40 percent of the income of whites, income inequality would be one-sixth less if there were no racial discrimination. Thus, racial discrimination is capable of explaining half of Brazil's super-inequality."[37]

Opinion survey data mentioned earlier shows that either the sociologists have effectively persuaded the populace that racial discrimination is rife in Brazil or else they have been preaching to the converted. The 1995 *Folha de São Paulo*/Datafolha São Paulo survey figures demonstrate that almost 90 percent of the population acknowledge the presence of racial discrimination in Brazil. As mentioned above, the ISER/CPDOC figures on Rio de Janeiro for 1996 indicate that 68.2 percent of the inhabitants of Rio de Janeiro agree that blacks suffer more than whites from the "rigors of the law." So far, so good. However, the São Paulo survey data also reveals that Brazilians continue to extol the virtues of racial democracy and deny having any prejudice themselves. As many as 87 percent of respondents who classified themselves white and 91 percent of those who defined themselves as brown claimed to have no prejudice against blacks, while 87 percent of the blacks interviewed denied having any prejudice against whites. Even more surprisingly, 64 percent of the blacks and 84 percent of the browns denied having themselves suffered from racial prejudice. The *Folha de São Paulo* researchers, by analyzing the replies to questions designed to measure degrees of racial discrimination, showed convincingly that 48 percent of nonblacks showed some degree of prejudice. It would appear that while the majority of Brazilians of all colors agree that racism exists, they themselves either do not discriminate, discriminate but deny it, do not suffer discrimination, or do suffer discrimination without recognizing it. Furthermore, the vast majority adhere to the values of "racial democracy." As Paulo Singer comments, "most Brazilians don't believe in racial democracy and yet at the same time attempt to practice it, or at least give the impression that they do so. . . . Whites, blacks, browns and others share the same convictions and fantasies around the issues of 'racial democracy.'"[38]

The demonstration and recognition of the reality of racism did more than merely deny the myth of racial democracy; it suggested that the myth had the powerful function of masking discrimination and prejudice and of impeding the formation of a large-scale black protest movement. In this way, Brazilian racism became more insidious because it was officially denied. This argument is presented in its most sophisticated form by Michael George Hanchard in his analysis of the black movement in Brazil.[39] What he calls a "racial hegemony" in Brazil neutralizes racial identification among nonwhites, promoting racial discrimination while simultaneously denying its existence, thus "assisting the reproduction of social inequalities between whites and non-whites while simultaneously promoting a false premise of racial inequality between them." In other words, the "myth of racial democracy" is seen constantly to defuse "consciousness" of racial discrimination and inequality. By the same token, the myriad color categories present in Brazil, in particular the differentiation of mulattos from blacks and whites, also have a "function." As Carl Degler would have it, the "mulattos" are the "escape hatch" which dissipates possible racial polarizations and animosities.[40] For these authors, what began as Brazil's glory is now its damnation. Racial democracy, far from being a splendid ideal, is relegated to the status of a mere ideology which masks discrimination in order to maintain it.

This analysis contains, of course, a hidden comparison with the United States, whose bipolar conception of "races" defined by the "one drop rule" and the relations between them is so powerful as to create the illusion that it is natural, or at least a necessary feature of "modernity." Talcott Parsons argued that racial polarization was a necessary and welcome feature of "modernity," stating:

> Relatively sharper polarization clearly favors conflict and antagonism in the first instance. Providing, however, other conditions are fulfilled, sharp polarization seems on the longer run to be more favorable to effective inclusion than is a complex grading of the differences between components, perhaps particularly where gradations are arranged on a superiority-inferiority hierarchy. To put cases immediately in point, I take the position that the race relations problem has a better prospect of resolution in the United States than in Brazil, partly because the line between white and Negro has been so rigidly drawn in the United States and because the system has been sharply polarized.[41]

Writing much more recently, Michael Hanchard expresses a similar opinion which is shared by many: "Conflicts between dominant and subordinate racial groups, the politics of race, help constitute modernity and the process of modernization throughout the world. They utilize racial phenotypes to evaluate and judge persons as citizens and non-citizens. . . . This is the politics of race between whites and blacks at the end of the twentieth century, and Brazil is no exception."[42] In comparison with the "normality" and "modernity" of the U.S., Brazil must be declared wanting: for not having polarized "races"; for defining a person's "race" by appearance rather than genealogy;[43] for not having produced a strong mass black movement; for not having been the stage for racial confrontation; and for officially subordinating the specificity of races to the importance of a firm belief in the equality of humanity. The "myth of racial democracy" is interpreted as the functional element, somehow "outside" Brazil's race arrangements, which "impedes" Brazil from being similar to the U.S.[44]

Another current of thought breaks with this tradition and understands the notion of racial democracy to be at the basis of, and therefore constitutive of, a radically distinct way of constructing "races" and the relations between them. It does not see Brazilian "race relations" as being better or worse than the rest of the world, but certainly different.[45] Roberto DaMatta, for example, argues that it is the hierarchical and relational nature of social relations in Brazil that favors the production of the celebration of "mixture," "syncretism," and "intermediaries" in general. In the "individualistic" United States, racial polarization and segregation are the necessary outcome. DaMatta notes: "In Brazil we have multiple systems of social classification, while in the United States, there is a clear tendency to produce a system of classification of the type "all or nothing," direct and dualist, a tendency which seems to me to be directly correlated with individualism, egalitarianism and, obviously,—as Weber showed— with the Protestant ethic."[46] Anthropologist Robin Sherrif, who spent two years of field research in a Rio de Janeiro shantytown (*favela*), argues that "racial democracy" is as real for the shantytown dwellers with whom she lived as discrimination. "Racial democracy," she suggests,

> is certainly a myth, but it is also a dream in which the majority of Brazilians of all colors and social classes desire to believe with passion. While the myth obviously allows for tremendous hypocrisy and obscures the reality of racism, it is also a moral discourse which affirms that racism is obnoxious, unnatural and contrary to being Brazilian. . . . [I]t was only when poor Afro-Brazilians insisted repeatedly that "all people are equal," that "the blood is the same," as they generally say, that I was able to recognize the prescriptive and moral power of the dream. They were not telling me about the social world that they believe to exist, but which they think should be. At the same time that the myth denies the reality of their oppression, it also gives them the certainty of their fundamentally inherent equality, and reminds their oppressor how [s/]he should behave as a good Brazilian. The myth provides the moral high ground to Afro-Brazilians.[47]

And so we come full circle. Racial democracy returns, no longer in its prior glory as the achievement of harmony and equality, but as an aspiration, a "dream," a principle of such strength that it impedes the recognition and subsequent punishment of those who would deny it.

Once it is possible to grasp the fact that most contemporary Brazilians deny racism, hold racist beliefs (by which I mean Lamarckian assumptions that social characteristics are transmitted genetically), and yet deny that they themselves practice racial discrimination against those who are darker than themselves, it is also possible to understand why the Caó law has not fulfilled its promise. The police, the technicians of the judiciary,[48] magistrates, juries, judges, the accused, and even at times, the accusers, share a reluctance to allow conviction unless there is incontrovertible evidence of racism. They would prefer to maintain racial discrimination as an abstract evil rather than a real and concrete fact of life.

The question which must now be posed is a practical one. What is being done and can be done to reduce prejudice and discrimination against the poor in general and against people of darker color in particular?

Over the past three years organizations related to the wider black movement have undergone an important change. Previously, they laid the greatest emphasis on establishing a specific black identity. They felt that Brazil's complex and gradational system of racial classification, as part of the myth of racial democracy, was responsible for "masking" the true bipolar division of Brazilians into whites and blacks, *brancos* and *negros*. The building of a racial identity continues to inspire many organizations, but there has been a growing emphasis on addressing the concrete issues of inequality in the workplace, in the educational system, in relation to health, and in religious organizations. As a result, black caucuses have emerged in the trades unions, pre-university courses for young blacks and other disadvantaged people have been organized countrywide, special efforts have been made to reach black women concerning their reproductive health, and black priests and pastors have organized themselves to fight racism within the Catholic, Protestant, and evangelical churches.[49] With a reduction of emphasis on forging identity, parts of the movement have also become more inclusive, seeking alliances beyond the small core of black activists and recognizing that not all Brazilians favor foregoing their complex system of racial classification for the bipolar model.[50] At the same time, the movement has re-doubled efforts to bring cases of racism into the courts. The Center for the Articulation of Marginalized Populations (CEAP) in Rio de Janeiro has employed a full-time lawyer to help bring cases before the courts, a recent example being the case of Tiririca cited previously. The black women's organization, Geledês, of São Paulo, has instituted a similar project and undertaken research on the discrimination of blacks in the criminal justice system.[51] One of their conclusions is that the very harshness of the law may be one of the impediments to its utility and utilization.[52] What is particularly interesting and important about these actions is that they represent efforts to "de-radicalize" public space in Brazil, to narrow the gap between the ideal of racial democracy and the common practice of racial prejudice and discrimination. The difficulties, as I have noted above, lie in establishing strong and convincing evidence in a society averse to recognizing racism in a concrete sense. But the recent victory of Vicente Francisco do Espírito Santo and the furor around the Tiririca case indicate that with or without victory in the courts, the mere fact of bringing racism to the forefront of public debate must help to erode it in the long term. The law may be beginning at last to provide the public "moral high ground" for black Brazilians. Although it appears that conviction under the Caó law remains taboo, the social dramas engendered by public accusations provide an important opportunity for public debate of the issues involved. Significantly, they do this through consistently denying specific characteristics of "blacks" or "whites" by focusing on the essential equality of all Brazilians.[53]

At the same time as the movement has shifted its emphasis from culture to justice, the federal government, from the Ministry of Culture to the Ministries of Labor and Justice, has extended its concern for Afro-Brazilian issues.[54] Previously, most government activity in relation to Afro-Brazilians was restricted to the Palmares Foundation in the Ministry of Culture, which administered a minuscule and unpredictable fund to promote mainly cultural events. In 1996, the government launched its National Human Rights Program, which contains a series of planned activities in the interests of the black population. These include support for "the inter-ministerial working group—created by Presidential decree on November 20, 1995—for drawing up activities and policies to valorize the black population," and a Working Group for the Elimination of Discrimination in the Workplace and in Careers within the Ministry of Labor. In relation to the legal system, the program will:

> stimulate State Secretaries of Public Security to promote refresher courses and seminars on racial discrimination. . . . Adopt the principle of the criminalization of racism in the Penal and Code and Penal Process. . . . Disseminate the International Conventions, articles of the Federal Constitution and infra-constitutional legislation dealing with racism. . . . Support the production and publication of documents contributing to dissemination of anti-discriminatory legislation.

These measures can be classified as "anti-discriminatory." They are aimed basically at strengthening individual rights and freedoms as established by the federal constitution. They may be defined as attempts at "de-racialization."

However, the National Human Rights Program goes beyond this goal to propose interventions that aim to strengthen a bipolar definition of race in Brazil and to implement specific policies in favor of black Brazilians. For example, the government plans to bring the Brazilian system of racial classification in line with that of the United States, instructing the Brazilian Institute for Geography and Statistics (IBGE), which is responsible for collecting official census data, "to adopt the criterion of considering mulattos, browns and blacks [*os mulatos, os pardos e os pretos*] as members of the black population." In addition, the program will "provide support for private enterprises which undertake affirmative action," "develop affirmative action for the access of blacks to professional courses, the university and areas of state of the art technology," and "formulate compensatory policies to promote the black community economically."

These actions are, of course, radically distinct from the deracializing ones of combating racism. Instead of denying the significance of "race," they celebrate the recognition and formalization of "race" as a criterion for defining and targeting policy. For the first time since the abolition of slavery, the Brazilian government has not only recognized the existence and iniquity of racism, but also has chosen to contemplate the passing of legislation which recognizes the existence and importance of distinct "racial communities" in Brazil. Brazilian president Fernando Henrique Cardoso, whose academic career as a sociologist began with research on race relations as a spin-off of the UNESCO project, announced in his presidential speech on Independence Day, 1995: "We wish to affirm, and truly with considerable pride, our condition as a multi-racial society and that we have great satisfaction in being able to enjoy the privilege of having distinct races and distinct cultural traditions also. In these days, such diversity makes for the wealth of a country."

In this spirit, the Brazilian government promoted a Conference on Affirmative Action and Multiculturalism in July 1996 at which a number of Brazilian and U.S. academics discussed the issue of affirmative action in Brazil. Thomas Skidmore, after outlining the spirit of affirmative action in the U.S., posed eight "Questions for Brazil" including:

· Is Brazil fully committed to equality of opportunity or to a diverse society?
· Is Brazil ready to acknowledge historic injustice against minorities and women?
· If Brazil is ready to answer yes to the above questions, then how will it define minority categories?[55]
· How will promotion of racial minorities be reconciled with Brazil's highly hierarchical society in which personal and family connections are all-important?
· Are Brazilian minorities, especially Afro-Brazilians and women, ready to fight for affirmative action in their country?
· Is the Brazilian elite ready for the social conflict that will inevitably result from introducing affirmative action?
· Is Brazil prepared for the long haul on this issue?
· Is Brazil prepared to be accused of copying the U.S.?[56]

In my view, these questions are innocuous and relatively easy to answer in comparison with a more basic one which Skidmore does not ask, namely: Is Brazil prepared to forego its historic official denial of "race" as a criterion for government action by lending government approval to (a) the concept of race and (b) to policies that target the specific racial communities thus created? To repeat, it is one thing to follow policies designed to minimize the significance of race in social life, i.e., those designed to combat racism in the workplace, in schools, in the courts, etc. It is quite another to design and follow policies which are themselves based on the assumption that "race" should be a criterion for the distribution of public resources. Whether or not affirmative action contributes to redressing the social and economic imbalance between one category and another, it most certainly consolidates beliefs in racial difference by ratifying race as a legitimate criterion for public action. Affirmative action is the other side of the coin of racial discrimination, a fact which is tacitly recognized by the government of Brazil in translating the term as "positive discrimination."

It is not my intent to take sides on this issue, but merely to point to the wider implications of the decisions taken at this time. If the Brazilian government wishes to continue along its path of "racial democracy," combating racism and opening up opportunity to all Brazilians regardless of sex and color, then it will restrict its actions to exposing and punishing the evils of racism and racist thought, while developing truly effective public policies to reduce what Paes de Barros has called Brazil's super-inequality. Policies that target the poorest areas of Brazil will automatically include large numbers of darker Brazilians. If, on the other hand, it wishes to combat racism by also adopting affirmative action policies, then it may not only engender conflict, as Thomas Skidmore himself has noted, but more importantly, it will also strengthen the "racialization" of Brazil by adding the rubber stamp of government policy to the neo-Lamarckian popular belief that races are natural phenomena after all. The discourse of the constitution and the Caó law is an anti-racialist and an anti-race discourse in the sense that although it implicitly recognizes the "reality" of race, it refuses to recognize its relevance in the distribution of social rights and obligations. The discourse of affirmative action, on the contrary, recognizes the reality of "race" and promotes it as an attribute which should be relevant in the distribution of such social rights and obligations. Thus, it questions racial democracy and the canons of democracy *tout court*.

Even if Skidmore did not pose the basic question, Brazilians are posing it themselves, and in oblique but significant ways providing replies. In the 1986 election survey in São Paulo, respondents were asked what blacks and mulattos should do to defend their rights. Eight percent of the whites and 11.3 percent of the nonwhites felt that each person should demand that his or her rights be respected on an individual basis. Five and two-tenths percent of the whites and 7.2 percent of nonwhites felt that the problem should be resolved by "a movement composed of blacks and mulattos only." The solution proposed by the great majority (83.1 percent of the whites and 75.3 percent of the blacks) was the organization of a movement "in which whites who are concerned about this problem would also participate."[57]

One of the most interesting aspects of the three surveys I have mentioned in this chapter, the São Paulo election study of 1986, the Datafolha survey of 1995, and the ISER/CPDOC survey of 1996, is that blacks, browns, and whites tend to agree on every major issue, including racism. The fact that Brazilians of all colors share the same basic values and concepts points to the extent of the political and cultural homogeneity of Brazilian society and of the dubious sociological validity of such concepts as "the black community" other than as a figure of rhetoric. What these same surveys also show is that the factors which differentiate opinion are educational and income levels. Paulo Singer argued on the basis of the Datafolha survey that "[t]he poor and those with less formal schooling perceive less prejudice, but are in favor of the implementation of affirmative action in Brazil. More of those who are better off and have more schooling perceive the existence of racial prejudice but are opposed to affirmative action."[58] This difference could be explained by the self-interest of those who have gained their wealth and education without the aid of affirmative action. But such an interpretation does not deny their commitment to a nonracial ideology.

On November 20, 1995, not long after Louis Farrakhan's March on Washington, various black organizations in Brazil organized a

"March on Brasilia" to celebrate the anniversary of the death of the maroon leader and national hero Zumbi and to protest against racial discrimination. Two students who participated in the march returned with the clear sensation that they had participated in a very "Brazilian" affair. In contrast to the besuited masculine seriousness of the Washington march, the Brazilian version consisted of men and women of all possible colors, who danced their way to the center of power dressed in the brightest garb, rather in the manner of a carnival samba school. The students commented that it was as if "Brazil" had refused to accept a racial division within social and political life, even when it came to the issue of racism itself.[59]

At the same time, however, the demand for the recognition of "racially-based demands" continues apace. A group of professors and students at the University of São Paulo has drawn up a document arguing the case for establishing entry quotas for Afro-Brazilian students and suggesting complex mechanisms for deciding who might qualify as such. And a small number of U.S.-based multinational companies have initiated affirmative action policies.

All the evidence, therefore, suggests that Brazil will continue to produce divergent points of view and actions in relation to the question of equity between people of different colors. Whichever of these wins the backing of the Brazilian state will have acquired a most powerful ally. The position taken by the state on the issue of race is as critical to the ways in which race will be framed in the future as it has been in the past.

NOTES

I would like to thank Joan Dassin, Antonio Sérgio Guimarpes, Pamela Reynolds, Olívia Cunha, and Yvonne Maggie for their useful comments on an earlier draft of this chapter.

1. VEJA, no. 128, July 31, 1996, at 9. The Tiririca case resulted in criminal proceedings with impassioned positions for and against.
2. VEJA, *id.* at 11.
3. O GLOBO, Oct. 8, 1996, at 11.
4. According to Barros: "The degree of inequality in Brazil is about 50 percent higher than the world average when measured by the Gini coefficient (0.4 for developed countries and 0.6 for Brazil). As a consequence of this

greater degree of inequality, the average income of the 10 percent most wealthy in Brazil is about 29 times greater than that of the 40 percent of the most poor while the world average is about three times greater." R. P. Barros, *Diferenças entre Discriminação Racial e por Gênero e o Desenho de Políticas Anti-discriminatórias*, 4 ESTUDOS FEMINISTAS 183, 189 (1996).

5. A research project entitled "Law, Justice and Citizenship: Victimization, Access to Justice and Political Culture in the Metropolitan Region of Rio de Janeiro" conducted a random survey of 1,574 individuals in Metropolitan Rio earlier this year. I am grateful for the authors for permission to utilize figures from the first print-outs of their data.

6. DaMatta explores the perennial tension between the roles/concepts of *malandro* (trickster) *e caxias* (named after the hero of the Brazilian army, the Duke of Caxias) in his now classic work, CARNIVALS, ROGUES AND HEROES: AN INTERPRETATION OF THE BRAZILIAN DILEMMA (University of Notre Dame Press, 1991).

7. I here translate the Brazilian terms "branco," "pardo," and "preto," which are used by the national census. The question of classification is of the greatest importance and will be addressed later in this chapter. The patience of the reader will certainly be taxed by the apparently excessive use of quotation marks, but there seems no other way of maintaining analytical distance from the native terms and concepts.

8. C. HASENBALG & NELSON DO VALLE SILVA, ESTRUTURA SOCIAL, MOBILIDADE E RAÇA 155 (Rio de Janeiro: Vértice [Editora Revista dos Tribunais], IUPERJ, 1988).

9. For example, a survey conducted by the *Folha de São Paulo* and Datafolha in 1995 revealed that 89 percent of white respondents, 88 percent of brown respondents, and 91 percent of black respondents believe that whites hold prejudice against blacks.

10. L. Sansone, *Cor, classe e modernidade em duas áreas da Bahia*, 23 ESTUDOS AFRO-ASIÁTICOS 143, 163 (1992).

11. PAULO SÉRGIO PINHEIRO, ESCRITOS INDIGNADOS (São Paulo: Brasiliense, 1984).

12. M. De.P. Teixeira, *Raça e Crime: Orientação para uma Leitura Crítica do Censo Penitenciário do Rio de Janeiro*, 64 CADERNOS DO ICHF 1, 4 (1994).

13. Sérgio Adorno, *Discriminação Racial e Justiça Criminal em São Paulo*, NOVOS ESTUDOS CEBRAP 45, 53 (1995).

14. *Id.* at 59.

15. *Id.* at 63.

16. Florestan Fernandes, *A Luta contra o Preconceito de Cor*, in RELAÇÕES RACIAIS ENTRE NEGROS E BRANCOS EM SÃO PAULO (Roger Bastide & Florestan Fernandes eds., São Paulo: Editora Anhembi, 1951). Such behavior was the result of the anomie resulting from the difficulties of adapting to social life after the abolition of slavery.

17. B. FAUSTO, CRIME E COTIDIANO: A CRIMINALIDADE EM SÃO PAULO (1880–1924) 55 (1984).

18. *Id.*

19. C.A.C. RIBEIRO, COR E CRIMINALIDADE: ESTUDO E ANÁLISE DA

Justiça no Rio de Janeiro (1900–1930) 72 (Rio de Janeiro: Editora UFRJ, 1995).

20. For an excellent analysis of the thinking of "positivist" legal thinkers during the Old Republic, *see* Marcos César Alvarez, Bacharéis, Criminologistas e Juristas: saber jurídico e nova escola penal no Brasil (1889–1930), Universidade de São Paulo, doctoral thesis (1996).

21. Raymundo Nina Rodrigues, As Raças Humanas e a Responsibilidade Penal no Brasil 134 (Rio de Janeiro: Libraria Progresso Editora, 1957 [1894]).

22. *Id.* at 162.

23. O.M.G. de Cunha, *1933: Um Ano em que Fizemos Contatos*, 28 Revista USP 142 (1996).

24. Peter Eccles, *Culpados até prova em contrário: os negros, a lei e os direitos humanos no Brasil*, Estudos Afro-Asiáticos 135, 138 (1991).

25. As quoted in *id.* at 141.

26. Florestan Fernandes, writing about the Afonso Arinos law in the year in which it was introduced, comments on the skepticism of many members of the São Paulo Black Movement in relation to the efficacy of the law in combating racism. Fernandes, *A Luta contra o Preconceito de Cor, supra* note 16. What neither he nor they anticipated, however, was the difficulty of bringing miscreants to book under it.

27. Article 68 of the 1988 Constitution states: "Definitive property rights of the descendants of maroon communities (*quilombos*) who continue to occupy their lands are recognized and the State is obliged to issue the respective titles."

28. Eccles, *supra* note 24, at 146.

29. Isto É, no. 14045, Sept. 4, 1996, at 78.

30. M.G. Hanchard, *Black Cinderella? Race and the Public Sphere in Brazil*, 7 Public Culture 165 (1995).

31. Stefan Zweig, Brasil: País do Futuro (Rio de Janeiro: Editora Civilização Brasileira, 1960 [1944]); and L. Spitzer, Lives in Between: Assimilation and Marginality in Austria, Brazil, West Africa, 1780–1945 (Cambridge University Press, 1989).

32. "Whether it be the influence of our Portuguese origin, and the tendency of the Iberians to cross [*sic*] with the inferior races; whether it is a special virtue of our white population, which I don't believe; or whether it might be finally one more influence of the character of the Brazilian people, indolent, apathetic, incapable of strong passions, the truth is that color prejudices, which certainly exist among us, are little defined and intolerant on the part of the white race. In any event, much less than it is said that they are in North America." Rodrigues, *supra* note 21, at 149–50.

33. I am very grateful to Verena Stolcke for permission to cite from her work in progress on UNESCO and its research projects in Brazil.

34. Stolcke, *id., quoting* Alfred Métraux.

35. *Id.* at 3.

36. Carlos Hasenbalg, *Entre o Mito e os Fatos: racismo e relações raciais no Brasil*, 38 no. 2 DADOS 361 (1995).

37. Barros, *Diferenças entre Discriminação Racial e por Gênero e o Desenho de Políticas Anti-discriminatórias*, *supra* note 4.

38. Paulo Singer, *Racismo Cordial: a mais completa análise sobre o preconceito de cor no Brasil*, E GUSTAVO VENTURI 80–81 (C. Turra, São Paulo: Editoria Ática, 1995).

39. Hanchard, *supra* note 30.

40. C. DEGLER, NEITHER BLACK NOR WHITE: SLAVERY AND RACE RELATIONS IN BRAZIL AND THE UNITED STATES (Madison: University of Wisconsin Press, 1986).

41. Talcott Parsons, *The Problem of Polarization on the Axis of Color*, in COLOR AND RACE 352–53 (J.H. Franklin ed., Boston: Beacon Hill Press, 1968).

42. Hanchard, *supra* note 30, at 182–83.

43. O. NOGUEIRA, TANTO PRETO QUANTO BRANCO (São Paulo: T.A. Queiroz, 1985).

44. I have argued this point and the fact that language itself helps create the illusion of Brazil's "failure," in Peter Fry, *Why Brazil is Different*, 4836 TIMES LITERARY SUPPLEMENT 6–7 (1995); and Peter Fry, *O que é que a Cinderela Negra tem a dizer sobre a "política racial" no Brasil*, REVISTA USP 122 (1996).

45. For the clearest exposition of this point of view, *see* ROBERTO DAMATTA, RELATIVIZANDO: UMA INTRODUÇÃO À ANTROPOLOGIA SOCIAL 58–85 (Petrópolis: Vozes, 1981).

46. *Id.* at 81.

47. Robin E. Sherrif, Woman Slave Saint: A Parable of Race, Resistance and Resignation (1993), at 5 (manuscript); and Hasenbalg, *Entre o Mito e os Fatos*, *supra* note 36, at 366.

48. *See* M. CORRÊA, MORTE EM FAMÍLIA (São Paulo: Graal, 1983).

49. Caetana Maria Damasceno, Cantando Para Subir: Orixá no Altar, Santo no PEJI, Programa de Pós-Graduação em Antropologia Social, Universidade Federal do Rio de Janeiro, master's thesis, 1990; JOHN BURDICK, LOOKING FOR GOD IN BRASIL: THE PROGRESSIVE CATHOLIC CHURCH IN URBAN BRAZIL'S RELIGIOUS ARENA 53 (Berkeley: University of California Press, 1996).

50. Cunha, *1933: Um Ano em que Fizemos Contatos*, *supra* note 23.

51. Adorno's research, cited *supra* note 13, was conducted in conjunction with Geledês.

52. This opinion was expressed by one of the Geledês' lawyers at the 19th Annual Meeting of the National Association of Graduate Programs in the Social Sciences (ANPOCS) in 1995.

53. Olívia Cunha and Marcia Silva drew my attention to the "positive" aspects of the failure of the judicial system to bring cases of racism to court.

54. Yvonne Maggie drew my attention to this significant shift of emphasis, having herself observed the notable emphasis on culture and identity during the events surrounding the 1988 centenary of the abolition of slavery

in Brazil. She observed that the vast majority of events were of a cultural nature while few addressed the issues of inequality. Yvonne Maggie, *Cor, Hierarquia e sistema de classificação: a diferença fora do lugar*, 14 ESTUDOS HISTÓRICOS 149 (1994).

55. "It is sometimes said that Brazil has no clearly defined racial categories. In fact, of course, such categories have been defined and applied in collecting census data. The two-color, bipolar breakdown of the US contrasts with the multi-racial classification in Brazil. Establishing racial categories would undoubtedly be one of the greatest practical difficulties to applying affirmative action to Brazil." Thomas E. Skidmore, *Affirmative Action in Brazil? Reflections of a Brazilianist*, paper presented at the conference on Affirmative Action, Brasília, 1996 (photocopy), at 13.

56. *Id.*

57. C. Hasenbalg & Nelson do Valle Silva, *Notas sobre a desigualdade e política*, 25 ESTUDOS AFRO-ASIÁTICOS 141, 156 (1993).

58. Singer, *supra* note 38, at 81.

59. José Renato Perpétuo Ponte and Denise Ferreira da Silva, personal communication.

13 Comments on Fry

Joan Dassin

PETER FRY HAS WRITTEN an exceptionally lucid treatment of some of the most perplexing issues of Brazilian society. Asking how color (not "race," which his inverted commas indicate to be a social construct, subject to historical and cultural interpretation) interacts with the rule of law and the underprivileged, Fry holds up some seeming paradoxes for analysis. He argues that the apparent contradictions are at the root of the Brazilian racial experience, and must therefore be understood in their full historical and anthropological dimensions before asking how legal instruments can remedy the negative effects of racial discrimination. He is less interested in the law per se and more interested in the workings of law in society—an appropriate point of departure to which policymakers should pay more heed.

The first "paradox" is implicit in the chapter's opening anecdotes, which immediately give us the characteristics of racism in Brazil. Racism is pervasive in culture, in the workplace, and in everyday life. At the same time, even the targets have trouble recognizing it, and when they do, there is no recourse, no sustained attention. Even in the rare case when a race-based grievance is redressed, the delay is so significant that personal sacrifices are inevitable. Tiririca, the songwriter who was puzzled by the (short-lived) furor over his presumably "racist" song, Luciano Ribeiro, the nineteen-year-old black bicycle rider who died because he was left unassisted by the white driver who hit him and the white neurologist who neglected to attend to him (neither of whom suffered any consequences), and Vicente Francisco do Espírito Santo, who waited three years before winning a court decision readmitting him to a job from which he had been clearly sacked on racial grounds—they each suffered from the same malady. Racism is everywhere but nowhere in Brazil; it is as difficult to prove or identify as it is to redress.

A second seeming paradox that Fry implicitly raises is based on the deeply entwined nature of class and race in Brazil. He makes the point that "the potential for the corruption of justice by wealth and power"—present in every liberal democracy—is exacerbated in Brazil by that country's "status as world leader in the inequality of wealth and income." He clearly believes in the importance, if not primacy, of economic and social inequality, e.g., "class" as opposed to "race." This is especially critical in regard to the law. Fry cites data indicating that 93.8 percent of the population believe that if a wealthy person and a poor person commit the same crime, the latter will be treated with greater rigor. This perception is supported by empirical research.

At the same time, race *can* be separated out as an independent variable and seems to be the dominant factor driving the biased treatment blacks and mulattos receive from the law in Brazil. Hence, research cited by Fry substantiates that in 1986 in São Paulo, a high percentage of whites, blacks, and browns felt that blacks and mulattos were more persecuted by the police than whites. Adorno, examining criminal records for cases of theft, drug trafficking, rape, and armed robbery in São Paulo in 1990, came to the conclusion that "color [was] a powerful instrument of discrimination in the distribution of justice." Fausto's work on crime in the city of São Paulo during the period 1880–1924 reported "overwhelming discrimination" as a key reason for the disproportionate arrest of blacks and mulattos, while Antonio Costa, using quantitative methodology to analyze court records of crimes brought to trial by jury in Rio de Janeiro between 1880 and 1930, found that blacks and mulattos, although tried in the same proportion as whites, had a higher chance of being convicted than white defendants. For Costa Ribeiro, "the color of the defendant was the most significant factor determining conviction." On the one hand, economic and social status act as powerful social differentiating factors, and color may be secondary (compare the old

Brazilian saying, *o dinheiro embranquece*, "money whitens"). On the other hand, racial discrimination may itself be partially responsible for Brazil's overall inequalities of wealth and income. Which takes precedence? Fry does not decide, but rather implies that the *relation* between class and race inequality is the real bedrock of Brazilian social relations.

A third seeming paradox stems from legal institutions and their standing in Brazilian society. In our more "legalistic" Anglo-Saxon culture, even hard evidence of rampant discrimination and abuse do little to diminish legal authority. In Brazil, in contrast, the rule of law itself is not an uncontested value. As Fry points out, the culture admires those who take advantage of their cunning, wealth, and/or social position to circumvent the law, while disparaging those who fail to take advantage of their comparative privilege. (One recalls the Brazilian fascination with U.S. President Nixon, who was widely admired for his *esperteza*, and the contempt for President Carter, whose Southern Baptist earnestness placed a moral straightjacket around his use of American superpower.) At the same time, with only one exception until 1951, successive Brazilian constitutions and penal codes have upheld the formal value of equality before the law. On the one hand, then, manipulation of the law by those who have the privilege and status to do so (by definition, whites, rather than blacks or most mulattos) is seen as a positive value; on the other hand, most Brazilian law and the vast bulk of Brazilian jurisprudence—presumably also expressing the nation's most positive instincts—provide for equal treatment of formally equal citizens.

Further complicating the picture is the undercurrent of thought represented by Nina Rodrigues and other "positivist" legal thinkers who claimed that since "criminal responsibility varied from individual to individual, . . . the penal system should provide unequal treatments for unequal individuals." Fry points out that while these ideas were largely kept at a distance from the formal apparatus of the criminal justice system, they operate "as a semi-clandestine counterpoint to the formal value of equality before the law." Fry's ability to substantiate his argument deep in Brazilian social thought—rare among analysts of the contemporary scene—is one of his great strengths.

A fourth paradox also involves cultural issues and the law. Fry recounts the fate of legislation specifically intended to penalize race-based discrimination. The first, the so-called Afonso Arinos law, was invoked only three times between 1951 and 1991, resulting in two convictions. (It is interesting that the law itself was a response to an embarrassing incident suffered by a black American who was refused entry to a São Paulo hotel. Apparently the commonplace occurrence of similar incidents among Brazilians themselves did not merit a legal remedy.) Subsequent legal instruments were harsher. The 1988 Constitution, for example, defined racist practice as a crime rather than a mere misdemeanor. And in accordance with the new constitution, Alberto Caó's law denied bail to those accused of "crimes resulting from racial or color prejudice" and stipulated prison sentences of from one to five years. Furthermore, crimes resulting from racial or color prejudice may never lapse. As Fry concludes, however, the new law has been no more effective than the old in either stemming racism or punishing "racist practice." Despite increasingly punitive legislation available to prosecute "racial crimes," and despite the fact that the majority of Brazilians of all colors agree that racism exists, they are generally reluctant to seek legal remedies.

In the most creative and original part of the chapter, and at the core of his argument, Fry notes that much recent research has sought to denounce the "myth of racial democracy." Along with the active but relatively small black movement, Fry argues that this research has helped create a drastic reversal of Brazil's image and self-image. If until the early 1950s Brazil was seen as a model of tolerance and "racial harmony" (the Freyrean idyll), Brazil "is now held to be as racist, if not more, than the United States with which it had previously been so favorably compared."

Here Fry sets up a bit of a straw man, setting the stage for his repudiation of two key points: one, that the "myth of racial democracy" is somehow "outside" Brazil's race arrangements, rather than an intrinsic part of "race relations" themselves; and two, that Brazil's complex and gradational racial system is too ambiguous—an insidious, infiltrating, guerrilla-style enemy, as it were—and therefore inferior to the clearly demarcated U.S. racial system, whose easily identifiable distortions are easier to correct. Fry is at his historical and anthropological best in this part of his chapter. He traces the image of

Brazil from the turn of the century until the 1940s, when black U.S. leaders were so impressed with racial harmony in Brazil that some apparently even advocated emigration there. The turning point was a post-war study by UNESCO which opened the "Pandora's box" of racial democracy and revealed its underlying racism. Since then, re-searchers—especially social scientists seeking to document racial inequality in the workplace, the educational system, and the criminal justice system (the so-called "hard" areas of social life where being black *does* cause problems)—have provided strong evidence of the mutually reinforcing patterns of discrimination. Fry's description of Carlos Hasenbalg's research is particularly compelling in this regard. Nonwhites suffer at every stage of the life cycle, from health conditions at birth, to education, insertion in the labor market, and social mobility. This compounding aspect of discrimination is also clear from Sérgio Adorno's work on the criminal justice system, where blacks lose out at every stage in the judicial process.

However—and here is the central "paradox" the chapter addresses—despite the demonstration of the reality of racism, and the fact that most Brazilians of all colors agree that racism exists, most also claim that they do not discriminate or even suffer from discrimination. This suggests that the real debate should be around the "myth of racial democracy." Does the myth, as Hanchard and others argue, mask discrimination and prejudice? Even more insidious, does the myth help "neutralize" racial identification among non-whites, creating the famous "mulatto escape hatch" which confuses "clear" color lines? Fry obviously takes a different view—closer to those held by Paulo Singer and anthropologist Robin Sherrif—which sees in "racial democracy" "an aspiration, a 'dream,' a principle of such strength that it impedes the recognition and subsequent punishment of those who would deny it."

This then provides Fry with another explanation (beyond general ambivalence toward the law) for why legal instruments are of such limited use in remedying Brazilian racism. As he argues, the vision of all parties, even victims, is shaped by the powerful cultural norm of "racial democracy." Hence, they are reluctant to bring cases and still more reluctant to convict, unless the evidence is incontrovertible.

To his credit, Fry then takes up an extremely important practical question: "What is being done and can be done to reduce prejudice and discrimination against the poor in general and against people of darker color in particular?" Demonstrating the currency of his knowledge, Fry provides an excellent summary of changes in Brazil's black movement over the past three years. He notes that the building of a "racial" identity—to counteract the "masking" of the true bipolar division of Brazilians into whites and blacks by Brazil's gradational racial classification system—is still an objective for many organizations.

Nonetheless, there has been a growing emphasis on addressing the concrete issues of inequality in precisely those "hard" areas of social life where they have been best documented: in the workplace, in the educational system, in relation to health, and in religious organizations. This has given blacks real targets in the struggle against the economic and social consequences of discrimination. Significantly, organizations such as the Center for the Articulation of Marginalized Populations (CEAP) in Rio and Geledês in São Paulo are intensifying their efforts to bring cases of racism into the courts. Despite the deeply entrenched resistance to the recognition of racism, these organizations are trying to use the courts as a "moral high ground" for black Brazilians. They argue, in effect, that the law should fulfill its promise of guaranteeing racial democracy in Brazil.

Fry ends his chapter with a clear warning note about one of the hottest issues in Brazil today, the debate over affirmative action. He notes with satisfaction the unprecedented efforts of the federal government in Brazil to strengthen individual rights and freedoms through a series of decrees and working groups to promulgate and disseminate antidiscriminatory measures. At the same time, he is very critical of proposed interventions by the National Human Rights Program that would "strengthen a bipolar definition of race in Brazil and . . . implement specific policies in favor of black Brazilians." An example is a plan to bring the Brazilian system of racial classification in line with that of the United States, so that census data would consider mulattos, browns, and blacks as "blacks." Similarly, the government would provide support for compensatory economic and educational programs for blacks. Fry bristles at the idea of formalizing "race" as a criterion for defining and targeting policy.

Furthermore, he is shocked that the government of as reputable a sociologist as Fernando Henrique Cardoso would contemplate passing legislation "which recognizes the existence and importance of distinct 'racial communities' in Brazil." This really does beg the question of why the Cardoso government—which would make a truly historical contribution by officially recognizing the existence of racial discrimination and designing programs to combat its effects in the workplace, in schools, and in the courts—would want to go farther and promote *discriminação positiva*, as affirmative action is often translated.

The U.S. experience has made it abundantly clear that while affirmative action has undeniably forced open important doors for blacks, women, and other victims of discrimination, resulting in real gains in many cases, it has also polarized debate about the best routes for minority and women's advancement. In addition, affirmative action laws and policies have perversely reinforced deeply entrenched beliefs in racial (or gender) differences—the beginning of the slippery slope toward belief in racial (or gender) inferiority and inequality—by ratifying race (or gender) as a legitimate criterion for public action.

That the debate very quickly becomes acerbic and even literally violent was evident in the hate campaign mounted by self-avowed "progressive" advocacy groups against Ward Connerly. Himself a successful African-American businessman, said to have personally profited from affirmative action measures in his own building and contracting business, Connerly is a University of California regent who led the campaign for Proposition 209, a proposal to eliminate all racial preferences in public employment, contracting, and education in the state of California. On November 5, 1996, the proposition passed, 55 percent to 45 percent, opening the way for other states to follow suit, with potentially dramatic consequences for public policy and race relations in the U.S. Significantly, Proposition 209 has so far been upheld by the courts, withstanding legal challenges brought by powerful pro–affirmative action advocacy groups. In the U.S., at least, this battle will very likely be fought out in the legal arena for the foreseeable future. Affirmative action will also continue to be a contentious political issue, especially in populous states like California, Texas, and Florida, where long-established minority groups must compete for still-scarce economic resources with successive waves of diverse immigrant groups.

For his part, Fry does take sides on this issue, despite protestations to the contrary. He reaffirms his belief that "racial democracy" is a valid aspiration, and that the Brazilian government should restrict its actions to "exposing and punishing the evils of racism and racist thought," while targeting "super-inequality," the underlying problem in Brazil. Again he indicates his belief that poverty is the fundamental issue, since "policies that target the poorest areas of Brazil will automatically include large numbers of darker Brazilians." Above all, the government should not strengthen the "racialization" of Brazil. Data indicates that Brazilians of all colors share the same basic values. This, after all, is one of the country's unique assets, as compared, say, to Guatemala or the Andean countries, where the chasm between Spanish-speaking and indigenous populations is centuries deep, affecting both the concept and the practice of the nation-state. What separates Brazilians from one another is their educational and income levels. Accentuating their racial divides as well would be highly destructive.

Fry lays down the gauntlet for a broader debate on these issues. His nuanced, historically-grounded contextualization of both "race" and the "law" holds both concepts up to serious examination. Without this perspective, well-intentioned policymakers could be lulled into simplistic solutions doomed to fail, as have so many programs intended to promote legal and judicial reform, poverty alleviation, and an end to race- and gender-based discrimination.

PART

III

Institutional Reform,
Including Access to Justice

14 Institutional Reform, Including Access to Justice: Introduction

Juan E. Méndez

THE PRECEDING SECTIONS have described the limits of Latin American democracy at the twilight of the twentieth century. The empirical approach to each segment of society demonstrates what is perhaps the most dramatic flaw: the exclusion of vast sectors from the benefits of democracy. The reasons are varied and specific to each country and to each issue, and they thus defy simple generalizations. Nevertheless, there are common crucial underlying factors: the weakness of state institutions to protect the victims of abusive behavior, to grant them redress, and to provide them with a forum for the resolution of disputes. The situation of the administration of justice in the whole continent probably does not by itself explain the prevalence of violence of all sorts, nor is it the sole reason behind the invidious discrimination that excludes large sectors of our populations from the benefits of democracy. But it is fair to say that if our court systems were functional and effective in making the letter of the law a reality, these problems would not have such a devastating effect on the quality of our democracies.

It would be inadequate to paint the situation of the judiciary in the whole continent with a single stroke. There are great differences between countries and even between regions and jurisdictions within a single country. There are also gaping differences in professionalism and even probity between the judiciaries of one country and another. But these are, in essence, differences of degree. No single country can boast a judiciary that is up to the daunting task of "giving to each his and her own" in the current complicated circumstances of our societies. To varying degrees, all judicial branches in Latin America are in grave need of modernization and adaptation to new societal problems.

Modernization alone, however, would not be enough, even if approached in earnest. Judiciaries have lagged behind in relation to the region's economic growth and in comparison to the changes that other state institutions have made for facing new realities. In fact, in most places the courts have been experiencing serious regressions. The proportion of state budgets allocated to them are, almost invariably, too small to support the needs of their users, and the tendency in many places is to shrink financial allocation even further. Buildings, equipment, and other physical capacities simply do not keep pace with the growth in the demand for judicial services. Specific training for judges, magistrates, and court personnel is virtually nonexistent, and in most countries the jobs are so unattractive in pay, benefits, and social prestige that recruitment for them takes place among mediocre students and professionals, at best.

Substantive and procedural laws that courts apply are outdated; yet they are rarely, if ever, amended to apply to changing social realities. Judges are discouraged from experimenting with creative adaptation of antiquated laws to the problems they have to solve on a daily basis. The law, shaped by the legal philosophy of positivism, has not been allowed to evolve, and the result is a stultifying formalism that forces the facts of life into obsolete legal categories or simply throws the facts of life out of court. When excessive formalism is not by itself an obstacle to justice, inordinate delays and incessant red tape have the same effect.

Courts have been losing ground in another aspect which is crucial to their effectiveness: their credibility and prestige in public opinion. To a large degree, the loss of respect in society is the legacy of years of neglect and of generations of complacency with the status quo on the part of leaders of the bench. But unquestionably, this already worrisome problem has been exacerbated in recent years by design; some elected leaders have not hesitated to interfere with the judiciary in order to ensure its alignment with their own vision of power. In country after country, elected leaders of Latin America's most recent vintage have undermined the independence of the judiciary and manipulated the courts to their advantage. In some cases, the practical purpose has been to ensure that no uncomfortable inquiries are made into allegations of corruption; in others, the goal is more ideological: guaranteeing that the leader's highly personal view of the country's needs is not hampered by any serious checks and balances. This has been true even in countries where the judiciary had achieved high credibility in the transition years by producing credible prosecutions of the crimes of the recent past. Manipulation of appointments and of procedures for removal, creation of new seats or of whole new jurisdictions, the use of "faceless" judges and prosecutors, and a special predilection for the sanctity of military jurisdiction, all have turned independence and impartiality of the judiciary into an idle concept. The result is an alarming lack of credibility for the notion of justice in public opinion in all Latin American countries.

There has been a trend in international cooperation to emphasize promoting the capacities of the administration of justice in underdeveloped countries. Some of the reasons for this trend are explored in the following pages. Whatever the reasons may be, in just a few years those concerned with the promotion of democracy have resolutely added a salutary concern for the relative health of the administration of justice to their traditional interest in free and fair elections. However, if this is a promising development in international relations, some initial results described in this section can definitely be called disappointing.

The judiciaries, and those who lead them, have been particularly resistant to change. This is not surprising in elite bodies that are usually among the most conservative sectors and institutions of society and the state. In Latin America, however, they have not generally rejected offers of outside assistance, but in many cases they have been particularly unimaginative as to how they could best use that assistance or in identifying opportunities and needs for serious reform. For that reason, if too much money has been wasted on infrastructure (e.g., buildings, equipment, and organization) without a clear sense of how they would be used to improve a clearly deficient service, the fault does not lie entirely with the *naiveté* and inexperience of international donors.

The international community has clearly committed its own mistakes in this process. Its priority has been the efficient delivery of services, particularly in fighting crimes of international interest and in expeditious resolution of investment disputes. This has resulted in an interest in organization and infrastructure, including computerized systems and additional personnel (though not necessarily better trained or qualified). In contrast, there has been relatively little interest in emphasizing the overall fairness of processes and any decisions resulting from them. The leverage of foreign assistance has seldom been used to nudge Latin American judicial systems into looking for ways to streamline cumbersome procedures and modernize jurisdictional norms so as to adapt the capabilities of judges and prosecutors to the demands of everyday life.

An unwarranted deference to false issues of sovereignty has muted preoccupations with principle, particularly with the cardinal principle of any democratic judiciary: independence and impartiality of courts. In fact, in an effort to cut corners, cooperation funds have flowed to secret courts and "faceless" judges and prosecutors in some countries, despite the obvious fact that their very existence contradicts basic notions of autonomy and independence of the judiciary from other branches of government. In part, these errors stem from the fact that international donors have invested large amounts of money without appropriate consultation with users of judicial services or with beneficiary communities. Indeed, consultation has been limited to a few functionaries in the Justice and Foreign Relations Ministries of recipient governments, with little participation even by magistrates and court officials. Fortunately, lawyers, bar associations, and nongovernmental organizations with an interest in the administration of justice are making their voices known and demanding to be consulted in future support programs.

The proliferation of international assistance programs has had another advantage: there is now more awareness of and expertise about what is most clearly wrong with the present state of the administration of justice. Without prejudice to the very real problems of lack of independence, impartiality, and efficiency, what is most sorely needed in Latin America today is a clear-eyed view of what it will take to make justice a reality for the marginalized, the underprivileged, and the excluded in our midst. The real problem is that women, children, indigenous peoples, landless peasants, inmates, the institutionalized, and other similarly deprived sectors of our societies simply do not have access to justice.

That is why this section of this book dedicates special attention to this problem. On one hand, it is clear that inefficiencies in the delivery of judicial services disproportionately affect the poor, since they do not have the benefit of litigating with a reserve of money and resources to offset the losses caused by delays and unresponsiveness. Excessive formalism also affects them disproportionately, because formalism favors cleverness and obstructionism over reason and substantive fairness, and cleverness and obstructionism—not to be mistaken with good lawyering—are market commodities that can be obtained for a price.

Nevertheless, the problems of access to justice go beyond the ill effects of inefficiency and outdatedness. Legal services for the poor are largely unavailable except through volunteerism, and even those efforts are generally discouraged, if not actually persecuted. There is also little, if any, effort to simplify processes or to make them understandable to the users of judicial services. Language support and interpretation, at least for criminal proceedings, are explicitly enshrined in some constitutions and solemn international obligations freely entered into by states, but are very rare in reality.

There is a critical need to take a serious look into alternative conflict resolution methods, not only to simplify the process but also to help lighten the heavy weight of the backlog of cases. At the same time, facile solutions will not do; it is important to be serious and tough-minded when we contemplate alternative systems of justice, whether we create them anew or modify old traditions and practices. It would be a travesty if alternative mechanisms became a form of "second-class justice." At the very least, constitutional review and other forms of supervision by professional courts must be preserved, especially for courts that are entrusted with the protection of fundamental human rights. Surely, review and supervision must be made consistent with prompt, effective, and simplified justice.

In the end, accessible justice for the underprivileged is probably the key to the most pressing need in our end-of-century democracies: the challenge of inclusion. Unless we solve the problems of marginalization and exclusion, the regimes that we create and consolidate will not deserve the adjective "democratic." In the following chapters, we attempt to open up the debate as to how to make the administration of justice meaningful to the vast sectors of our society that currently have little chance of ever obtaining redress from a court of law. Unless we achieve broad and universal access, the right to justice will continue to be a privilege, not a right.

15 International Aspects of Current Efforts at Judicial Reform: Undermining Justice in Haiti

Reed Brody

The need for a judicial system that will bring [human rights abusers] to justice is the major concern, the major desire, and the major issue for most Haitians. We need to see that justice is done and that those who have committed such heinous crimes—crimes against humanity—will be brought to justice.

JEAN-BERTRAND ARISTIDE[1]

ONE OF THE KEY PRINCIPLES of development assistance is that the intended beneficiaries should participate in determining the priorities and modalities of that assistance.[2] International assistance to judicial reform, like all international development assistance, must be shaped by those who will be most immediately affected. It often appears, however, that political development assistance, and in particular assistance to judicial reform, ignores this fundamental principle. Judicial "reform," like the judiciary and the law itself, is not "neutral." It seeks to promote given interests.[3] The interests of the donor country may be different from those of the recipient country. In many cases today in Latin America, as Jorge Correa Sutil has pointed out,[4] the donor may see judicial reform as necessary for facilitating transition to a free-market economy which will open opportunities for the donor.[5] International development assistance should also enhance rather than impede the enjoyment of human rights.[6] The 1993 U.N. World Conference on Human Rights called on "international and regional finance and development institutions to assess . . . the impact [of] policies and programmes on the enjoyment of human rights."[7]

The case of U.S. "assistance" to Haitian efforts at reform illustrates the disastrous results when the democratically-determined priority of the recipient country—a priority dictated by international human rights standards—clashes with the policy interests of the donor country which run counter to those standards.

Throughout Haitian history, repressive rulers and their henchmen have literally gotten away with murder. The law has been used to reify and reinforce the domination of a small elite over the great mass of poor peasants and workers, and has almost never functioned to punish even in the case of the worst massacres. Even when dictatorial leaders have been overthrown, they have usually been allowed to leave the country to join their bank accounts. As a result, the Haitian poor justifiably have little faith in the Haitian state in general and the legal system in particular.[8]

The latest, and perhaps most tragic, episode in this unbroken cycle of repression and impunity began with the 1991 *coup d'état* against President Jean-Bertrand Aristide, a grass-roots leader overwhelmingly elected with the support of the underprivileged on a platform calling for radical social change. The coup led to a three-year reign of terror during which between three thousand and five thousand people were executed by the military and their paramilitary allies. Thousands more suffered arbitrary arrests, torture, rape, and beatings, while an even larger number faced threats and extortion. Popular organizations and local activists were particularly hard hit. Hundreds of thousands of Haitians fled the terror by seeking exile abroad or going into hiding.

With the return of President Aristide, Haitians looked forward to the possibility that their tormenters would be brought to justice. The elected government listed justice for coup victims as one of its key priorities,[9] and popular organizations made it one of their principal demands.[10] Haiti's duty under international human rights standards also required that it prosecute these grave violations and allow victims to seek compensation.[11]

While decades of authoritarian rule—consistently supported by the United States[12]—had left the Haitian legal system weak at best and predatory at worst, President Aristide recognized that if the courts could deliver justice for the victims of the most recent repression, some measure of popular confidence in the system could be restored. He also saw that prosecution and victim compensation could help empower the poor by providing official recognition of the importance of their suffering. Indeed, he stated that of the several reasons why Haiti needed a "functioning independent judiciary," the "most important" was "for the prosecution of those who have committed crimes against the Haitian people."[13]

Yet, two years after the restoration of democracy, only a handful of lower-level criminals have been convicted and sentenced.[14] Impunity has been nearly total and people see their tormenters armed and freely circulating. Haitians' confidence in their justice system is as low as ever, and the possibility of meaningful reform is evaporating.

There are many reasons for this failure. The judicial and prosecutorial system remains extremely weak. The popular thirst for justice is not reflected in a judiciary and legal profession largely drawn from the small upper strata of Haitian society—a sign itself of how the poor remain disempowered in formally democratic Haiti. The disarmament of former soldiers and paramilitary agents has proceeded at a snail's pace, in large part because of deliberate inaction by the U.S.-led Multinational Force and the U.N. peacekeeping mission,[15] and fear of this *macoute* element still stalks city and countryside,[16] inhibiting people from coming forward to denounce their repressors. Even when class bias does not get in their way, inadequately trained, poorly paid, and totally unprotected judges have little incentive to order the arrest of these armed criminals. Without arresting the street-level killers, of course, nailing those who gave the orders is next to impossible. The police are entirely new and inexperienced, particularly in investigative methods. The Haitian government itself has been inconsistent in its efforts at investigation and prosecution,[17] while a Truth Commission, whose report has never been released, diverted attention and resources away from prosecutions.[18] The failure to put known criminals away creates a vicious cycle, since people who might otherwise summon the courage see little benefit in stepping forward. They thus resign themselves to the continuation of the historical pattern of impunity and domination.

The heaviest responsibility rests with the United States and, to a lesser degree, other international actors. The United States, whose wishes are fated to become Haiti's commands, has actively obstructed the justice process, while the United Nations and other donors have refused to help in significant ways.

U.S. Obstruction of Justice

The Bush and Clinton administrations consistently, but unsuccessfully, pressed exiled President Aristide to grant an amnesty for murder and torture to the coup leadership—many of whom had been on the payroll of U.S. intelligence agencies—as a part of any settlement allowing for his return.[19] Such an amnesty would have been in violation of Haiti's obligation to prosecute those guilty of gross abuses of human rights.[20] The Clinton administration went as far as to present Haiti's Minister of Justice with draft amnesty laws covering serious human rights abuses.[21] As American troops prepared to enter Haiti, former President Jimmy Carter, with the backing of the Clinton administration, even promised Haiti's military leaders a general amnesty which, fortunately, the U.S. could not unilaterally implement. Having failed to achieve a *de jure* amnesty, however, U.S. actions since the restoration of democracy have contributed to *de facto* impunity.

American troops entering Haiti in September 1994 simply allowed most top criminals to leave. Many officials of the paramilitary Front for the Advancement and Progress of Haiti (FRAPH), as well as army and police *attachés* who were arrested by Haitian authorities or field-level U.S. troops, were released after the intervention of senior U.S. officials.[22]

In October 1994, soon after landing in Haiti, U.S. troops entered the central and regional headquarters of the FRAPH and the Armed Forces. They found "trophy photographs" showing FRAPH members with the people they were killing or torturing[23] and some 160,000 pages of documents. These materials reportedly include documents revealing the finances, membership, and criminal activities of the military and FRAPH. They are also said to identify arms caches still hidden throughout the Haitian countryside. Without notifying the Haitian government, the U.S. seized these materials and shipped them to the Pentagon. Haitian authorities have spent almost two years trying to recover these records.

In December 1995, after American newspapers reported on the stolen records, the U.S. Ambassador in Haiti offered to return materials to Haitian law enforcement officials, but only if Haiti agreed to keep them secret and only if the U.S. could "delete or remove names or other information identifying individual U.S. citizens,"[24] thereby covering up the U.S. role in the terror and protecting many dual nationals. As a State Department spokesperson explained, "We wanted to redact, to take out of some of those documents and references that we thought might be damaging to individuals, even perhaps to some American interests or concerns. It was on that basis that we offered the documents to the Haitian Government."[25] Then-President Aristide, supported by a U.S. Congressional study,[26] insisted on Haiti's right to recover the stolen materials "in the form in which they were taken." The Haitian government has argued that the evidence seized is necessary to determine responsibility and build proper cases against former military and paramilitary officials for gross human rights abuses committed during *de facto* rule. Any details on arms caches could also be used by the Haitian government to disarm the thugs who still terrorize Haiti.

The U.S. has also obstructed Haitian justice by actively protecting leading criminals, as exemplified by its actions on behalf of FRAPH President Emmanuel Constant. Described by the *New York Times* as the country's "most wanted man" for his role in the repression,[27] Constant has admitted to receiving regular payments and encouragement from the CIA while he built his terror network.[28] Constant is wanted at home to face charges of murder, torture, and arson, and Haiti has asked for his extradition. In one case I investigated, Constant allegedly led his men in the torching of a pro-Aristide shantytown, burning 1,053 houses and killing over thirty people.

After Aristide's return, Constant was ordered to appear in court for questioning about his involvement in FRAPH's crimes, but he fled the country. He entered the United States as a result of what was said to be a bureaucratic lapse. After attention was called to his presence in the U.S., he was arrested in New York in March 1995 and his visa was revoked. U.S. Secretary of State Warren Christopher, calling FRAPH "an illegitimate paramilitary organization whose members were responsible for numerous human rights violations in Haiti," asked the Justice Department for his immediate deportation to Haiti, asserting that "[t]o permit Mr. Constant to remain at large in the United States . . . will appear as an affront to the Haitian government, and will cast doubt on the seriousness of our resolve to combat human rights violations."[29]

Constant was not deported, however. Rather, he was kept in INS detention until June 1995, when he was released onto the streets of New York. Although the State Department depicted the decision to release him as a mere "delay" in Constant's deportation in order to allow Haiti's judicial system to better prepare, a secret agreement between the U.S. government and Constant—revealed by the *Baltimore Sun*—purportedly allowed the death squad leader to "self-deport" at any time to a third country of his choice, effectively allowing him to escape justice in Haiti.[30] Constant's release also appears to violate the United States' commitment under the U.N. Torture Convention to extradite or bring to trial suspected torturers.

According to the State Department, Constant's "return to Haiti at this time would place an undue burden on Haiti's judicial and penal system."[31] Yet the Haitian authorities thought otherwise, filing an extradition request for his return. In Haiti, his release caused an outcry from human rights groups and representatives of victims of the repression.

The Role of the United Nations in the Fight against Impunity

Although the government of Haiti ranked the fight against impunity as one of its top programmatic priorities, no foreign donor could be found to assist in this effort. Together with the Minister of Justice, I met with representatives of the European Union and the U.N. Center for Human Rights in Geneva to discuss a proposal for creating a Special Prosecutor's Office to centralize prosecutions in the hands of well-trained and well-protected professionals who could devote full time to this task. However, both decided on other priorities.

The United Nations/OAS Civilian Mission in Haiti (MICIVIH)

played an outstanding role in recording and calling attention to abuses committed during the *de facto* government. It was particularly disappointing, therefore, that MICIVIH took the position that helping the government of Haiti prosecute human rights crimes was outside its broad mandate to "assist the judicial system to reinforce the legal means guaranteeing the exercise of human rights and the respect of legal procedures." Many, both within the mission and within the government, pointed out that prosecution of human rights crimes was Haiti's human rights duty.[32] Yet MICIVIH refused a direct request by President Aristide in October 1994 to assign staff to work with the Ministry of Justice on prosecuting human rights crimes and only parsimoniously turned over information it had collected during the coup years on such crimes.[33] Idealistic MICIVIH staff chafed at the headquarters' ban on helping victims pursue legal remedies. One regional office complained of "a practice of MICIVIH [headquarters] staff to discourage or caution observers following important human rights cases to avoid virtually any form of advice, assistance, or, in at least two cases, even mere observation."[34]

USAID Assistance to Justice Reform

Ironically, at the very same time that the U.S. was blocking justice for coup victims—the gateway to reform which the government of Haiti has determined to be the number one priority in the justice field—the U.S. Agency for International Development (USAID) was undertaking generous (if often poorly targeted) support for other aspects of "judicial reform," allocating $18 million over six years, much of it through its Washington, D.C.–based contractor, Checchi & Co.[35] Emergency training was provided to approximately four hundred judges and prosecutors. In February 1995, a Judicial Mentors program provided copies of laws to judges and undertook an inventory of all courts, prisons, and needed commodities. In July 1995, the National Magistrates' School was opened, fulfilling a mandate of the 1987 Constitution, and began training justices of the peace, prosecutors, investigating justices, and trial court judges. The U.S. Department of Justice, the Ministry of Justice, the National Center for State Courts, and Haitian law school faculty members worked together to develop a judicial training curriculum. Since the school's opening, training has consisted of three two-week programs with forty judicial personnel per class.[36]

With USAID support, an Office of Judicial Supervision was established within the Ministry of Justice to monitor the performance of judges and prosecutors throughout the country. Moreover, court facilities have been renovated at two sites to serve as prototypes for additional renovations, and eighteen other courthouses have been rehabilitated through community development initiatives. Efforts continue to improve Haitian law schools, establish a public law library, and strengthen the magistrate's school.[37] USAID is also funding local NGOs to provide legal assistance to indigent defendants. From January to May 1996, some 1,507 cases were received by the different NGOs.[38]

These programs, though generous, have been sharply criticized by both Haitian and U.S. human rights groups, principally because they were designed with little input from local actors.[39] For more than a year, USAID and Checchi had virtually no contact with Haitian human rights groups[40] or that (small) portion of the private bar that collaborates with human rights NGOs.[41] In October 1995, Human Rights Watch reported:

> [A] group of Haitian lawyers and law professors organized a three-day symposium on legal reform in early June. The discussions were intense, provocative, and illuminating. One of the organizers lamented, however, that despite receiving three invitations, no one from either AID or the US embassy had attended the conference. When asked what they think of the AID judicial reform project, several prominent Haitian lawyers responded that they knew nothing about it so they could not comment. A senior official in the Haitian justice ministry said the same.[42]

Little attempt was made to draw on MICIVIH's knowledge in developing the program. Haitian government officials have also complained that the U.S. and not Haiti was determining which kinds of reforms were being funded.

These criticisms—which USAID later undertook important steps to address—pale, however, when compared to outright U.S. obstruction of accountability for coup-era crimes, an obstruction which is undermining the entire reform effort. For as long as Haitians see that their tormenters roam the country with impunity and that the judicial system cannot or will not touch them, they will continue to regard the system as alien, an instrument of the ruling elite.

The Malary Trial

The effect of U.S. obstruction was dramatically illustrated by the chain of events leading to the July 1996 acquittal of two alleged gunmen in the 1993 murder of former Justice Minister Guy Malary.[43] The notorious Port-au-Prince Police Chief Michel Francois, thought to have ordered the Malary killing (and reported by NBC to have been on the U.S. payroll), had been allowed by U.S. forces to slip away in 1994 to the Dominican Republic. There, in a bizarre and unexplained move, he was arrested in 1996 and sent not to Haiti, where he had already been convicted in absentia in another political murder, but to Honduras. Brig. Gen. Philippe Biamby, the Haitian army chief of staff, also assumed to be connected to the murder, was also allowed to leave. One of their associates, former U.S. Drug Enforcement Agency asset Marcel Morissaint, was arrested in Haiti, however, and charged in the Malary killing. Morissaint was cooperating with my team of investigators on the Malary case and may have gone on to do so in other high-profile cases in which he was also implicated. In September 1995, however, he was mysteriously sprung from jail. Haiti's Justice Minister alleged that Morissaint was whisked away under U.S. protection,[44] a charge U.S. officials have denied. Haitian prosecutors also did not know that the U.S. was withholding a CIA report stating that Constant and Biamby "coordinated the murder of Justice Minister Guy Malary."[45] With the ringleaders and the informant gone under U.S. sponsorship, and the U.S. still blocking access to army and police records, while concealing other records, the case against the two alleged hitmen rested on eyewitness testimony. Because of the pervasive fear which still grips Haiti due to the failure to disarm the terror squads, only two street beggars acknowledged seeing the broad-daylight killing. Their stories were dismissed by an upper-class jury,[46] however, and the two defendants were acquitted.[47]

Conclusion

The priorities for external assistance to judicial reform should be democratically determined by the host country, should be in accordance with international human rights norms, and should be implemented in consultation with the groups most affected. In the case of Haiti, the democratically elected Haitian government had determined, in keeping with international standards of human rights, that its first judicial priority—a necessary step to restoring popular confidence in the judicial system and paving the way for more lasting judicial reform—was to establish accountability and justice for coup-era crimes. The United States, the principal donor to the Haitian justice system, has opposed accountability and justice and actively undermined the pursuit of these goals.

NOTES

This chapter is based on the author's experiences in 1995 and 1996 as part of a team of international lawyers convened by President Aristide to assist in bringing to justice those responsible for crimes committed during the coup regime. The views expressed are his own.

     1. President Jean-Bertrand Aristide, *The Role of the Judiciary in the Transition to Democracy*, in TRANSITION TO DEMOCRACY IN LATIN AMERICA: THE ROLE OF THE JUDICIARY (Irwin P. Stotsky ed., Boulder: Westview Press, 1993).

     2. *See*, e.g., ORGANISATION FOR ECONOMIC CO-OPERATION AND DEVELOPMENT (OECD), PARTICIPATORY DEVELOPMENT AND GOOD GOVERNMENT (Paris: OECD, 1995) (participatory development—defined as a "process by which people take an active and influential hand in shaping decisions that affect their lives"—is a "central concern in the allocation and design of development assistance." The "developing countries themselves are ultimately responsible for their own development"). *See also* InterAction, *InterAction Standards for Private Voluntary Organizations* (Washington, D.C.) ("7.1.2 Participants from all groups affected should, to the maximum extent possible, be responsible for the design, implementation, and evaluation of projects and programs") (available at http://www.interaction.org/ia/mb/pvo/standards.html). Unfortunately, this principle is all too often ignored. *See* GRAHAM HANCOCK, LORDS OF POVERTY: THE POWER, PRESTIGE, AND CORRUPTION OF THE INTERNATIONAL AID BUSINESS (New York: Atlantic Monthly Press, 1989).

     3. In the 1980s, for instance, the impetus for U.S. political development assistance in Latin America was to help "resis[t] the spread of leftism by promoting incremental transitions from right-wing military governments

to moderate, elected civilian governments." Tom H. CAROTHERS, IN THE NAME OF DEMOCRACY: U.S. POLICY TOWARD LATIN AMERICA 223 (Berkeley: University of California Press, 1991).

4. *See generally* the chapter in this volume by Jorge Correa Sutil.

5. As a World Bank official responsible for developing and evaluating judicial reform programs in Latin America stated: "Acknowledgment of the need for judicial reform is growing because of increasing recognition that political and judicial reform are key corollaries of *economic* reform. A *free and robust market* can thrive only in a political system where individual freedoms and property rights are accorded respect and where redress for violations of such rights can be found in fair and equitable courts." Maria Dakolia, *A Strategy for Judicial Reform: The Experience of Latin America*, 36 VA. J. INT'L L. 167–68 (1995) [emphasis added]. Indeed, the World Bank only assists reform efforts aimed at the "development of a legal framework appropriate to a market economy" and will not assist projects solely addressing criminal law reform. Lawyers Committee for Human Rights and Venezuelan Program for Human Rights and Education, *Halfway to Reform: The World Bank and the Venezuelan Justice System* 25 (New York: Lawyers Committee for Human Rights, 1996).

6. *See InterAction Standards for Private Voluntary Organizations, supra* note 2, at 71.4: "In its program activities, members shall respect and foster human rights, both socio-economic and civil-political."

7. *Vienna Declaration and Program of Action*, June 25, 1993, at Part 2, art. 2.

8. *See especially* Lawyers Committee for Human Rights, *Paper Laws, Steel Bayonets: Breakdown of the Rule of Law in Haiti* (New York: Lawyers Committee for Human Rights, 1990).

9. *See* Aristide, *supra* note 1.

10. *See, e.g.,* Larry Rohter, *As Haiti's People Call for Justice, Its Penal System Is Slow to Reform*, NEW YORK TIMES, Jan. 29, 1995 ("Three months after President Jean-Bertrand Aristide returned to power promising justice and reconciliation, Haitians are clamoring for his Government to begin prosecuting the soldiers, police officers and paramilitary gunmen who killed, robbed and pillaged during three years of military dictatorship").

11. According to the Inter-American Commission on Human Rights, "the State has a legal duty . . . to take reasonable steps to . . . use the means at its disposal to carry out a serious investigation of violations committed within its jurisdiction, to identify those responsible, to impose the appropriate punishment and to ensure the victim adequate compensation." *Velasquez Rodriguez*, IACHR, Judgment of 29 July 1988, Series C N/4, para. 174.

12. As one leading human rights group has noted, "US policy toward Haiti for the past 80 years hardly demonstrates a commitment to the rule of law and this record restricts the nature of US involvement in reform efforts." *Paper Laws, Steel Bayonets, supra* note 8, at 214.

13. Aristide, *supra* note 1. As Jaime Malamud-Goti has said, referring to Argentina, "Our sense of worthlessness, of shame and guilt demands a 'political remedy.' Only public admission by political institutions that we were wronged will legitimize us in our own eyes." Jaime Malamud-Goti,

Human Rights Abuses in Fledgling Democracies, in Transition to Democracy in Latin America: The Role of the Judiciary 225, 231, *supra* note 1.

14. In August 1995, military *attaché* Gérard Gustave, alias "Zimbabwe," was convicted in the killing of prominent businessman and Aristide supporter Antoine Izmery, while numerous others, including Police Chief Michel Francois, were convicted in absentia. Several dozen military and paramilitary agents are currently in detention and some trials have gone forward. In May 1996, for instance, a court in Mirebalais convicted two ex-Corporals and an *attaché* of the illegal arrest and torture of a leader of a popular organization. In July 1996, a court in nearby Hinche convicted a former soldier and an assistant section chief in the 1994 murder of another peasant leader. Former Captain Castera Cenaflis, commander of the Gonaives zone, is in detention awaiting trial for his role in the April 1994 massacre in the Raboteau slum of Gonaives. Charges of murder, torture, and arson have also been filed against FRAPH leader Emmanuel Constant, whose extradition is being sought from the United States (see below).

15. "[C]aution kept soldiers from the necessary jobs of disarming and arresting members of the Haitian military and a brutal paramilitary group known as Fraph." Editorial: *Danger Signs in Haiti,* New York Times, Sept. 9, 1996.

16. Laurie Richardson, *Disarmament Derailed,* NACLA Report on the Americas (May/June 1996), at 11.

17. The Haitian government has been hampered by a lack of continuity in justice efforts. Between early 1995 and early 1996, the country had no fewer than four Ministers of Justice. President Aristide established "complaint bureaus" (*bureaux de doleances*) and later a nationwide *Bureau d'Assistance Legale* to assist victims in filing complaints. Some three hundred cases of abuse were presented through these mechanisms, which never received adequate funding or publicity, however, and eventually died without producing concrete results. In the summer of 1995, President Aristide created the *Bureau des Avocats Internationaux,* an international team of lawyers and investigators of which the author was a part, to work with the Haitian authorities in investigating crimes against human rights. The Bureau helped to found, in October 1995, a new Criminal Brigade of the Haitian police to investigate seventy-seven leading crimes against human rights. In addition to its lack of experience (like all Haitian police) the Brigade has been hampered in its work by a lack of guidance and support and the inability to develop a consistent relationship with the judiciary and prosecutors. Despite entreaties to do so from the Truth Commission, the *Bureau,* MICIVIH, and others, the government never implemented the idea of creating a special prosecutor's office to centralize human rights prosecutions.

18. In December 1994, President Aristide established the National Commission for Truth and Justice (CNVJ) with three Haitian and three international commissioners. The CNVJ 's report—completed in February 1996 but still kept secret except for its recommendations—includes some six hundred pages of text and six hundred pages of data, took ten months to pre-

pare, and involved testimony from 5,450 witnesses nationwide. It identified some 8,600 victims and nearly 20,000 human rights violations committed during the coup era. The recommendations included detailed proposals for urgent changes to be made within the judiciary, the prosecutorial system, the police force, and the Haitian legal code. It called for the immediate prosecution, by a special prosecutor's office, of those listed in an annex.

Most of the information gathered by the CNVJ was taken from victims' statements, however, and was therefore largely known to the public. The Commission was denied access by the U.S. to Haiti army, police, and paramilitary files (see below), a fact which it denounced. More importantly, the CNVJ used resources which could have gone to prosecutions and it took the complaints of thousands of Haitians who might have otherwise turned to the justice system.

19. According to Human Rights Watch, "Aristide was under consistent pressure from UN Special Envoy Caputo and from Amb. Lawrence Pezzullo, special envoy for President Clinton, to make concessions on the Haitian army's accountability for its crimes," including General Cedras' demands for immunity for the high command. HUMAN RIGHTS WATCH WORLD REPORT 1994 108 (New York: Human Rights Watch, 1994). Further, "[d]uring the first half of 1994, US officials actively promoted a blanket amnesty for human rights violations committed since the coup." HUMAN RIGHTS WATCH WORLD REPORT 1995 101 (New York: Human Rights Watch, 1995).

20. In two important 1992 decisions, involving Argentina and Uruguay, the Inter-American Commission on Human Rights found that amnesties for grave human rights abuses violate the American Convention on Human Rights, in particular the state's duty to ensure and to protect human rights, and the right of the victims to seek justice. Annual Report of the Inter-American Commission on Human Rights 1992–93, OAS Doc. Ser. L/V/II/83 doc. 14, corr. 1. Report 28/92 (Argentina) at 41 and Report 29/92 (Uruguay) at 154. *See also* Diane Orentlicher, *Settling Accounts: The Duty to Prosecute Human Rights Violations of a Prior Regime*, 100 YALE L. J. 2537 (1991); Jaime Malamud-Goti, *Transitional Governments in the Breach: Why Punish State Criminals?*, 12(1) HUM. RTS. Q. 12 (1990); Robert E. Norris, *Leyes de Impunidad y los Derechos Humanos en las Américas: una respuesta legal*, 15 REVISTA IIDH 47 (Instituto Interamericano de Derechos Humanos, 1991).

21. Human Rights Watch/Americas and National Coalition for Haitian Refugees, TERROR PREVAILS IN HAITI: HUMAN RIGHTS VIOLATIONS AND FAILED DEMOCRACY 35 (New York: Human Rights Watch, 1994).

22. *See* Allan Nairn, *Haiti Under the Gun*, THE NATION, Jan. 8–15, 1996, at 11; Editorial: *Danger Signs in Haiti*, NEW YORK TIMES, Sept. 9, 1996 ("Since the intervention, American troops have allowed some men wanted for brutal crimes to escape Haitian justice, and even released several after their arrest").

23. Larry Rohter, *Haiti Accuses US of Holding Data Recovered by GI.'s*, NEW YORK TIMES, Nov. 28, 1995, at 1.

24. Memorandum of Understanding Concerning the Return of Haitian Documents and Other Materials (undated draft), para 7.

25. U.S. Department of State Daily Press Briefing, June 24, 1996.

26. Memorandum of Harry Gourevitch, American Law Division, Congressional Research Service, Library of Congress, Dec. 12, 1995 ("Under international law, the American military was not authorized to seize the documents").

27. Larry Rohter, *A Haitian Set for Deportation Is Instead Set Free by the US*, NEW YORK TIMES, June 22, 1996, at 5.

28. *See* Allan Nairn, *Behind Haiti's Paramilitaries*, THE NATION, Oct. 24, 1994. The U.S. apparently used FRAPH as a way to pressure Aristide into making concessions to the military. According to Lawrence Pezzullo, former U.S. Special Envoy to Haiti, FRAPH was "a political offset to Lavalas (Aristide's political movement)." *Id.* Colonel Patrick Collins, Constant's former handler for the Defense Intelligence Agency, "praised Constant for balancing the 'extreme' of Aristide." Allan Nairn, *He's Our S.O.B.*, THE NATION, Oct. 31, 1994.

29. Letter from Secretary of State Warren Christopher to Attorney General Janet Reno, March 29, 1995.

30. Myers, *Haitian's Deal with US Could Let Him Avoid Trial in Atrocities*, BALTIMORE SUN, July 27, 1996.

31. Rohter, *A Haitian Set for Deportation Is Instead Set Free by the US*, *supra* note 27.

32. *See* note 11, *supra*.

33. Many Haitians who complained to MICIVIH (and to the Truth Commission) believed, incorrectly, that such a complaint opened the way to the possibility of prosecution or of economic compensation. In 1995, the government of Haiti encouraged MICIVIH to make a systematic effort to recontact complainants to ascertain whether they had followed up their complaints by seeking legal redress and whether they would consent to having their complaints transferred to the Haitian authorities. MICIVIH eventually turned over to the Haitian police file summaries for a number of top-priority crimes.

34. In the internal memorandum, the regional office cited several cases. One, in particular, stands out:

> In the case of slain Aristide supporter ["X"]—a case brought before the judicial system by the popular organization [NGO "Y"]—the observer asked if, with the victim's family's consent, MICIVIH might release probative information in its files to the Haitian judicial authorities. The response from [MICIVIH headquarters] was replete with such admonitions as "we are unable to offer technical assistance", "we cannot act as legal counsel" and "we cannot offer to provide evidence". The relatives did sign an informally drafted release, modeled after the one for the Truth Commission. [MICIVIH headquarters] found it unacceptable but, nevertheless, provided no form of their own. At a recent hearing on the matter, a former FAdH named in the *plainte* exonerated himself, claiming he was ["X"]'s friend and that he had tried to help him. The observer had to sit quietly, knowing that his own files contained

declarations made by ["X"] himself to MICIVIH before his death wherein he named that very soldier as one of those who were after him and were declaring that, because he was "lavalas," he had "no right to live" and that when they found him again he would "be finished." Memorandum from Regional Office X to MICIVIH headquarters, Base [Z] Weekly Report, Oct. 2–8, 1995, MICIVIH (on file with author.)

The acquitted former soldier was placed in charge of the *caserne* where an *attaché* who was also being held in the X murder escaped shortly thereafter. In the same case, the *Juge d'Instruction* sought permission to use the regional office's fax machine to relay important arrest warrants to another city. According to the regional office, "Given the facts that one arrest had already taken place the previous day and that word of it was sure to spread quickly resulting in the probable flight of the accused, time was of the essence. Nevertheless, Montagne Noire's response was that such assistance was 'not in the mandate' and that to comply would set a 'bad precedent.' No contrary provision of the mandate was cited and none exists." MICIVIH Memorandum, *id.*

35. As of late 1995, other contributions included: France FF86 million over two years; Canada CDN$ 8.65 million over two years; UNDP US$ 467,000 over two years; and European Union 439,000 ECUS over one year. *See* Ministère de la Justice, *Contribution des Bailleurs de Fonds au Secteur Justice* (Port-au-Prince, Haiti, 1995).

36. In May and June 1996, some 342 judicial personnel participated in ordinary sessions, 104 in a one-week session on relations between judges and police and 30 in a one-week session on the administration of the *parquet* Projet d'Administration Judiciare Mai-Juin 1996.

37. *See* Ministère de la Justice, *supra* note 35.

38. Projet d'Administration Judiciare, Mai–Juin 1996. USAID's choice of NGO grantees has been questionable at best. None is known in the human rights community or has any experience providing legal assistance. Memorandum from Robert Weiner, Lawyers Committee for Human Rights, *Observations on Judicial Reform*, April 18, 1996 [hereinafter Weiner Memo]. One group in Gonaive, which was apparently created only when USAID money became available, was instrumental in its first month of work in obtaining the release of two alleged coup-era criminals because the warrants against them were not translated into Creole as required by the constitution but rarely done in practice.

39. *See* Human Rights Watch/Americas and National Coalition for Haitian Refugees, *Haiti: Human Rights After President Aristide's Return*, Oct. 1995, at 21–22; Weiner Memo, *supra* note 38. This also violates a key principle of development assistance. *See InterAction Standards for Private Voluntary Organizations, supra* note 2, at 7.1.3: "A member shall give priority to working with or through local and national institutions and groups, encouraging their creation where they do not already exist, or strengthening them where they do."

40. According to the Platform of Human Rights Organizations, the

umbrella for the leading Haitian human rights NGOs, as of early 1996, no Checchi representatives had visited the Platform.

41. Weiner Memo, *supra* note 38.

42. *Haiti: Human Rights After President Aristide's Return, supra* note 39, at 23.

43. Ironically, it was Malary, among others, who rebuffed U.S. attempts to foist an amnesty law on Haiti—an amnesty that would have covered his killers.

44. Allan Nairn, *Our Payroll, Haitian Hit,* THE NATION, Oct. 9, 1995.

45. The document, *Haiti's Far Right: Taking the Offensive [word blacked out]*, dated October 28, 1993, was released to the New York–based Center for Constitutional Rights in September 1996, as part of a lawsuit.

46. The class bias of the judicial system reaches into the jury box as well. The jury pool is composed of names submitted by Justices of the Peace. In an overwhelmingly illiterate country, almost all of the two hundred persons in the pool for the trial session which included the Malary case were professionals, and some 30 percent were lawyers. Only twenty-eight potential jurors appeared for selection, however. Of the fourteen jurors and alternates chosen, at least six were lawyers and two were law students. One was a television anchorman during the coup period.

47. *See* Reed Brody, *Impunity Continues in Haiti,* NACLA Report on the Americas, Sept.–Oct. 1996, at 1.

16 Comments on Brody and a Discussion of International Reform Efforts

Leonardo Franco

RECENT EXPERIENCE by the international community in supporting reform processes in Latin America and elsewhere in the world has underscored the importance of judicial reform as a vital element in strengthening and upholding the rule of law. Indeed, progress in judicial reform has become inextricably linked with the transition to democracy and broad-based socioeconomic change. In this delicate and often painful process, the judiciary is frequently the focus of citizens' aspirations or frustrations and acts as the barometer of progress in the process of societal reform.

While national legal systems may differ widely, fundamental human rights and related procedural guarantees, namely, the due process of law, have the status of general principles of international law, normally enshrined in the national constitutions and main implementing legislation. The importance of an independent, efficient, and accessible judiciary in relation to the rule of law is clear, and is based on the accepted notion that

> within a state, rights must themselves be protected by law; and any disputes about them must not be resolved by the exercise of some arbitrary discretion, but must be consistently capable of being submitted for adjudication to a competent, impartial and independent tribunal, applying procedures which will ensure full equality and fairness to all the parties, and determining the question in accordance with clear, specific and pre-existing laws, known and openly proclaimed.[1]

Yet, while there is growing recognition of the central role of judicial reform in the societal change process, current experience points to a certain lack of coherence, if not a failure, of concerned international actors, be they bilateral or multilateral institutions or private-sector groups, to adapt judicial reform efforts to societies which are deeply fractured by a history of conflict, widespread human rights violations, and ingrained traditions of authoritarian rule and military domination, not to mention socioeconomic inequality.

The chapter by Reed Brody illustrates many of the typical weaknesses found in internationally supported judicial reform efforts to date, both inside and outside of Latin America. The key point made in his chapter is that bilateral donors actively prevented—or at least did not support—application of justice to human rights violators in Haiti while at the same time providing financial and technical support for a judicial reform program in the country.[2]

International Efforts in Judicial Reforms and in Strengthening Human Rights Institutions

Brody's chapter raises fundamental questions about the preconditions, principles, and best practices in the field of capacity-building and technical assistance in support of judicial reform and strengthening of the rule of law. Similar concerns may also emerge from an examination of a variety of internationally supported initiatives aimed at judicial reform, legal capacity-building, and strengthening human rights institutions. It is obvious that the task of empowering national institutions is fundamentally a national responsibility. However, the present international concern for good governance and the importance given to the rule of law and human rights observance in the transition to democracies, and consolidation thereof, has served as an impetus for promoting growing multinational and bilateral actions in support of national initiatives.

It would be useful—though perhaps oversimplified—to distinguish three international approaches involving different overall motivations, methodologies, and institutional backgrounds and to examine their respective impact on justice and human rights strengthening, namely, the United Nations post-conflict peace-building efforts, the U.N. human rights field missions, and the international financial institutions.

Post-Conflict Peace-Building

Even though the post–World War II experiences in European reconstruction do not serve as applicable examples in today's world, post-conflict peace-building remains a significant aspiration of the international community in its attempt to rebuild countries devastated by internal strife. As noted by a recent U.N. report, "to be truly successful, U.N. peace-keeping operations are often followed by efforts to consolidate peace which are generally known as post-conflict peace-building. Such measures, designed to address root causes of a conflict, include not only promotion of development or humanitarian assistance" but also, *inter alia*, "building or strengthening of the judiciary and other public institutions and promoting human rights."[3] It must be recognized, however, that for the time being, such peace-building efforts are but work still in progress.

From the perspective of a United Nations High Commissioner for Refugees (UNHCR), judicial and legal capacity-building in states disrupted by prolonged conflict is viewed primarily as a means to "enhance the capacity of states to meet their international legal obligations and strengthen the rule of law and respect for human rights in those States."[4] UNHCR views such measures as essential to ensure smooth reintegration of refugees in countries of origin, thereby constituting a source of prevention of renewed displacement and refugee flows. These concerns were discussed in the context of a workshop, held in October 1996, jointly organized by the World Bank and UNHCR.[5] The workshop addressed "best practices" and "lessons learned" in relation to capacity-building in general, including rule of law strengthening as an indispensable and complementary component of the rehabilitation and socioeconomic recovery strategy normally supported by the international community. At the critical phase of war-to-peace transition, strengthening of the rule of law would normally involve support in establishing democratic institutions, restoring or reforming the national legal framework (the constitution and criminal and civil law), ensuring respect for fundamental human rights, strengthening the administration of justice and access thereto, promoting conflict resolution mechanisms at community levels, and establishing a civilian police force to restore and maintain public order and security.

However, as noted during this workshop, internationally supported capacity-building is often ill-adapted or even debilitating when applied in fragile post-conflict conditions:

> Sometimes, training approaches and/or materials are inappropriate or insensitive to local cultural and linguistic contexts. Training in itself does not necessarily build capacity. Good training can be given for a bad cause or vice versa. Usually, perceived incapacity does not stem simply from an absence of technical know-how alone, which can be remedied through an externally driven "quick fix" approach, but also from deeply rooted political and structural factors which can only be addressed through national commitments and political will in the society concerned. As an example, efforts to build an independent judiciary cannot rely simply on training seminars to provide judges with better knowledge of the law. The root causes for the lack of independence must be diagnosed and simultaneously addressed as part of a comprehensive sector strategy.[6]

Despite growing awareness of the importance of strengthening the rule of law in the context of the war-to-peace transition, national reconciliation, and recovery, such activities are not always addressed as part of internationally supported reform efforts. While a clear lack of technical and financial resources for this task may be part of the problem, it is also true that legal and judicial reform, especially in relation to the criminal justice system, often involves a difficult relationship with national governments and powerful national special interest groups, some of which may be implicated in human rights violations. This may complicate relations between traditional U.N. agencies and governments. As a result, the approach to date has been a fragmented one on the part of both bilateral and multilateral agencies.

More recently, however, it seems that judicial reform may be moving from the sidelines to center stage. This move is indicated in recent developments in two different aspects of international efforts, i.e., activities of the U.N. human rights field missions and of international financial institutions (IFIs).

U.N. Human Rights Field Missions (The Guatemala Experience)

In recent years, experiences of United Nations human rights field missions (in El Salvador, Haiti, Guatemala, and most recently, Rwanda), have increasingly found that human rights monitoring and verification must be complemented by an effort to strengthen judicial institutions. Indeed, the Aspen Institute recommendations are clear on this point: "The United Nations should encourage institution-building, legal reform, and education for human rights; such long-range projects should be considered important elements of UN human rights field operations."

The United Nations Mission for the Verification of Human Rights in Guatemala (MINUGUA) represents the "second generation" of human rights verification missions and the first formal U.N. experiment in combining human rights verification and support for institution-building from its inception. In Guatemala, the parties to the peace negotiation, the Government of Guatemala and the Unidad Revolucionaria Nacional Guatemalteca (URNG), asked the United Nations to verify compliance with human rights by both parties, while recognizing the inherent weaknesses of the state to effectively protect those rights. The Comprehensive Accord on Human Rights, signed by the parties on March 29, 1994, entrusted the United Nations with the strengthening of national governmental and nongovernmental entities that protect human rights even before the signing of a final peace accord. To these responsibilities were added human rights–related verification and institution-building aspects of the Accord on the Identity and Rights of Indigenous Peoples, signed by the parties in March 1995. This was a particularly significant development, given the historic exclusion of the country's majority indigenous Mayan population.

Since November 1994, under the management of its own specialist team, MINUGUA has provided technical support to various institutions relating to the protection of human rights (i.e., the Judicial Branch, Office of the Prosecutor General, Human Rights Ombudsman, the penal system, and the police, the latter two as "auxiliary organs" of the justice system), as well as the nongovernmental sector. At the core of the Mission's institution-building strategy was the fight against impunity, an endemic problem in Guatemala, pointed out in MINUGUA's first report of March 1994:

> Impunity in Guatemala is a phenomenon which goes beyond the human rights sphere and affects other aspects of national life. The Mission is equally concerned at the impunity enjoyed by ordinary criminals, which creates a feeling of defencelessness among Guatemalan society and undermines basic values such as public safety, the concept of justice and equality before the law. It should also be pointed out that everyone living in Guatemala has the fundamental right to be able to live a life free from fear and disruption and to be safe from attacks on his or her life, integrity, safety and freedom.

> The State must identify and tackle the root causes of impunity in order to eliminate it. The Mission, taking into account the evidence uncovered in the course of its verification, wishes to stress, "*inter alia*, the defective functioning of the administration of justice."[7]

The institution-building programs of the Mission pursued a two-track strategy of improving justice administration, on one hand, and "promoting a culture of human rights observance in Guatemala," on the other. To this end, a comprehensive sector approach was designed, involving:

- · A preliminary "diagnosis" of the justice system, carried out prior to the program's start-up, in consultation with concerned sectors of Guatemalan society (e.g., Human Rights NGOs) and the donor community. This exercise is especially important, not only to reveal the distinct features of the different institutions, but also to ensure that the international efforts do not inadvertently strengthen a repressive state apparatus.
- · A program strategy consisting of first, both short and longer term interventions, designed with support from UNDP, and benefiting from firm and indispensable donor support. The aim of the short-term strategy (financed via a Trust Fund program of some US $7 million over 2 years) was to generate im-

mediate and tangible changes in the functioning of the justice system as a vital confidence building measure for the ongoing peace process. To this end, international experts were hired to accompany and give in-service training to national counterparts in the different institutions. Initially priority was given to the Office of the Prosecutor General in order to improve application of the then recently enacted code of criminal procedure. This new code provided for oral trials, a system of judicial interpreters, free provision of public defenders and creation of the Office of the Prosecutor General with exclusive powers for criminal prosecution, separate and distinct from the Attorney General responsible for the defense of the state. The second program strategy consists of firm national commitments to program objectives, specified in formal agreements with the various national counterparts.

- Support for increased access to justice, especially for the country's indigenous Mayan population, through a series of local-level projects, involving training of the judiciary in customary law and indigenous rights, legal aid programs, and integrated justice centers in remote, war-affected parts of the country. It must be noted that the historic exclusion of this population will only be addressed through much broader and far-reaching socioeconomic reform.
- Support for priority legal reform, through technical support to the Guatemalan Congress, in areas crucial for human rights protection (e.g., regulating prison conditions and limiting the scope of military justice).
- An intense program of human rights education, promotion, and dissemination, using methods and materials adapted to the needs of largely illiterate, traditionally isolated, rural communities.

What is the outcome of these efforts to date? In Guatemala, as in many other countries, the long-term nature of the judicial reform process cannot be overemphasized, given the inherent complexity of the sector and powerful vested interests against reform. In such a context, a short-term program such as MINUGUA can, however, create better possibilities for long-term reform. Such efforts are in turn closely related to measures to address the chronic socioeconomic inequality affecting the indigenous populations. In view of the competent staff involved in the institution-building program, key "lessons learned" are that:

- Overall, the state institutions have been receptive to external support, although absorption capacity has varied among them, some of which lack an organized agenda of priorities, leading to long implementation delays. This is especially true in the case, for instance, of the police forces.
- A natural resistance to change has also proven difficult to overcome, making it necessary to develop a wider range of actions and assistance in newer and smaller public institutions (e.g., the Office of the Prosecutor General and the Public Defender's Office).
- The interinstitutional nature of the change implies a need to initiate significant advances in more than one institution at a time, in order to see measurable results. For example, improved criminal investigation capacity requires improvements at various levels in the police system, public ministry, and courts.

It seems to me, therefore, that the Mission's program is having a tangible impact on human rights protection in Guatemala, through improved technical capacity of judicial and related organs, and by stimulating public awareness of justice issues, resulting in a clamor for reform. Undoubtedly, progress made to date is largely due to the public impact of information on institutional functioning gained through verification of human rights, acquired through the Mission's nationwide field office network and publicized regularly in the Mission Director's reports to the United Nations Secretary-General. It is also due to the indispensable political will and commitment demonstrated by the government to initiate reform measures, including, for example, those limiting the power and influence of the military.[8]

International Financial Institutions

Given the inherently long-term structural changes and investments (both national and external) implied in public sector reform, including the justice sector, it is worth noting the evolving policies in this area of international financial institutions (IFIs), such as the World Bank and the Inter-American Development Bank.

A study carried out by the Lawyers Committee for Human Rights and the Venezuelan Program for Human Rights Education contains valuable information on the subject of experiences of the World Bank and judicial reform in Venezuela in particular, and in Latin America in general.[9] This study is all the more important for revealing that the World Bank—which has come to view the rule of law as the "enabling environment" for economic investment—is today the major non-state actor in this field worldwide. World Bank–supported reform efforts have not been without controversy, however, since its legal department has concluded that the World Bank's charter limits the kinds of reform initiatives that can be supported to those directly related to economic matters.

In their evaluation of the World Bank's performance in Venezuela, the following points are of particular relevance:

· The project was not part of a comprehensive reform strategy;
· There was no broad government commitment to reform;
· Reform strategies failed to address crucial structural impediments to judicial independence;
· The reform strategies were premised on artificial economic and noneconomic distinctions in key areas;
· Access to justice concerns were not addressed; and
· There was no broad-based participation in the design and development of the project.

Yet, as the report demonstrates, the World Bank's involvement in judicial reform is relatively recent and continues to evolve, particularly in light of experience gained in the collapse of authoritarian regimes in Latin America, Eastern Europe, and Africa. There is evidence that the World Bank has begun to recognize that "without a sound legal framework, without an independent and honest judiciary, economic and social development risk collapse."

For its part, the Inter-American Development Bank (IADB) has unequivocally adopted justice reform, respect for human rights, and strengthening of civil society as indispensable features of its policy for modernization of the state and promoting conditions favorable to economic growth and stability. Bank-led programs support countries in the establishment of a justice system which is independent, effective, and nondiscriminatory, prioritizing innovative and strategically vital areas such as alternative methods of conflict resolution and legal aid/education programs directed at the general population.

Conclusions

Taking into account the various approaches and experiences outlined above in relation to international aspects of strengthening of the rule of law, I submit the following basic conclusions for consideration:

- One cannot separate the reform of justice administration from justice for human rights violations. This point highlights another crucial issue already confronted in both Latin America and elsewhere: the practice of granting amnesties as the political price to pay in the transition to democracy, when the cause of justice may be sacrificed in the interest of national reconciliation.
- "Quick fix" and disjointed approaches (such as "crash" courses and donations of equipment) to judicial reform cannot be successful in the long term unless they are linked to measures to address the deeply rooted political, technical, and structural factors which inhibit effective functioning of the judiciary. Too often international efforts seek to apply foreign models which are ill-adapted to the fragile structures of emerging democracies.
- "Top down" approaches to judicial reform—without seeking to involve civil society, including lawyers' associations and NGOs—are bound to fall short of their objectives. Indeed, a major challenge is to promote a popular demand for justice, on the part of traditionally excluded populations, as part of a le-

gitimate expectation for increased accountability and transparency from government structures in general.

- Judicial reform is not neutral in any society—the change process will suit certain societal interests and conflict with those of other powerful groups.

- Human rights concerns should form a central focus of judicial reform and efforts to strengthen the rule of law, within the context of a comprehensive sector approach based on a diagnosis which is both action-oriented and participatory. This should include a program strategy covering legal reform, access to justice, and human rights education and promotion, especially through NGOs and civil society.

- In post-conflict situations, internationally supported capacity-building efforts should aim to build up radically different and alternative structures that are able to "heal the wounds of war," especially at the community level, rather than merely strengthening discredited structures which existed prior to the conflict.

NOTES

The author is former Director of the United Nations Human Rights Verification Mission to Guatemala (MINUGUA) and former Director of International Protection, United Nations High Commissioner for Refugees. The views expressed in this chapter are my own, and do not necessarily reflect those of the United Nations. This chapter was prepared with the valuable contribution of Jenifer Otsea, based on her participation in the International Conference on Central American Refugees (CIREFCA) and MINUGUA.

1. PAUL SIEGART, THE INTERNATIONAL LAW OF HUMAN RIGHTS 18 (Oxford: Clarendon Press, 1983).

2. No formal amnesty was agreed upon during the political transition in Haiti. Yet, as Ian Martin, the Director of the U.N. Human Rights Mission at the time, stated: "The UN/OAS and US negotiators obviously regarded the amnesty pledge as necessary to secure the peaceful departure of the military leadership. Beyond this, there was a great concern to promote reconciliation and avoid vengeance. Aristide's reluctance regarding a blanket amnesty came to be regarded as justifying suspicions that he would promote vengeance; there was little understanding that when acts of popular vengeance have occurred in Haiti, they have been a symptom of a situation in which severe human rights violations have been perpetrated and there is

no hope of justice through due process of law. The international community came to expect Aristide to be able to promote reconciliation and prevent vengeance, while wanting to deny him the ability to do so by promising truth and justice." (*See* HONOURING HUMAN RIGHTS AND KEEPING THE PEACE: LESSONS FROM EL SALVADOR, CAMBODIA AND HAITI—RECOMMENDATIONS FOR THE UNITED NATIONS 114 (Aspen Institute, 1995).

    3.   H.L. Hernández & S. Kuyama, *Strengthening the United Nations System Capacity for Conflict Prevention* 35 (U.N. Joint Inspection Report, New York: United Nations, 1995).

    4.   *UNHCR's Role in National Legal and Judicial Capacity Building*, UNHCR Executive Committee Doc. No. EC/46/SC/CRP.31 (May 1996).

    5.   "Adapting Capacity Building Strategies to the Needs of War-Torn Societies" (Washington, D.C., Oct. 21–24, 1996).

    6.   Jenifer Otsea, "Adapting Capacity Building Strategies to the Needs of War-Torn Societies," UNHCR Document (Oct. 1996).

    7.   MINUGUA, "U.N. Human Rights Verification Mission to Guatemala," U.N. Doc. A/49/856, March 1994, at para. 202. The other elements of impunity mentioned in the above-referred report include the following: the existence of illicit associations linked with drug trafficking, car theft, timber smuggling, and financial and other interests which may enjoy the support, the complicity, or the tolerance of state agents; the autonomy enjoyed by the army in its counter-insurgency and anti-subversive activities and also the procedures it uses in this sphere and the broad interpretation it gives to those concepts; the control exerted over rural communities by military commissioners and CVDCs (Civil Defence Patrols); and the proliferation of and lack of control over possession of firearms in the hands of private individuals. *Id.*

    8.   It is important to highlight the fact that after this paper was presented to the Notre Dame workshop, the final Peace Agreement was signed by the Government of Guatemala and the URNG in December 1996 in the presence of the U.N. Secretary General. Furthermore, one of the sectorial agreements that preceded the signing of the final agreement specifically dealt with the issue of strengthening the role of the state and the civil authorities.

    9.   Lawyers Committee for Human Rights and the Venezuelan Program for Human Rights Education and Action, *Halfway to Reform: The World Bank and the Venezuelan Justice System* (New York: Lawyers Committee for Human Rights, 1996).

Judicial Reforms in Latin America: Good News for the Underprivileged?

Jorge Correa Sutil

ANY ATTEMPT to show a general and systematic picture of the process of judicial reforms in Latin America has several risks. The first one is that the observer may become dizzy with the amount, nature, and degree of different initiatives. More changes are being proposed, approved, or are in the process of implementation than the judicial institutions can tolerate.

Recently, nearly all the Latin American countries have decided to or attempted to change the way their judicial branches are governed. In the last decade, and frequently as an important part of their transitions to democracy, Peru, Argentina, El Salvador, Panama, Costa Rica, Colombia, Paraguay, and Ecuador have changed their constitutions in order to create *Consejos de la Magistratura* to govern their judicial branches, following the European post-war model.[1] Chile, Guatemala, Honduras, and Nicaragua have recently discussed similar efforts to amend their constitutions to create these new bodies. In contrast, Uruguay repealed its own *Consejo* immediately after recovering democracy. One will find a similar number of countries that have amended their constitutions in order to guarantee that a percentage of their public budget goes to the judiciary, frequently establishing, at the same time, the right of the *Consejos* to administer that budget.[2] Furthermore, a number of countries have changed in the last years the rules that govern the ways their judges are appointed and their terms in and conditions of office.[3] Not less is the number of countries that are making efforts to change their criminal procedures into a more oral and less inquisitorial model, and trying to bring about enormous changes in their public prosecutor's offices, *Ministerios Públicos*.[4]

In nearly all Latin American countries one finds efforts to improve the education of judges, including the creation of national judicial schools that offer programs for preparing judges or for continuing their education.[5] In every country in Latin America, there are programs for reinforcing the public defender's office, discussions to create or give more or less jurisdiction to the *Defensores del Pueblo* (derived from the Swedish model of people's advocate, or ombudsman), and efforts to create or reinforce systems of alternative dispute resolution, to reform the police, and to create specialized jurisdictions.

It is time for judicial reform in Latin America. USAID has granted no less than $200 million between 1985 and 1995 for the modernization of justice in Costa Rica, Honduras, Guatemala, El Salvador, and Panama. The same agency established programs for modernizing the judiciary in Argentina, Chile, Uruguay, Bolivia, Colombia, and Paraguay. The World Bank has also been active in this arena, especially in Bolivia and Venezuela, and recently in Paraguay and Argentina. In Venezuela, the World Bank approved a loan of $30 million for the modernization of the judiciary, with the understanding that the Venezuelan government will add another $30 million to the same project.[6] The Inter-American Development Bank has recently restructured its legal department and created a full new branch to deal with the modernization of the state and especially with judicial reform.[7]

Substantial efforts have been made in the last decade to change the judiciary throughout Latin America. However, there are risks involved. It is not easy to assess where those changes are heading. It is also difficult to identify the efforts which will be effective, and to foresee how they will change the situation of the poor.

A second risk when trying to describe recent efforts of judicial reform in Latin America is to naively accept the rhetoric of reform and believe that it is enough to put good ideas on legal paper in order to create new realities. The amount of efforts and initiatives certainly does not guarantee success or even better judicial services for the people. I know of very few studies that evaluate the impact of what has been done. Yet, one can find important voices warning that most of these efforts will be unsuccessful because they are not focused on the most relevant problems that the Latin American judicial systems experience.[8]

A third risk that is present in any effort to evaluate recent judicial reforms is to confuse judicial reform with judicial instability. In most Latin American countries, the judiciary traditionally has been an unstable institution, principally due to its lack of independence from politics and the pervasive instability of democracy in the region.

This chapter tries to recognize the presence of the underprivileged groups in the process of changing the judicial systems in Latin America and to foresee the impact of the changes on these groups. The next section attempts to characterize current efforts to change relevant aspects of the judiciary in Latin America. Because a list of the reforms that have been approved or are under serious discussion would be lengthy, this section analyzes where the reform process is heading and the impact it could have on the underprivileged.

A Characterization of the Efforts to Reform the Judiciary: Their Causes and Goals
Why So Many Changes Now?

Any observer of Latin American history should be surprised by the amount of efforts presently being deployed. The judiciary has not been in the forefront of the issues that have mattered to Latin American ruling groups. Though many of the Latin American elites of the nineteenth century who made efforts to build constitutional systems looked at the law as a privileged instrument to bring about the values of enlightenment, it is difficult to recognize programs which were established with the purpose of empowering the judiciary. The continental European model our codifiers of the last century were following was not that of a branch of government that could control the others, as in the United States, but that of "inanimated figures" who would mechanically apply the law. They were looking for honest civil servants who would become "the mouth that pronounces the words of the law." Consequently, notwith-standing the importance that some enlightened Latin American elites of the nineteenth century attributed to the law,[9] they did not pay much attention to the judiciary.

The movement towards a welfare state that occurred in many Latin American countries from around 1920 onwards also did not focus on the judiciary. This branch of government was not the one to distribute benefits. It was a period when the executive branch and its bureaucracy grew. The elites did not empower the judiciary to control or limit the expansion of the state and its regulatory powers; they did however, with the support of the people and in the midst of populism, consolidate the endemic Latin American imbalance in favor of the executive branch, a process that ran to the detriment of the other two branches of government, if not also of civil society.

During this period, the judicial branch became another part of the bureaucratic apparatus of Latin American governments. It was one more institution for the political powers to control, one more office where they could appoint their partisans in order to reward them, guarantee their loyalty, and make sure no decisions were taken by judges that could damage the interests of the ruling party.

During the 1950s and 1960s, the years of dominance of the ideology of import substitution and state-centered development, neither the law nor the judiciary were in the forefront of strategies to redress underdevelopment. Law was seen by the new elites, comprised especially of engineers, economists, and social scientists, as an obstacle for change, a realm that had to be curtailed in its influence in order to make sure that it would not frustrate the new ways of organizing production and labor. The judiciary was also insignificant for the revolutionary left which, influenced by the Cuban revolution, became important during the late 1960s and the early 1970s. The revolutionaries were too concerned with issues of structural social justice to focus on the perceived minor issues of individual justice in the courtrooms.[10] On their part, the authoritarian military regimes of the 1970s and the 1980s certainly did not have the will to empower a judiciary that could limit their repressive policies.

For nearly two centuries of independent history, the judicial systems of Latin American countries have played a minor, if not irrelevant, role. In many cases, the judiciary was no more than another office of government, highly politicized, too weak to enforce the law against the government or any other dominant groups, and frequently weakened by corruption.[11] What has changed in the late 1980s and the 1990s that has resulted in so much more being said, debated, invested, and programmed for the judiciary? In trying to answer this question, I will focus on different factors that have influenced judicial reform and try to characterize the type of reform or reforms that each factor is provoking.

Transition to Democracies: The Need to "Democratize" the Judiciary

The first factor pushing for judicial reform in Latin American recent history is the establishment of, or the return to, democratic political regimes. In many Latin American countries, the history of their recent transitions to democracy has been so entangled with their history of dealing with past human rights violations, that it is nearly impossible to talk about one without also discussing the other.[12]

Perhaps the best example is the Argentine transition, whose starting point nearly coincided with the public trial of the generals who had been in power and who were tried for their responsibilities in human rights violations. The trials were fully viewed on television. A criminal prosecution, a working courtroom, and the decisions of judges were probably the most graphic and dramatic scene of transition that the Argentines experienced. The judges and their ability to enforce the rule of law appeared as the main actors of the new political times. Some observers have argued that from those days onwards, the Argentinean judiciary may be transforming itself into a forum where citizens voice, discuss, and legitimate many of their political demands.[13]

Most importantly, the new rhetoric of human rights protection, the acknowledgment of the poor role that judges played in most countries in dealing with human rights violations during dictatorships, and the feeling that judicial independence was a crucial factor

for the consolidation of democracy have been key elements in explaining some of the reform efforts.[14] Of course, in each pattern of
change one can also find a series of different concurrent motives that
vary from country to country. Yet, in the transition to democracy one
can trace the main cause of two reforms that, with different degrees
and nature, have been present in the last decade in many Latin
American countries. Both are efforts to establish a new relationship
between the judiciary and other branches of government. I would
like to think that they are efforts to integrate the judicial branch with
democracy, by making the judges attuned with and bound by democratic values, while still independent of short-term interests of political parties in government.

One of these reforms has been related to the creation or strengthening of judicial careers. In some Latin American countries, judges
do not have life tenure positions and are, according to law or tradition, *de facto* removable by changing political authorities. El Salvador,
Honduras, Panama, Guatemala, Paraguay, Peru, Chile, Venezuela,
and Bolivia have recently changed or are discussing major changes in
the laws governing the ways judges may be appointed, evaluated,
held accountable, or sanctioned for their wrongdoings.[15]

Another reform, common in many Latin American countries, has
been, as previously mentioned, the aim to create new institutions
that mediate and make more transparent the relations between the
political branches and the judiciary. Following the post-war European model, Peru, Argentina, El Salvador, Panama, Costa Rica,
Colombia, Paraguay, and Ecuador have recently created *Consejos de la
Magistratura* or *Consejos del Poder Judicial.*[16] Chile, Guatemala, Honduras, and Nicaragua have discussed bills in the same direction. In
most cases, the creation of these councils has responded to the aim of
avoiding the political control of the judiciary by the executive branch
or political party elites. The councils are institutions comprised of individuals who are appointed by all branches of government, but
who are not supposed to represent the branches' immediate interests,
and who cannot be removed by or made accountable to the executive
or the legislative branch. The councils typically have an important
participation in the nomination of judges and in judicial policies, in-

cluding the right to propose the budget of the judiciary, administer its resources, and propose bills related to the judiciary.

It is probably too early to evaluate these changes. One must be careful of becoming too optimistic about both reforms. Immediate political interests have been present in their implementation; frequently, under the rhetoric of establishing the basis for an independent judiciary, members of the judicial councils have been appointed in ways that are far from guaranteeing the independence of the judges. In some cases, the councils have had conflicts with the Supreme Court or have been accused of weakening the political independence of judges.[17]

Free Market Economies:
The Decentralization of Fora for Dispute Resolution

The last decade in Latin America has been dominated by trends toward open market economies. Except for Cuba, all countries have experienced a change from regulatory and welfare states to freedom of markets. While there are differences in the degree of such shifts and the degree of political consensus they generate from one country to another, the same trends appear in each and every one of them.

An open market economy decentralizes the fora of dispute resolution. While the state was the great investor in Latin American societies and controlled prices, trade unions, and most jobs, the political parties and the offices of the executive and legislative branches were the most important institutions in which to locate expectations and solve the disputes among social groups. As the state intervention is dismantled, conflicts that arise are not necessarily resolved by the politicians. The most important conflicts that arise nowadays in Latin America do not usually end up as requirements for the government to change the way social benefits are distributed. Rather, private actors confront each other either in the market or in the courtrooms. In an open market economy, courts are a frequent and important fora for enforcement of the rules that regulate markets and for resolution of disputes that the market is not able to solve. The deregulation of the economy in Latin America has changed dramatically the amount and nature of judicial litigation. This phenomenon lies at the origin of a number of efforts to reform the judiciary.

Free Market Economies and More Conflicts in the Judiciary: How Much Judiciary? Requirements for Improving Efficiency

The process of opening the markets and allowing them to allocate more resources than ever before has multiplied the amount of litigation. This is especially true because the transition from highly regulated markets to more open and free ones has provoked many bankruptcies and the firing of public workers. Litigation related to collecting debts increases in an exponential way in such periods, collapsing judicial systems. Something similar happens with labor conflicts and litigation related to interpretation or enforcement of contracts.

The first reaction of most Latin American countries was to create more of the same, by increasing the judicial budgets and the number of courts available.[18] Soon the need for more sophisticated answers became clear, in part because the demand for justice is rather inflexible, and in part because the spending did not work in favor of the poor; the richest groups tended to absorb all the new resources that the system created.

New trends of reform are now appearing on the Latin American horizon in order to cope with the increment of litigation. One trend is the attempt to increase judicial service through the improvement of court efficiency. Although there are inadequate systems of judicial statistics throughout Latin America, it is clear that court operations have severe inefficiencies. One study showed that in 1991 the civil courts in Argentina could resolve only 6 percent of the cases initiated in that year. In Bolivia, the average length of a criminal procedure is five years. In Paraguay, only one case is solved for every eleven cases that enter the system.[19]

A new rhetoric of efficient administration, coming from the private sector, has invaded the public offices of Latin America. The courts are no exception. In every country, the concept of court administration has blossomed. It has created wide controversy in judiciaries not used to the idea of being held accountable for the amount and quality of the service they deliver to the public. It is bothersome for a formally independent branch of government to have external agencies intervening or giving opinions about the administration of their resources and evaluating their performance.

Many countries have increased the financial resources they allocate to their judicial system. A significant number have established in their constitutions that no less than a determined percentage of their public budget should go to the judicial systems. The figures are not low, ranging between 2 and 6 percent. However, the constitutional rule is seldom honored.[20] At the same time that countries increase the amount they invest in their judicial systems, they require control in order to guarantee that the effort effectively improves the judicial services for the general population. This supports the need to have increased and better information about court performance and to introduce the knowledge and instruments of modern administration into the old structures and procedures of the judicial systems.

Free Market Economies and the Growth of Judicial Conflicts: The Search for Alternative Dispute Resolutions

Even if court administration improves, the court system is not expected to be able to cope with the amount of new litigation. Most judicial experts and actors in Latin America are convinced that the increasing amount of litigation must not be confronted with a weak judiciary and that it is no solution simply to multiply the number of courts in a system that has not only been poorly financed but which also suffers from an inadequate structure and professional culture. Consequently, Latin America has joined enthusiastically a worldwide movement for creating mechanisms of alternative dispute resolution.

However, except in Peru, there are few experiences of informal fora created by the people and tolerated or recognized by the state for solving disputes.[21] Latin American countries, other than Peru, Guatemala, Mexico, and in some ways, Ecuador, have not looked at their own historical traditions of dispute resolution but have instead tended toward building on or strengthening mediation and arbitration from models which have been successful in France and the United States. International agencies, especially the Inter-American Development Bank, have been actively encouraging these initiatives.[22]

Enthusiasm has been such that the Argentinean government, even before knowing what to do regarding alternative dispute resolutions, declared in a presidential decree that mediation was a matter of national interest.[23] In order to give impulse to alternative dispute resolutions, most countries have recently changed their civil procedure codes, authorizing or requiring the judges, at the beginning or during the trial, to call the parties and try to settle the dispute. This change in the law has not yet been successful, because judges and judicial institutions are collapsing under the work load and have little or no experience in mediating or guiding agreements. At the same time, there are a series of other reforms in many Latin American countries that try to establish arbitration as a regular forum for dispute resolution, especially those related to commercial matters. What may be more important for the poor is that some countries have enacted or are discussing bills to establish mediating agencies where some issues have to be addressed before they reach the judicial procedure. These experiences are becoming especially popular for family conflicts.[24]

It is too early to say if these initiatives are good news for the poor. It is uncertain if the efforts to create alternative fora will mean that the poor will finally have a place where they will be heard, confront their counterparts, and try solutions without the unintelligible judicial structure and language that typically marginalize them, or if this is going to be another inefficient and lengthy hurdle that the poor will have to overcome before reaching a judicial decision.

Free Market Economies—Not Only More Conflicts
but More Complex Ones: Judicial Education as a Response

Deregulating the economy, diminishing the role of government, and opening of markets has not only produced an increase in the amount of litigation in Latin America, it has also changed the nature of litigation, expanding the complexity and diversity of the disputes the judges must confront. New methods of trading, subtle ways of controlling markets or violating antitrust laws, difficulties in protecting information in data banks, and other problems of high complexity dramatically entered into the Latin American countries, markets, and courts well before their legal systems could regulate them or the judges could understand the problems these issues entail.

Judges must increasingly respond to very relevant and sophisticated issues surrounding the economy, including issues related to the right to limit or ban some industrial projects in order to protect the environment.[25] The cost-benefit analysis in which the judge has to involve her/himself in order to solve this type of problem is far removed from the skills Latin American judges have needed traditionally. Tradition and culture are serious obstacles for judges, who must adapt to new roles that include resolving issues that are novel or which, in Latin America, have historically been in the hands of regulatory agencies.

This problem has been one of the main factors behind the pressure for more and better judicial education. Judicial schools have flourished throughout Latin America.[26] They are usually one of the first initiatives proposed under the umbrella of judicial modernization, a slogan that is often used but seldom defined. These judicial schools or academies are normally state agencies, organized as autonomous entities or dependent on the Supreme Court or the *Consejos de la Justicia*. The Spanish and French models have been influential, along with some inspiration on contents and methodologies contributed by U.S. agencies.

The private sector has been generally supportive of these judicial schools. Their demand is basically for judges with more knowledge, especially knowledge related to commerce, economy, and business. Other members of the private sector, as well as other social actors, view the judicial schools as an opportunity for achieving judicial independence and for strengthening judicial power against corruption. Their demand is for educational contents related to judicial ideology and culture. Still others view judicial schools as a good opportunity to introduce judges to ideas of modern administration, so as to make them truly care for efficiency and for better service to the people.[27]

Crime and Insecurity:
Reforms of the Criminal Justice System

Another trend of important reforms in the Latin American judiciary is related to the increase in crime and the way it seems to undermine democracy. The relation between crime and democracy may be established in two ways in Latin America. First, following the transitions to democracy, the demand for security has become one of the main issues and sources of popular unrest in Latin American countries. The new democratic regimes are often accused of not being able to cope with the growth of crime in the cities.[28] Second, the control of organized crime, especially crime involving drugs and corruption, has become a key issue in these democracies. Both problems are related to judicial performance.

Some observers of these problems in Latin America have accused the judiciary of being inefficient in dealing with regular crime and coping with organized crime. From this perception springs another demand for judicial reform, sometimes expressed dramatically. For example, President Fujimori of Peru interrupted the functioning of the other branches of government on April 5, 1992. One of his arguments was that the judiciary was corrupt and inefficient to such a degree that it was provoking the loss of prestige of democracy and law. Fujimori intervened in the judiciary and removed many judges.[29] Another example is the frustrated Venezuelan *coup d'état* of February 1992, where one of the main grievances of the rebelling soldiers was the complete lack of confidence in the Supreme Court and the incapacity of the judges to cope with corruption.

The critics and reformers of criminal justice who are promoting more efficiency against crime have been joined by liberal groups concerned about the gaps between due process and criminal procedures in Latin American countries. For years these groups have denounced violations of human rights, including the number of prisoners held without a final criminal verdict in Latin American prisons. Although among the two groups there is some tension, they constitute a common reform movement, seeking efficiency in crime repression and protection of the rights of the accused. International agencies, especially from the U.S., have supported these efforts.

These changes in the Latin America criminal justice system can be characterized as changes in structure, procedure, and ideology. They are an effort to move from the written and inquisitorial model of criminal justice that most countries inherited from the Spanish tradition to an oral procedure in which there is direct involvement of a judge in the main stages of the trial. There is also a widespread effort to reorganize the public prosecutor's offices, and especially to provide them with better means to investigate crime and to control the police.[30]

To what extent these are good news for the poor or other underprivileged groups is difficult to say, both because of the complexity of the issues involved and because most reforms are at an early stage of legislative discussion or implementation.[31] The poor in Latin America are certainly among the most frequent victims of crime;[32] thus, if the system for sanctioning crime becomes more efficient and crime diminishes, the poor should theoretically be better off. However, the reforms have not yet reached the point where it is possible to accurately measure their impact on the crime rate. On the other hand, those accused of crime by the police and tried by the criminal judicial system are nearly all poor. The poor are the main clients of the criminal system and the primary victims of its excesses and human rights violations.[33] It is in their interests if police brutality is decreased by the public prosecutors' new roles; it is against their interests if the perceived need for security in the cities increases illegal repression and civil authorities continue to tolerate it.

The Reforms and the Underprivileged in Latin America

The aforementioned efforts are not all of the judicial reforms being tried in Latin America, but the preceding discussion is a fair description, together with some explanation of their causes, of the most important and common ones.

Do these reforms mean good news for the underprivileged? In this chapter, I have been able to mention the poor of Latin America only twice as having some relation to these reforms. I have not mentioned them as part of an organized movement promoting reform, as a group whose interests inspire the reforms, or as a target sector to be beneficially affected by them. One could explore more subtle relations between the poor and the reforms of the judiciary than I have attempted here. Also, one could focus on other judicial reforms more closely related to the poor, such as the creation of *Defensores del Pueblo,* or people's advocates, and various efforts to strengthen the systems of public defense. However, these are not the areas where most of the resources are being directed in Latin America.

The fact is that one could give a general description of the most important reforms of judicial systems in Latin America, analyzing their causes and goals, without ever referring to the poor as relevant actors. A preliminary and not very optimistic conclusion would be that judicial reforms in Latin America are definitively linked more with the opening of markets than with any other factor. They are not provoked by underprivileged groups, and they do not have those groups as targets. One should only hope for some minor side effects that may benefit underprivileged groups. Yet, such a conclusion has to be qualified; there is too much focus on judicial reform and probably too little attention to the changes that such reforms may ultimately produce.

If I were to talk of one great shift in the judicial systems of Latin America, I would say that there is a shift of power and of fora of decision making and dispute resolution. All I can attempt here is a description of this shift and a short analysis of the risks and opportunities that the situation entails for the poor.

What Is Changing?

The most important change in Latin America involves the role of governments. Throughout most of the twentieth century, groups that were marginalized came into the political system and gained social benefits through political organization and participation. Political parties and a share of governmental power was the most important way through which numerous Latin Americans achieved some power and a share of the social benefits, such as housing, health care, and education. Today, however, governments are radically diminishing their roles. They are also becoming less important as fora for participation and as vehicles of social mobilization. The era of the welfare state in Latin America is coming to an end. Most of the decision-making processes and much of the power the government is losing is being transferred to the market. The market is now the main forum where groups advance their interests and resolve their conflicts.

This is bad news for the poor. Markets are not the best place for the poor to fight for their causes. For the underprivileged, it is in the marketplace that their weakness is most eloquently displayed. The losers in the market must find other arenas where they can demand better conditions, and this venue is often advanced under the rhetoric of social justice and human dignity. While this type of argument does not count in the marketplace, it may count in public institutions.

Throughout the twentieth century in Latin America, governments, political parties, and various public institutions were places where the language of social justice and human dignity was used. The underprivileged learned for more than fifty years how to integrate into society and to achieve social benefits through those political channels. But as previously noted, today these political channels have lost most of their weight. The judiciary, which in the Latin American tradition has not been an important forum for the underprivileged to voice their demands, may finally become, under the new conditions, an important place to advance social justice. This assertion is more than wishful thinking. There are some recent signs that underprivileged groups are taking their causes and cases to the judicial system in order to improve their situation. For example, there are cases in which public interest law and public interest litigation has been used to advance the interests of underprivileged groups.[34]

Using the judiciary to protect the underprivileged is new in Latin America. Litigation to protect and publicly promote the cause of human rights in defense of the dissidents of military regimes during the 1970s, especially in Chile, may be highlighted as an early example. In Argentina, there are a number of cases that have been adjudicated in order to protect minorities. There are also a number of cases of police brutality that were tried in the courts as public interest litigation. In Central America, Brazil, and the Caribbean, cases are being brought to the courts in order to protect indigenous groups and the environment. Colombia has had active public interest litigation in the courts on the issue of environmental protection. In Peru, there are cases of public interest law in the areas of human rights and consumer protection. These cases are novel, and not yet an important feature of public life in Latin America. Yet they may constitute a trend that should be followed closely. For the underprivileged, they may mean the most important institutional change in the Latin American judicial systems.

Limits and Opportunities of This Emerging Trend

It is too early to analyze in full the opportunities and limits that the new practices of using the judicial forum entail for the advancement of the interests of the underprivileged. The judiciary is a forum where arguments of fairness, equality, discrimination, and injustice may find a proper place. At the same time, using the judiciary to advance socioeconomic rights represents serious risks, especially in countries where judges are not accustomed to hearing arguments based on social science data or foreseeing the general effects that a particular decision produces on society. One could wonder if a forum that has traditionally not been accustomed to public interest litigation will be able to cope wisely with the new problems. One could also ask if the judiciary has not lost too much legitimacy in the eyes of the underprivileged for them to use it.

   If the picture presented in this chapter is correct, the judiciary is being reformed in Latin America in order to respond to various social demands for a wider and stronger role. Even though such a role is not being demanded by underprivileged groups or adopted in order to protect them, these groups may nonetheless benefit from the process. If reforms result in a stronger judiciary, with judges being more independent and attuned to democratic values, then the underprivileged of Latin America may find a new forum to advance their interests.

   Furthermore, the judicial forum has two procedural characteristics that may become very important in cases involving the protection of the underprivileged. First, in the judicial process the parties have to confront each other. This means that powerful groups are not able to simply ignore the arguments of the underprivileged. They have to confront them. This is not a minor issue when one is talking of the demands of groups that are systematically marginalized in public discussion. Second, in the judicial process the parties must base their arguments on shared principles or norms. The judicial forum may thus give a voice to the underprivileged that is not heard in the marketplace or the political arena. Finally, in order to add corrections and limits to the outcome of the competition, in the judicial forum the poor can use the same rhetoric that is so common to courts and lawyers: the language of discrimination.

NOTES

1. The *Consejos de la Magistratura* or *Consejos del Poder Judicial* are conceived as bodies created to govern the judicial branch. Their role is to participate, in a relevant way, in the appointment of superior judges, to exercise some disciplinary role over the judiciary, to prepare and propose the judicial budget, to deal with court administration, including general supervision of it and the making of proposals for its improvement, to direct or supervise educational programs for judges, and the like.

Normally these bodies are composed of representatives of the three branches of government. Such composition is designed, on the one hand, to avoid judicial isolation. Because of this goal, the *Consejos* are not composed exclusively of judges, so that the views of people from outside the judiciary and with direct or indirect popular representation are integrated. On the other hand, it is a way to protect judicial independence, making sure that judicial appointments or the public policies on judicial matters are not only in the hands of politicians, but partially in the hands of the judges. In many Latin American countries, the creation of the *Consejos* has been part of the agendas for initiating or consolidating democracy.

For a comparative overview of the role of the *Consejos* in Latin America, *see* MARIO VERDUGO MARINKOVIC, LOS CONSEJOS DE LA MAGISTRATURA EN LATINOAMÉRICA Y EL PROYECTO CHILENO SOBRE LA INSTITUCIÓN (Cuadernos de Trabajo, Departamento de Investigación, Santiago: Universidad Diego Portales, 1992); Héctor Fix Zamudio, *Gobierno y Administración de los Tribunales. El Consejo de la Magistratura*, paper presented at the seminar *Justicia y Sociedad*, Mexico, D.F., Sept. 1993. For an overview of the same institution in European countries, *see* Andrés De la Oliva Santos, *El Consejo de Magistratura en España*, in JUSTICIA Y SOCIEDAD (Universidad Nacional Autónoma de Mexico, 1994); Augusto Víctor Coelho, *El Consejo de Magistratura en*

Portugal, in JUSTICIA Y SOCIEDAD, *id.*; and Giovanni Giacoblie, *El Consejo de Magistratura en Italia*, in JUSTICIA Y SOCIEDAD, *id.* For an interesting critical analysis of the topic, *see* EUGENIO RAÚL ZAFFARONI, DIMENSIÓN POLÍTICA DE UN PODER JUDICIAL DEMOCRÁTICO (Quito: Corporación Latinoamericana para el Dessarrollo, 1994).

2. The following chart shows the countries that have a constitutional or legal provision that guarantees that a certain percentage of the state budget is applied to the judiciary. The second column shows the amount of such percentage, as guaranteed in the constitution. The third column shows the amount really expended in the judiciary in those same countries in 1994.

Country	% of the State Budget Guaranteed to the Judiciary in the Constitution	% of the State Budget Effectively Expended on the Judiciary in 1994
Costa Rica	6%	5.5%
El Salvador	No less than 6%	3.6%
Guatemala	No less than 2%	1.8%
Honduras	No less than 3%	1.0%
Panama	2%	0.5%
Bolivia	3%*	N.A.
Paraguay	No less than 3%	2.4%
Ecuador	2.5%**	N.A.

* The constitution talks of "a percentage," not fixing its amount. The *Ley de Organización Judicial* established that percentage at 3 percent. That was suspended through the budget law.
** Only in a legal provision valid for years 1994 to 1996.

3. Some of the countries that have recently changed in a significant way the rules governing the career of their judges, or the way they are appointed, are the following:
  • Argentina reformed its Constitution in 1994. Through the creation of the *Consejo de la Magistratura*, the system for judicial appointments should change. It is not yet in force.
  • Uruguay repealed its *Consejo* when the country returned to a democratic system.
  • Immediately after their return to democracy, most countries in Central America amended their constitutional provisions related to judicial appointments and established rules for a judicial career. That was the case of El Salvador and Panama in 1991, Honduras in 1992, and Guatemala in 1985. In Costa Rica, a major reform was made in 1993.
  • In Colombia, major changes were introduced in the systems of judicial appointments with the creation of the *Consejo Superior de la Judicatura* in 1991.
  • In Paraguay, the system changed in 1992.
  • In Ecuador, there should be changes to adapt the legislation on judicial appointments to the constitutional reform of 1992.
  • In Chile, there were changes on the system of judicial career in 1995, especially on the way judges are selected and their work is evalu-

ated. The constitution was not changed. In 1997, a bill was being discussed in Congress to change the composition of the Supreme Court.

• In Peru, judges were removed or declared removable after the *Fujimorazo* in April 1992.

4. The next chart shows the status of criminal procedure rules in most Latin American countries:

Argentina	Relevant reform approved in 1991
Costa Rica	Reformed in 1973. New projects being discussed
El Salvador	Reformed in 1973, and again in 1997
Guatemala	Reformed in 1973. New projects under discussion
Nicaragua	Changed in 1979
Honduras	Changed in 1984
Panama	Changed in 1984
Colombia	Reforms, especially dealing with the creation of independent public prosecutors, being implemented
Chile	A major reform presently being discussed in Congress. A constitutional amendment was passed in 1997 creating the Ministerio Público.

5. Some of the Latin American countries that have recently created judicial schools are as follows: Costa Rica established its judicial school in 1964, El Salvador in 1991, Guatemala in 1992, Honduras in 1991, and Panama in 1993. Bolivia created an *Instituto de Capacitación de la Judicatura y el Ministerio Público* that has not yet performed its role in a regular way. Colombia has its *Escuela Judicial,* called *Rodrigo Lara Bonilla.* In Paraguay, the Constitution of 1992 mandates its creation. In Chile, the *Academia Judicial* was created in 1995 and began functioning for preparation of judges and ongoing education of all the judicial personnel in 1996. Peru has a long-standing tradition of judicial education. It put to work a national school called *Academia de la Magistratura* in 1996. In Uruguay, the *Centro de Estudios Judiciales,* dependent on the Supreme Court, has been developing education for judges, especially to prepare them for adapting to procedural reforms.

6. For a description and appraisal of the Venezuelan Project and generally on the World Bank policy towards judicial reform in Latin America, *see* Lawyers Committee for Human Rights and the Venezuelan Program for Human Rights Education and Action, *Halfway to Reform: The World Bank and the Venezuelan Justice System* (New York: Lawyers Committee for Human Rights, 1996). For a description of World Bank policies, *see* Malcom Rowat, Waleed Malik, & Maria Dakolias, *Judicial Reform in Latin America and the Caribbean,* World Bank Technical Paper no. 280 (Washington, D.C.: World Bank, 1995).

7. For a description of views of the Inter-American Development Bank, *see* Strategic Planning and Operational Policy Department, Frame of Reference for Bank Action in Programs for Modernization of the State and Strengthening of Civil Society (Washington, D.C.: IDB, 1996).

8. SITUACIÓN Y POLÍTICAS JUDICIALES EN AMÉRICA LATINA, Cuadernos de Análisis Jurídico no. 2 (Jorge Correa ed., Santiago: Universidad Diego

274   JUDICIAL REFORMS IN LATIN AMERICA

Portales, 1993). The same skeptical view may be found in *Halfway to Reform*, *supra* note 6; and Jose María Rico, Report to the IDB (Inter-American Development Bank) on judicial reform in Central America, Washington, D.C., IDB (unpublished).

9. The ideology of codification, with its faith in reason, raises optimistic expectations. If law in the codes is clear, operative, just, effective, and capable of regulating almost any relevant case, then the judges' role is reduced to a largely mechanical one.

10. The only exception in Latin America is Peru, which developed some important judicial policies in the period. For an overview of the lack of judicial policies in Chile, *see* Jorge Correa Sutil, *Formación de Jueces para la Democracia*, in FILOSOFÍA DEL DERECHO Y DEMOCRACIA, REVISTA DE CIENCIAS SOCIALES no. 34/35 (Valparaíso: Universidad de Valparaíso, 1989–90).

11. The picture is homogeneous in Latin America. Costa Rica is an exception with a reasonably stable and independent judiciary. Uruguay has a tradition of a powerful judiciary and a better public image than most other Latin American countries. Chile has had a weak judiciary that played a minor role until the 1980s. Nevertheless, it has been very stable and has a high standard of independence, even from political interference. For an analysis of Chilean judicial independence, *see* Jorge Correa Sutil, *The Judiciary and the Political System in Chile: The Dilemmas of Judicial Independence during the Transition to Democracy*, in TRANSITION TO DEMOCRACY IN LATIN AMERICA (Irwin P. Stotzky ed., Boulder: Westview Press, 1993). Argentina is a complex case. With no regulated judicial career and with a tradition of political interference on the Supreme Court, it has had a tradition of stability in the lower courts and a high number of judicial appointments of individuals that come from the judicial career and are recommended by superior judges. Probably one of the most important risks of the judiciary of the countries of the Southern Cone is a corporative isolated spirit among its members. For a description of this phenomenon, *see* EUGENIO R. ZAFFARONI, ESTRUCTURAS JUDICIALES (Buenos Aires: EDIAR, 1994); and Correa Sutil, *The Judiciary and the Political System in Chile, supra*.

12. For an overview of the relation between transition to democracy and the issue of dealing with past human rights, *see* TRANSITIONAL JUSTICE: HOW EMERGING DEMOCRACIES RECKON WITH FORMER REGIMES (Neil J. Kritz ed., vol. 1, Washington, D.C.: U.S. Institute of Peace Press, 1995). Especially related to this topic are the articles by José Zalaquett, Guillermo O'Donnell, Philippe C. Schmitter, David Pion-Berlin, and Ruti Teitel included in TRANSITIONAL JUSTICE, *id. See also* TRANSITIONAL JUSTICE AND THE RULE OF LAW IN NEW DEMOCRACIES (A. James McAdams ed., University of Notre Dame Press, 1997).

13. Catalina Smulovitz, *Ciudadanos, Derecho y Política*, in LAS ACCIONES DE INTERÉS PÚBLICO (Felipe Gonzalez ed., Santiago: Cuaderno de Análisis Jurídico Serie Publicaciones Especiales, no. 7, 1997).

14. In the case of Chile, for the relation between the role played by judges during the military regime and the efforts deployed to reform the ju-

diciary during the first period of transition to democracy, *see* Jorge Correa Sutil, *No Victorious Army Has Ever Been Prosecuted*, in TRANSITIONAL JUSTICE AND THE RULE OF LAW IN NEW DEMOCRACIES, *supra* note 12.

15. For a brief overview of judicial careers in Latin America, *see* LUIS SALAS & JOSÉ MARÍA RICO, CARRERA JUDICIAL EN AMÉRICA LATINA (San José: CAJ, 1990).

The status of judicial stability and recent relevant changes in the norms related to judicial careers are shown in the following chart:

Country	Year of the most recent reform	Main subject of the reform or actual status of a judicial career.
Costa Rica	1993	After a year in office judges cannot be removed.
Honduras	1992	Provisions have changed in order to guarantee a career. To be seen if effective against a long-lasting tradition of political intervention.
Panama	1991	Judges cannot be removed.
Guatemala	1985	No laws make effective constitutional general provisions guaranteeing independence.
Venezuela		No legal changes have been effective to put an end to traditional political interventions in Venezuelan judiciary.
Peru	1992	Judges are actually removed by a body designated by political authorities.
Bolivia		A tradition of political intervention in the judiciary.
Chile	1994	A judicial career since the nineteenth century. Most recent changes deal especially with the way judges are periodically evaluated by their peers in superior courts. A change in the way Supreme Court judges are appointed should be approved in 1997.
Colombia	1991	The creation of the *Consejo Superior de la Judicatura* gives this body the right to appoint judges. They cannot be removed.
Paraguay	1992	The new constitution establishes independence of the judiciary and lifetime tenure. Traditionally judges have been elected every five years, which makes them highly vulnerable to political majorities.
Ecuador	1992	Notwithstanding constitutional provisions, judges are highly dependent on the political leaders.
Argentina	1994	There is a high degree of *de facto* participation of the sitting judges in the nomination of new judges. The performance of the *Consejo* created in the new constitutional reform is to be seen. It is not yet functioning due to political tension about its integration. A tradition of presidential intervention in the removal of the Supreme Court judges every time the country loses or recovers democracy.

16. For an explanation of these terms, *see* note 1, *supra*.

17. The Venezuelan *Consejo* has been frequently accused of strengthening

political intervention in the judiciary. In Colombia, the activity of the *Consejo Superior de la Judicatura* has created frictions with the Supreme Court.

18. For a description of this trend in Colombia, *see* EDUARDO VELEZ ET AL., JUECES Y JUSTICIA EN COLOMBIA (Bogotá: Instituto Ser de Investigación, 1987); for the case of Argentina, *see* MARTÍNEZ A. CAVAGNA ET AL., EL PODER JUDICIAL DE LA NACIÓN: UNA PROPUESTA DE CONVERSIÓN (Buenos Aires: La Ley, 1994); in the case of Chile, *see* Carlos Peña González, *Poder Judicial y Sistema Político*, in PODER JUDICIAL EN LA ENCRUCIJADA, Cuadernos de Análisis Jurídico no. 22 (Santiago: Universidad Diego Portales, 1992).

19. Universidad Externado de Colombia, *La Administración de Justicia en Argentina, Bolivia, Ecuador, Jamaica, México, Panama, Paraguay y Uruguay*, in JUSTICIA Y DESARROLLO EN AMÉRICA LATINA Y EL CARIBE (Washington, D.C.: IDB, 1993).

20. See *supra* note 2.

21. To a large extent, the *Justicia de Paz* in Peru has been a popular creation, recognized by the central state, rather than created by it. This is certainly the case of the *Rondas Campesinas*. For a bibliography of Peruvian systems of popular justice, *see* HANS J. BRANDT, JUSTICIA POPULAR: NATIVOS CAMPESINOS (Lima: Centro de Investigaciones Judiciales de la Corte Suprema de Justicia, Fundación Friedrich Naumann, 1986); and HANS J. BRANDT, EN NOMBRE DE LA PAZ COMUNAL: UN ANÁLISIS DE LA JUSTICIA DE PAZ EN EL PERU (Lima: Fundación Friedrich Naumann, 1990).

22. For an overview of this trend, and the strong support of the Inter-American Development Bank, *see* Nestor-Humberto Martínez Neira, *El BID y la Administración de la Justicia*, in JUSTICIA Y DESARROLLO EN AMÉRICA LATINA Y EL CARIBE, *supra* note 19; *Primer Encuentro Interamericano sobre Resolución Alternativa de Disputas, Reporte Final* (Buenos Aires: National Center for State Courts, Fundación Libra, 1994).

23. The presidential decree declaring mediation an issue of national interest is no. 1480 of 1992, *cited in* Carlos Manuel Garrido, *Informe sobre Argentina*, in SITUACIÓN Y POLÍTICAS JUDICIALES EN AMÉRICA LATINA, *supra* note 8.

24. In Uruguay there is a constitutional provision requiring conciliation or settlement efforts in the Peace Court system before bringing a civil suit. Juan Enrique Vargas, in a report to IDB, cites an unpublished paper, *Mediación, Negociación y Conciliación*, by Luis Torello, then president of the Uruguayan Supreme Court. In this paper, this authority states that the statistics show that the functioning of this system, especially the one of previous conciliation, has not reached the desired results. The constitution of Costa Rica establishes the right to arbitration. In 1993 the Supreme Court of this country, with the help of USAID, created a program in alternative dispute resolution. In Paraguay, Ecuador, El Salvador, Guatemala, Honduras, Bolivia, and Panama, there are legal provisions for encouraging arbitration and settlement of disputes during the judicial process, apparently with few effective results. In Colombia, after the constitutional reform of 1991, there have been efforts to stimulate programs of alternative dispute resolution. They

have been developed in arbitration, centers for settlement of disputes, the capacity of police officers to settle minor offenses, and the bargaining process authorized in the public prosecutor's office. Argentina had some failed experiments with settlement of disputes by judges, and in 1995 started a program for transferring disputes from the courts to mediation centers outside the courts before continuing the judicial procedures. Chile has a well-established tradition of arbitration, especially of commercial disputes. On the other hand, the efforts to make judges settle disputes have been quite ineffective, except in labor and family courts. There are some interesting experiences of mediation in legal aid offices, and recently in family disputes.

25. This is especially true in the cases of Colombia and Chile. Smulovitz, *supra* note 13.

26. For an overview of judicial education programs in Latin America, *see* SITUACIÓN Y POLÍTICAS JUDICIALES EN AMÉRICA LATINA, *supra* note 8; EUGENIO R. ZAFFARONI, ESTRUCTURAS JUDICIALES, *supra* note 11; and MARÍA JOSEFINA HAEUSSLER, EXPERIENCIAS COMPARADAS DE FORMACIÓN JUDICIAL (Santiago: Corporación de Promoción Universitaria, 1993).

27. For an analysis of the goals and a critical approach of expectations on judicial education, *see* Jorge Correa Sutil, *Capacitación y Carrera Judicial en Hispanoamérica*, in JUSTICIA Y SOCIEDAD, *supra* note 1.

28. For a description of this phenomenon in six Latin American countries, *see* ACCESO DE LOS POBRES A LA JUSTICIA (Franz Vanderschueren & Enrique Oviedo, eds., Santiago: Ediciones Sur, 1995).

29. In his address the day President Fujimori decided to close the Congress and intervene in the judiciary, he stated that "corruption and political influence has come to a stage where it is present throughout all the instances of the judiciary." "In Peru," he added, "justice has always been a commodity that you buy or sell at the best price the parties can pay." Lorenzo Zolezzi, *Informe sobre Peru*, in SITUACIÓN Y POLÍTICAS JUDICIALES EN AMÉRICA LATINA, *supra* note 8.

30. For some of the efforts to reform the public prosecutor's office, see the articles included in chapter 2 of the book JUSTICIA Y SOCIEDAD, *supra* note 1; *see also* EL MINISTERIO PÚBLICO (Santiago: Corporación de Promoción Universitaria, 1994).

31. *See supra* note 4 for a chart describing the most recent changes in criminal procedure. For description of these reforms, *see* REFORMAS PROCESALES EN AMÉRICA LATINA (Santiago: Corporación de Promoción Universitaria, 1993).

32. ACCESO DE LOS POBRES A LA JUSTICIA, *supra* note 28.

33. *Id. See also* EUGENIO R. ZAFFARONI, SISTEMAS PENALES Y DERECHOS HUMANOS EN AMÉRICA LATINA (Buenos Aires: Depalma, 1986).

34. *See* LAS ACCIONES DE INTERÉS PÚBLICO, *supra* note 13.

18

Access to Justice for the Poor in Latin America

Alejandro M. Garro

LAW IS SUPPOSED TO WORK as the great equalizer, because rich and poor alike are free to vindicate their rights in court in order to obtain "equal justice under the law." The ability of those with few resources to access the courts has been used as a key measurement of the level of consolidation of an accountable democracy.[1] Access to justice is also critical for small and medium-size businesses attempting to enforce contracts, establish accountability for wrongful acts, defend intellectual property rights, and vindicate basic constitutional rights. The significance of "access to justice" needs to be reconsidered in light of the globalization and deregulation of the economies of Latin American countries. Their recent experience with economic change, by moving from a state-directed to a free-market model, brought home the relevance of "legal security" and access to justice as essential components of sustainable economic development.[2] The persistence of traditional patterns of income inequality, now aggravated by the short-term impact of neoliberal economic policies, suggests that subsidized programs of legal assistance to the poor might play some role in assuring more equitable patterns of income distribution.[3] There is, therefore, more than one reason to be concerned with "access to justice."

In modern legal systems, the claim for access to justice operates under the assumption that in a civilized society the state should guarantee its citizens the possibility of vindicating their rights, whether against fellow citizens or the state itself. Modern liberal democracies proclaim that access to justice is a fundamental right, which may be characterized as a civil and political right on the one hand, or as a "social" and "economic" right on the other. But leaving aside academic discussions and lofty proclamations, the finest legal system in the world would still not provide justice if most people did not have access to it. Courts and legal services are in theory available to all, just like the Sheraton Hotel—anybody can enter, all that is needed is money.[4] The truth of the matter is that justice is an expensive commodity, even in those countries with the highest levels of education and a generous allocation of expenditure in social welfare.[5] In Latin America in particular, the sad truth is that the machinery of justice has historically been beyond the reach of the mass of the population, which happens to receive a small part of the national income.

The term itself, "access to justice," implies that "justice" is imparted by some people or institutions, and that there are obstacles in the way to reach those people and institutions. Both in rural and urban areas, the poor have virtually no access to legal services, courts, and formal legal institutions. Out of ignorance, lack of bargaining power, cynicism, or even fear that the judicial machinery (which is assumed to be manipulated by elitist power interests) will operate against them, lack of confidence in the judiciary is a pervasive problem in Latin America,[6] particularly on the part of low-income citizens.[7] This perception is a reflection, rather than a cause, of how limited the service of administration of justice has been for the poor. "Access" and "justice," however, may be given a meaning beyond formal access to subsidized programs, lawyers, courts, and the judicial process. If we include the many varieties of preventive legal advice and collective legal actions on behalf of vulnerable sectors of society, access to and use of those kind of legal services is even more rare and difficult.

Despite this somber scenario, one is unlikely to encounter much debate in Latin America as to whether access to justice should be guaranteed to all. "Equality before the law" has been traditionally declared by the constitutions, the organized bar, and the judiciary in Latin America as an essential component of the administration of justice. Giving the poor effective participation in the legal processes is widely thought to be necessary in order for the legal system to live up to its written standards. All Latin American legal systems profess commitments to the legal equality of their citizens and to the rule of law, and several programs of legal assistance for the poor have been in place for quite a long time in most countries of the region.[8] However, rules and principles as to how institutions are supposed to work are poor indications of what actually happens. This gap between theory and practice may be present everywhere, but idiosyncratic Latin American particularisms regarding actual enforcement of the law have aggravated the problems surrounding access to justice for the poor.[9]

Because the terms of the debate on "access to justice" are not centered on whether the poor should have access to justice, but rather on how to make it more accessible, the focus of this chapter is accordingly narrowed to discuss the different approaches that have been adopted and their potential to make a difference. Thus, the purpose of this chapter is not to discuss the plans for legal aid that are in place (which have been inadequate for one reason or another), but rather to reflect on those approaches that have the greatest chance to make a difference. A related subject is the relationship between "access to justice" from the perspective of legal assistance programs for the poor and the ongoing programs of legal reform in Latin America. To what extent do the needs for legal assistance and the overall success of legal aid programs depend on the judicial processes within which courts and lawyers operate?

The answer to this question is that overall changes in the legal system and the judicial process are an essential component of any legal aid program. In jurisdictions where the administration of justice is characterized by extensive and formalistic procedural requirements, an equally extensive bureaucracy and its attendant costs pose the greatest obstacles to access to justice for the poor. Even under a body of well-conceived regulations for legal assistance to the poor, and under the most generous efforts of government subsidy for legal aid, the level of economic growth and concomitant welfare state development of most countries of the region is unlikely to satisfy the massive need of legal assistance. Legal aid probably could not survive without subsidy, but whatever the type of legal assistance program in place, its benefits will not reach the majority of society's marginal elements unless the problems of access are tackled as part of those that affect the legal system as a whole. If access to justice is viewed as part of an overall process of change, in which civil society and political actors become actively involved, then legal assistance programs, coupled with legal and judicial reform, are likely to secure some relief from social injustice.

The first part of this chapter presents a typology of legal services programs, discussing, in terms of their efficacy, the different kinds of legal services for the poor that have been in place in most Latin American countries. The second part argues that the traditional goal of these services has been individually focused, reactive, and court-oriented, thus incapable of having a substantial impact on the high demands for access to justice for the poor. The third and final part presents an outline of those areas of institutional reform which, if conceived as essential components of an overall process of facilitating access to justice by the poor, are most likely to produce a significant change for disadvantaged groups in Latin America.

Typology of Existing Legal Service Programs

The available literature on legal services programs in Latin America resorts to various classification criteria in order to describe different approaches to legal aid for the poor. Each of these programs attempts in its own way to provide effective participation in the legal process, but most are poorly organized, overburdened, understaffed, and generally underfinanced. Not surprisingly, these legal aid programs reach only a small number of the poor.

One of the criteria for distinguishing among different programs of legal assistance is based on the areas of the country served by those legal aid plans. Accordingly, one may distinguish between legal services aimed at reaching marginal sectors of society living in urban squatter settlements adjoining major Latin American cities (e.g., the *barrios* of Caracas, *pueblos jóvenes* of Lima, *villas miserias* of Buenos Aires, or *favelas* of Rio de Janeiro), as opposed to programs aimed at the more remote rural areas. The bulk of the poor live outside the market economy, and penetration of the formal legal structure into rural communities is usually either incomplete or nonexistent. Real power lies in the hands of local landholders; most disputes are settled, if at all, by the *patrón* or local leaders.[10] Because members of the legal profession are clustered in the cities, as are the influential bar associations and universities, most of the organized legal aid plans in Latin America function only in the nation's capital or in the provincial capitals.[11] Very few legal services reach down to the rural interior.[12]

Another method of distinguishing among legal aid programs is based on the subject matter of the dispute or specific claim. Thus, one may distinguish among the legal services available to criminal defendants, workers, tenants (whose claims may be related to agricultural land or to urban housing), indigenous peoples, women (with claims often relating to alimony, domestic violence, rape, or other gender issues), and other low-income people who are likely to bring long-standing claims to basic services in such areas as health and public utilities. Within a similar range of low-income populations, some groups face a disproportionately higher barrier to justice than other social groups. Women, for example, are not only more likely to be poorer than men, but they also experience higher levels of illiteracy.[13] They are generally at the center of family disputes, which constitute as much as one-third of the cases handled by courts in Latin America.[14] Access to justice to indigenous peoples is impeded not only by poverty and lack of familiarity with the official court system, but also by language barriers,[15] so that in this particular field, access to justice also entails availability of adequate translation services.

Legal aid programs have also been distinguished according to the institution that sponsors the program of legal services. Thus, one may refer to programs of legal aid sponsored by the government (at the national, state/provincial, or municipal level); those relying on the court-assigned counsel system (also referred to as the judicare system); those provided in the context of clinical education programs run by law schools; and those provided by bar associations, church-supported community groups, and other nongovernmental organizations focusing on legal representation of the most vulnerable groups in society.

The typical publicly-funded program relies on lawyers paid by the state on a full-time basis. These are government-provided lawyers (*fiscales* or *procuradores*) who staff the office of the Public Ministry or other departments of the central or local government. Legal services provided by public-salaried attorneys are the most popular in Latin America. Criminal defendants (whether poor or not) may be entitled to free legal representation by a public defender (*defensor de oficio, defensor oficial*) in order to implement the constitutional guarantee of the right to counsel.[16] Some jurisdictions include government-provided lawyers not only for criminal defendants, but also for other vulnerable groups such as minors, workers, and rural or indigenous populations.[17] Almost invariably, the quality of the legal representation provided by these government lawyers is very low[18]—the office of the public defender is likely to be understaffed and overburdened[19] and the nature of the public defender's function or service is often negatively perceived by both the public defender and the person whom he or she represents.[20] The public-salaried model is also in crisis in the United States, especially after Congress cut much of the funding and placed several restrictions on the Legal Services Corporation, which since 1974 had been representing the poor in civil matters.[21]

State-supported legal services employing attorneys who work on a part-time basis also report an immense caseload.[22] In some jurisdictions, government-funded plans of legal aid rely on the bar associations to provide the poor with legal assistance, either on the basis of *pro bono* representation assumed by bar members or with the support of the government.[23] However, even in Chile, a country referred to as a leader in Latin America in terms of legal programs for the poor, where this type of service has been in place the longest with a relative degree of success, it is widely acknowledged that staff attorneys are undercompensated and overburdened with a heavy workload.[24]

The so-called "assigned counsel" or "judicare system" relies on private practitioners appointed by the court. In some countries of Latin America, the judiciary plays a major administrative role in requiring private lawyers to provide free legal assistance in noncriminal cases to "indigent persons." According to this scheme, the court hearing the case is generally responsible for making a determination, after hearing the other party, whether the applicant qualifies as "indigent."[25] Obtaining the privilege to litigate without costs (*beneficio de litigar sin gastos*, also referred to as *amparo de pobreza* or *privilegio de pobreza*) generally hinges upon demonstrating that the case has a sufficient prospect of success and is not frivolously asserted. Some jurisdictions establish a fixed financial ceiling on income to determine whether the applicant can afford to pay legal fees;[26] others apply a flexible test to determine indigence.[27]

In some jurisdictions, the applicant may choose the attorney who will represent him or her without costs and, failing that option, the court makes the appointment from a list-at-large of practicing attorneys in the judicial district. In terms of their level of success in the quality of legal representation, the most relevant distinction among programs of assigned counsel or judicare appears to be based on whether the program provides for compensation of the attorneys or simply relies on their volunteer services. Not surprisingly, jurisdictions which provide for compensation of the attorneys serving the poor are likely to succeed in providing more effective legal aid than those purely relying on the voluntary or enlisted services of the legal community.[28]

Legal aid lawyers may and do, however, receive some compensation through shifting fees of litigation to the losing party. This is called the "English rule" in the United States, though it is practiced in most civil-law countries, in which the costs of litigation borne by the loser include the payment of the attorney's fees of the winning party. Those who qualify for assistance are exempted from the payment of attorney's fees if they lose the case, although in some jurisdictions the assisted person who lost the case may still have to pay filing fees, stamp taxes, and bear other costs such as those of his or her own witnesses and experts.[29] On the other hand, if the assisted party wins, the assigned counsel is entitled to recover the value of their fee from the losing party. The court-assigned counsel mostly operates in labor disputes and those involving domestic relations, such as divorce, alimony, or child support. In those cases, the prospects of winning the case and recovering attorney's fees does not operate as a sufficient financial incentive in relation to the amount of work required from counsel.[30]

Clinical education programs run by law schools provide another organizational scheme aimed at broadening access to justice by the poor. In some jurisdictions in Latin America, law schools provide for different clinical programs that function on a voluntary basis; other jurisdictions have established such programs as a compulsory requirement for university graduation (Trinidad and Tobago);[31] and still other jurisdictions impose this requirement after graduation as a prerequisite to be admitted to practice (Chile).[32] Although these clinical education programs have obvious advantages in terms of organizational independence, many of them have faced serious financial constraints.[33] Admittedly, legal aid plans relying on law school clinics have a twofold objective: to provide practical training to the students and to provide legal advice and representation to the poor. However, the success of these programs has been mostly measured in terms of the educational experience gained by students, rather than in terms of their actual success in meeting legal needs affecting the poor.[34]

In some Latin American countries, legal aid projects have been sponsored by nongovernmental organizations who attempt to organize and provide legal assistance to various poverty groups. Some of these private organizations provide legal aid to criminal defendants, workers, tenants, women, peasants, and indigenous peoples, as well as to poor dwellers in the large metropolitan areas who are squatters on government or private land.[35] Without any financial support from the government or bar associations, lawyers for nongovernmental organizations provide as much honest and competent legal assistance as they can. The emergence of these new interest groups is noteworthy and is expected to grow.[36] However, the absence of a tradition of charitable giving and of public-interest lawyering severely limits the capacity of these privately-funded organizations to reach the poor.

Traditional Goals of Legal Services for the Poor

Most of the legal services programs outlined above are geared either towards defending individual claims in court or administrative proceedings or in bringing judicial complaints for the purpose of securing a specific individual gain or avoiding a specific individual loss. Thus, the overall scheme of legal aid is basically reactive, in the sense that services are provided to the poor on an individual basis and for the purpose of generating access to the courts through free or affordable representation. Legal services thus provided are therefore directed toward courtroom work. This approach, individually focused and court-oriented, though capable of correcting injustices in individual cases, is unlikely to bring equal justice to the poor.[37]

Providing the poor with free counseling and representation, assuring their day in court, is consistent with constitutional mandates of due process and the traditional role of the lawyer, i.e., an advocate who is trained to manipulate technical and abstract doctrines to benefit individual clients. But this type of advocacy is unlikely to have an overall impact on shaping the rules of law for the purpose of increasing the legal bargaining power of the poor. It may suffice to push for the effective enforcement of those rules that favor the poor in an individual case, but the rule thus applied is likely to have little impact because of the traditional gap between the "law in the books" and the "law in action." Some other kind of "legal service" is required in order to actually change the rules and responses which operate against the interests of the poor. Admittedly, it is necessary to ensure the availability of lawyers who advocate an interpretation of the law that fairly takes into account existing inequalities in the distribution of income. Yet it is also necessary to put in place a legal system operated by independent judges who handle disputes under a reasonably expedient judicial process capable of ensuring that existing rules are actually enforced. This requires changes which go beyond legal aid plans.

First, it calls for an image of the lawyer that exceeds that of an advocate in individual cases before courts of law. That image is closer to a policy-minded jurist whose main role is that of a "social engineer" searching for innovative solutions for the poor. Such a role of the lawyer does not imply revolutionary changes, but it does require the active participation of lawyers in programs or initiatives of reform specifically aimed at changing governmental decisions affecting equality of opportunities and distribution of income. Secondly, the lawyering functions envisaged by this proposal call for the emergence of grass-roots organizations capable of bringing collective actions on behalf of poor or marginalized persons. Thirdly, this type of legal service can only be provided within an institutional framework conducive to collective advocacy and favoring the settlement of disputes in a manner that is expedient and fair. In brief, in order to succeed, any governmental or nongovernmental program aimed at increasing access to justice by the poor must be accompanied by institutional reform. It is to the essential features of that program of reform that our attention now turns.

Access to Justice and Institutional Reform

Legal aid, regardless of the form it takes, is a basic but not sufficient attribute of access to justice. Law reform is an essential component of any program aimed at providing legal assistance to the poor, and projects for judicial reform in Latin America, as noted by Correa Sutil, are currently carried out by, or at least are part of the program of, several international agencies.[38] Admittedly, it remains to be seen whether the programs will actually benefit underprivileged groups,[39] but even assuming some misguided efforts on the part of the reformers, any resulting system can hardly be worse than one characterized by long delays, corruption, and tendencies to favor those with deep pockets. Because the threshold hurdle to access to justice is the ignorance of the potential users about their rights, any reform initiative must promote access by addressing the main economic, psychological, informational, and physical barriers that have traditionally impeded access to justice. Then, it is necessary to orient the reform efforts towards a legal system that is worthy of access, because easy and equal access to questionable tribunals operating under questionable rules is unlikely to bolster the rule of law. Finally, it is necessary to provide for legal reforms that allow the legal system to cope with and respond to an increased access.

Several areas calling for institutional reform come to mind. These include reducing the costs of litigation and the causes of delay; establishing expedient and informal proceedings for small claims; promoting greater incentives to reach an early settlement and alternative means of dispute resolution; liberalizing rules of standing; and embracing the ideal of "public interest lawyering" as an essential component of legal education, professional training, and practice of law. A glimpse at each of these areas follows.

Court costs and delays. Incidental costs to litigation include not only attorney's fees, but also filing fees, stamp taxes, and the like, not all of which are fair and affordable in proportion to the type of case and claimant. Excessive costs of litigation in some Latin American countries were already noted in the 1970s Florence Access-to-Justice Project.[40] Excessive court delays in a few other countries have been more recently measured and diagnosed by the World Bank.[41] The reasons why costs are high and cases are delayed are many and complex. Some of the causes relate to the futile ritualistic nature of many rules of procedure aimed at providing due process but actually bogging down cases in a mass of technicalities. Other delays result from interlocutory appeals or complicated rules of evidence. One of the causes of increasing costs of litigation is obviously related to the length of the proceedings, which is related in turn to causes such as complicated or vague laws or the need to regulate the same issues repeatedly due to lack of reliance on precedents.[42] The absence of incentives for plaintiffs or defendants to reach an early settlement also contributes to litigation that drags on for years.[43] Some jurisdictions do not permit contingency fee agreements (*pacto de cuota litis*), thus effectively preventing access to justice to poor plaintiffs with sizable damage claims.[44] Costs of litigation may also include "informal" pecuniary incentives aimed at motivating court personnel. It is well known, though hardly ever documented, that corruption plagues the administration of justice of many Latin American countries.[45] This represents a major threat both to the underprivileged (who are the least likely parties to afford paying bribes) and to the integrity of the justice system.[46] Even if many of the accusations of corruption were unfounded, the absence of a relatively speedy, transparent, and credible judicial process to ascertain undue influence or bribery taints the credibility of justice and erodes even further confidence in the courts.

Procedural reforms aimed at widening access to justice. Many of the problems affecting the poor involve a large number of individuals suffering from similar injuries arising from the same causes. It is not difficult to perceive that the costs of litigation are likely to decrease if one party or organization is entitled to bring a single claim on behalf of the group of plaintiffs considered as a whole. Also the actual and preventive impact of the ruling would increase if such a ruling were to redress not the wrong against one individual but against a whole group of individuals. The technical design and actual implementation of procedures aimed at merging and simultaneously settling a large number of closely related individual claims is one of the greatest and most urgent challenges to increasing judicial access.

Latin American legal systems allow the joinder of plaintiffs against a common defendant (*litisconsorcio activo*) and the joining of different cases (*acumulación de autos*) which have been filed separately, as long as certain requisites have been met (e.g., the claims must be supported by the same facts and share a common cause, they must not be inconsistent, and all of them must independently satisfy the jurisdictional requirements).[47] However, this aggregation of plaintiffs, claims, or suits does not necessarily entail cost advantages or a significant reduction in the length of the proceedings. First, none of the plaintiffs may assume the representation of the group as such, unless and to the extent that each individual plaintiff confers powers of attorney on the representative. Secondly, each individual claim remains substantively distinct despite the joinder, meaning that each plaintiff retains the right to be heard and produce evidence separately, as if the joinder had not taken place. Thirdly and most importantly, the ruling handed down in the case is not binding, and hence has little consequence, on persons not joined in the action but who remain subject to the same threat that affected the plaintiffs who brought the action.[48]

In order to enhance access to justice, Latin American legal systems need to broaden standing to sue as the most cost-effective means to spell out rights to enforce regulations for, and prevent damage to, thousands of people. Enhancing standing to sue is likely to increase the power of the judiciary and change the social policy of the administration. However, it is not altogether clear whether states are willing to accept or ready to cope with the type of class-action suits that has become one of the hallmarks of the American civil justice system. Some kind of procedural mechanism ought to be devised for the representation of "collective" or "diffuse" interests, thus reducing not only psychological and informational barriers, but also minimizing the costs of bringing suits for each individual. Experience has shown that giving power to public prosecutors to independently initiate suits on behalf of the underprivileged (e.g., minors, absentees, and incompetents) or in defense of the "public interest" has largely failed.[49] It is thus necessary to grant standing to associations and nongovernmental organizations (environmentalist, consumer, and human rights groups) so that they may sue on behalf of the public interest or common good.[50]

Establishment of courts and informal proceedings to handle small claims. Another option to reduce case backlogs and improve access to justice is to establish tribunals whose composition and procedure are specifically designed to handle claims up to a certain monetary amount. Experience with small claims courts and neighborhood tribunals in Latin America has been mixed. In some countries, the system of justices of the peace (*juzgados de paz*) or municipal judges, created for the purpose of handling small claims expeditiously, has become increasingly bureaucratized.[51] In other countries, the experience has been extremely favorable.[52] A simplified oral and concentrated procedure, where parties may appear *pro se*, is likely to allow for the settlement of disputes which, due to backlogs and delays in ordinary courts, would be otherwise left without remedy.

Legal reform in certain substantive areas of the law. Access to justice may also be enhanced through the adoption of reforms of substantive law geared towards a more expedient resolution of issues affecting the most vulnerable sectors of society. Labor disputes concern issues such as formalization of employment contracts and unfair termination of employment. Property and contract law often concerns disputes affecting peasants and dwellers of shantytowns which are aimed at securing formal legal title, tenants' rights to agricultural land, or precarious urban settlements.[53] In the area of family law, the most recurrent issues involving the underprivileged are those related to divorce and distribution of marital property,[54] child custody and support, paternity actions,[55] and pension rights. The availability and distribution of rights to drinking water, irrigation, and protection against pollution of the environment also affect the poor. Issues related to police violence, human rights abuses, and crime in general find the poor as its regular clients, be it as victims or accused. Each of these issues cries out for legal reform of the most varied nature which is aimed at simplifying the rules or the proof of facts that are likely to determine the outcome of a dispute. Efforts toward reform must take into account that most protagonists of disputes are unlikely to be informed of their rights or able to afford a lawyer to represent them.

Alternative dispute resolution. Alternative means of dispute resolution (ADR) such as mediation, conciliation, and arbitration are to be encouraged because, depending on the nature of the dispute, they may offer a more attractive option than the conventional, slow, and at times unpredictable judicial process.[56] ADR is an important alternative to the delays or corruption that characterize much of the formal/judicial method of settling disputes. Arguably, resorting to systems of private justice embraced with increasing success by the U.S. entrepreneurial model may single out a first and second level of judicial administration in which the underprivileged are left to settle their disputes in the congested public courts while the privileged enjoy a speedy resolution of their conflicts through ADR. This allegation is too sweeping to detract from the merits of ADR, though it should be considered seriously. First, most methods of ADR are meant to be consensual, and if the mediation is to be imposed as a prerequisite of litigation, the mediator's decision is not binding on the parties. Secondly, the suitability of a particular form of ADR depends much on the nature of the dispute and the parties involved, and it is not meant to replace the public courts in those areas touching matters of public policy which are not arbitratable, e.g., domestic violence and violent crimes. Thirdly, in addition to realizing that ADR is not a panacea to the structural problems affecting the administration of justice, it is even more important to emphasize that ADR is not likely to succeed unless it gains both the understanding and support of the public courts. Indeed, the best approach to experimenting with and gradually introducing mediation and arbitration is through pilot programs sponsored and supervised by the ordinary courts.[57] Recent attempts to introduce ADR in some Latin American jurisdictions have reported a substantial rate of success.[58] Although the establishment of mediation programs is too recent to allow sufficient conclusions as to their success, there is no question that ADR opens a new avenue that is worth pursuing.

Legal education and training. One of the primary problems with access to justice is the absence of legal training specifically geared towards an understanding of legal, economic, and social imbalances, and this deficiency lessens or prevents access to justice by the poor. If lawyers do not perceive themselves as having any role to play in changing the rules responsible for many of the legal problems affecting the poor, this is in large measure the result of the absence of legal training oriented towards public service. Current law school curricula in most Latin American law schools offer little in the way of discussing and examining what law does to and for low-income people. There are no courses on public interest law and the term as such is mostly unknown. Indeed, traditional law school curricula tends to be highly theoretical, divorced from the practicalities of the legal profession and the realities confronted by the poor.[59] The absence of academic perspectives on public interest law and the lack of consciousness on part of the private bar on public interest lawyering should be one of the main areas of concern of justice reform programs in Latin America. After all, the primary responsibility for securing equal justice under the law rests not on legal aid programs, but rather on private lawyers, the organized bar, and nongovernmental organizations. Legal services for the poor and enhanced access to justice are likely to come in the long run more through a new generation of public interest lawyers, sound incremental law reform, increased resort to ADR, and adequate staffing of courts and training of judges, than through "band-aids" provided by subsidized representation of individual indigent plaintiffs or defendants.

NOTES

1. During the decades of military dictatorship, civil war, and authoritarian rule, judicial control of the executive action and protection of civil liberties took a back seat. The democratization process that swept the region during the late 1980s has brought with it a greater realization of the need for a legal system capable of enforcing individual rights against the state. Only when the rule of law was asserted as the basis of legitimate authority did claims for access to justice gain prominence. Much of the initial frustration suffered in the wake of the transitions from authoritarian to democratic regimes was felt in the inability of the newly elected governments to bring to justice those responsible for past human rights abuses.

2. In order to be "efficient," an operational market economy also requires a certain level of fairness to operate, calling for a clearly defined set of property rights, predictable rules of the game, and neutral tribunals for resolving business disputes. Thus, access to fairly independent courts and expedient judicial processes is critical for both large and small businesses attempting to enforce contracts, seek monetary redress against wrongful acts, or obtain injunctions against trademark, patent, or other violations of intellectual property rights.

3. For a conceptual analysis of ways in which legal services for the poor might influence income distribution, *see* David M. Trubek, *Unequal Protection: Thoughts on Legal Services, Social Welfare, and Income Distribution in Latin America*, 13 TEXAS INT'L L. J. (1978).

4. Lord McCluskey, *Problems of Access to Justice in International and National Disputes*, keynote address at the 22nd Biennial Conference of the International Bar Association, Buenos Aires, Sept. 1988. *Reproduced in* INTERNATIONAL LEGAL PRACTITIONER 13 (1988).

5. Erhard Blakenburg, *Comparing Legal Aid Schemes in Europe*, 11 CIVIL JUSTICE QUARTERLY (1992).

6. All surveys attempting to measure public attitudes towards the judiciary in Latin America indicate that the level of public confidence in the judiciary is alarmingly low. *See*, e.g., Eduardo Buscaglia Jr., *Judicial Reform in Latin America: The Obstacles Ahead*, LATIN AMERICAN AFFAIRS 4 (Fall/Winter 1995), World Bank Technical Paper no. 350, which compares the level of public confidence in the judiciary in thirty-five developed and developing countries. All Latin American countries, with the exception of Chile, rank in the bottom 15 percent. Indeed, "[S]urveys conducted in Argentina, Brazil, Ecuador and Peru show that between 55 and 75 percent of the public have a very low opinion of the judicial sector. More specifically, in Argentina, 46 percent of those surveyed perceived the judicial sector as inaccessible. The same occurs in Brazil, Ecuador, and Venezuela, where the percentages are 56, 47, and 67 percent, respectively." *Id.*

7. Thus, it has been reported in Chile that poor people who have had no experience with the judiciary have a 20 percent confidence rate in the judiciary, but those individuals who have had experience with the judiciary have a somewhat improved level of confidence *See* María Dakolias, *A Strategy for Judicial Reform: The Experience in Latin America*, 36 VA. J. INT'L L. 167–68 (1995).

8. For a comprehensive survey of different legal aid programs in Latin America, *see* LEGAL AID AND WORLD POVERTY: A SURVEY OF ASIA, AFRICA, AND LATIN AMERICA 77–131 (C. Foster Knight ed., New York: Praeger, 1974).

9. *See* Guillermo O'Donnell, *Another Institutionalization: Latin America and Elsewhere*, Kellogg Institute Working Paper no. 46 (Kellogg Institute, University of Notre Dame, 1995), referring to clientelism, patronage, nepotism, favors, "*jeitos*," and other "particularisms" which flavor the actual enforcement of formal rules of law. *See also*, with particular reference to the impact of those particularisms in the legal system as a whole, Keith Rosenn, *Brazil's Legal Culture: The Jeito Revisited*, 1 FLA. INT'L L. J. (1985). As to the consequences of these structural or cultural features in the way of doing business and providing legal counsel to U.S. clients, *see* Michael Gordon, *Of Aspirations and Operations: The Governance of Multinational Enterprises by Third World Nations*, 16 INTER-AM. L. REV. (1984); and Eugene Robinson, *The South American Graft*, WASHINGTON POST, Dec. 1990.

10. *See* Dwight B. Heath, *New Patrons for Old: Changing Patron-Client*

Relationships in the Bolivian Yungas, in STRUCTURE AND PROCESS IN LATIN AMERICA: PATRONAGE, CLIENTAGE, AND POWER SYSTEMS 101, 120 (Alan Strickon & Sydney Greenfield eds., Albuquerque: University of New Mexico Press, 1972); KENNETH KARST, MURRAY SCHWARTZ, & AUDREY SCHWARTZ, THE EVOLUTION OF THE LAW IN THE BARRIOS IN CARACAS (Los Angeles: University of California, 1973), *reproduced in part in* LAW AND DEVELOPMENT IN LATIN AMERICA: A CASE BOOK 574–628 (Keith Rosenn & Kenneth Karst eds., Berkeley: University of California Press, 1975).

11. For example, the Peruvian Ministry of Justice has established seven legal aid offices in the city of Lima alone, and only eight additional offices to serve the rest of the country. Dakolias, *supra* note 7, at 208.

12. LEGAL AID AND WORLD POVERTY, *supra* note 8, at 104. There is a scarcity of information with respect to the practice of law in Latin America. Figures on the total number of licensed attorneys may occasionally be found. Luis Bates Hidalgo & Ira Leitel, *Legal Services for the Poor in Chile,* in LEGAL AID AND WORLD POVERTY, *id.* at 132, 134, report a ratio of 400 Chilean lawyers for each million inhabitants in 1970. This figure is quite low if compared with the figures of lawyer density in industrialized countries. Edward Bankenburg, *Comparing Legal Schemes in Europe,* 11 CIVIL JUSTICE Q. 106, 109–10 (April 1992), reports a ratio of 300 California lawyers per 100,000 of the population of the state, and comparable figures of 150 barristers and solicitors per 100,000 inhabitants in England and Wales, 77 in West Germany, and 37 in the Netherlands. These figures in themselves do not have great significance, unless coupled with information as to the functional and territorial distribution of the services and the quality of the professional service provided by these attorneys. Thus, despite the prevalent idea that there is an excess of lawyers in all major capital cities of Latin America, scarcity of legal services may still result from the inadequate distribution of those services with respect to the overall needs, especially the needs of the poor for legal assistance.

13. Latin American women have a 34 percent probability of sharing the bottom 20 percent of the income distribution as compared to a 15 percent probability shared by men. George Psacharopoulos, Samuel Morley, Ariel Fizbein, et al., *La pobreza y la distribución de los ingresos en América Latina: Historia del decenio de 1980,* World Bank Technical Paper no. 350 (Washington, D.C.: World Bank, 1993). Shahid Javed Burki & Sebastión Edwards, *Consolidating Economic Reforms in Latin America and the Caribbean,* FINANCE & DEVELOPMENT 7–8 (March 1995), found that the impact of poverty increases in recent years has fallen the heaviest on Latin American women; that the second most significant factor for determining poverty is gender; and that single women heads of households, likely to be below the poverty line, are now a common phenomenon. According to CARLOS PEÑA GONZÁLEZ, EL ACESO A LA JUSTICIA (1995), 30.5 percent of Chilean women, as compared to 21.7 percent of men, have a low level of knowledge about their rights and the role of the judicial system to protect those rights. A 1995 report from The Comisión Permanente de los Derechos de la Mujer y del Niño notes that

73 percent of the Peruvian population that are illiterate are women, and that women who live in rural areas are even more likely to be disadvantaged educationally than those living in the cities. (Ed. note: see also the chapter by Acosta in this volume.)

14. *See* María Dakolias, *The Judicial Sector in Latin America and the Caribbean: Elements of Reform*, World Bank Technical Paper no. 319 (Washington, D.C.: World Bank, 1996). Disputes involving alimony and custody are reported as the most frequently processed type of claim by the legal aid clinics of the Lima Bar Association. The World Bank, *Peru: Judicial Sector Assessment*, Internal World Bank Document no. 13718-PE (Washington, D.C.: World Bank, 1994).

15. Dakolias, *A Strategy for Judicial Reform, supra* note 7, at 212–13. The Ecuadorean legal system fails to provide translation services for indigenous people who do not understand or speak Spanish. *Id.*

16. Statutory provisions relating to the office of the public defender are found in the codes of criminal procedure or occasionally in special legislation This office is usually attached to the different levels of criminal courts, and in many countries public defenders work full-time as employees of the Ministry of Justice.

17. Thus, Venezuelan law provides for government counsel in criminal matters (*defensores públicos*), for workers and minors, and for rural and indigenous populations. Lawyers Committee for Human Rights and the Venezuelan Program for Human Rights Education and Action, *Halfway to Reform: The World Bank and the Venezuelan Justice System* (New York: Lawyers Committee for Human Rights, 1996).

18. For a criticism of the quality of the representation exercised by public defenders in Latin America, *see* LEGAL AID AND WORLD POVERTY, *supra* note 8, at 79 ("As a practical matter, the machinery for fulfilling the right to counsel is not effective for most of the poor. Defendants may not have counsel assigned (if at all) until after the major stages of the prosecution have been completed. The courts make little or no effort to provide for the expenses necessary to pay witnesses or conduct an investigation on behalf of the accused. Furthermore, the quality of legal representation provided by assigned counsel is very low, owing to the lack of a financial incentive"). At the Notre Dame workshop, Judge Schiffrin noted that within the jurisdiction of the Federal Circuit Court of La Plata (Argentina) where he sits, 7 full-time public defenders take up approximately 80 percent of all criminal cases handled by 4 investigative magistrates and 2 trial courts. In the City of Buenos Aires, 41 public defenders represent all criminal cases before 73 investigative magistrates (*jueces de instrucción*), 49 trial courts, and 15 appellate courts.

19. *See Halfway to Reform, supra* note 17, referring to the fact that in Venezuela the number of public defenders is insufficient to handle the existing caseload; 157 public defenders shared a total of 45,702 cases, an average of 291 cases per lawyer. "The [Venezuelan] Judicial Council estimated that it needed a minimum of eighty-four additional public defenders for 1994 to meet national needs, but only two lawyers were hired. The ratio of cases per

lawyer subsequently increased to 348 in 1995. In several states, the 1995 average was 450 cases per lawyer; in the state of Sucre, that number jumped to 625." It has been reported that Ecuador has a total of twenty-one public defenders, Quito and Guayaquil (with a population of more than 2 and 3 million people, respectively) having only four public defenders each. *As cited by* Dakolias, *supra* note 7, at 208.

20. Thus, it has been noted that public defenders in Venezuela generally "sense a great social distance between themselves and their clients, view them as guilty and clearly are not disposed to make any effort to defend them." Rafael Pérez Perdomo, *Informe sobre Venezuela*, in SITUACIÓN Y POLÍTICAS JUDICIALES EN AMÉRICA LATINA, CUADERNOS DE ANÁLISIS JURÍDICO 588 (Jorge Correa Sutil ed., Santiago: Universidad Diego Portales, 1993). The same author refers to equally dysfunctional perceptions of the prisoner whom the public defender is meant to represent. "Contact between defendants and public defenders is so superficial that many interviewed prisoners ignore the fact that they have public counsel and when asked about the role of the public defender at court hearings where the presence of counsel is required, the prisoners make no distinctions among the roles [of the judge and public defender]; rather, all of the judicial functionaries are viewed together as 'those who want to screw' [the prisoners]," *Halfway to Reform*, *supra* note 17, at 65. It is worth repeating that this flaw in the function of the public defender is also perceived in other jurisdictions.

21. *See* David Barringer, *Downsized*, ABA JOURNAL 60–66 (July 1996); and Richard C. Reuben, *Keeping Legal Aid Alive*, ABA JOURNAL 20 (November 1996). Indigent defense programs for criminal defendants have been suffering severe problems in several jurisdictions of the United States. *See* American Bar Association, *P.D. Funding Struck Down*, ABA JOURNAL 18 (May 1992), referring to the "mind-boggling work load" of the city of New Orleans, which fails to "meet our minimum standards of competence." Unable to afford a full-time staff of public defenders, many municipal courts in the United States must rely on a court-assigned counsel system, in which criminal defendants are represented by lawyers who may never have seen the inside of a courtroom. According to the *New York Times*, "In about 40 percent of New Jersey's municipal courts, there are no paid public defenders. Instead, defense lawyers are picked at random, often at the last minute, and must work for nothing. These are assignments that the bar calls mandatory pro bono and that many lawyers call unconstitutional—unfair to lawyers and defendants alike." *New Jersey's Public Defender System Pleases Few*, NEW YORK TIMES, Feb. 24, 1994.

22. According to an official report on a legal services program run in Brazil by the state of Rio de Janeiro, the program employed 160 attorneys on a part-time basis who had contacts with 45,000 persons per month, and who completed 90,000 cases in 1976, which means that attorneys averaged ten minutes per completed case. *See* Associação da Assistência Judiciaria do Estado do Rio de Janeiro, *O Atendimento Judiciário Gratuito do Estado do Rio de Janeiro* (1977), *cited in* David M. Trubek, *Unequal Protection: Thoughts on Legal*

Services, Social Welfare, and Income Distribution in Latin America, 13 TEX. INT'L L. J. 243, 260 (1978). For a criticism of other legal assistance programs in Brazil, *see* LEGAL AID AND WORLD POVERTY, *supra* note 8, at 77, 86 ("[T]he underlying objective is limited to the provision of free representation of indigents in court proceedings. Free representation in civil cases is, in general, limited to defendants. Absent to any significant extent is the notion that legal services include preventive law/community legal education and law reform activity.... No real effort is made to reach the poor. This approach effectively eliminates 90 to 95 percent of the poor, who are not inclined to bring their problems to a legal aid office organized by rich and more powerful people").

23. In Peru, the bar association reportedly funds sixteen legal aid clinics, each one with one lawyer and five employees, which handled a total of 19,719 cases in 1992. *See Peru: Judicial Sector Assessment, supra* note 14, *cited by* Dakolias, *A Strategy for Judicial Reform, supra* note 7, at 208.

24. Chile's main national program of legal aid is financed by the government but administered by the Chilean Bar Association since 1928, first through a *Servicio de Asistencia Judicial* (SAJ) and since 1981 through the *Corporaciones de Asistencia Judicial* (CAJ). There is one CAJ in each Metropolitan Region, Valparaíso and the Bío-Bío Region, and a fourth CAJ based in Iquique was established in 1987 for Antofagasta and Tarapac. Michael A. Samway, *Access to Justice: A Study of Legal Assistance Programs for the Poor in Santiago, Chile*, 6 DUKE J. INT'L & COMP. L. 347–49 (1996). Despite SAJ's and CAJ's beneficial effects for the poor, it has been reported that they are inadequate to meet the needs of the nation's poor. According to Knight in LEGAL AID AND WORLD POVERTY, *supra* note 8, at 89, SAJ staff attorneys are badly paid, law graduates are overburdened with a continuing workload of some 80 to 90 cases, and SAJ offices (except perhaps the Central Office) are poorly furnished (lacking library facilities, desks, typewriters, heat during the winter, and so on). Knight also asserts: "Budget considerations make it impossible to provide a staff adequate to meet the demand. The attitude of recent law graduates toward SAJ is not one of dedication to the task of assisting the poor while perfecting professional skills. The cumulative weight of these factors suggests that the quality of legal assistance provided through the SAJ is not good." *Id.* Legal aid offices in the CAJ are staffed by 130 attorneys who earn approximately US $440 per month; the thirty social workers who staff the CAJ earn significantly less; and recent law school graduates (*postulantes*) perform their services without pay. Samway, *supra*, at 358.

25. The codes of civil and commercial procedure of many Latin American countries generally include provisions on how to qualify for the "privilege to litigate without costs." After a determination of the applicant's income, a "certificate of poverty" is issued and the applicant is exempted from the payment of court costs and attorney's fees. *See*, e.g., National Code of Civil and Commercial Procedure Argentina (Código Procesal Civil y Comercial de la Nación), at arts. 78–86 [hereinafter ArgCCivComProc].

26. Due to high demand for legal services in proportion to the resources available, some jurisdictions have established miserable levels of income in

order for a person to qualify for legal aid. *See* Dakolias, *A Strategy for Judicial Reform, supra* note 7, at 208 (referring to the legal aid office in Trinidad and Tobago, which in 1993 received more than 10,000 requests for assistance and accepted less than 10 percent due to the low income threshold requirement).

27. *See*, e.g., ArgCCivComProc., *supra* note 25, at art. 78, para. 2, which states: "The granting of the privilege to litigate without costs shall not be prevented because the applicant is able to afford his living expenses, regardless of the source of his income." This provision has been construed in the sense that proof of indigence is not required, for it suffices a showing that the applicant lacks the income needed to pay the legal expenses. M. SERANTES PEÑA & J.F. PALMA, CÓDIGO PROCESAL CIVIL Y COMERCIAL DE LA NACIÓN Y NORMAS COMPLEMENTARIAS: COMENTADO, CONCORDADO Y ANOTADO CON JURISPRUDENCIA 86 (1993).

28. For a comparative discussion of "assigned counsel" or "judicare" models of legal aid in Western Europe and the United States, *see* Mauro Cappelletti et al., *Access to Justice: Variations and Continuity of a World-Wide Movement*, 54 REVISTA JURÍDICA DE LA UNIVERSIDAD DE PUERTO RICO 221 (1985), which compares the operation of such programs in Sweden, France, Belgium, Great Britain, and Germany; Heribert Hirte, *Access to the Courts for Indigent Persons: A Comparative Analysis of the Legal Framework in the United Kingdom, United States, and Germany*, 40 INT'L & COMP. L. Q. 91 (1991), which compares legal aid programs in England and Wales, The Netherlands, and Germany. In contrast, the compensation, if any, received by government-provided lawyers in developing countries is very low. Thus, legal aid lawyers in Trinidad and Tobago receive a fee which is usually one-sixth of the market rate. Dakolias, *A Strategy for Judicial Reform, supra* note 7, at 208.

29. It is reported that the courts, which should in theory bear these costs, generally are out of funds to bear those expenses. LEGAL AID AND WORLD POVERTY, *supra* note 8, at 80.

30. "To the extent that the assigned counsel system works at all, it probably operates mainly in criminal proceedings at the appellate level. In civil cases assigned counsel are used less frequently and primarily where the assisted party is a defendant. . . . It is not difficult to imagine that only a tiny fraction of Latin America's poor have had their rights vindicated by assigned counsel and public defenders." *Id.*

31. Second-year law students in Trinidad and Tobago are required to take at least one case in the law school's legal aid program in order to graduate. Dakolias, *A Strategy for Judicial Reform, supra* note 7, at 209.

32. Dakolias, *A Strategy for Judicial Reform, id.* at 209 and 218 n. 219 (referring to Chile and Venezuela as Latin American countries requiring practical training before conferring a license to practice law). Chilean recent law school graduates are required to complete a six-month unpaid internship with the legal aid office to receive a license to practice from the Supreme Court. *Id.* at 218 n. 220. *See also* STEVEN LOWENSTEIN, LAWYERS, LEGAL EDUCATION AND DEVELOPMENT: AN EXAMINATION OF THE PROCESS OF REFORM IN

CHILE (New York: International Legal Center, 1970). A typical graduate may handle between 80 to 110 cases in a six-month period. *See* Samway, *supra* note 24, at 358–59 ("The student *postulante* element is an important social welfare mechanism which sets Chile apart from other countries in the Americas, including the United States, which do not require post-law school legal aid service").

33. *See* LEGAL AID AND WORLD POVERTY, *supra* note 8, at 117 ("Faced with what they consider more pressing needs (such as higher faculty salaries or better physical facilities), Latin American law schools may be loath to provide the financing necessary for a legal aid project").

34. LEGAL AID AND WORLD POVERTY, *id.* at 104 ("The use of students is laudable when it provides an educational experience the students will find of value when they enter practice. But it must be recognized that student labor has value of a different sort—it can be cheap and can be easily manipulated through the creation of compulsory requirements for university graduation and the *licenciatura* (the license to practice). The best of the *consultorios jurídicos* are expensive, educationally valuable, and provide high-quality client service. The worst exploit student labor, foster student indifference or animosity toward the legal problems of the poor, and provide inferior client service").

35. *Id.* at 112.

36. *See,* e.g., the emergence of the Asociación Nacional de Abogados Democráticos (ANAD) in Mexico in 1991. It has been reported that as of 1993, ANAD comprised about 250 members in Mexico City and another 200 in twelve of Mexico's thirty-one states. Affiliated with ANAD are other nongovernmental organizations in charge of organizing training programs on legal education (El Despacho de Orientación y Asesoría Legal, DOAL, in Mexico City), handling women's family legal problems such as domestic violence (Mujeres en Acción Sindical, MAS, also in Mexico City), and representing campesinos and indigenous peoples (Tierra y Libertad in Mexico City and Chiltak in Chiapas). *See generally* Carl M. Selinger, *Public Interest Lawyering in Mexico and the United States,* 27 INTER-AMERICAN L. REV. 343, 352–53 (1995–96).

37. *See generally* LEGAL AID AND WORLD POVERTY, *supra* note 8, at 109 ("Equal justice should mean more than having the poor client's rights vindicated in a particular case; it should mean at least that the legal system operates to benefit the poor as a class in equal proportion to the recognized way it operates to benefit powerful social interests"); and Trubek, *supra* note 3, at 261 ("Publicly-funded legal services programs rarely, if ever, engage in collective advocacy, which may be essential if legal assistance is to have a substantial impact on social welfare program design or administration").

38. *See* Jorge Correa Sutil's chapter in this volume. Correa Sutil notes that USAID has granted not less than $200 million dollars from 1985 to 1995 for programs on the improvement of the administration of justice in Costa Rica, Honduras, Guatemala, El Salvador, and Panama. Other USAID programs are under way in Argentina, Bolivia, Colombia, Chile, Ecuador,

Paraguay, and Uruguay. The World Bank is carrying out a program in Venezuela, and other programs are envisioned for Bolivia and Paraguay. Finally, the Inter-American Development Bank, as part of its program on "Modernization of the State" in Latin America, is also planning to invest in judicial reform in some countries of Latin America.

39. *See* Correa Sutil, *id.*

40. *See* ACCESS TO JUSTICE: A WORLD SURVEY (Mauro Cappelletti & Bryant G. Garth eds., Milan: Giuffré, Sijthoff, 1978). At that time, court costs in Colombia were estimated at 50 percent of the value of claims involving $3,500 and approximately 60 percent of the amount of claims not exceeding $700. *See* M. Fernández, *Access to Justice in Colombia,* in ACCESS TO JUSTICE, *id.* at 398–99. In Uruguay, court costs for claims involving $5,000 were estimated at 32 percent of the amount in litigation, 40 percent of a claim for $500, and 50 percent of claims lower than $500. Enrique Vescovi, *Access to Justice in Uruguay,* in ACCESS TO JUSTICE, *id.* at 1028.

41. Eduardo Buscaglia & María Dakolias, *Judicial Reform in Latin American Courts: The Experience in Argentina and Ecuador* 3, World Bank Technical Paper no. 350 (1996). The authors note that in 1993 the median time spent before the disposition of a case in Argentina, Ecuador, and Venezuela was 2.5, 1.9, and 2.4 years respectively; these periods have increased 76 percent since 1987.

42. Although the rule of "stare decisis" is not part of the legal tradition in Latin America, the actual use of precedents to settle cases presenting similar material facts is more a matter of practice than dogma. *See* Raúl Brañes, *Access to Justice in Chile,* in ACCESS TO JUSTICE, *supra* note 40, at 368: "Judgments in individual cases can only benefit other potential claimants if the legal doctrine they support is consistently affirmed by subsequent cases. Otherwise, the principle of Civil Code, Article 3, that judicial decisions have no effect except in the cases in which they are announced, applies without exception." Compare Fernández, *Access to Justice in Colombia, supra* note 40, at 414, where the author observes that Colombian judges "do not use much 'case law' in reaching their decisions" despite the existence of a 1896 statute (Law No. 169) that encourages judges to apply the doctrine affirmed by three uniform decisions of the Supreme Court.

43. This has been one of the focal areas of recent efforts towards judicial reform in the United Kingdom, where the civil-justice system is said to be designed to satisfy lawyers rather than consumers. The latest official proposal on making civil justice cheaper was written by Lord Woolf, who headed a commission reporting that the civil courts in England and Wales "are a nightmare for those trapped in their Byzantine procedures." *See More Justice is More Just,* THE ECONOMIST, July 27, 1996, at 15. The message of Lord Woolf's report is that much of the blame is to be placed on the fact that lawyers have an interest in keeping cases going as long as they can. *See generally Lord Woolf's Access to Justice: Plusça change . . . ,* 59 MOD. LAW REV. 773–96 (1996).

44. An agreement between attorney and client, providing for compen-

sation expressed in terms of a percentage of the expected recovery, though a matter of everyday practice in the United States, is considered unethical and void in many, if not most, civil-law countries. *See* RUDOLPH SCHLESINGER, HANS W. BAADE, M. DAMASKA, & PETER HERZOG, COMPARATIVE LAW: CASES, TEXT, MATERIALS 358 (5th ed. 1988). Thus, under the "loser-pays-all" rule that prevails in most civil-law countries, a plaintiff who cannot retain a lawyer on a contingent fee basis and who is faced with the risk of having to pay his opponent's attorneys if the case goes the wrong way, will think twice before s/he initiates litigation.

45. For a country-based index of corruption, compiled from seven surveys undertaken by institutions from different countries, *see A Global Gauge of Greased Palms*, NEW YORK TIMES, Aug. 20, 1995, at 3. *See also A World Fed Up With Bribes*, NEW YORK TIMES, Nov. 28, 1996, at D-1.

46. *See* Keith Rosenn, *The Protection of Judicial Independence in Latin America*, 19 U MIAMI L. REV. 1, 13 (1987).

47. *See, e.g.,* Federal Code of Civil and Commercial Procedure (Argentina), arts. 87–89; Code of Civil Procedure (Bolivia), arts. 65–66; Code of Civil Procedure (Brazil), arts. 46–50.

48. *See* Vescovi, *Access to Justice in Uruguay, supra* note 40, at 1035–36; Brañes, *Access to Justice in Chile, supra* note 42, at 365–66; and Fernández, *Access to Justice in Colombia, supra* note 40, at 413–14.

49. *See, e.g.,* Vescovi, *Access to Justice in Uruguay, supra* note 40, at 1037 ("[D]espite the power of the Ministerio Público to represent collective interests, in practice the office has done nothing for the protection of consumers, constitutional freedoms, or the environment").

50. For a discussion of recently adopted Italian legislation aimed at broadening the standing to sue to associations, *see* Douglas L. Parker, *Standing to Litigate "Abstract Social Interests" in the United States and Italy: Reexamining "Injury in Fact"*, 33 COLUM. J. TRANSNAT'L. L. 259 (1995). For a discussion of the potential of collective action mechanisms for reducing litigation costs and change public policy, from the standpoint of public choice theory, *see* MANCUR OLSON, THE LOGIC OF COLLECTIVE ACTION: PUBLIC GOODS AND THE THEORY OF GROUPS (Harvard University Press, 1971).

51. *See* Fernández, *Access to Justice in Colombia, supra* note 40, at 399–400 (reporting on the experience of municipal courts in Bogotá, where proceedings last for an average of one year).

52. For a discussion of the Brazilian experience, *see* Marcos Afonso Borges, *La Justicia de Pequeñas Causas en el Brasil*, in JUSTICIA Y SOCIEDAD 657 (1994); for a discussion of the Mexican experience, *see* Héctor Molina González, *Tribunales de Mínima Cuantía*, in JUSTICIA Y SOCIEDAD 669 (1994). For a comparative study of small claims courts in common-law countries, where these courts have been developed more extensively than in civil-law countries, *see* Christopher J. Whelan, *Small Claims Courts: Heritage and Adjustment*, in SMALL CLAIMS COURTS: A COMPARATIVE STUDY 207 (Christopher J. Whelan ed., 1990).

53. The relaxation of formal requirements for labor contracts and

leases of urban real property have been mentioned as one of the aspects of Chilean law (Labor Code, art. 119; Decree-Law No. 964 of 1975) that took the situation of the underprivileged classes into account. *See* Brañes, *Access to Justice in Chile, supra* note 42, at 363–64.

54. *See* Vescovi, *Access to Justice in Uruguay, supra* note 40, at 1034–35 (referring to the procedural and substantive rules governing divorce action that go back to 1909 and are specifically geared to make the procedure relatively simple, inexpensive, and expeditious).

55. *See* Fernández, *Access to Justice in Colombia, supra* note 40, at 412–13 (referring to a 1968 reform aimed at simplifying the proof for establishing who is the father of a child born out of wedlock; whereas under former law the evidentiary burden for establishing paternity required a showing of "stable and notorious sexual relations," under the 1968 reforms paternity may be inferred from proof of sexual relations and conduct of the mother and presumed father).

56. *See generally* Mauro Cappelletti, *Alternative Dispute Resolution Processes within the Framework of the World-Wide Access-to-Justice-Movement*, 56 MOD LAW REV. 282 (1993).

57. *See* Dakolias, *The Judicial Sector in Latin America and the Caribbean, supra* note 14, at 52 (recommending that judicial reform programs include both court-annexed and private ADR as part of the programs).

58. *See* Dakolias, *A Strategy for Judicial Reform, supra* note 7, at 200 (reporting a 70 percent success rate for mediation proceedings in Chile); at 202 (reporting a 65 percent success rate for mediation proceedings in Argentina under a recently adopted scheme of mandatory mediation, and also reporting a high success rate for mediation proceedings in child support and alimony cases conducted by the Procuradoría in El Salvador).

59. For reference to Mexican legal education, *see* James E. Herget & Jorge Camil, *The Legal System of Mexico*, in MODERN LEGAL SYSTEMS CYCLOPEDIA 1.30.61–65 (Kenneth Robert Redden ed., Buffalo: W.S. Hein, 1988). The observations made with regard to legal education in most Mexican law schools may be extended to much of Latin America.

19 Polyarchies and the (Un)Rule of Law in Latin America: A Partial Conclusion

Guillermo O'Donnell

Aos meus amigos, tudo; aos meus inimigos, a lei.
(For my friends, whatever they want; for my enemies, the law.)
GETÚLIO VARGAS

Introduction

Impressed by the ineffectiveness, if not the recurrent violations, of many basic rights in Latin America, several authors in the present volume challenge the appropriateness of attaching the label "democracy" to most countries in this region. At the very least, as Juan Méndez puts it in his introduction to the section on lawless violence, these failures indicate a "clear abdication of democratic authority." The doubts and challenges to the democratic condition of these countries spring, on one hand, from justified outrage in view of the dismal situation that, in terms of basic rights of the vulnerable and the poor, most of the chapters in this volume document. On the other hand, these same doubts and challenges reflect the vague and fluctuating meanings attached to the term "democracy," not only in common but also in academic usage. The problem has become more acute since the number of countries from the South and East which claim to be democratic has greatly expanded in the last two decades. This expansion has forced democratic theory to become more broadly comparative than it used to be when its empirical referent was almost exclusively limited to countries situated in the northwestern quadrant of the world. However, I have argued in recent publications[1] that in broadening its geographical scope, democratic theory has carried too many unexamined assumptions,[2] reflecting in so doing the conditions prevailing during the emergence and institutionalization of democracy in the highly developed world. I also argued that, given the present range of variation among pertinent cases, some of these assumptions need to be made explicit and submitted to critical examination if we are going to achieve a theory of adequate scope and empirical grounding. In the present text, based on a discussion of the rule of law and its ramifications in terms of the conceptualization of democracy, citizenship, and the state, I attempt to advance in this direction.

Polyarchy

Country X is a political democracy, or a polyarchy: it holds regularly scheduled competitive elections, individuals can freely create or join organizations, including political parties, there is freedom of expression, including a reasonably free press, and the like.[3] Country X, however, is marred by extensive poverty and deep inequality. Authors who agree with a strictly political, basically Schumpeterian, definition of democracy would argue that, even though the socioeconomic characteristics of X may be regrettable, this country undoubtedly belongs to the set of democracies. This is a view of democracy as a type of political regime, independent of the characteristics of state and society. In contrast, other authors see democracy as a systemic attribute, dependent on the existence of a significant degree of socioeconomic equality, and/or as an overall social and political arrangement oriented toward the achievement of such equality. These authors would dismiss country X as "not truly" democratic, or as a "facade" version of democracy.

Contemporary literature has generated plenty of definitions of democracy.[4] If the options were limited to the two just sketched, I would opt for the first. The definition that conflates democracy with a substantial degree of social justice or equality is not analytically useful. Furthermore, it is dangerous: it tends to depreciate whatever democracy exists, and thus plays into the hands of authoritarianism—in Latin America, we learned this the hard way in the 1960s and 1970s. On the other hand, while I am persuaded that a "politicist," or solely regime-based, focus is necessary for an adequate definition of democracy, I do not consider it sufficient. Academic usage cannot completely ignore the historical origins and the normative connotations of the terms it adopts. The fundamental point which I will elaborate here is that there is a close connection of democracy with certain aspects of equality among individuals who are posited not just as individuals, but as *legal persons*, and consequently as citizens—i.e., as carriers of rights and obligations that derive from their membership in a polity, and from being attributed personal autonomy and, consequently, responsibility for their actions. Whatever the definition of democracy, since Athens until today this is its common historical core.

In contemporary democracies, or polyarchies, citizens have, at a minimum, the right to vote in competitive elections. This means that they are supposed to make a choice among no less than five options.[5] This choice would be senseless if they had not (more precisely, if they were not attributed by the existing legal/institutional framework) a sufficient degree of personal autonomy to consciously make such choices.[6] In this sense, democracy is a collective wager: even if grudgingly, every *ego* accepts[7] that all other adult *alter* have the same right (i.e., are equal with respect to) to participate in the momentous collective decision that determines who will rule them for a time. In spite of the infinitesimal weight of each vote in such decision, the feeling of not being mere subjects, but instead citizens exercising their equal right of choosing who would rule them, goes a long way in accounting for the huge enthusiasm that often accompanies the founding elections at the demise of authoritarian rule.[8]

The significance of the attribution of personal autonomy is even more clear in relation to other political rights. If, as entailed by the definition of polyarchy, I am granted the right to freely express opinions about public matters, I am presupposed to have sufficient autonomy to have such opinions (even if I am mimicking the opinion of others, it is still myself who has adopted them); this same autonomy makes me responsible for such opinions, for example, if they make me liable to a libel suit. This leads us into a second point: polyarchy as a political regime, together with the whole legal system of western (and westernized) societies, is built on the premise that everyone is endowed with a basic degree of autonomy and responsibility, unless there is conclusive and highly elaborate proof to the contrary. This is the presumption that makes every individual a "legal person," a carrier of formally equal rights and obligations not only in the political realm but also in contract, tort, criminal, and tax obligations, in dealings with state agencies, and in many other spheres of social life. This fact, which pertains as much to the history of democracy as it does to the history of capitalism and of the territorially-based state, means that in manifold social transactions we and the other parties in such transactions are assumed to be equally autonomous and responsible. Since Karl Marx, this kind of equality may be dismissed as "purely formal" or, worse, as a highly efficacious way to conceal the inequalities that really matter.[9] I believe this is a serious argument, but it does not cover the whole story: formal or not, these *are* equalities, and they have expansive potentialities for further equalization.

What I have noted is also true in relation to activities that require a higher investment of personal activity than voting or signing an already printed employment contract. For example, expressing opinions, participating in an electoral campaign, or joining a political party require not only that one has the autonomous disposition to do so but also resources, such as time, information, and even sheer energy,[10] as well as legal protections against the possibility of being sanctioned because of undertaking such activities. Lacking these propitious conditions, only some exceptionally motivated individuals carry out such activities. This also holds true at a less directly political level, such as suing an exploitative landlord, an abusive spouse, or a police officer who behaves unlawfully. As Amartya Sen has argued, the functionings of each individual (i.e., the activities that one may undertake) depend on the set of actual capabilities with which one is endowed by a broad constellation of social factors.[11] If in any given case certain actions (for instance, because of deprivation of necessary resources) are not within the set of the actor's capabilities, the freedom to act in that way would be spuriously attributed to such an actor. In this sense, if in country X there exists a pervasive condition of extreme poverty (which affects many more capabilities than those based solely on economic resources), its citizens are *de facto* deprived of the possibility of exercising their autonomy, except perhaps in spheres that are directly related to their own survival. If the deprivation of capabilities entailed by extreme poverty results in persons being hard pressed to exercise their autonomy in various spheres of their life, then it seems wrong, both morally and empirically, to posit that democracy has nothing to do with such socially determined impediments. Actually, saying that it has nothing to do is too strong: authors who accept a regime-based definition often warn that, if those miseries are not somehow addressed, democracy, even narrowly defined, will be in jeopardy. This is a practical argument, subject to empirical tests which, indeed, show that poorer and/or more inequalitarian societies are less likely to have enduring polyarchies.[12] This is an important issue, but not the one I deal with here.

Formal Rights

The preceding discussion implies that there is an intermediate dimension between the political regime and the broad socioeconomic characteristics of a given country. As such, this intermediary level is bound to be influenced by both regime and socioeconomic structure, so whatever this dimension is, it is—to resuscitate an admittedly ambiguous term—relatively autonomous from these two levels. I argue that this intermediary level consists of the extent to which the rule of law is effective across various kinds of issues, regions, and social actors, or equivalently, the extent to which full citizenship, civil and political, has been achieved by the entire adult population.

The "rule of law" (like terms that we shall see are partially concurrent, such as a *Rechsstaat, État de Droit,* or *Estado de Derecho*) is a disputed term. For the time being, let me assert that its minimal (and historically original) meaning is that whatever law there is, this law is fairly applied by the relevant state institutions, including, but not exclusively, the judiciary. By "fairly" applied I mean that the administrative application or judicial adjudication of legal rules is consistent across equivalent cases, is made without taking into consideration the class, status, or power differentials of the participants in such processes, and applies procedures that are preestablished and knowable. This is a minimum, but not an insignificant, criterion: if *ego* is attributed the same equality (and, at least implicitly, the same autonomy) as the other, more powerful, *alter* with whom the former enters into a crop-sharing arrangement, or employment contract, or marriage, then it stands to reason that the individual has the right to expect equal treatment from the state institutions that have, or may acquire, jurisdiction over such acts.

This is, it is important to note, formal equality in two senses. One, it is established in and by legal rules that are valid (at least[13]) in that they have been sanctioned following previously and carefully dictated procedures often ultimately regulated by constitutional rules. Two, the rights and obligations specified are universalistic, in that they are attached to each individual *qua* legal person, irrespective of his or her social position, with the sole requirement that the individual has reached adulthood (i.e., a certain age, legally prescribed) and has not been proved to suffer from some kind of (narrowly defined and legally prescribed) disqualifying handicap. These formal rights support the claim of equal treatment in the legally defined situations that both underlie and may ensue from the kind of acts above exemplified. "Equality [of all] before the law" is the expectation tendentially inscribed in this kind of equality.[14] At this moment, I want to notice a point to which I shall return: the premises and characteristics of these rights and obligations of the legal person as a member of society (which, in the interest of brevity, I will call civil rights or civil citizenship[15]) are exactly the same as those of the rights and obligations conferred in the political realm upon the same individuals[16] by a polyarchical regime. Actually, the formal rights and obligations attached by polyarchy to political citizenship are a subset of the rights and obligations attached to a legal person.

A Brief Overview of the Evolution and Sequence of Rights

Since Plato and Aristotle, we have known that formal equality is insufficient. It soon becomes evident to political authorities that, in order for these rights not to be "purely" formal, some equalizing measures must be undertaken. The corollary of this observation, together with the left's criticisms of "formal freedoms," has propelled two major achievements. One is recognizing the need for policies aimed at generating some equalization (or, at least, to redressing egregious inequalities) so that peasants, workers, women, and other underprivileged actors may have a real chance of exercising their rights. In some countries, this has led to the complex institutionality of the welfare state. The second achievement results from recognizing that, even if these equalizing measures are reasonably adequate for highly organized groups or constituencies with large memberships, there are still a number of situations that require even more specific measures, if formal equality is to be approximated at all. Consequently, various kinds of social and legal aid programs and initiatives for the poor or for those who for any reason have a hard time legally defending their rights have become another feature, especially of highly developed countries.

The overall result of these changes has been a significant decrease in the universalism of the law. Reasons of formal and substantive equalization were seen as demanding that legal rules specifically aimed at certain social categories be implemented. These decisions were in part the product of political struggles of the groups thus specified, in part the result of preemptive paternalistic state interventions in a mix that has varied across countries and time.[17] These processes have led, from the right and the left as well as from some communitarians, to stern criticism of the resulting "legal pollution."[18] I want to stress, however, that in this matter sequences are important: these criticisms imply that in the highly developed countries the particularization of the legal system was a later historical development, premised on the previous extension of formal, universalistic legislation. Some of the harshest critics of these legal systems seem to forget that their very ability to challenge the systems (even before courts) without personal risk is grounded in formal rights that persist quite vigorously in spite of the "legal pollution" that has taken place. We shall see that this is rarely the case outside of the highly developed world, and draw some conclusions.

Habermas has proposed a useful typological sequence.[19] He notes that in most European cases, the state that emerged out of absolutism went on to generalize the concept of the legal person as a carrier of "bourgeois" rights, typically embodied in civil and commercial codes. This was a first step toward the generalized juridification of society which, following Max Weber,[20] was at once the process of formation of national states and of the expansion of capitalism. The second step was that of the *Rechsstaat*, which established "the constitutional regulation of executive authority . . . [under] the principle of administrative legality," even though individuals were not yet granted political rights, including the right to elect their rulers. In Europe, this happened at a third stage, sometime during the nineteenth century, when through varied processes the adult male population acquired full political rights. The fourth stage that Habermas notes is that of the welfare state and its concomitant rights. This period marked a clear advance in social equity and democratization but diminished the legal universalism of the previous stages. Actually, this developmental typology is not truly adequate in relation to several of the European cases it purports to embrace and does not fit at all other important cases, such as the United States. Nevertheless, it is useful in two respects. The first, on which Habermas and other German authors have elaborated,[21] is the finding that the processes of social change referred to above included a dimension of intense juridification: "the expansion [by means of] the legal regulation of new, hitherto informally regulated social situations [and] the densification of law, that is the specialized breaking down of global into more individuated legal definitions."[22] The increased complexity of the bundles of rights and obligations attached to the concept of a legal person is an expression of this process. This, in turn, has been the product of the emergence of states that attempt to order social relations over their territory in several ways, an extremely important one of which is their own legislation.

The second aspect which I find useful in Habermas's scheme[23] is that it serves to highlight a crucial difference on which I want to insist: the expansion and densification of civil rights in highly developed countries basically took place well before the acquisition of political and welfare rights. Admittedly, there are important exceptions to this, prominently the much slower and, to a large extent, the different sequencing of the extension of rights to women and various racial minorities.[24] But even with these caveats, the difference stands:

in most contemporary Latin American countries, now that the political rights entailed by polyarchy have become generally effective, the extension of civil rights to all adults is incomplete, as the present volume abundantly attests.

Latin America

Now we can go back to our hypothetical country, the polyarchy X. It is, as noted, highly inegalitarian and a large part of its population lives in poverty. It is also one in which the rudiments of a welfare state exist. However, this welfare state is much less comprehensive and articulated than those of highly developed countries, its performance is even less satisfactory, it has grown almost exclusively by means of paternalistic state interventions, and it scarcely reaches the very poor.[25] To put some flesh on my example, what I have just described applies, with differences that are irrelevant for purposes of the present text, to all the contemporary polyarchies of Latin America—and, for that matter, to various new polyarchies in other parts of the world. Yet within this shared background there is a major difference that sets Costa Rica and Uruguay[26] apart from the rest. In these two countries there exists a state that long ago (and in spite of the authoritarian interruption suffered by Uruguay) established a legal system that, by and large, functions across its whole territory, and in relation to most social categories, in ways that satisfy the preliminary definition of the rule of law I gave above. These are countries where the rule of law is reasonably effective; their citizenships are full ones, in the sense that they enjoy both political and civil rights.

This is not the case with other Latin American countries, both those that are new polyarchies and those—Colombia and Venezuela—that have been so for several decades. In these countries, as I have discussed in other texts,[27] huge gaps exist, both across their territory and in relation to various social categories, in the effectiveness of whatever we may agree that the rule of law means. In what follows I briefly depict these failures.[28]

Flaws in the existing law: In spite of progress recently made, there still exist laws and administrative regulations that discriminate against women[29] and various minorities[30] and that establish for defendants in criminal cases, detainees, and prison inmates conditions that are repugnant to any sense of fair process.[31]

Application of the law: As the epigraph of this chapter makes clear, the discretionary, and often exactingly severe, application of the law upon the vulnerable can be a very efficient means of oppression. The flip side of this is the manifold ways by which the privileged, whether directly[32] or by means of appropriate personal connections,[33] exempt themselves from following the law. Latin America has a long tradition[34] of ignoring the law or, when acknowledging it, of twisting it in favor of the powerful and for the repression or containment of the vulnerable. When a shady businessman recently said in Argentina, "To be powerful is to have [legal] impunity,"[35] he expressed a presumably widespread feeling that, first, to voluntarily follow the law is something that only idiots[36] do and, second, that to be subject to the law is not to be the carrier of enforceable rights but rather a sure signal of social weakness.[37] This is particularly true and dangerous in encounters that may unleash the violence of the state or powerful private agents, but an attentive eye can also detect it in the stubborn refusal of the privileged to submit themselves to regular administrative procedures, not to say anything of the scandalous criminal impunity they often obtain.

Relations between bureaucracies and "ordinary citizens": Although this is part of the preceding observation, it bears independent comment. Perhaps nothing underlines better the deprivation of rights of the poor and vulnerable than when they interact with the bureaucracies from which they must obtain work, or a work permit, or apply for retirement benefits, or simply (but often tragically) when they have to go to a hospital or a police station.[38] This is, for the privileged, the other face of the moon, one that they mount elaborate strategies and networks of relationships to avoid.[39] For the others, those who cannot avoid this ugly face of the state, it is not only the immense difficulty they confront for obtaining, if at all, what nominally is their right, it is also the indifferent, if not disdainful, way in which they are treated and the obvious inequality entailed when the privileged skip these hardships. That this kind of world is far apart from the basic respect for human dignity demanded, among others, by Lane and Dworkin,[40] is evinced by the fact that, if one does not have the "proper" social status or connections, to act in front of these bureaucracies as the bearer of a right, not as the supplicant for a favor, is almost guaranteed to cause grievous difficulties.

Access to the judiciary and to fair process: Given my previous comments, I will not provide further details on this topic, which has proved quite vexing even in highly developed countries.[41] In most of Latin America (and aside from when it undertakes criminal procedures that tend to disregard rights of the accused before, during, and after the trial) the judiciary is too distant, cumbersome, expensive, and slow for the underprivileged to even attempt to access it. And if they do manage to obtain judicial access, not surprisingly the evidence available points to severe discrimination.[42]

Sheer lawlessness: This is an issue on which I placed more emphasis in a previous work where I argue that it is a mistake to conflate the state with its bureaucratic apparatus.[43] Insofar as most of the formally enacted law existing in a territory is issued and backed by the state, and as the state institutions themselves are supposed to act according to legal rules, we should recognize (as continental European theorists have long known,[44] and Anglo-Saxon ones ignored) that the legal system also is a constitutive part of the state. As such, what I call "the legal state" (i.e., the part of the state that is embodied in a legal system) penetrates and textures society, furnishing a basic element of stability to social relations.[45] However, in many countries of Latin America the reach of the legal state is limited. In many regions, including those geographically distant from the political centers and those in the peripheries of large cities, the bureaucratic state may be present, in the guise of buildings and officials paid out of public budgets, but the legal state is absent: whatever formally sanctioned law there exists is applied, if at all, intermittently and differentially. More importantly, this segmented law is encompassed by the informal law enacted by the privatized[46] powers that actually rule those places. This leads to complex situations, of which unfortunately we know too little but which often involve a continuous renegotiation of the boundaries between these formal and informal legalities, in social processes in which it is (at times literally) vital to understand both kinds of law and the extremely uneven power relations that they breed.[47] The resulting dominant informal legal system, punctuated by arbitrary reintroductions of the formal one, supports a world of extreme violence, as abundant data, both from rural and urban regions, establish. These are subnational systems of power that, oddly enough for most extant theories of the state and of democracy, have a territorial basis and an informal but quite effective legal system and that coexist with a regime that, at least at the center of national politics, is polyarchical.

The problems I have summarized in the present section indicate a severe incompleteness of the state, especially of its legal dimension. In most cases, in Latin America and elsewhere, this incompleteness has increased during democratization, at the rhythm of economic crises and the sternly antistatist economic policies that prevailed until recently. There is some evidence, too, that this deficiency has been fostered by the desire of national politicians to shape winning electoral coalitions and, consequently, to include candidates from the perversely "privatized" areas to which I am referring.[48] As Scott Mainwaring and David Samuels have noted with reference to Brazil, these politicians behave as "ambassadors" of their regions, with very few policy orientations except obtaining resources from the center for these regions.[49] These politicians use the votes they command and the institutional positions they attain at the center for assiduously helping the reproduction of the systems of privatized power they represent. For example, in Argentina and Brazil, legislators from "brown" areas have shown a keen (and often successful) interest in dominating the legislative committees that appoint federal judges in those same regions; this is surely an effective way of further cutting out their fiefs from the reach of the legal state.

It is difficult to avoid concluding that the circumstance I have just described must profoundly affect the actual workings of these polyarchies, including its institutions at the center of national politics. Admittedly, however, this conclusion is based on a sketchy description of complex issues. This is due in part to space limitations and in part to the fact that the phenomena I have depicted have been documented by some anthropologists, sociologists, and novelists, but with few exceptions,[50] they have not received attention from political scientists. Insofar as political scientists are supposed to have special credentials for describing and theorizing democracy and democracies, this neglect is problematic. It is obvious that for these purposes we need knowledge about parties, congresses, presidencies, and other institutions of the regime, and the many current efforts invested in these fields are extremely welcome. However, I believe that knowledge about the phenomena and practices I have sketched above is also important, both *per se* and because they may be surmised to have significant consequences upon the ways in which those regime institutions actually work and are likely to change.[51]

Furthermore, inattention to these phenomena leads to neglecting some problems and interesting questions, even at the level of the typological characterization of the regime itself. In the cases to which I am referring, the rights of polyarchy are upheld by definition. However, while this is true at the national level, the situation in peripheral areas is sometimes quite different. The sparseness of research in these areas does not allow me to make assured generalizations, but it is clear from the works already cited, as well as from abundant journalistic information and reports of human rights organizations, that some of these regions function in a less than polyarchical way. In these areas, for reasons that will not occupy me here, presidential elections and elections to national legislatures (particularly those that are held simultaneously with the former) are reasonably clean. But elections for local authorities are much less pristine and include cases tainted by intimidation and fraud. Worse, in all the countries with which I am reasonably acquainted (and with the exceptions of Costa Rica and Uruguay and, in this matter, also of Chile), these problems have tended to intensify, not improve, during the existence of the present polyarchies. Furthermore, many of these areas are rural, and they tend to be heavily overrepresented in the national legislatures.[52] This highlights the question of who represents and what is represented in the institutions of the national regime and, more specifically, of how one conceptualizes a polyarchical regime that may contain regional regimes that are not at all polyarchical.[53]

On the Rule of Law (or *Estado de Derecho*)

At this point, we must refine the initial definition of the rule of law. It is not enough that certain acts, whether of public officials or private actors, are ruled by law, i.e., that they act *secundum legem*, in conformity with what a given legislation prescribes. These acts may entail the application of a discriminatory law and/or one that violates basic rights, or the selective application of a law against some while at the same time others are arbitrarily exempted. The first possibility entails the violation of moral standards that most countries write into their constitutions and that nowadays, under the rubric of human rights, these countries have the internationally acquired obligation to respect. The second possibility entails the violation of a crucial principle of both fairness and the rule of law, that like cases be treated alike.[54] Still another possibility is that in a given case the law is properly applied, but that this results from the decision of an authority that is not, and does not itself feel, obligated to proceed in the same way on future equivalent occasions. The effectiveness of the rule of law entails certainty and accountability. The proper application of the law is an obligation of the relevant authority: it is expected that normally it will make the same kind of decision in equivalent situations and, when this is not the case, that another properly enabled authority will sanction the offending one and attempt to redress the consequences. This is tantamount to saying that the rule of law is not just a congerie of legal rules, even if all have been properly enacted; it is a legal system, a set of rules that has several fundamental characteristics in addition to having to be properly enacted. This argument will occupy us in the rest of the present section.

The concepts of the rule of law and of *estado de derecho* (or *Rechsstaat* or *état de droit*, or equivalent terms in other languages of countries belonging to the continental law tradition) are not synonymous. Furthermore, each of these terms is subject to various definitional and normative disputations.[55] In view of this, here I limit myself to some basic observations. To begin with, most definitions have a common core: the view that the legal system is a hierarchical one (usually crowned in constitutional norms) that aims at, although it never fully achieves, completeness.[56] This means that the relationships among legal rules are themselves legally ruled, and that there is no moment in which the whim of a given actor may justifiably cancel or suspend the rules that govern her/his performance.[57] Nobody, including the highest placed officials, is *de legibus solutus*.[58] It follows then that "the government shall be ruled by law and subject to it,"[59] including "the creation of law [which] is itself legally regulated."[60]

The legal system, or the legal state, is an aspect of the overall social order that, when working properly, "brings definition, specificity, clarity, and thus predictability into human interactions."[61]

For producing such results, a necessary condition is that the laws have certain characteristics in addition to those already noted. Among the many listings of such characteristics that have been proposed, here I adopt the one espoused by Raz:

> 1. All laws should be prospective, open and clear; 2. Laws should be relatively stable; 3. The making of particular laws . . . must be guided by open, stable, clear, and general rules; 4. The independence of the judiciary must be guaranteed; 5. The principles of natural justice must be observed (i.e., open and fair hearing and absence of bias); 6. The courts should have review powers . . . to ensure conformity to the rule of law; 7. The courts should be easily accessible; and 8. The discretion of crime preventing agencies should not be allowed to pervert the law.[62]

Points 1 to 3 refer to general characteristics of the laws themselves; they pertain to their proper enactment and content, as well as to a behavioral fact that this author and others stress: the laws must be possible to follow, which means that they (and those who interpret them) should not place unreasonable cognitive or behavioral demands on their addressees. The other points of Raz's listing refer to courts and only indirectly to other state agencies. Point 4 requires specification: that the independence of the courts (itself a murky idea[63] that I will not discuss here) is a valuable goal is shown, *a contrario*, by the often servile behavior of these institutions in relation to authoritarian rulers. But this independence may be misused only to foster sectorial privileges of the judicial personnel or unchallenged arbitrary interpretations of the law. Consequently, it also seems required "that those charged with interpreting and enforcing the laws take them with primary seriousness,"[64] and, I add, that they are attuned to the support and expansion of the polyarchy that, in contrast to the authoritarian past, confers upon them such independence. Obtaining this is a tall order everywhere, including in Latin America. In this region even harder accomplishments are implied by point 6, especially with respect to overseeing the legality of actions of presidents who see themselves as electorally empowered to do whatever they see fit during their terms.[65] The actual denial to the vulnerable of points 5 and 7 I have already mentioned, and it is amply illustrated by the works I have cited. The same goes for point 8, especially regarding the impunity of the police and of other (so-called) security agencies, as well as of violence perpetrated by private agents, together with the often indifferent, if not complicit, attitude of the police and the courts towards these acts.

At this point, we should notice that the English language expression "rule of law," and the type of definition I have transcribed, do not contain any direct reference, as do *estado de derecho* and equivalents, to state agencies other than courts. This is not surprising given the respective traditions, including the particularly strong role that the courts played in the political development of the United States.[66] Nevertheless, the whole state apparatus and its agents are supposed to submit to the rule of law, and in fact I already noted that most of the egregious transgressions of whatever legality exists are committed during interactions of these agents with the poor and vulnerable.

Furthermore, if the legal system is supposed to texture, stabilize, and order manifold social relations,[67] then not only when state agents but also when private actors violate the law with impunity, the rule of law is at best truncated. Whether state agents perpetrate unlawful acts on their own or *de facto* license private actors to do so, does not make much difference, either for the victims of such actions or for the (in)effectiveness of the rule of law.

The corollary of these reflections is that, when conceived as an aspect of the theory of democracy, the rule of law, or the *estado de derecho*, should be conceived not only as a generic characteristic of the legal system and of the performance of courts, but also as the legally based rule of a democratic state. This entails that there exists a legal system that is itself democratic, in three senses: first it upholds the political freedoms and guarantees of polyarchy; second, it upholds the civil rights of the whole population; and third, it establishes networks of responsibility and accountability[68] that entail that all agents, public and private, including the highest placed officials of the regime, are subject to appropriate, legally established controls of the lawfulness of their acts. As long as it fulfills these three conditions, such a state is not just a state ruled by law; it is a democratic legal state, or an *estado democrático de derecho.*

I want to insist that the rights of political and civil citizenship are formal, in the double sense that they are universalistic and that they are sanctioned through procedures that are established by the rules of authority and representation resulting from a polyarchical regime.[69] The political citizen of the polyarchy is homologous to the civil citizen of the universalistic aspects of the legal system: the rights of voting and joining a political party, of entering into a contract, of not suffering violence, of expecting fair treatment from a state agency, and the like are all premised on individuals who share the autonomy and responsibility that make them legal persons and agents of their own actions. This is a universalistic premise of equality that appears in innumerable facets of a democratic legal system. It underlies the enormous normative appeal that democratic aspirations have evinced, even if often vaguely and inconsistently expressed, under the most varied historical and cultural conditions.

Inequalities, the State and Liberal Rights

It might be argued that I am taking an excessively convoluted road for justifying the rule of law, when it can be sufficiently justified instrumentally,[70] by its contribution to the stability of social relations, or by arguing that its deficiencies may be so severe as to hinder the viability of a polyarchy. These are sensible arguments, and nowadays there is no dearth of them, especially in terms of the contribution that appropriate legislation makes to private investment and, supposedly, ultimately to economic growth. Presently, several international agencies are willing to support this goal, and legions of experts are busy with various aspects of it. However, I am persuaded that a proper justification of the rule of law should be grounded on the formal but not insignificant equality entailed by the attribution to legal persons of autonomous and responsible agency (and on the basic dignity and obligation of human respect that derive from this attribution, although I have not elaborated this point[71]).

Furthermore, in the present context of Latin America, the type of

justification of the rule of law one prefers is likely to make a significant difference in terms of the policies that might be advocated. In
particular, there is the danger derived from the fact that nowadays
legal and judicial reforms (and the international and domestic funding allocated to support them) are strongly oriented toward the perceived interests of the dominant sectors (basically domestic and
international commercial law, some aspects of civil law, and the more
purely repressive aspects of criminal law).[72] This may be useful for
fomenting investment, but it tends to produce a "dualistic development of the justice system," centered on those aspects "that concern
the modernizing sectors of the economic elite in matters of an economic, business or financial nature ... [while] other areas of litigation
and access to justice remain untouched, corrupted and persistently
lacking in infrastructure and resources."[73] For societies that are profoundly unequal, these trends may very well reinforce the exclusion
of many from the rule of law, while further exaggerating the advantages that the privileged enjoy by means of laws and courts
enhanced in their direct interest. In contrast, the substantive justification of the rule of law I am proposing here leads directly to the issue
of how it applies, or does not apply, to all individuals, including
those who have little direct impact on private investment.

Two comments are now in order. One, empirical and already
made, is that although there are variations from case to case, many
new polyarchies, in Latin America and in other regions, exhibit numerous points of rupture in the legal circuits I have delineated. To the
extent that this is true, we must reckon that in these cases the rule of
law has only intermittent and partial existence, if any. In addition,
this observation at the level of the legal state is the mirror image of
numerous violations of the law at the social level, which elsewhere I
have argued amount to a truncated, or low-intensity, citizenship.[74] In
the countries that concern us, many individuals are citizens with respect to their political rights, but they are not citizens in terms of their
civil rights.

The second comment is theoretical. In the preceding pages we implicitly reached an important conclusion that now I wish to highlight. There is one and only one specific difference between
polyarchy and other regimes.[75] It is that the highest positions of the

regime (with the exception of courts) are assigned as the consequence of elections that are free, fair, and competitive. The other
rights and guarantees specified in the definition of this regime are de-
rivative of the former, i.e., they are their prudentially assessed and in-
ductively derived conditions for the existence of that kind of
election.[76] On its part, the specific characteristic of the rule of law as
an attribute of the legal side of a democratic state, in contrast to authoritarian rule, is the existence of a full network of legally defined
accountabilities which entail that nobody is *de legibus solutus*. The
first specific characteristic pertains to the political regime, a polyarchy; the second one to the state, or more precisely the face of the
state that is embodied in a democratic legal system. Both are based
on the same type of (formal) rights and attributions of human
agency, and both are the product of long historical processes, origi-
nating in the northwestern quadrant of the world, of extension of political and civil rights.

For these reasons, I believe that, even if it opens intricate conceptual problems that we are spared if we reduce democracy solely to a
regime attribute,[77] we must think, in addition to the latter, of the de-
mocraticness of the state, especially of the state conceived in its legal
dimension. At this level the relevant question refers to the various
degrees and dimensions along which the three attributes of a democratic rule of law, or *estado de derecho*, are or are not present in a given
case. Democracy is not only a (polyarchical) political regime but also
a particular mode of relationship between state and citizens,[78] and
among citizens themselves, under a kind of rule of law that, in addition to political citizenship, upholds civil citizenship and a full network of accountability.

Another conclusion flows from this discussion. As I have defined
it, the full effectiveness of the rule of law has not been reached in any
country. It is a moving horizon, since societal change and the very acquisition of some rights trigger new demands and aspirations, while
the continued effectiveness of those that have been won can never be
taken for granted. Seen from this angle, democracy loses the static
connotations that it tends to have when conceived solely as a regime,
and shows that it is itself that moving horizon (and, for this reason, in
spite of innumerable disappointments with its actual workings, the

source and referent of intense normative appeal). If this is correct, our intellectual endeavors should be properly conceived as being about a theory of endless and always potentially reversible democratization, rather than about democracy *tout court*.

At this point, the reader has surely noticed that I made only passing references to issues of socioeconomic inequality. This is not because I consider these matters unimportant. Rather, in the first section I mention the main inconveniences generated by including overall equality (or any substantive measure of social welfare) into the definition of democracy. But I added that the intermediary level I was going to delineate is not independent of the broad structural characteristics of society. To begin with, Costa Rica and Uruguay (which, as already noted, are the only Latin American countries where, jointly with political rights, civil rights and horizontal accountability are reasonably effective) suggest that one of the directions of causation runs from these rights to social structure. These countries are among those in Latin America that have the lower proportion of poor. More significantly, Costa Rica and Uruguay have the least unequal income distribution in Latin America (except, presumably, Cuba). Finally, jointly with another relatively old but presently shaky polyarchy, Colombia, these countries, in sharp contrast with the rest, emerged from the past couple of decades of economic crisis and adjustment with basically the same (Costa Rica and Colombia) or even a slightly improved (Uruguay) income distribution.[79] Although this is another matter on which much research is needed, it seems that enjoying full citizenship fosters patterns of inequality that are less sharp, and socially and politically less crippling, than those in countries where, at best, only full political rights are upheld.

On the other hand, the apparently strongest link, albeit the most difficult to assess, is the causal direction that runs from an inegalitarian socioeconomic structure to the weakness of political and, especially, civil rights. There are, to my mind, two main factors. One, rather obvious, is the dramatic curtailment of capabilities entailed by deep inequality and its usual concomitant of widespread and severe poverty. The second, which seems to me as important as it is overlooked, is that the huge social distances entailed by deep inequality foster manifold patterns of authoritarian relations in various encounters between the privileged and the others. One consequence is the enormous difficulty of the former in recognizing the latter as equally autonomous and responsible agents. This pervasive difficulty, that an attentive eye can immediately discover in these countries,[80] is a major obstacle to the attainment of full citizenship. Structural inequality is a problem everywhere. Yet it is more acute in Latin America, a region that not only shares with others widespread poverty but that also has the most unequal income distribution. Rights and guarantees are not "just there"; they must be exercised and defended against persistent authoritarian temptations, and for this the capabilities that society furnishes to its members are crucial.

We should take into account that the law, in its content and in its application, is largely (like the state of which it is a part) a dynamic condensation of power relations, not just a rationalized technique for the ordering of social relations.[81] If, on one hand, poverty and inequality signal the long road to be traversed toward the extension of civil citizenship (not to mention the achievement of significantly more equal societies), what I have just said about the law suggests a beacon of hope and a general strategy. The point is that being the carrier of formal rights, social or political, is at least potentially an aspect of empowerment of individuals and their associations.[82] This has been recognized throughout the world in innumerable struggles of subordinate sectors which have aimed at the legal validation of the rights they claimed. With this they contributed to the process of intensive juridification I mentioned before and made of the law a dynamic condensation of the power relations in play. In spite of the criticisms that formal rights have elicited from various quarters, it seems clear that, when conquered and exercised, they provide a valuable foundation for struggling for more specific and substantive rights.

This holds true even though this same legal system is the law of a capitalist society and, as such, it textures and guarantees some social relations that are inherently unequal. Yet irrespective of how unequal a given relationship is, if *ego* can impose her civil and political rights on others, she controls capabilities that help protect her and project her own agency, individual and collective, into the future.[83] Jointly with the political freedoms of polyarchy, civil rights are the main support of the pluralism and diversity of society. As a consequence, it is wrong to think of the legal state as in a zero-sum position in relation to society, even if in some situations it may be true in relation to the bureaucratic state. Quite the contrary, the more the legal state extends itself as the democratic rule of law, the more it usually supports the independence and the strength of society. A strong democratic legal state—one that effectively extends its rule over the whole of its territory and across all social sectors—is a crucial correlate of a strong society. Conversely, the ineffectiveness of civil rights, whether under authoritarian rule or under a weak legal state, hinders the capability of agency that the law nominally attributes to everyone.

It is time to remember that civil rights are basically the classic liberal freedoms and guarantees. This leads to an apparently paradoxical situation: the Latin American cases I have been discussing may be properly called democratic in the sense that they uphold the democratic rights of participation entailed by polyarchy, but they scarcely exhibit another component of the democracies existing in the highly developed world, the liberal one. Furthermore, for reasons I cannot discuss here,[84] another important component, republicanism, is also weak in these cases. A consequence on which I want to insist is that, insofar as we are dealing with cases where the liberal component of democracy is weak while at the same time the political rights of polyarchy are effective, in most of Latin America and elsewhere, there is a reversion of the historical sequence followed by most highly developed countries. It follows that the implicit assumption of effective civil rights and of accountability, made by most extant theories of democracy, is untenable in relation to many new polyarchies. Rather, as I have been insisting, the absence or marked weakness of these components, as well as of republicanism, should be explicitly problematized by any theory that purports to embrace all presently existing polyarchies. Without sliding into the mistake of identifying democracy with substantive equality or welfare, our theories must come to terms with the great practical and analytical importance of the relative effectiveness of not only political but also civil citizenship and accountability in each case—or, to put it in equivalent terms, the extent to which a polyarchical regime coexists with a properly democratic rule of law (or an *estado democrático de derecho*). For this purpose, as I also have been insisting, even though it greatly expands the scope and complexity of the analysis, it is necessary to conclude that a solely regime-based focus is insufficient.

These reflections pose what is perhaps the curious task of democratic, progressively oriented politics in Latin America: to undertake liberal struggles for the effectiveness of formal, universalistic civil rights for everyone. Even if in the origins of polyarchy liberalism sometimes (often, throughout the history of Latin America) acted as a break to democratic impulses, in the contemporary circumstances of this and other regions of the world the more promising democratizing impulses should come from demands for the extension of civil citizenship. This, of course, is worthwhile in itself. It is also the road to the creation of areas of self-empowerment of the many who nowadays are truncated citizens. On the horizon of these hopes is a much less inequalitarian society, one that through the generalization of the democratic rule of law becomes a decent one—one, as Margalit put it, "in which the institutions do not humiliate people."[85]

Concluding Remarks

The reader has had to bear with me the oddity of a lexicon that speaks of democracies that are democratic *qua* polyarchies but are not democratic, or are very incompletely so, as seen from the angle of the rule of law and the legal state; of cases that are usually called "liberal democracies" but that are scarcely liberal; of regimes that are polyarchical at the national but sometimes not at the subnational level; and of democracy pertaining as much to the legal face of the state as to the regime. In addition to my scant literary talents, the reason for this awkwardness is that our vocabulary has been shaped by the restricted theoretical scope resulting from the implicit assumptions mentioned at the beginning of this chapter and discussed during it. Despite these shortcomings, I hope I have shown that the themes of the state, especially the legal state, and of the effective extension of civil citizenship and accountability under the rule of law should be considered as much a central part of the *problématique* of democracy as is the study of its (polyarchical) regime.

I believe that it is in the context of the analyses and the concerns

I have presented here that some political aspects of the rich, fascinating, and often justifiably somber chapters of this volume should be interpreted. Most of the Latin American countries to which these chapters refer are polyarchies. Having reached this condition is, indeed, important progress in relation to the utter arbitrariness and violence of the authoritarian systems that in most cases preceded those polyarchies. In this specific, regime-centered sense, I do not share the reluctance of some of our authors in calling these cases "democracies," although I prefer to label them polyarchies, or political democracies. On the other hand, and as these same authors make abundantly clear, the achievement of a fuller democracy that includes the democratic rule of law is an urgent and, under the circumstances spelled out in this volume, huge and apparently distant achievement. That the struggles toward this goal may be grounded, as they should be, in the political freedoms of polyarchy signals the potential of this kind of regime, even if marred by truncated citizenship and weak accountability.

NOTES

I appreciate the comments of David Collier, Ernesto Funes, Gabriela Ippolito-O'Donnell, Ary Kacowicz, Xochitl Lara, Marcelo Leiras, Scott Mainwaring, Sebastián Mazzuca, Juan Méndez, José Molinas, Gerardo Munck, Paulo Sérgio Pinheiro, Dietrich Rueschemeyer, Héctor Schamis, and Ruth Zimmerling, as well as the participants in the academic workshop and the public policy forum that were at the origin of the present volume. I also appreciate the comments of the participants in the panel "The Quality of Democracy and Democratic Consolidation," Annual Meeting of the American Political Science Association, Washington, D.C., Aug. 28–31, 1997.

1. *See generally* Guillermo O'Donnell, *On the State, Democratization and Some Conceptual Problems: A Latin American View with Glances at Some Postcommunist Countries,* 21(8) WORLD DEVELOPMENT 1355–69 (1993); *Delegative Democracy,* 5(1) J. OF DEMOCRACY 55–69 (1994); *Illusions about Consolidation,* 7(2) J. OF DEMOCRACY 34–51 (1996); *Poverty and Inequality in Latin America: Some Political Reflections,* in POVERTY AND INEQUALITY IN LATIN AMERICA: ISSUES AND NEW CHALLENGES (Víctor Tokman & Guillermo O'Donnell eds., University of Notre Dame Press, 1998); and *Horizontal Accountability and New Polyarchies,* in THE SELF-RESTRAINING STATE: POWER AND ACCOUNTABILITY IN NEW DEMOCRACIES (Andreas Schedler, Larry Diamond, and Mark Plattner eds., Boulder: Lynne Rienner Publishers, 1999). Since these publications, like the present one, are part of a larger effort in which I analyze the characteristics and dynamics of new polyarchies, I apologize in advance for the various references that I make here to my own writings.

2. Or, as Dahl put it, "These half-hidden premises, unexplored assumptions, and unacknowledged antecedents [that] form a vaguely perceived shadow theory [of democracy]." ROBERT DAHL, DEMOCRACY AND ITS CRITICS 3 (New Haven: Yale University Press, 1989).

3. *See especially* DAHL, *id.* at 221. The attributes stated by Dahl are: (1) elected officials; (2) free and fair elections; (3) inclusive suffrage; (4) the right to run for office; (5) freedom of expression; (6) alternative information; and (7) associational autonomy. In O'Donnell, *Illusions about Consolidation, supra* note 1, I have proposed adding: (8) elected officials (and some appointed persons, such as high court judges) should not be arbitrarily terminated before the end of their constitutionally mandated terms; (9) elected officials should not be subject to severe constraints, vetoes, or exclusion from certain policy domains by other, nonelected actors, especially the armed forces; and (10) there should be an uncontested territory that clearly defines the voting population (for persuasive arguments about this latter point, *see especially* JUAN LINZ & ALFRED STEPAN, PROBLEMS ON DEMOCRATIC TRANSITION AND CONSOLIDATION: SOUTHERN EUROPE, LATIN AMERICA, AND POST-COMMUNIST EUROPE [Baltimore: Johns Hopkins University Press, 1996]). These ten attributes I take as jointly defining polyarchy.

4. See the interesting account of the numerous adjectives added to the term "democracy" in David Collier & Steven Levitsky, *Democracy with Adjectives: Conceptual Innovation in Comparative Research,* 49(3) WORLD POLITICS 430–51 (1997). For reflections on the changing meanings of democracy in a specific context—France—which in several respects is closer than the United States to the Latin American tradition, *see* PIERRE ROSANVALLON, LA MONARCHIE IMPOSSIBLE: LES CHARTES DE 1814 ET DE 1830 (Paris: Fayard, 1994).

5. Assuming that for these elections to be competitive at least two political parties are required, these options are: vote for party A, vote for party B, cast a blank ballot, cast a null ballot, and do not vote.

6. The theme of personal autonomy and its correlates has elicited a lot of attention in political philosophy, but until now it has not much influenced democratic theory. The basic bibliography on this theme and a thoughtful discussion may be found in Jack Crittenden, *The Social Nature of Autonomy,* 54 THE REVIEW OF POLITICS 35–65 (1992). For contributions that I found particularly illuminating on this matter, *see* JOSEPH RAZ, THE MORALITY OF FREEDOM (Oxford: Clarendon Press, 1986); JOSEPH RAZ, ETHICS IN THE PUBLIC DOMAIN: ESSAYS IN THE MORALITY OF LAW AND POLITICS 195–211 (Oxford: Clarendon Press, 1994); and JEREMY WALDRON, LIBERAL RIGHTS, COLLECTED PAPERS 1981–1991 (Cambridge UK: Cambridge University Press, 1993).

7. The history of this often grudging acceptance is that of the incorporation to citizenship of urban workers, peasants, women, and others. Conversely, its refusal is the stepping-stone to authoritarian rule: guardians, enlightened vanguards, military *juntas,* theocracies, and the like have in common the denial, at least in the political realm, of the autonomy of their subjects.

8. For a discussion of these elections and the collective mood that usually surrounds them, *see* GUILLERMO O'DONNELL & PHILIPPE SCHMITTER, TRANSITIONS FROM AUTHORITARIAN RULE: TENTATIVE CONCLUSIONS ABOUT

UNCERTAIN DEMOCRACIES (Johns Hopkins University Press, 1986). I examined the micromotivations underlying these phenomena in Guillermo O'Donnell, *On the Fruitful Convergences of Hirschman's 'Exit, Voice, and Loyalty' and 'Shifting Involvements': Reflections From the Recent Argentine Experience*, in DEVELOPMENT, DEMOCRACY, AND THE ART OF TRESPASSING: ESSAYS IN HONOR OF ALBERT HIRSCHMAN 249–68 (Alejandro Foxley, Michael McPherson, & Guillermo O'Donnell eds., University of Notre Dame Press, 1986).

9. Of course, the classic statement of this argument is Karl Marx, *The Jewish Question*, in KARL MARX: ESSENTIAL WRITINGS (New York: Harper & Row, 1972). *See also* Otto Kirchheimer, *The 'Rechsstaat' as Magic Wall*, in THE CRITICAL SPIRIT: ESSAYS IN HONOR OF HERBERT MARCUSE 428–52 (Barrington Moore Jr. ed., Boston: Beacon Press, 1967).

10. For research on the United States that shows the importance of these and other resources in terms of various kinds of political participation, *see* SIDNEY VERBA, HAY L. SCHLOZMAN, & HENRY BRADY, VOICE AND EQUALITY: CIVIC VOLUNTARISM IN AMERICAN POLITICS (Harvard University Press, 1995).

11. AMARTYA SEN, INEQUALITY REEXAMINED (Harvard University Press, 1992). *See also* PARTHA DASGUPTA, AN INQUIRY INTO WELL-BEING AND DESTITUTION (Oxford: Clarendon Press, 1993); and, from a more philosophical and also extremely interesting perspective, *see* Charles Taylor, *What's Wrong with Negative Liberty*, in PHILOSOPHY AND THE HUMAN SCIENCES, PHILOSOPHICAL PAPERS 2. 211–29 (Cambridge UK: Cambridge University Press, 1985).

12. This is borne out by the work of Adam Przeworski and his associates, in Adam Przeworski, Michael Alvarez, José Antonio Cheibub, & Fernando Limongi, *What Makes Democracies Endure?*, 7(1) J. OF DEMOCRACY 39–56 (1996); and Adam Przeworski & Fernando Limongi, *Modernization: Theories and Facts*, 49(2) WORLD POLITICS 155–83 (1997).

13. With this parenthetical expression I am sidestepping some complex issues of legal theory with which I do not need to deal here.

14. Research in the United States shows that most people place high value on feeling that they are treated by means of fair processes by courts and the police, to an extent largely irrespective of the concrete outcome of the process. TOM R. TYLER, WHY PEOPLE OBEY THE LAW (Yale University Press, 1980). In Robert Lane, *Procedural Goods in a Democracy: How One is Treated Versus What One Gets*, 2(3) SOCIAL JUSTICE RESEARCH 177–92 (1988), Lane argues persuasively that an important, albeit neglected, topic in democratic theory and practice is not only who gets what by what means from whom but also the degree to which institutions are fair and respectful of the equal dignity of all individuals. Legal theorist Ronald Dworkin has made being treated "with equal consideration and respect" the hallmark of a properly ordered society. RONALD DWORKIN, TAKING RIGHTS SERIOUSLY (Harvard University Press, 1977).

15. I use the term in this context with some hesitation, due to the strong criticisms made of T.H. Marshall's influential scheme. T.H. MARSHALL, CLASS, CITIZENSHIP AND SOCIAL DEVELOPMENT (University of

Chicago Press, 1950). *See,* among others, Michael Mann, *Ruling Class Strategies and Citizenship,* 21(3) SOCIOLOGY 33–54 (1987); and Bryan Turner, *Outline of a Theory of Citizenship,* 24 (3) SOCIOLOGY 189–217 (1990).

16. With the exception, of course, that political rights are usually reserved for nationals.

17. There is a large literature on this matter. Within the works that stress the legal aspects of this topic, I found particularly useful: Ulrich Preuss, *The Concept of Rights and the Welfare State,* in DILEMMAS OF LAW IN THE WELFARE STATE 151–72 (Gunther Teubner ed., New York and Berlin: de Gruyter, 1988); Ulrich Preuss, *Two Challenges to European Citizenship,* 44 (3) POLITICAL STUDIES 534–52 (1996); ROGER COTTERRELL, THE POLITICS OF JURISPRUDENCE: A CRITICAL INTRODUCTION TO LEGAL PHILOSOPHY (University of Pennsylvania Press, 1989); Jürgen Habermas, *Law as a Medium and as an Institution,* in DILEMMAS OF LAW IN THE WELFARE STATE 203–30, id.; and JÜRGEN HABERMAS, BETWEEN FACTS AND NORMS (MIT Press, 1996).

18. As expressed by Teubner in DILEMMAS OF LAW IN THE WELFARE STATE *supra* note 17. Actually, the issue is more complicated. Attacks on the present legal systems of highly developed countries refer both to their remnants of "formal" universalism and to the innumerable pieces of particularized legislation issued not only by legislatures but also by administrative agencies, basically in the context of regulation and welfare policies. Unhappiness about these systems is broadly shared, but there is no agreement about why and in what direction they should be changed.

19. Habermas, *Law as a Medium and as an Institution, supra* note 17. For a more detailed discussion, *see* HABERMAS, BETWEEN FACTS AND NORMS, *supra* note 17.

20. MAX WEBER, ECONOMY AND SOCIETY: AN OUTLINE OF INTERPRETATIVE SOCIOLOGY (2 vols., Berkeley: University of California Press, 1978). For an analysis of Weber's sociology of law and its elective affinities with the development of capitalism, *see* ANTHONY KRONMAN, MAX WEBER (Stanford: Stanford University Press, 1983).

21. *See especially* the works cited in note 17, *supra.*

22. Habermas, *Law as a Medium and as an Institution, supra* note 17, at 204.

23. And the developmental typology, in this respect not too different, of T.H. MARSHALL, CLASS, CITIZENSHIP AND SOCIAL DEVELOPMENT (University of Chicago Press, 1950).

24. In relation to women's rights, *see especially* Sylvia Walby, *Is Citizenship Gendered?,* 28(2) SOCIOLOGY 379–95 (1994).

25. On the characteristics of the welfare state in Latin America, the basic works are CARMELO MESA-LAGO, SOCIAL SECURITY IN LATIN AMERICA: PRESSURE GROUPS, STRATIFICATION AND INEQUALITY (University of Pittsburgh Press, 1978); and JAMES MALLOY, THE POLITICS OF SOCIAL SECURITY IN BRAZIL (University of Pittsburgh Press, 1979). *See also* James Malloy, *Statecraft, Social Policy, and Governance in Latin America* (Working Paper no. 151, University of Notre Dame, Kellogg Institute, 1991). For analyses of the contemporary

situation of Latin America in terms of poverty and inequality, see the studies included in POVERTY AND INEQUALITY IN LATIN AMERICA: ISSUES AND NEW CHALLENGES, *supra* note 1.

26. In this sense, Chile is a marginal case. Various kinds of civil rights are more extensive and effective in this country than in most of the rest of Latin America. However, not only the political constraints imposed by the constitution inherited from the Pinochet regime but also a judiciary, also inherited from this period, that is highly penetrated by authoritarian views lead me not to classify this country jointly with Costa Rica and Uruguay.

27. *See particularly* O'Donnell, *On the State, supra* note 1.

28. From other angles, these failures are abundantly, if dismally, detailed in this volume.

29. *See* Mariclaire Acosta, *Overcoming the Discrimination against Women in Mexico: A Task for Sisyphus,* and the "Comment" to this chapter by Dorothy Thomas, in this volume.

30. *See* Jorge Dandler, *Indigenous Peoples and the Rule of Law in Latin America: Do They Have a Chance?,* and Peter Fry, *Color and the Rule of Law in Brazil,* as well as the respective "Comments" to these chapters by Shelton Davis and Joan Dassin, in this volume.

31. *See* Juan Méndez, *Problems of Lawless Violence: Introduction,* and Nigel Rodley, *Torture and Conditions of Detention in Latin America,* in this volume.

32. The work of DaMatta, especially his analysis of the expression "Você sabe con quem está falando?" is an excellent illustration of this. ROBERTO DAMATTA, CARNIVALS, ROGUES, AND HEROES: AN INTERPRETATION OF THE BRAZILIAN DILEMMA (University of Notre Dame Press, 1991); and DaMatta, *The Quest for Citizenship in a Relational Universe,* in STATE AND SOCIETY IN BRAZIL: CONTINUITY AND CHANGE 307-35 (John Wirth et al. eds., Boulder: Westview Press, 1987).

33. In O'Donnell, *Illusions about Consolidation, supra* note 1. I stress the importance that particularistic relationships of various kinds have in the social and political functioning of these countries.

34. The colonial times' dictum "La ley se acata pero no se cumple" ("The law is acknowledged but not implemented") distills this tradition. This is not an exclusively Latin American phenomenon. For post-communist countries, including Central European ones, *see,* among others, Aleksander Smolnar, *Civil Society in Post-Communist Europe,* paper presented at the conference "Consolidating the Third Wave Democracies" (Taipei, August 1995); Martin Krygier, *Virtuous Circles: Antipodean Reflections on Power, Institutions, and Civil Society,* 11(1) EAST EUROPEAN POLITICS & SOCIETIES 36–88 (1997); and THE RULE OF LAW AFTER COMMUNISM (D. Czarnota & Martin Krygier eds., Aldershot: Dartmouth Publishing, 1997). But, as in the case of Latin America, I have not yet seen systematic attempts to link these phenomena to the workings of the respective regimes.

35. CLARÍN, May 10, 1997, at 8.

36. Or naïve foreigners or potential suicides, as would be the case if, when driving, one would follow the formal rules of traffic. I have com-

mented on this theme in Guillermo O'Donnell, *Y a mi qué me importa? Notas Sobre Sociabilidad y Política en Argentina y Brasil* (Working Paper no. 9, University of Notre Dame, Kellogg Institute, 1984), also included (in English) in my COUNTERPOINTS: SELECTED ESSAYS ON AUTHORITARIANISM AND DEMOCRATIZATION (University of Notre Dame Press, 1999).

37. This important but often neglected point is discussed in DaMatta, *The Quest for Citizenship in a Relational Universe, supra* note 32; DAMATTA, CARNIVALS, ROGUES, AND HEROES, *supra* note 32; and Marcelo Neves, *Entre Subintegracao e Sobreintegracae: A Cidadania Inexistente,* 37(2) DADOS 253–75 (1994).

38. The terrible and recurrent violence to which the poor are subjected in many parts, rural and urban, of Latin America has been analyzed with particular detail and eloquence in the work of Paulo Sérgio Pinheiro and his associates at the University of São Paulo. *See especially* Paulo Sérgio Pinheiro, *The Legacy of Authoritarianism in Democratic Brazil,* in LATIN AMERICAN DEVELOPMENT AND PUBLIC POLICY 237–53 (Stuart S. Nagel ed., 1994); and Paulo Sérgio Pinheiro & Malak El-Chichini Poppovic, *Poverty, Marginalization, Violence and the Realization of Human Rights,* Preparatory Committee, United Nations World Conference on Human Rights (Geneva, April 1993, multicopied). About the police, *see* PAUL CHEVIGNY, EDGE OF THE KNIFE: POLICE VIOLENCE IN THE AMERICAS (New York: New Press, 1995); and Paul Chevigny, *Defining the Role of the Police in Latin America,* and the "Comments" by Jean-Paul Brodeur, in this volume. A fascinating, if dismal, ethnographic account of police behavior in Brazil may be found in GUARACY MINGARDI, TIRAS, GANSOS E TRUTAS: COTIDIANO E REFORMA NA POLICIA CIVIL (São Paulo: Página Aberta, 1992).

39. Which may go a long way to explain why the current efforts to enhance the workings of the state apparatus have been so neglectful of this side. I discuss this matter in O'Donnell, *Poverty and Inequality in Latin America: Some Political Reflections, supra* note 1.

40. *See,* among others, DWORKIN, *supra* note 14; and Lane, *supra* note 14.

41. On this matter, *see* Jorge Correa Sutil, *Judicial Reforms in Latin America: Good News for the Underprivileged?,* and Alejandro Garro, *Access to Justice for the Poor in Latin America,* in this volume. *See also* Pilar Domingo Villegas, *Rule of Law and Judicial Systems in the Context of Democratization and Economic Liberalisation: A Framework for Comparison and Analysis in Latin America* (Mexico, D.F.: CIDE, 1994, multicopied); Pilar Domingo Villegas, *The Judiciary and Democratization in Latin America,* paper presented to the "Vienna Dialogue on Democracy and Institutionalization of Horizontal Accountability" (Vienna, 1997); and Hugo Fruling, *Judicial Reform and Democratization in Latin America* (Miami: North-South Center, 1995, multicopied).

42. In addition to the works already cited, it bears mentioning that in a survey I took in December 1992 in the metropolitan area of São Paulo (n: 800) an overwhelming 93 percent responded "no" to a question asking if the law was applied equally in Brazil, and 6 percent didn't know or didn't answer. In

a similar vein, in a survey recently taken in the metropolitan area of Buenos Aires (n: 1,400, Guzmán Heredia y Asociados) 89 percent of respondents indicated various degrees of lack of confidence in the courts, 9 percent expressed they had some confidence, and only 1 percent said they had a lot of confidence.

43. O'Donnell, *On the State, supra* note 1.

44. *See,* e.g., NORBERTO BOBBIO, DEMOCRACY AND DICTATORSHIP: THE NATURE AND LIMITS OF STATE POWER (University of Minnesota Press, 1989). An extreme position, fully conflating the state with the legal system, was influentially articulated by Kelsen. *See* HANS KELSEN, GENERAL THEORY OF LAW AND STATE (New York: Russell & Russell, 1945); HANS KELSEN, PURE THEORY OF LAW (Berkeley: University of California Press, 1967).

45. Or, as Rawls puts it, "the law defines the basic framework within which the pursuit of all other activities takes place." JOHN RAWLS, A THEORY OF JUSTICE 236 (Harvard University Press, 1971).

46. I use the term "privatized" to indicate that these actors often are private ones acting jointly with others who have some kind of state employment but who gear their behavior toward goals that have very little to do with such affiliation.

47. Blanca Heredia, *Making Economic Reform Politically Viable: The Mexican Experience,* in LATIN AMERICAN POLITICAL ECONOMY IN THE AGE OF NEOLIBERAL REFORM: DEMOCRACY, MARKETS, AND STRUCTURAL REFORM 265–96 (William C. Smith, Carlos Acuña, & Eduardo Gamarra eds., Brunswick: Transaction Publishers, 1994); DAMATTA, CARNIVALS, ROGUES, AND HEROES, *supra* note 37; and Villegas, *Rule of Law and Judicial Systems in the Context of Democratization and Economic Liberalisation, supra* note 41. These authors point out the complex manipulations of the intersections between formal and informal legal systems that are required by successful social navigation in this kind of world. Interesting studies of this kind of navigation by underprivileged sectors may be found in Boaventura de Souza Santos, *The Law of the Oppressed: The Construction and Reproduction of Legality in Pasargada,* 12 LAW AND SOCIETY 5–126 (Fall 1977); James Holston, *The Misrule of Law: Land and Usurpation in Brazil,* 33(4) COMP. STUDIES IN SOC. & HIST. (1991); and James Holston & Teresa P.R. Caldeira, *Democracy, Law and Violence: Disjunctions of Brazilian Citizenship,* in FAULT LINES OF DEMOCRATIC GOVERNANCE IN THE AMERICAS (Felipe Agüero & Jeffrey Stark eds., Miami: North-South Center & Lynne Rienner Publishers, 1998). However, as Neves stresses, through these processes enormous power differentials are expressed and reproduced. Neves, *supra* note 37. For a few examples among many of the degree to which various kinds of privatized (and basically criminal) systems of territorially-based power exist, *see* America's Watch, *Forced Labor in Brazil Revisited,* 5 AMERICA'S WATCH (1993); HUMAN RIGHTS WATCH/AMERICAS, POLITICAL VIOLENCE AND COUNTERINSURGENCY IN COLOMBIA (New York: Human Rights Watch, 1993); HUMAN RIGHTS WATCH/AMERICAS, POLICE BRUTALITY IN URBAN BRAZIL (New York: Human Rights Watch, 1997); Centro de Estudios Legales y Sociales (CELS), *Informe sobre la Situación de los Derechos Humanos en la Argentina:*

Año 1994 (Buenos Aires, Universidad Nacional de Buenos Aires, 1995); CARLOS MEDINA GALLEGO, AUTODEFENSAS, PARAMILITARES Y NARCOTRÁFICO EN COLOMBIA (Bogotá: Editorial Difusora Periodística, 1990); COMISIÓN COLOMBIANA DE JURISTAS, COLOMBIA, DERECHOS HUMANOS Y DERECHO HUMANITARIO: 1996 (Bogotá: Comision Colombiana de Juristas, 1997); and JORGE MONTENEGRO & NICOLÁS ZICOLILLO, LOS SAADI (Buenos Aires: Legasa, 1991).

48. *See* O'Donnell, *On the State, supra* note 1, for a description and discussion of these "brown" areas, territorially based systems of domination barely reached by state law, which can cover huge extensions, sometimes bigger than a middle-sized European country (*see, e.g.*, VEJA, Oct. 7, 1997; and COMISIÓN COLOMBIANA DE JURISTAS, COLOMBIA, DERECHOS HUMANOS Y DERECHO HUMANITARIO: 1996, *supra* note 47.

49. Scott Mainwaring & David Julian Samuels, *Robust Federalism and Democracy in Contemporary Brazil,* paper presented at the meeting of the International Political Science Association (Seoul, August 1997). For concurrent observations about Argentina, *see* Edward Gibson & Ernesto Calvo, *Electoral Coalitions and Market Reforms: Evidence from Argentina* (Northwestern University, 1996, multicopied); and Edward Gibson, *The Populist Road to Market Reform; Policy and Electoral Coalitions in Mexico and Argentina,* 49(3) WORLD POLITICS 339–70 (1997).

50. Mainly, to my knowledge, the already cited works of Paulo Sérgio Pinheiro and his associates, *supra* note 38; as well as Jonathan Fox, *The Difficult Transition from Clientelism to Citizenship,* 46(2) WORLD POLITICS 151–84 (1994); Jonathan Fox, *Latin America's Emerging Local Politics,* 5(2) J. OF DEMOCRACY 105–16 (1995); MARCOS NOVARO, PILOTOS DE TORMENTAS: CRISIS DE REPRESENTACIÓN Y PERSONALIZACIÓN DE LA POLÍTICA EN LA ARGENTINA (1989–1993) (Buenos Aires: Letra Buena, 1994); and ANTHONY W. PEREIRA, THE END OF THE PEASANTRY: THE RURAL LABOR MOVEMENT IN NORTHEAST BRAZIL, 1961–1988 (Pittsburgh University Press, 1997). For vivid sociological descriptions of situations of *de facto* legal statelessness, *see* JORGE PARODI, LOS POBRES, LA CIUDAD Y LA POLÍTICA (Lima, Peru: CEDYS, 1993); and SERGIO ZERMEÑO, LA SOCIEDAD DERROTADA: EL DESORDEN MEXICANO DE FIN DE SIGLO (Mexico, D.F.: Siglo XXI, 1996).

51. I suspect that another reason for this neglect is that the institutional level of the regime lends itself more readily to empirical research than the phenomena I pointed out above. Political scientists are not trained to observe the latter, and the usually highly disaggregated and qualitative kind of data (often of an ethnographic character) they tend to generate is of difficult interpretation, especially in terms of their implications for the functioning of national-level politics. Furthermore, insofar as some of these phenomena are closely related to legal matters, they also require knowledge that is seldom provided in our discipline, while the lawyers who study these often informal phenomena are also few and quite marginal in their own discipline. In settings where career and promotion patterns place a prize on working on mainstream topics and approaches, the transdisciplinary skills required by these phenomena and, at least for the time being, the difficulties in translat-

ing findings into solid and comparable data sets are a discouraging factor for this type of research.

52. *See especially* LINZ & STEPAN, PROBLEMS ON DEMOCRATIC TRANSITION AND CONSOLIDATION: SOUTHERN EUROPE, LATIN AMERICA, AND POST-COMMUNIST EUROPE, *supra* note 3; and Mainwaring & Samuels, *supra* note 49.

53. We may remember that the secular authoritarianism of Southern states in the United States, interwoven with a national polyarchical regime, generated an interesting literature that may be usefully reexamined by political scientists working on the kind of case I am discussing here. *See* KIM Q. HILL, DEMOCRACY IN THE FIFTY STATES (Lincoln: University of Nebraska Press, 1994), and the literature cited therein.

54. *See especially* Peter Ingram, *Maintaining the Rule of Law*, 35 PHILOSOPHICAL QUARTERLY 141, 359–81 (1985).

55. For discussions centered on the United States, *see especially* THE RULE OF LAW: NOMOS XXXVI (Ian Shapiro ed., New York University Press, 1994); and in continental Europe, *see* Michel Troper, *Le Concept de l'État de Droit*, 15 DROITS: REVUE FRANCAISE DE THÉORIE JURIDIQUE 51–63 (1992); JACQUES CHEVALIER, L'ÉTAT DE DROIT (2d ed., Paris: Montchrestien, 1994); and Léo Hamon, *L'État de Droit et son Essence*, 4 REVUE FRANCAISE DE DROIT CONSTITUTIONNEL 699–712 (1990).

56. For a detailed analysis of this theme, *see* CARLOS ALCHOURRÓN & EUGENIO BULYGIN, NORMATIVE SYSTEMS (New York and Vienna: Springer-Verlag, 1971). Arguments from various theoretical perspectives about the tendential completeness of legal systems are found in DWORKIN, *supra* note 14; H.L.A. HART, THE CONCEPT OF LAW (Oxford: Clarendon Press, 1961); Ingram, *supra* note 54; and KELSEN, PURE THEORY OF LAW, *supra* note 44.

57. It goes without saying that this is an idealized description, which is not fully satisfied by any country. But the degrees and frequency of departures from this norm exhibit and entail important differences across cases.

58. In contrast, the distinctive mark of all kinds of authoritarian rule, even those that are highly institutionalized and legally formalized (a *Rechsstaat*, in the original sense of the term), have somebody (a king, a *junta*, a party committee, or what not) that is sovereign in the classic sense: if and when they deem it necessary, they can decide without legal constraint.

59. Joseph Raz, *The Rule of Law and Its Virtue*, 93 LAW QUARTERLY REV. 196 (1977).

60. HART, *supra* note 56, at 97.

61. JOHN FINNIS, NATURAL LAW AND NATURAL RIGHTS 268 (Oxford: Clarendon Press, 1980).

62. Raz, *The Rule of Law and Its Virtue*, *supra* note 59, at 198–201. For similar listings, *see* FINNIS, *supra* note 61; and LON FULLER, THE MORALITY OF LAW (Yale University Press, rev. ed. 1969).

63. For apposite discussion, *see* MARTIN SHAPIRO, COURTS: A COMPARATIVE AND POLITICAL ANALYSIS (University of Chicago Press, 1987).

64. FULLER, *supra* note 62.

65. In O'Donnell, *Delegative Democracy, supra* note 1, I labeled as "dele-

gative" these plebiscitary, inherently anti-institutional views and the kind of regime they tend to generate.

66. Stephen Skowronek, Building a New American State: The Expansion of National Administrative Capabilities (New York: Cambridge University Press, 1982); Martin Shefter, Political Parties and the State: The American Historical Experience (Princeton University Press, 1994); and Theda Skocpol, Protecting Soldiers and Mothers: The Political Origins of Social Policy in the United States (Harvard University Press, 1992).

67. Or, as Krygier puts it while making cogent remarks about the deficiencies of the rule of law in contemporary Central Europe: "At a bare minimum . . . the point of the rule of law—and its great cognitive and normative contribution to social and political life—is relatively simple: people should be able to rely on the law when they act. That requires that it exists, that it is knowable, that its implications be relatively determinate, and that it can be reliably expected to set bounds within which all major actors, including the government, will act." Krygier, *Virtuous Circles, supra* note 34, at 47.

68. Because of space restrictions and because I have discussed this issue quite extensively in a recent work, (*see Horizontal Accountability and New Polyarchies, supra* note 1), in the present text I will make only passing reference to accountability. However, I hope it will be clear that I consider accountability, including what I term the "horizontal" kind (i.e., the control that some state agents exercise over the lawfulness of the actions of other such agents), as one of the three constitutive dimensions of the democratic rule of law.

69. Recently, Habermas insisted on this aspect as a central characteristic of law in contemporary democracies. See Habermas, Between Facts and Norms, *supra* note 17.

70. For discussion of various kinds of justification of the rule of law, *see* Margaret Jane Radin, *Reconsidering the Rule of Law*, 69 Boston U. L. Rev. 4, 781–819 (1989).

71. In this sense, Raz is on the mark when he asserts that "the rule of law provides the foundation for the legal respect for human dignity." Raz, *The Rule of Law and Its Virtue, supra* note 59, at 204–05.

72. We must also consider a discernible trend toward hardening the criminal justice system against "common" suspects. In another pertinent issue, human rights organizations have expressed serious concerns about procedures that egregiously violate the principle of fair trial, adopted—with assistance from foreign agencies that would not dream of establishing similar procedures in their own countries—against suspects in the drug trade.

73. Villegas, *Rule of Law and Judicial Systems, supra* note 41. For further substantiation of these concerns, *see* Villegas, *The Judiciary and Democratization in Latin America, supra* note 41; as well as chapters by Correa Sutil and Garro in this volume.

74. O'Donnell, *On the State, supra* note 1.

75. Neither elections *per se*, universal adult vote, the temporal limitation

of mandates, or the division of powers pertain exclusively to polyarchy. For an enlightening discussion on this matter, *see* GIOVANNI SARTORI, THE THEORY OF DEMOCRACY REVISITED: I. CONTEMPORARY DEBATES (Chatham: Chatham House, 1987).

76. I suspect that this (probably unavoidable) prudential and not analytical derivation is the reason for the endless disputations about which are the proper attributes of polyarchy, even among those who agree on the usefulness of this and similar concepts. I elaborate on this and related matters in work currently in preparation.

77. Parsimony is a virtue of theory, but it should not be achieved at the expense of its proper scope. On a related matter, I am under the impression that the rising interest on the "quality" of democracy (*see especially* LINZ & STEPAN, PROBLEMS ON DEMOCRATIC TRANSITION AND CONSOLIDATION: SOUTHERN EUROPE, LATIN AMERICA, AND POST-COMMUNIST EUROPE, *supra* note 3) expresses concerns and intuitions pointed in the same direction that I have been pursuing here. In this sense, the present text may be seen as an effort to conceptually refine and make more empirically amenable the connotations of the term "quality" as used in this context.

78. This point is argued in Philippe Schmitter & Terry Lynn Karl, *What Democracy Is . . . and Is Not*, 2 J. OF DEMOCRACY 3, 75–88 (1991).

79. *See* Oscar Altimir, *Inequality, Poverty, and Employment in Latin America*, in POVERTY AND INEQUALITY IN LATIN AMERICA: ISSUES AND NEW CHALLENGES, *supra* note 1.

80. I invite some unscientific but relevant observations: look at any kind of interaction between individuals in high and low social positions in Costa Rica and Uruguay, and compare these interactions with similar ones in other countries that have a tradition of deep inequality. The highly deferential, almost servile, attitude you will see in the latter you will very rarely see in the former. Argentina is a somewhat deviant case of past relative egalitarianism, similar to that of Costa Rica and Uruguay, that still reverberates in this kind of interaction; but it was achieved under populism, not democracy, and in contrast to the other two countries, it was sharply reversed in the past two decades. For further discussion of these matters, *see* O'Donnell, *Y a mi qué me importa?*, *supra* note 36.

81. There is an interesting parallelism between the claims of a political technical rationality made by some jurists and those made by many mainstream economists. As we know, the latter are enormously influential and the former are becoming so, especially under the auspices of instrumentally inspired efforts to enhance the legal systems of new polyarchies.

82. For arguments in this respect, *see* JEAN COHEN & ANDREW ARATO, CIVIL SOCIETY AND POLITICAL THEORY (London: MIT Press, 1992); and, even though he focuses on constitutional rules while here I am referring to the whole legal system, *see also* Stephen Holmes, *Constitutionalism*, in THE ENCYCLOPEDIA OF DEMOCRACY (S.M. Lipset ed., London: Routledge, 1995).

83. This characteristic of autonomy as agency projected toward the future is stressed by Raz, *The Rule of Law and Its Virtue*, *supra* note 59.

84. I discuss this theme in O'Donnell, *Horizontal Accountability, supra* note 1, including its implications in terms of weak horizontal accountability.

85. Avishai Margalit, The Decent Society 1 (Harvard University Press, 1996).

Appendix
The Rule of Law and the Underprivileged in Latin America
Workshop

I. Problems of Lawless Violence
Chair: Tom Farer, University of Denver

1. Defining the Role of the Police
   Paper by: Paul Chevigny, New York University Law School
   Discussant: Jean-Paul Brodeur, University of Montreal
2. Conditions of Detention
   Paper by: Nigel Rodley, University of Essex, England
   Discussant: Ligia Bolívar O., PROVEA, Venezuela
3. Rural Conflicts
   Paper by: Alfredo Wagner Berno de Almeida,
      Social Anthropologist, Brazil
   Discussant: Roger Plant, UN Mission to Guatemala

II. Overcoming Discrimination
Chair: Rebecca Cook, University of Toronto

1. Indigenous Peoples
   Paper by: Jorge Dandler, International Labor Organization,
      San José, Costa Rica
   Discussant: Shelton H. Davis, World Bank
2. Racial Discrimination
   Paper by: Peter Fry, Universidade Federal do Rio de Janeiro,
      Brazil
   Discussant: Joan Dassin, Inter-American Dialogue

3. Women
   Paper by: Mariclaire Acosta, Comisión Mexicana de Defensa
   y Promoción de los Derechos Humanos
   Discussant: Dorothy Q. Thomas, Women's Rights Project,
   Human Rights Watch

III. Institutional Reform, Including Access to Justice
   Chair: Juan Méndez, Inter-American Institute on Human Rights

1. International Aspects of Current Efforts at Judicial Reform
   Paper by: Reed Brody, U.S.A.
   Discussant: Leonardo Franco, UNHCR; Former Director, UN
   Mission to Guatemala
2. Judicial Reform
   Paper by: Jorge Correa Sutil, Law School, Diego Portales
   University, Chile
   Discussant: Leopoldo Schiffrin, Federal Court of Appeals,
   Argentina
3. Access to Justice
   Paper by: Alejandro Garro, Columbia University Law School
   Discussant: Sérgio Adorno, University of São Paulo, Brazil

Public Policy Forum Panelists

Mariclaire Acosta
President, Comisión Mexicana de Defensa y Promoción de los
Derechos Humanos

Fernando Carrillo-Flórez
Senior Advisor, State and Civil Society Unit, Inter-American
Development Bank

Fernando Cepeda Ulloa
Journalist, Colombia

Adama Dieng
Secretary-General, International Commission of Jurists, Geneva

Graciela Fernández Meijide
Senator, Argentina

Jaime García Parra
Former Minister and Ambassador of Colombia

Nelson A. Jobim
Minister of Justice, Brazil

Jorge Madrazo
President, Comisión Nacional de Derechos Humanos Mexico

Emilio Mignone
President, Center for Legal and Social Studies, Argentina

Fernando Moreira Salles
Fundação Vitae, Brazil

Mark L. Schneider
Assistant Administrator, Bureau for Latin America and the
    Caribbean, U.S. Agency for International Development

Contributors

Mariclaire Acosta
President, Mexican Commission for the Defense and Promotion of Human Rights (CMDPDH), Mexico City, Mexico

Ligia Bolívar O.
Director, Legal Defense Program, Venezuelan Program for Human Rights Education and Action (PROVEA), Caracas, Venezuela

Jean-Paul Brodeur
Professor and Senior Researcher, School of Criminology and International Center for Compared Criminology, University of Montreal, Canada

Reed Brody
Advocacy Director, Human Rights Watch; former Deputy Chief of the United Nations Secretary General's Investigative Team in the Democratic Republic of Congo

Paul Chevigny
Professor of Law, New York University Law School, New York, U.S.A.

Rebecca J. Cook
Professor of Law and Associate Dean for Graduate Studies, Faculty of Law, University of Toronto, Canada

Jorge Correa Sutil
Professor of Law and former Dean, Diego Portales Law School, Santiago, Chile

Jorge Dandler
Senior Specialist on Rural Employment and Indigenous Peoples, Area Office for Central America and Panama, International Labor Organization, San José, Costa Rica

Joan Dassin
Independent Consultant; former Vice President of the Inter-American Dialogue, Washington, D.C., U.S.A.

Shelton H. Davis
Lead Social Development Specialist, Environmentally and Socially Sustainable Development Department, Latin America and Caribbean Region, The World Bank, Washington, D.C., U.S.A.

Leonardo Franco
Former Director, United Nations Human Rights Verification Mission to Guatemala; former Director of International Protection, United Nations High Commissioner for Refugees

Peter Fry
Professor of Anthropology, Department of Social Sciences, Universidade Federal do Rio de Janeiro, Brazil; Member, Nucleo Interdisciplinar para o Estudo das Desigualdades Sociais (NIED)

Alejandro M. Garro
Adjunct Professor of Law, Columbia University; Senior Research Scholar, Parker School of Foreign and Comparative Law, New York, U.S.A.

Juan E. Méndez
Director, Inter-American Institute on Human Rights, San José, Costa Rica; former General Counsel, Human Rights Watch, New York, U.S.A

Guillermo O'Donnell
Helen Kellogg Professor of Government and International Studies; Fellow and former Academic Director of the Helen Kellogg Institute for International Studies, University of Notre Dame, U.S.A.

Paulo Sérgio Pinheiro

Professor of Political Science and Director, Center for the Study of Violence, University of São Paulo, Brazil; former United Nations Special Rapporteur for Rwanda

Roger Plant

Independent Consultant; former Head of the Socioeconomic Area and Indigenous Issues Adviser of the United Nations Mission to Guatemala

Nigel S. Rodley

Professor of Law, University of Essex, United Kingdom; United Nations Special Rapporteur on Torture

Dorothy Q. Thomas

Consultant, Shaler Adams Foundation; former Director, Human Rights Watch Women's Rights Project, Washington, D.C., U.S.A.

Index

Inter-American Indian Congress,
126
International Convention on the
Elimination of All Forms of Racial
Discrimination, 118–19
International Covenant on Civil and
Political Rights (ICCPR), 31
International Covenants on Human
Rights, 118
International Decade for the Indige-
nous Populations of the World
(1995–2004), 124
international declarations of rights,
83–84
international development assistance, 227–28
international financial institutions:
court delays measured by, 288; and
indigenous peoples, 126–27; and
judicial reform, 157, 251–52, 256; in
Mexican economic crisis, 162;
against poverty, 101
International Fund for Agricultural
Development (FAO), 89–90
International Labor Organization,
119, 158. See also ILO Convention
No. 169
International Money Fund (IMF),
162
International Year for the Indigenous Populations of the World
(1993), 124

J

joinder of plaintiffs, 289
judges, accountability of, 223, 224,
255, 260
judicare systems, 282, 283–84
judicial education, 233–34, 256,
264–66, 291–92
Judicial Mentors program (Haiti),
233
judicial reform: access to justice,
287–92, 317; background, 257–59;
dispute resolution fora, 261–62;
economic reform linked with,
251–52, 268, 278; government of ju-

dicial branches, 255–57; importance of, 243; international assistance to, 227–30; and international
community, 157, 243, 244–45,
251–52, 256; introduction, 11–13;
and legal assistance programs, 280;
oriented toward dominant sectors,
320; and poor, 267–71; priorities
for, 236; top-down approach, 252;
in transition to democracy, 259–61;
USAID assistance to, 233–35
judiciaries: access to, 313; accountability, 23, 255, 260; independence
of, 317; modernization of, 222; and
police impunity, 58; reform of, 66;
resistance to change, 223–24
juridification of society, 310
justice of peace systems, 290
justice systems: class bias, 229, 235;
corruption, 187–88; credibility,
222–23; financial resources, 263;
gender discrimination, 173; improvement strategies, 224, 248–49,
262–63; inequality, 215; racial discrimination, 189–94, 201, 212

K

kidnapping, police collaboration in,
63–64
kleptocracy, 75
Krenak, Airton, 129
Kuhlmann, Stella, 62

L

labor law reform, 290
labor legislation, 91, 95, 96, 102
labor unions, 167
laissez-faire economics, 91, 94
land (see also indigenous communal
lands): cultural significance of, 104,
120; of Indians, 129–30; of indigenous peoples, 120–21, 128, 131–33,
135–36, 146; private ownership
limitations, 94–95
land privatization, 94, 103–4
land reform. See agrarian reform
Lane, Robert, 312–13